Ki: A Road That Anyone Can Walk

A Road
That Anyone
Can Walk

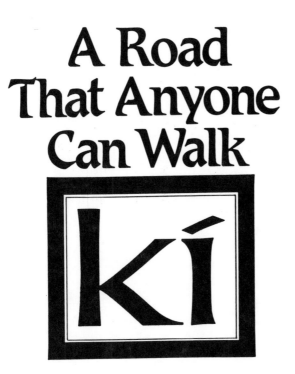

William Reed

Japan Publications, Inc.

Note to the reader. Those with health problems are advised to seek the guidance of a qualified medical or psychological professional before implementing any of the approaches presented in this book. It is essential that any reader who has any reason to suspect serious illness seek appropriate medical or psychological advice promptly. Neither this nor any other related book should be used as a substitute for qualified care or treatment.

Published by JAPAN PUBLICATIONS, INC., Tokyo and New York

Distributors:
UNITED STATES: Kodansha America, Inc. through Farrar, Straus & Giroux, 19 Union Square West, New York, N. Y. 10003. CANADA: Fitzhenry & Whiteside Ltd, 91 Granton Drive, Richmond Hill, Ontario, L4B 2N5. BRITISH ISLES AND EUROPEAN CONTINENT: Premier Book Marketing Ltd., 1 Gower Street, London WC1E 6HA. AUSTRALIA AND NEW ZEALAND: Bookwise International, 54 Crittenden Road, Findon, South Australia 5023. THE FAR EAST AND JAPAN: Japan Publications Trading Co., Ltd., 1–2–1, Sarugaku-cho, Chiyoda-ku, Tokyo 101.

First edition: May 1992
Second printing: May 1993

LCCC No. 91–060394
ISBN 0–87040–799–6

Printed in U.S.A.

Dedicated to Koichi Tohei

A man who though thirty years my senior,
born a nation and a language apart
in a country once at war with my own,
changed the course of my life and showed me the Way.

In Praise of the Ki of the Universe

Vast is the universe and boundless with Ki.
What superb vitality it contains.
Spinning the heavenly bodies, ruling the earth,
Moistening mountains with streams throughout the four seasons.
Filling us full of life.

Without color or odor or form,
Mystery to our forebearers,
Who thought it to be beyond the grasp of Man.

At last the time has come
When here and now we can experience the essence of Ki
With our own minds and bodies.

–Koichi Tohei
October 28, 1990

Preface

People in every walk of life suffer limitations of one sort or another, in health, human relationships, job or career. Ironically, many people know what they should do to overcome their difficulties, but lack the energy, discipline, or will-power to take action.

Health problems are often aggravated, if not caused by stress and bad habits. A smoker may know that tobacco is injurious to health, but be unable or unwilling to quit smoking. A sedentary person may know that he is not getting enough exercise, but remains inactive. A relationship gone sour might be salvaged by efforts to improve it, if only the other person would take the first step. A career change could benefit a person enormously, yet somehow inertia prevents him from taking positive steps for a change. The world is full of good advice, much of it in print. Why then does so little of it get put into practice? It takes tremendous energy to realize your potential and do your best in life. This energy is called *Ki*.

Everyone is able to do his or her best some of the time. But fatigue brought on by stress can prevent a person from maintaining that condition long enough to make a difference. Not even the best professional sports players are immune from slumps. A prolonged decline may force a player into premature retirement, during what should be the most productive years.

Much has been written about human potential. The lives of men and women of exceptional talent remind us that we all could be more than we are. Certainly talent, and to a degree physical and mental vitality, are largely influenced by genetics. But no one yet has clearly established what a human being's potential is, and most people would agree that their lives could be improved in many ways. What then, is holding them back?

Very simply, they suffer from a lack of Ki, or life energy. Some fault fading youth, bad luck, or lack of opportunity. Others blame their parents or environment for their inability to act. Life energy is usually assumed to be determined by one's constitution, and not something that you can do anything about. If you accept this supposition, that what you have is all you get, you must be prepared to live with it. If not, you have a good reason to learn about Ki.

The disease which is predicted to be the AIDS of the 1990s, is in fact not a life-threatening illness at all, but a condition known as *chronic fatigue syndrome* (CFS). Although CFS does not kill, it robs a person of all but the minimum energy needed to stay alive. Furthermore, doctors have found no clear cause for this affliction. Like AIDS, it seems to affect the immune system. It renders a person exhausted, miserable, and essentially unable to function as a normal or productive member of society. It seems to strike people who have been active and healthy, even high achievers. Saddest of all is that it strikes in youth or middle age, consigning its victims to a joyless existence. CFS is an internal energy crisis. Without energy and motivation to live well, how can we ever solve the many external problems that beset us?

If it were possible, not just for the sick and tired, but for normal and productive people to increase their Ki energy, the world would certainly benefit greatly. This book aims to show that it not only is possible, but practical; and has been done by a great number of people, many of whom had to work against great odds or handicaps. These people have learned a simple but powerful secret: the art of unifying mind and body. Successful people in ages past have all been able to do this, yet very few have been able to pass the secret on to other people.

One man has not only discovered how to coordinate mind and body and strengthen Ki, but has also created a simple set of principles and practices which enable anyone to do the same. This man is Koichi Tohei, the founder of the Ki Society International and the man who developed both Aikido with Mind and Body Coordination and Kiatsu Therapy.

Koichi Tohei was born on January 20, 1920, in the Tochigi Prefecture of Japan. He was quite frail as a child. His parents were so worried about his health that they frequently took him to the doctor. His father had a fourth degree (*dan*) black belt in Judo, and at his father's insistence, he took up Judo training to build his strength. By the age of fourteen, he had earned the first dan black belt in Judo.

At the age of sixteen, he enrolled in the Keio Gijuku University Preparatory program. After he was injured in Judo practice, he came down with pleurisy, and was forced to stay out of school for one year. It is said that sickness brings people to their senses, and indeed during this recovery period he had much opportunity to reflect on his inadequate and weak condition. In an effort to strengthen both mind and body and to speed his recovery, he engaged in enthusiastic practice of Zen meditation and *misogi* breathing methods.

He studied Zen with the head priest of Daitokuji in Kyoto, Jôsei Ohta, and *misogi* from one of Tesshû Yamaoka's top students, Tetsuju Ogura and his successor, Tessô Hino. At the age of nineteen, he began training in the martial art of Aikido with Morihei Ueshiba, from whom he eventually obtained the highest grade of black belt, the tenth degree. Upon graduation from the Keio Gijuku University at the age of twenty-three, he was drafted into the thirty-sixth unit of the Utsunomiya Military Forces and sent to central China as a second lieutenant. It was on the battlefield where he first realized the critical difference between martial arts as a sport and the fearful uncertainties of modern warfare. While one rarely risks life or limb in sports, even a small mistake in war can be fatal. It was through this experience that he learned how to truly calm the mind under pressure.

After the war was over, he returned to the practice of Zen and *misogi*, in an effort to apply his insights and experience to the art of Aikido. Between 1953 and 1979, he made twenty-two trips to the United States, beginning in Hawaii, and gradually branching out to twenty states to teach the principles and techniques of Aikido. On September 16, 1971, he formed the Ki Society International, to teach the principles of Ki, and Mind and Body Coordination. In 1974, he formed the Shin Shin Tôitsu Aikido Kai, to teach Aikido with Ki. He noticed that as people began to have more leisure and more money, ironically they seemed to become more susceptible to disease. In an effort to help people strengthen mind and body by stimulating their own original life-force (Ki), he formed a school to teach Kiatsu therapy in 1980. To further spread Ki principles to the world and to help people overcome difficulties and lead a more positive life, in 1981 he formed the Ki no Genri Jissenkai, an organization dedicated to the application of Ki principles in daily life. In 1983, he established the Aikido Instructors School at the Ki Society Headquarters, to train instructors who could help teach Ki principles throughout the world.

In October of 1990, Koichi Tohei established a new Ki Society World Headquarters campus, located near Utsunomiya City in Tochigi Prefecture, just north of Tokyo, Japan. This campus, which includes a Ki Museum, the largest privately owned *dôjô* training facility in Japan, and a number of separate buildings for various types of Ki training, is

Tohei's contribution to society and to the future. The Ki Society will use this complex as a means of conveying Tohei's teachings to the world.

Only a fortunate few will be able to visit these facilities, particularly from overseas. Limitations of time, distance, and expense will prevent many people from having direct access to the Headquarters. But there is an even more critical limitation keeping people from knowing about this valuable and inspiring approach to the problems of life: the language barrier. Although two or three of Tohei's early books have been translated into English, nothing yet has appeared which presents how his teachings have developed over the past thirty years. This information is available in Japanese and his most recent book has achieved best-seller status in Japan, but this means nothing to the rest of the world outside Japan.

This book closes the gap. Based on my own years of experience studying with Tohei Sensei (teacher/master) since 1972, my experience as a special instructor at the Ki Society Headquarters, and having bilingual access to all that Tohei has written in Japanese, as well as his special blessing for the project, including many dozens of hours of private interviews, I am prepared to tell his story. I have attempted to reproduce his words, stories, and teachings as faithfully as possible, based on his books and articles in Japanese, endless notes taken during his lectures and classes over nearly two decades, and many hours of private interviews. Tohei himself is averse to exaggerated tales of things which happened in the past, particularly if they cannot be repeated or performed by anyone in the present. However, a degree of uncertainty is inevitable in any oral history, as no human memory is infallible. Those who were actually present at some of the incidents described in this book may remember them somewhat differently. Quite possibly, some of the people in these stories may have inadvertently been transformed into composite characters, rather than actual individuals. But I believe such errors have been kept to an absolute minimum and there is certainly no deliberate exaggeration or intentional distortion of the truth. My apologies for any variations which may have entered into the telling since the actual event.

Acknowledgments

This book has existed in potential for some time, and in a sense is overdue. Much of the information contained was drawn from books which have been in print in Japanese for many years and therefore unavailable to most of the English speaking world. Most of the episodes are still well within the living memory of many readers and students of Ki. Human memory grows less reliable with time and some things may be lost altogether if not captured while still fresh.

Sometimes it takes a little push to get people to do what they know should be done. In this regard, special thanks goes to a friend and fellow instructor of Ki, Dr. David Shaner, Professor of Philosophy at Furman University in South Carolina. During a visit to Japan in 1989, Dr. Shaner suggested to his teacher Koichi Tohei, that someone should write his biography in English. I believe he spoke for Mr. Tohei's many overseas students, who having met this remarkable man, were extremely eager to know more about his life. Barriers of geography and language seemed to put this knowledge hopelessly out of reach. But Tohei Sensei liked the idea. He liked it so much that he asked me to see the project through drawing on his many books in Japanese, and promising full cooperation in interviews.

With considerable help from Dr. Shaner in writing interview questions, I conducted about twenty-five hours of interviews with Tohei Sensei in Japanese. Gradually the project grew from the original idea of a simple biography, to a comprehensive digest of Tohei's teachings. In addition to the interviews, I based my research on as many as five books which Koichi Tohei had written in Japanese, books which had never been translated into English. Since that time the fruits of Tohei's lifelong study have appeared in a very tangible form, a new Ki Society Headquarters campus complex in Tochigi Prefecture, north of Tokyo, Japan. This Headquarters, known as Ki no Sato, is certain to become the mecca for students of Ki from around the world. Whether or not you decide to visit it in person, it is worth knowing the story behind it.

I would also like to acknowledge the profound and inspiring influence of my own teachers, beginning with Master Tohei, and including my senior instructors Koretoshi Maruyama, Taketoshi Kataoka, and Yutaka Otsuka, at the Ki Society Headquarters in Japan, as well as George Simcox, the chief instructor of the Virginia Ki Society. Their long-standing generosity and patience have helped me to digest vast amounts of experience and make it available to others. Also important are the many Ki Society members with whom I have trained, as well as my students over the years, whose remarkable progress has convinced me that Ki training works, and works for all. Lastly, I would like to thank the readers of my two previous books, *Ki: A Practical Guide for Westerners* and *Shodo: The Art of Coordinating Mind, Body and Brush* (both by Japan Publications, Inc.), whose correspondence and encouragement helped me to produce this book.

Perhaps the most important person who made this book possible is my friend and mentor, the late Mr. Iwao Yoshizaki, president of Japan Publications, Inc. His vast editorial and publishing experience guided me through the stages of research and book design. His enthusiastic support gave me the confidence as well as the opportunity to start a writing career. And his strong belief in the importance of Ki, and respect for Tohei Sensei's integrity and noble character prompted him to make this a priority, regardless of short-term financial concerns. Mr. Yoshizaki deserves special thanks from us all. A word of appreciation is also due to Yotsuko Watanabe, chief editor at Japan Publications, Inc. for her endless patience and thorough professionalism in editing the final manuscript.

Introduction

Thomas Jefferson said that happiness is not being pained in body or troubled in mind. This is an enviable and all too rare condition in the modern world. Need that be the case? Is genuine health and enduring peace of mind a remote ideal or an attainable reality?

Unhappy people have much in common. They spend most of their time regretting the past, worrying about the future, and complaining about the present. The irony is that much of this fretting is self-fulfilling prophesy. Such a life is empty, because it is missing an essential element: the life energy and vitality we call Ki. Unhappy people spend their lives trying to prove to others just how miserable they are, and they usually succeed.

Happy people do just the opposite. They see themselves as essentially happy, sound in body and full of vitality, and naturally seek out ways to express it. Given a choice between a plus life and a minus life, they choose plus. When you choose a plus life and do everything in your power to bring it about, your life is naturally full of Ki. This book explains what this means in philosophical as well as practical terms, and offers numerous examples and illustrations of how it can be done. The ideas presented are not mine. I have absorbed, digested, and synthesized them from nearly twenty years of study with a man who has lived and breathed them: Koichi Tohei.

Mr. Tohei is best known in the West for having introduced the martial art of Aikido to America in 1953 and then throughout Europe and other countries. Though he is best remembered by long time students of the martial arts for his uncanny ability to throw multiple attackers much larger than himself, and other demonstrations of the power of Ki such as the "unbendable arm" or the "unliftable body," his achievements go far beyond this. He has published a great number of books in Japanese, though only a few in English. In this book I have attempted to synthesize the best of his teachings, including many which have never appeared in English until now.

This book is partly a biography of his life, the experiences which led him to discover and articulate Ki principles in a form that could be useful to others. The result of his life-long effort is a remarkably reasonable and teachable Way of life, a road that anyone can walk. Every aspect of Ki training can be applied practically to daily life.

Even though the concept of Ki appears frequently in the Oriental martial and healing arts, I have avoided making lengthy comparisons. You may indeed find similar ideas expressed in these traditions, though there are some significant differences as well. I have borrowed from their imagery when it seems useful or appropriate, but do not consider them as necessary authorities to support the idea of Ki. After all, if a philosophy of life truly has universal application, it need not depend on specialized knowledge or esoteric study. We can retain what is useful from these traditions, but need not stick blindly to their forms, which were created by and for people living under entirely different circumstances from our own.

Ki is not an esoteric power available to a select few. It should not be confused with supernatural power, or demonstrations of magic tricks, even though it is often popularized in this way. As a young man, Tohei underwent many types of training, from Zen to *misogi*, to the martial arts. He gradually weeded out what was real from what was fake, what worked from what did not. He had little patience for mysticism and rejected outright that which could not be taught and done by anyone. Whatever he demonstrated he always taught how to do, often explaining that teaching it to others was the best way to learn it yourself.

Can Ki training really give a person more control over his or her destiny? Life comes to us without a guarantee. From the highway to the stock market we take a chance in everything we do. But life differs from gambling in two important ways: it is not a game and the odds are not fixed. As human beings we have the power to do something to influence the outcome of events. As successful people throughout history have demonstrated, our potential is limited only by our belief and imagination.

The experience and achievements of other people, both historical and contemporary, remind us of all that is possible for man. Now with television reaching to virtually every part of the globe, no way of life is totally beyond our imagination. Naturally we want to know how to avoid the negative possibilities that we see, such as war, poverty, and disease. But we also want to know how to improve the quality of our lives through our own efforts, not just relying on government and society's institutions.

As long as a person lives and breathes, his potential remains unknown. Only death makes this potential apparent, because no action taken can erase what happened in the past. This means that we should try our best to fulfill that potential while we are still alive. This requires tremendous energy, to overcome inertia, to solve problems, to act on our goals, to leave the world a better place than we found it. To have this potential and waste it out of ignorance is tragedy; to do so out of negligence is folly.

The fundamental principle of Ki training is unification of mind and body. By beginning with simple concepts which are easy to understand, Koichi Tohei developed a series of Ki tests or experiments, which show whether or not this principle is being properly applied. Through this approach, anyone can learn to experience Ki and its applications in daily life. Physical and mental health depend on an abundant supply of vital Ki energy. By totally integrating and coordinating your mental and physical being, you renew and strengthen your life energy. Surely this is the secret to both happiness and success.

A Brief Note on Japanese Words, Personal and Place Names

I have tried to avoid the use of Japanese terms, except where they are useful or necessary in explaining Ki concepts. However, particularly in the biographical portion of the book, frequent use of Japanese personal and place names was unavoidable.

The Japanese custom is to put the family name first and the personal name second. I have favored the Western approach here putting the family name last and reinforcing it with Mr., where appropriate. Exceptions are made for names which are well known in the West, such as Miyamoto Musashi, where the family name is listed first, in the Japanese tradition. The title *Sensei* (teacher) also appears after the family name.

My teacher's name, Koichi Tohei, appears so frequently throughout the book, that I have dropped the usual term of respect, Sensei or even Mr., in order not to burden the reader with excessive repetition. In most cases the name appears simply as Tohei. This is an editorial convenience, for in conversation the proper term of respect is the title Sensei, or even *Sôshu* (founder).

Japanese pronunciation, while not that important for this book, is fairly simple. Vowels are always pronounced in the same way:

       a   as in c*a*lm
       i   as in *ea*st
       u   as in p*u*ll
       e   as in n*e*t
       o   as in s*o*lo

Some vowels are long as in ô or î. The most important word to pronounce correctly is Ki (as in *key*).

Contents

PART I

A Life of Ki: The Story of Koichi Tohei

To know that which lies before us in daily life,
Is the prime wisdom.
—John Milton

Chapter 1: Making of the Man

Tough Ancestral Roots

Mahatma Gandhi considered his whole life as an experiment of the spirit. Koichi Tohei considers his as an experiment of Ki, one without end. But where and why did it begin?

The Tohei family moved to Akabane in Tochigi Prefecture just before the Edo military government was established in 1600. During the Keichô year period (1596–1615), Iga Tohei moved toward the east to Shimo Akabane. His son, also named Iga, moved during the Kan-ei year period (1624–1644) to Kami Akabane. His second son Hachiya settled in this area. The head of the household was appointed chief magistrate of Tochigi Prefecture, Akabane, and the Tohei ancestral home was recognized as a Magistrate's Mansion, or Daikan Yashiki. This mansion still stands today, located in Tochigi Prefecture, 60 miles north of Tokyo, in Haga County, Ichikai Township, Akabane, and is one of two magistrate residences remaining in the area. The grounds cover 130,680 square meters (250 acres) and the house is surrounded by Japanese cedars and a moat. On the grounds is a 1,000 year old zelkova tree.

Koichi's grandfather, Kin-ichirô was a very influential man in both business and political circles. He moved to Utsunomiya City in Tochigi, and went into business as president of the Shimotsuke Newspaper Company. At the same time he worked as the Patent Office Manager, and was one of the officials in the main administrative office of the Democratic Party (Minseitô). The party had just been formed, and as he was a big landowner, the Dietmen practically took his word as law. Everyone tried to flatter him to receive favors. People encouraged him to become head of the Shimotsuke Bank, to help rescue it from financial difficulty. He reluctantly took on this task, feeling that he had assumed a significant burden.

He had political enemies in the Seiyûkai party, cabinet members Hara and Takahashi, who used their influence on the director of the legislative office, Sen-nosuke Yokota, to put the Shimotsuke Bank out of business. Caught in the political cross fire and loaded with debt, the bank was quickly forced into bankruptcy. Kin-ichirô assumed an enormous debt of ¥700,000. During the period between the Taishô and Shôwa eras (late 1920s), Keio University graduates earned monthly starting salaries of ¥25 to ¥35; so in present-day terms, that debt was more like several billion yen, or many millions of dollars.

Most parents want to leave an inheritance for their children, but Kin-ichirô had had a large debt forced upon him. He left the bank when it went bankrupt, and became president of the Shimotsuke Newspaper. After Koichi's grandfather's bank failed, he moved far from the ancestral home to Ichino-hori, in order to cultivate a large plot of land. This venture was quite successful, and he received a plaque from the Minister of Agriculture during the Meiji period (1868–1912) from Viscount Tôsuke Hirata, inscribed with the words, "Nine square miles of land, a hundred years of prosperity." Through his efforts and business ability, he was eventually able to build a large home for ¥50,000.

Koichi's father graduated in economics from Keio Gijuku University and went to work for a bank in Tokyo, which is where Koichi was born. His father Makoto and mother Tomiko married as students, which was very unusual at the time. Koichi was three years old when the family moved back to Akabane in early 1923. His father Makoto was forced to go back against his wishes, under the insistence of Koichi's grandfather Kin-ichirô, in order to help maintain the ancestral residence.

On September 1, 1923 a terrible earthquake shook the entire eastern plains of Japan, centering on Tokyo. This disaster destroyed much of the Shitaya area near Ueno in Tokyo, from which the Tohei family had moved just several months before. Even sixty miles north in Tochigi, during the earthquake they were unable to stand in the corridors of the house and could see flames rising in the sky in the direction of Tokyo. This left a major impression on Koichi as a small child. If the family had not moved from Tokyo, none of them would have survived.

On their move to Tochigi, Koichi's parents were surprised to find that the large country property, including fields and forests, was already thrice mortgaged. The debt of ¥700,000 was so enormous, nearly impossible to return by ordinary income, that Koichi's father considered selling the family estate and moving to Manchuria. The responsibility of succeeding the family home would have gone to the first son, Koichi's older brother Ken-kichi, but he had been drafted while still a student at Keio University during the Russo-Japanese War, and had died of an illness on the battlefield.

Koichi's mother Tomiko stopped them from selling the estate and moving away. Her father Chôemon Yaguchi, from the Shioya County of Tochigi Prefecture, was a large tax-payer as well as an aristocratic Diet member from an old family. He also refused to let them allow the Tohei estate to leave the family, considering it unforgivable in the eyes of their ancestors. Under Tomiko and her father's pressure, Makoto gave up on the idea and agreed to stay on. Koichi's mother showed enormous grit in arranging bank loans, and eventually restored the property to full family ownership, completely paying off the loan by the end of World War II. Many times she faced tough gangster types who came to demand payments. But she was very strong-willed, and ultimately succeeded in her goal of protecting the family home.

The Frail Youth

Koichi was very weak as a child. When Tomiko was pregnant with Koichi, she contracted a nearly fatal case of pneumonia. The doctors all but gave up on her, but she survived. After Koichi was born, he was incredibly overprotected by his mother. If he but sneezed, she kept him home from school. He never protested, and up to the second year of grade school he only attended about half of his classes. His mother even hired a man to walk with him to and from school as a bodyguard to protect him from other kids. His mother's over-concern for his health actually made him worse, and he frequently got sick. His younger sister by two years was always healthy, never even catching a cold. People often said that he should have been the girl, and she the boy. One day his father discovered in the bath that his son was wearing many layers of clothes. Koichi's father got angry, stripped his son down and doused him with cold water. At his father's insistence, from that time on Koichi wore only two layers of clothes, but never caught cold as might be expected, even though the temperature frequently drops more than several degrees below zero (centigrade) during the winter. This strengthened his body in a way that no number of layers of clothing could have done.

Koichi studied Judo from his father, who had earned a fourth degree black belt in the art at Keio University and was quite strong. At that time, he was the administrator of an agricultural college (now Kiyohara Agricultural Junior College in Utsunomiya) and taught Judo to the students there as part of their education. He decided to begin teaching his son from the age of nine. Koichi always trained at the college with older and larger boys, so he gradually grew stronger and rarely got sick anymore. By the time he entered the Utsunomiya Middle School at age of fourteen, he had earned his first degree of black belt.

In April of 1937, at the age of sixteen Koichi entered Keio Preparatory School. Usually people entered this school after their fifth year of middle school, but it was possible to enter after just four years, which his father encouraged him to do. He enrolled in the intensive program, the tests for which were so rigorous that it was impossible to memorize everything. He frequently studied English vocabulary all the way up to the examination hall. Some problems on the test he recognized as having just learned the morning of the test. With a combination of optimism and good luck he eventually passed, graduating in the upper ranks.

His grandfather's brother was in the second graduating class of the Keio Preparatory School. His father's older brother had also attended the school, but had been killed in a war. Even his father graduated from there in 1915, so he was pretty much expected to do the same.

At Keio he joined the Judo division. Only three people were selected from the three class years of students to compete in the school competition. He was selected for this group and because the group won he was admitted to the Judo division. But during spring training he was thrown very hard by a large senior student and badly injured his chest. He experienced severe pain for about an hour, which recurred each evening. Koichi was diagnosed at the Shiya Keio Hospital as having pleurisy, and was immediately hospitalized.

The next day the fever went down, so he thought it was nothing serious. After seventeen days he was released from the hospital, and assumed he could resume normal student life. He asked the chief of internal medicine, Dr. Matano, when he could resume Judo practice. The doctor became quite angry, saying that such a thing was out of the question. He could not practice Judo, tennis, or even ping pong. Not now, or ever. Dr. Matano told him that his body was as fragile as a cracked tea bowl. The most exercise he could expect to get was by taking a brief walk. Koichi was told not to raise his left arm too high, to avoid all shocks to the chest, not even to raise his voice. The doctor's words were so disheartening, that he felt that his young life had suddenly grown dark, without any possibility of improvement.

Koichi returned home, growing weaker and weaker as he tried to follow the doctor's advice. He never raised his voice above a whisper, to avoid giving any shock to his body. He was painfully careful to avoid stumbling on any small stone, and if he did, he felt a sharp pain in his chest. He became so nervous and weak, that his father told him he should go to a rehabilitation center on the Oarai coast of Ibaraki Prefecture, until he was able to recover and lead a normal life.

After he spent some time there, the patient in the next room pointed out that he seemed to be even weaker than when he came, saying that the coastal air was too rough for pleurisy and that he should have gone to mountains instead. This warning worried Koichi, and once after taking a walk by the sea, he got a forty degree (centigrade) fever. The doctor diagnosed it as a recurrence of pleurisy. After staying in bed for three days, he returned home to Akabane.

On the way home, he was traveling in an open air truck. They passed some children by the road, who were carrying the flag of Japan, a red sun on a white background, the flagpole wrapped at the top in strips of black cloth. They seemed to be saluting him as he passed. He later realized that the children had mistaken him for a soldier killed in the war with China. His body was so white and ashen as to be mistaken for a skeleton. The horror of this discovery made him realize that he had to rid himself of this sickness, which was of his body, not of his mind or inner self. Though the body may get sick, the mind discouraged, Ki itself is without such limitations. In Japanese, a distinction is made between physical illness (*byôki*) and weakness of Ki (*Ki no yamai*). By strengthening one's Ki, it is possible to overcome physical illness.

Strengthening Mind and Body with *Misogi*

Now determined to take his life in hand, young Tohei began reading everything he could find about self-improvement. As soon as he was able to sit up in bed, he began reading anything around the house that he thought would be of benefit: Confucius' Analects, Mencius, the Bible, the great books of both East and West, and especially the Chinese *Saikontan*, which he practically memorized. Gradually he became able to walk, and after a year of absence, was at last able to return to school. During that year, he realized many things and became increasingly dissatisfied with reading books alone. He found that while reading Plutarch's writings on great heros, he felt as if he himself were a very brave and strong man, but as soon as he put the book down he was his own sick and weakly self again. He wanted something more, but what?

One day his sister presented him with a book which she had found at a bookstore in Kanda, which she thought her older brother might like entitled, *My Teacher*, by Tetsuju Ogura, which described the words and actions of Ogura's teacher, Tesshû Yamaoka (a famous swordsman and calligrapher who lived in the late nineteenth century). This volume was a great inspiration. The book described in detail how Tesshû repeatedly risked his life in pursuit of truth, never compromising for anything false. Tohei was deeply moved. At the end of the book, it told of how Tetsuju Ogura was still healthy and alive, teaching at the Ichikûkai *misogi* dôjô in Nakano, Tokyo.

Tohei decided immediately that this was his way to salvation, and without telling a soul, especially his mother, he went to the dôjô (training hall) the next day. There he met an extremely dignified woman, the current head of the dôjô, Tessô Hino's wife, Michie. He explained everything about himself, his illness, and how he had discovered the book, and how much he wanted to train at the Ichikûkai dôjô. But her response was cold and indifferent. She told him that he had better give up on the whole thing, that their training involved calling out in a loud voice, and slapping the back very hard. This was no place for a weak boy from Keio to train. If he had pleurisy, the training would probably kill him. He pleaded earnestly against her refusal to be admitted, until her husband came out. Mr. Hino sympathized with Tohei's plight, and agreed to let him join, as long as he started with Zen meditation (*zazen*). After he strengthened his body through *zazen*, he would be allowed to participate in the more rigorous breathing and loud chanting of *misogi*.

The training was held only three days each month, but they had to train under the chief priest of Daitokuji Temple in Kyoto, Jôsei Ohta. The priest enjoyed doing intensive meditation sessions (*sesshin*, meaning, "encounter the mind") with the Ichikûkai members, because they trained so diligently. He lectured them before sitting each night, warning them that they would never be able to understand the meaning of his lectures. He was right, no one ever did understand his lectures. But this was real *zazen* training, nothing for the idly curious. The priest approved of Tohei because he was able to keep up without slacking off, sitting in meditation all night long. Within six months he could do this without effort. In August of 1937, Tohei finally received permission to begin *misogi* training. This was the day after the Incident at Rokô Bridge in China, which started World War II.

Misogi was an old Shinto (a word meaning Way of the Gods, representing the religion indigenous to Japan) breathing method, which had been passed down in secret and practiced in closed warehouses since the Edo period (1603–1868). The military government had attempted to oppress it, seeing it as a political threat. But more likely, they were uncomfortable with the presence of individuals possessing strong will-power, who were less easily subject to authoritarian controls. Tetsuju Ogura had gathered money from friends and relatives to start a *misogi* dôjô. He named it the Ichikûkai, "The Nineteenth Society," respresenting the day of his teacher's death, and from the fact that 1 + 9 =10, symbolic of the goal of self-completion. He said *misogi* was good for young people, because it pushed the body to the limit, and strengthened the will-power.

This combination of *zazen* and *misogi* was a very severe form of training. When a person joined a *misogi* session, he had to write in an attendance book his name, age, and where he attended school. Participants had to surrender their wallets, watches, tobacco, and shoes, so that no one could escape in the night. Even so, there were those who did. Unable to endure the hard training, one person took the toilet sandals and walked a full three miles from Nakano to Yotsuya.

The training began at 6:00 P.M. on Thursday evenings. Participants were told that they must put their lives on the line with each chant. Unlike other forms of training, Ichikûkai members would be pushed to the limit. The first night they were taught the basic method of breathing and how to do the chant in a loud deafening voice. This introduction lasted until 8:30 P.M., after which they were told to get some sleep. The next morning they were awakened by a loud drum, and shortly had to appear in the dôjô wearing a white pleated skirt (*hakama*), which was tied at the lower abdomen. Beginners (*shogaku*) lined up in rows. On the right sat the chief (*osa*), and on the left two assistants (*kagura*). Behind them sat the "gatherers" (*tsudoi*), who sat with forbidding expressions. As seniors, their job was to strike the backs of the beginners with open palms just as they exhaled, in an effort to encourage the lazy or weak-willed among them. The *osa* began the chant and the *kagura* took up the lead, swinging metal bells (*suzu*) formed of metal canisters containing small steel pellets, with a long stemmed handle. The bells were held in the right hand, high overhead, and brought down with a vigorous cutting motion, reminiscent of the swift cut of the sword, on which the arm movement was based. Members sat in the *seiza* position, sitting erect with the calves folded under the thighs. This cutting motion was designed to focus the will-power with the cutting power of a sword. The metal pellets would strike the bottom of the canister with a loud pealing sound, which would mingle with and amplify the sound of the chants.

The chant was based on the words of an old Shintô prayer, containing three essential images: the sword, the mirror, and the jewel. The words chanted were *TO HO* (a double edged sword or spear, meaning the power to cut or discern), *KA MI* (the mirror, or the mind which is calm and unclouded, and hence reflects all things clearly), *E MI* (the smile, or state of joy which comes from meditation), *TA ME* (the jewel, which is not only the treasure of wisdom, but a round and flawless object, which can roll freely about, representing the mind which can adapt freely to changing circumstances). Members would first chant these eight syllables *TO HO KA MI E MI TA ME*, then compress them to five, *TO HO KAMI EMI TAME*, then to two *TOHOKAMI EMITAME*, gradually blending to sound like *TO-EI*. This is not to be confused with the name To-hei, which only accidentally sounds similar. This *misogi* breathing was based on an old Shintô breathing method called *Eisei no Den*, which means, "Teaching of the World Eternal."

The chanting continued for one or two hours each session, a form of training which truly pushed the legs, the arms, the voice, the breath, and the mind to the limit. There was one session before breakfast, three sessions during the morning, three sessions again in the afternoon, and one session after dinner. Eight sessions per day, with one hour allowed for the meal, and only two twenty minute breaks. The *tsudoi* would go around and strike the backs of the beginners very hard as they chanted. Many students got swollen and bleeding backs from this, but no one was allowed to rest or slow down.

The *osa* would swing the bell with the right hand, starting from straight overhead, aiming at the right knee, and swinging with full force, as if cutting with a sword. No slackness was permitted, as *misogi* was considered a form of life and death training.

Under these tough conditions the voice begins to fail in half a day, and becomes harsh and husky after that. Tohei was almost voiceless for a week. Everything he did at Ichikûkai was against the doctor's orders. In fact, his chest began to develop sharp pains and he thought he had contracted pleurisy again. But having joined with total commitment to finish the training, he was determined not to quit, even if it killed him. By the time he finished the three day session the pain was gone. And it never came back. A year later he was diagnosed again at Keio Hospital and the pleurisy was gone without a trace. This was very unusual, as serious illnesses usually remain in some form, or leave their mark throughout a person's life. This *misogi* session was the first experience Tohei had that taught him how training the spirit could indeed overcome a physical weakness.

After graduating from the first part of the *misogi* training, participants move on to the *tsudoi* role. He thought that it certainly must be easier to strike the backs of the beginners than to be hit relentlessly from behind. But in fact this was even harder, because very quickly your hands would begin to swell from the pounding. The pain was even made worse by the blisters which formed on the hands from swinging the bells hour after hour. This pain was far worse than that of being hit on the back, because it reverberated up the arm to the head. Furthermore, the *tsudoi* were expected to practice harder than the beginners, so the chanting placed an even greater strain on the voice.

A full three-day program, consisting of eight sessions per day with little time to rest, was called a *maru-tsudoi*, or "*tsudoi*-round." Before graduating from Keio University, Tohei completed sixty *maru-tsudoi*, the only person before or since to finish that many sessions.

Three days of *misogi* were followed by three days of *zazen*, and he never failed to complete either one. But this took a toll on his school studies. *Misogi* was a full-time committment, so during these sessions Tohei missed all of his classes at the university. *Zazen* started in the evening, but lasted all night long, and he went to school directly from the meditation hall. Having slept little or none at all during the night, he slept through most of his classes, but always maintained an upright and immovable posture. This earned him the nickname of "Sleeping Buddha." Somehow he was able to take notes on the lecture, while catching up on his sleep during the moments when other students were called on to answer questions.

Students were frequently called on to translate aloud during the German lecture. The professor would often try to catch him with a question while he was sleeping, but each time he would call out "YES!" in a loud voice, and manage to translate it properly. One day he did this five times during the class. The professor was so impressed that he never called on him again. Had he been truly asleep, he could never have answered the professor's questions, but on that particular day he just pretended to be sleeping, sensing that a grilling was coming. The professor told the class that some students go all the way to Kamakura (outside of Tokyo) to practice *zazen*, but that there was one student among them who did it right there in the classroom. It was not unusual for college students to be interested in Zen at the time, since the war with China had already begun, and many students studied philosophy thinking about how to prepare for death.

Through his intensive *misogi* training, Tohei had restored his health and greatly strengthened his body. He then returned to Judo training, but was dissatisfied with the emphasis on physical strength and technique alone, and no emphasis on training the mind. He was particularly bothered by the fact that among equally ranked black belts, the larger one would always win. As his body was not large, this meant that he was severely limited from the start. He tried Kendo and Karate but encountered the same problems in these disciplines. He wanted real strength which could help him face any opponent, not just a relative physical advantage.

Encounter with Aikido

One of the former graduates of his school, Môri Matsudaira (who later had a career as a Diet member, Minister of State Affairs, and Director of the Environmental Agency), at the time worked for the Japan Manchurian Railroad. He had just come back to Tokyo on business, and told Tohei about an extremely powerful martial arts teacher whom he highly recommended. He wrote Tohei a letter of introduction and took him to Wakamatsu-chô in Tokyo to meet this remarkable man. The sign outside read, "Imperial Martial Arts Society, Aikido, Ueshiba Dôjô." This was his first encounter with Morihei Ueshiba and the martial art of Aikido.

The Sensei was out, but a live-in student (*uchi-deshi*) named Matsumoto ushered him in. Tohei asked what kind of martial art Aikido was, and without a word of explanation Matsumoto told Tohei to stick out his hand. Suspecting that something might happen, and being right-handed, he extended his left hand. Matsumoto wrenched it with an incredibly painful wrist lock. Tohei deliberately showed no reaction on his face, but only continued to look back at him. He had offered his left hand thinking to leave his stronger right hand free, recalling the story of the man on expedition in Korea who met a tiger, got his left arm bitten off, then calmly proceeded to kill the tiger with the knife in his right hand. Matsumoto must have sensed a possibility of a counterattack, for when there was no sign of the wrist lock taking effect, he immediately let go.

Thinking you can know the level of a teacher by looking at his students, Tohei was greatly disappointed in this first encounter with Aikido. But just as he was about to leave, Ueshiba Sensei returned. A small man with a white beard, good complexion, and expansive smile, he hardly fit the image of a strong martial artist. Surprised and curious, he presented the letter of introduction from Mr. Matsudaira, and was taken right away to the dôjô to be shown some Aikido techniques. When Ueshiba began throwing men much bigger than himself seemingly without effort, it looked fake to Tohei. In Judo, the larger man was usually able to throw the smaller. How then could the reverse be possible? It all seemed staged.

Then Ueshiba asked him to remove his jacket and step onto the mat. Tohei had never been thrown before by a man that size, but the moment he reached out to take hold of Ueshiba's lapel, he found himself laying flat on his back. He had no idea of how he could have been thrown so easily, much less of what he could have done to prevent it. He knew then that this was the martial art he had been searching for. He began daily training from the very next morning.

One of the exercises which they were taught was called *Kokyû Dôsa*. It involved both partners sitting on the mat facing each other in the *seiza* position, with back erect and calves folded under the thighs. One partner would extend both arms out at chest height, and the other would take hold of each of his wrists. The object was for the one being held to try to push his partner over, without raising his hips out of his seated position. The partner holding the wrists was to try to remain upright. The *seiza* posture is inherently stable, quite low to the ground, forming a triangular base between the two knees and the point where the big toes touch and cross. With training, both partners learn to lower their center of gravity, making it truly seem like a contest between an immovable object and an irresistible force. This was Tohei's first experience with *Kokyû Dôsa*, and in the beginning he could not figure out how it worked. Everyone could push him over, even a junior high school student. However, one morning after a three day *misogi* session, he found that no one but Ueshiba himself could move him. Within six months he could do this consistently, especially as he continued his training in *misogi* and *zazen*. Everyone in the dôjô was amazed at his progress.

The extraordinarily rigorous training at the Ichikûkai had helped him to discover a vital point: that the only way to survive difficulties was to relax completely. The discovery that relaxation also made one stronger was a major insight. Through it he could easily throw anyone who tried to rely on physical strength. Ueshiba himself relaxed completely when he did *Kokyû Dôsa* and the Aikido techniques, but he never instructed his students to do this.

Around this time Tohei had an opportunity to practice Judo with a former Judo partner from Keio University. This man had always been able to throw Tohei, but now the situation was reversed, even though Tohei had not practiced Judo for some time. His friends in the Judo club thought it strange that he could get stronger by taking time off.

Tohei was later given Aikido teaching responsibilities by his teacher. He taught the Military Police Academy in Nakano, the O-kawa Shûmei Private School in Meguro, The Matsudaira Dôjô on the farm at Sanrizuka, and even gave private lessons to the president of the Shiomizu Harbor Sugar Manufacturing Company at the home of Kôsaburô Okada.

Though he held a black belt rank (dan) in Judo at the time, he had never been formally ranked in Aikido. Few people believed that he had no rank in Aikido, and when asked if he did not even hold a *kyû* rank, he replied that throughout the whole year he was without *kyû*, a play on words suggesting that he had neither rank nor holiday. Later when he was drafted into the army, Ueshiba sent him a certificate for fifth dan, the fifth degree of black belt, usually reserved for professional martial arts instructors. This was the first rank which Tohei received in Aikido.

The Military Test

By December of 1941, the Japanese army was becoming more and more involved in fighting on all fronts, especially China and the invasion of the Malaysian Peninsula, and seemed to be moving inland with incredible speed. The tide of the war turned against Japan at the Battle of Midway in June of 1942. This put the Japanese army under pressure to draft college students before they had finished graduating, or to give them permission to graduate early. Under this arrangement, Tohei finished college six months early, graduating on September 30, 1942. He was twenty-three years old. He passed the conscription test and on October 1, joined the Eastern Army Unit 36, as a Second-Class Private. He was ordered to begin military training near the place where he grew up, Utsunomiya City of Tochigi Prefecture.

The lower officers and middle-ranked soldiers smiled and treated them like welcome guests. The new recruits were quite relieved by this, because they had all heard rumors of how newcomers were abused and hit by the officers. However the welcoming atmosphere only lasted the first day. Beginning the next day the officers turned mean. Recruits were yelled at whatever they did. On Tohei's second night in the army, after the senior officers on night duty went to sleep, the middle-ranked officers came into the barracks and woke up all of the new recruits. The ranking officer sat in the only chair, while the others made sure that no lights could be seen from the outside. They said they were there to do an inspection of personal effects. But this had already been done in the daytime. They just used that as an excuse for their real purpose: to "educate" the new recruits through rough treatment and threats.

The officers would ask stupid questions, looking for any excuse to hit the young soldiers. The man interrogated before Tohei was named Yamakawa; he was the first victim. He had just gotten married three days before joining the army, so they asked him if he missed his wife. He said no, thinking that was the answer they wanted. They accused him of lying and hit him for it. So he changed his answer, saying that in fact he did miss his wife. They hit him again, for daring to talk about his sweetheart in front of a superior officer. Whatever he answered their response was the same.

Soon it was Tohei's turn. He decided the only thing to do was to play the fool. They spoke to him in low voices, for fear of being heard by the senior officers. If they got caught mistreating the new recruits, they too would have been punished. Suddenly Tohei got an idea. He would answer in a loud voice, an easy matter for someone with that much *misogi* training. First they asked him his name. He called it out, loud enough to be heard outside. They told him to shut up, so he answered in a quiet voice, "Yes, sir." They asked where he was from and he called out his answer, again in a piercing voice. Afraid of being found out, they warned him to keep his voice down. He said that he would in a soft voice, but when he answered their third question in his original full and penetrating voice, they ordered him to go back to his room. Of all the soldiers present, he was the only one who was never hit by an officer.

The army showed no respect for ability or intelligence, in fact they did all that they could to suppress it. The higher-ranked and senior officers all lived together and their constant preoccupation was fault-finding. Care of bayonets and rifles, mending of clothing, polishing shoes, whatever they could find to complain about. It was like being a new bride in a home with 1,000 mother-in-laws.

There is a proverb in Japanese which says that, if you learn how to live in a place, wherever you are can be home. Once you understand the patterns of behavior and how things work, nothing is too difficult to handle. Since the officers constantly intimidated the recruits, Tohei had plenty of opportunity to observe and second-guess their behavior. In this way he never became their prey.

For example, he realized that if they did a shoe inspection one day, they would check the bayonets the next. By figuring out their habits, he could stay one step ahead. However, it was important to play the fool, because they had it in for college boys in particular, and resented their higher education. Military training was very easy for him, being a small challenge compared to what he had already undertaken of his own free will.

He had not expected the Ichikûkai training to have any practical applications, but it did. Every morning they were awaken at 6:00 A.M. by a bugle call, and all had to scramble outside for a dry towel rubbing, wearing only their military pants. The senior officers watched closely to see who was first and who was late. If you were late, you could expect certain punishment, but no one was allowed to get up before the bugle call. The purpose of this training was to develop readiness for unexpected enemy attacks.

His *misogi* training had been so much harder, that mornings here were easy. At Ichikûkai he had to rise much earlier, at 4:30 A.M. There they did extremely hard training all day long, to the point of exhaustion, without much time for sleep. The *misogi* leader would beat a drum three times and suddenly slide open the doors to their rooms. He had trained himself to leap out of bed at the first drum beat, so that he was never once caught sleeping. Naturally, in boot camp he was always the first one out front. But a few times he found that a man named Seki was beating him there. He asked Seki how he did it. Seki said that he woke up before the bugle, got dressed, and hid in the toilet, running out on call and pretending to have taken his time. He did this thinking it was the only way he could hope to become a candidate for officer's training. Tohei felt sorry for him and decided to let him continue the practice unexposed, himself remaining number two. Later, Seki was nominated for officer's training.

Boot camp required training in hand-to-hand combat, including bayonet practice with wooden sticks. New recruits were supposed to face off against well-trained officers in bayonet practice. The outcome was always clearly in the officers' favor. But Tohei had learned something which none of the officers knew: that you are stronger if you relax completely. Therefore when he faced his opponent, he held the wooden stick very lightly. The officer said to think of him as the enemy and attack with all of his might. He asked in a big voice if it was really all right to think of him as the enemy. This officer was well-experienced and full of confidence. He said to go ahead. Tohei approached slowly with the stick extended out front. The officer tried to knock it out of his hand. Had he held it tightly, as new recruits always did, it would have been knocked out of his hands. Instead the stick snapped back in front of the officer's face, as if it were fastened to him by a strong elastic cord. Tohei then sped up like a wild animal and began striking the officer here, there and everywhere. The officer screamed out for him to stop, crying for help. Tohei stopped at once and stood at attention. The officer called him an idiot for being so rough, but Tohei apologized, saying that he had only followed the officer's orders. Once more, the officer called him a fool, but never harassed him again.

After that incident the other men treated him with great respect and he was never abused by any of the officers. They did not know what to make of him. Was he a great man, or simply a fool? He learned from this experience that when you are in a position to lead others, you must never take advantage of them, make unreasonable demands, or fail to respect their opinions. If you want them to follow you willingly, you must always put yourself in the place of the people you lead. He determined never to humiliate or cause his men to suffer shame. After that, even on the battlefield, he never hit any of his men, nor was he ever hit by any superior officers.

Having finished boot camp, after passing the examination for officer candidates, Tohei entered the Toyohashi Officers Preparatory Academy in April of 1943. His performance on the test was the highest of the entire company. The Toyohashi training camp was reputed to be the best in Japan. It was about forty kilometers across from east to west and twelve kilometers from north to south, containing hills, valleys, and varied terrain. Every day they had to run across it carrying rifles and heavy gear. They had to learn how to use quick firing antitank guns, even though the Russian army's tanks were already so thick-skinned as to render these guns useless. They were told that what they lacked in fire power, they could make up for in fighting spirit. To help build this fighting spirit, there was a military song which all officer trainees were expected to sing during their severe training at Tenpaku field:

Tenpaku is the devil's field,
Under the guardians at Hell's Gate.
Our trail of tears feeds the Umeda River.

But the Officer's Preparatory Academy was not as bad as boot camp. The men selected were highly qualified and the best were to be selected from among them to become officers. Unlike the training at boot camp, here you were recognized for your abilities and there was no petty meanness. There was no longer any need to play the fool. Tohei felt like a fish returned to water. He was in good shape, filled with Ki, and did not find the training hard.

He wrote in his military diary: "They called it the devil's field under the guardians at Hell's Gate, so I expected something very strenuous. But when I arrived, I found it involved nothing more than a little light exercise." These diaries were issued by the school, so everyone suspected in the beginning that their diaries would be inspected some day. For the first month or two, all of the officer trainees wrote in them faithfully, careful to put only what they thought they were expected to write. But when no inspection came, many stopped writing, those who continued to write put down their complaints about the food, or how tired and short on sleep they were. Only Tohei continued to write in his diary daily. One day after training, they returned to find that all of their diaries had been collected. Everyone paled when they were called to the main hall for a lecture. As might be expected, they were scolded severely. How could they expect to lead the country, much less go to war, if all they could do was complain? Otozô Yamada, the company leader, reprimanded them intensely for an hour.

At the end of his lecture however, he said there was one man who was an exception to his remarks. One man's diary revealed an excellent spirit and good writing, a man whose words reminded him of the best military leaders of the past. This man was Tohei. This was not surprising, for he had borrowed many phrases from the Chinese classic, *Saikontan*, which he had practically memorized when sick with pleurisy. He had written extensively in his diary, partly in anticipation that the diaries would sometime be collected, but also in an effort to retain the various philosophical sayings which had inspired him as a youth; for they were allowed no books in the officer's camp.

The entry in Tohei's diary about finding the training to be nothing more than a little light exercise won him great approval from the senior officers. But that remark provoked great resentment from the lower officers who were actually conducting the training, for it made it seem like they were being too soft on the men. They tried to get back at him by making the training more severe, but this apparently had no effect on Tohei, and actually caused a number of the recruits to drop from exhaustion. At one point they even had to suspend training for a while, as it was taking its toll on everyone, except the man it was intended to punish, Tohei.

The training at officer's school went on for eight months. It culminated in three days and three nights of continuous hard training, marching all night long, with no time for sleep. This was followed by a written test, which would have been hard for anyone that short on sleep, no matter how easy the questions. In actuality, no one could get through the training without some sleep, though it had to be stolen at odd and precious moments. Tohei had learned to stay up all night sitting in *zazen*, without ever falling over or losing his meditation posture. When marching, he held the tail of the horse in front of him, and let it pull him along. In this way he could easily catch up on sleep, even while walking, for they would march for long periods. Other trainees kept walking off of the road or falling into the ditch. The teaching officer himself had fallen off of his horse several times during the night and was getting embarrassed over this loss of face. He offered anyone to change places with him, hoping to embarrass someone else instead. Everyone knew his purpose, so no one volunteered, except Tohei. To a man who could sleep while standing or walking, sleeping while sitting up was a simple matter. Tohei slept even more soundly on the horse and never fell off, instead enjoying many pleasant dreams. Compared to the daytime drills, riding on horseback was like paradise. The teaching officer kept waiting for him to fall off, which he never did, so on the third night he refused to let him ride. This time Tohei resumed sleep walking. His mind was fresh for the test, and he became the first student in the history of the school to get 100 percent of the questions right.

Once a month they had a lecture from Saburô Nakazawa, a major general in the Japanese infantry. The lecture dragged on for a full two hours, and was not very interesting. In fact, it put many men to sleep, particularly because they were already quite tired from their training. But anyone who slumped in the chair would be hit on the head by the school officers with the hard sheath of a military sword. Anyone who got sleepy was instructed to stand up. Though everyone was tired, no one would admit it, except Tohei, who was the only one to stand up. The top officer of the school scolded them after one lecture, saying they were too timid and calculating to be honest. Instead of standing up, they would try to steal a bit of sleep and risk getting hit with the sword. However that day, for the first time in the history of the school, one man had been honest enough to admit he was sleepy and stand up, Koichi Tohei. For this Tohei got great praise. His friends said they would have stood up too if they could sleep while standing. Everyone was afraid of falling over, and getting punished even more severely than for slumping in the chair. Because Tohei was standing, none of the senior officers ever suspected that he was really asleep.

In the second half of the eight month period, with graduation approaching, the instructors sprung many surprise tests on the officer candidates. The purpose of these tests was to select winners of the recognition of appreciation and merit in learning. Only a few people could win it out of the 1,500 enrolled in the school. But to win this award was a great honor, and if you won it you had the option of further training to become a major general.

The officer who trained them at boot camp had told them not even to try anything so foolish as to aim for this award (the *Kyôiku Sôkanshô*). For most people it was out of reach, and the attempt to earn it was so strenuous as to be nearly fatal. He encouraged them just to try to get enough rest and survive the training. In the whole history of the Utsunomiya Eastern Division thirty-sixth class, only one person had ever earned this award and it was not worth breaking your back trying to get it, only to be rejected in the end.

One of the hardest tests was being able to ride a particularly wild horse without being thrown to the ground. They were instructed to grip the horse's sides tightly with their knees and hold the reigns securely. Tohei suspected that this was probably a bad idea, as it would no doubt only further irritate the horse if you tried to control it or pulled too hard on the bit. He decided to try it bareback and just stay as relaxed and light as possible. The horse did its best to throw him, but to everyone's surprise, Tohei managed to stay on top. The horse eventually reared up so high that Tohei slid down its back and landed squarely on his feet. No one could accuse him exactly of having been thrown off, so they agreed that he therefore must have gotten off on purpose. In any event, he passed the test.

If you made even one mistake during training, you were disqualified. Many well-qualified people were dropped for being caught sleeping on sentry duty. But Tohei was able to sleep while standing straight up and he could sense it when the officers were coming to check on him. Since he also performed well on all of the other tasks that they were given, he became the only one in his group to win this recognition of appreciation and merit in learning from the academy.

On graduation he received the award from General Otozô Yamada. Other students complained that it was only an award for sleeping. In December of 1943 he graduated and went back to the original training field for observation. The first Class Privates there were all shocked that the man who they had always thought part fool, part wise could have won such a coveted prize. But the regiment officer was extremely pleased and came out to greet Tohei on horseback.

Trial by Fire

In February of 1944 he received orders to proceed to the battle front in China. With no guarantee of safety or return, he determined to take advantage of any and every opportunity to train himself. Up to that time, he had no more than a vague idea about what Ki was, but he assumed that this wartime experience would help make everything clear. He determined to practice a breathing method he had learned at Ichikûkai for 200 times each day, without fail. This method involved exhaling and inhaling slowly and steadily, at a rate of only one breath per minute. To breathe in this way 200 times would take three hours and twenty minutes. Yet life in the military, particularly on the front, would allow no time to sit down or concentrate on such training. He had to do it during whatever spare moments he could find, while walking, sitting, or lying down.

His company quietly set out from Moji Harbor in Yamaguchi Prefecture for Tsing Tao Bay in China. Each soldier had to take turns standing sentry duty at night to watch for enemy submarines, which would sneak up close and launch their torpedos. If you saw a submarine coming in time, you could avoid the torpedoes by suddenly changing the direction of the ship. Sentries were relieved every twenty minutes, after which most were exhausted from the strain of never being able to take their eyes off of the ocean surface.

At last they reached the famous rough seas off of the Genkai coast. The seas were particularly choppy one night and Tohei was given sentry duty on the ship's stern. This was the easiest place to get seasick, especially if you looked at the wake of the ship. Most of the men on board were already throwing up, and were in no condition to take sentry duty. Even though Tohei was still on observation-learning duty and did not yet have to take sentry duty, he volunteered.

He removed his overcoat and stood at attention with sword out front, legs apart, and looked over the sea, then began the long exhalation of the breathing exercise. Somehow he forgot the cold night air and never felt dizzy. Time and again the men would call out asking if he wanted to be replaced, but he told them not to mind, to get some rest themselves, and that he would call when he wanted to be replaced. As this was a perfect opportunity to practice the breathing exercise, he never called for a replacement until he had finished his goal of 200 breaths. He knew they must have thought him crazy or possessed, but he never flinched or lost concentration in his sentry duty. He was the youngest man on board, and all of the others had already had some battle experience. Many had an attitude of superiority toward him, as well. Yet after his extraordinary performance on sentry duty, their attitude toward him changed completely.

Many of the troop transport ships had been sunk in transit, so when they arrived at Tsing Tao Harbor, Tohei was greatly relieved. He learned later that three days after it left port on its next mission, their transport ship was sunk by an enemy torpedo.

Even on the march he continued practicing 200 breaths per day. If he missed a day, the next day he forced himself to do 400, which was enough of an incentive to keep him practicing daily. But he found it difficult to do a full minute's breath while walking and often had to stop and start again. This was partly because you use more oxygen while walking than sitting, particularly if you are carrying a heavy load. It was also difficult to maintain calm and steady breathing if you were not completely relaxed. Eventually he learned how to relax and allow his breathing to become naturally deep and full. This was the basis for what he later came to call Ki Breathing.

Their original orders were to go to Peking (Beijing). But the war had begun to turn against the Japanese army and they were forced to go first to north China, then central, then to the south, Nankin, Kankô, Gakushû, Chôsa, and Shôtan, and deep into central China, fighting much of the way. When they arrived at Shôtan, he was requested to return to the Toyohashi Preparatory Officers School as a teaching officer, but he refused. He said that he could not abandon the men with whom he had shared such danger and be the only one to go back to safety. His men were extremely pleased at this decision. Later he realized that he was probably safer in China than back in Japan, which was then suffering heavily under the air raids of the B29 bombers.

One night, on the march from Nankin to Kankô, they came under enemy attack for the first time. It was pitch-black, with almost no way to tell where the enemy was. They could hear the sound of the enemy guns, but against an unseen enemy, their own quick-firing rifles were almost useless.

It was then that his mind grew truly fearful, for this was not how or where he wanted to die. He knew that anyone killed that night would be left as food for wild dogs. He had practiced *zazen*, passed many of the Zen problems (*kôan*) given to measure their progress. At the Shôganji Temple in Ifuka he had firmly determined to face death with an immovable mind on the battlefield. But now confronted with the real possibility of dying, he wanted desperately to get out of there. It had been easy to face death sitting on a *tatami* mat in a peaceful temple. The forceful resolution he had felt in Japan deserted him completely now that he needed it. A man may preach or study great philosophy, but caught here between the cross fire, all it took was a single bullet to snuff out your life. Despite all of the training he had had, the whole experience made him painfully aware of his own lack of maturity. In his training he had to face artificial problems, but now for the first time he was faced with a real dilemma, a life-and-death predicament which seemed to have no solution.

Then he suddenly realized that if life had meaning and the universe had heart, it would not kill him in such a way. For what purpose had he trained? He had done nothing yet in his life to truly help others or make the world a better place. He decided that if he were to die such a meaningless death, such a world was not worth living in, and therefore there could be no regret in leaving it. Tohei made up his mind under fire to leave his fate entirely up to the universe. With this decision he suddenly felt very much at ease. The sound of the bullets ceased to bother him. He was able to relax completely, with all of the strength that it had given him before whenever he faced a problem bigger than himself. Later he always told his men to follow him without being afraid, often telling them they had nothing to fear from such slow moving bullets. Right through to the end of the war, none of his men were ever hit. At the time he only vaguely realized that when you are completely relaxed you are full of Ki and can move safely through life. Eventually he came to see that total relaxation was not only the key to facing physical danger, but any sort of problem or pressure.

He tried many times to calm his mind by sitting in Zen meditation, but this seemed of little use now that death was a real and constant threat. It was commonly taught in Zen and the martial arts that if you put strength into your lower abdomen, your mind would become fearless and immovable. He found that under enemy fire, if he did not tighten his lower abdomen, he would shake like a leaf. But by doing so, his whole body became so tense that he could not move. When patrolling enemy territory at night, he found that putting strength in the lower abdomen created both fatigue and anxiety and he could not continue it for long. However, if he ignored his lower abdomen, he found that he was afraid to do anything at all. It was then on the battlefield that Tohei first realized that the lower abdomen was a place to focus the mind, not a place to put strength. When he focused his mind there, he found both courage to act and a greatly heightened and accurate perception of danger. He later came to call this point of focus, the One Point in the lower abdomen, or simply the One Point.

With practice, he found that by concentrating on the One Point he could easily relax. However, sometimes on night patrols, he could not feel relaxed about a place that they were in. Something bothered him about the shape or configuration of the mountain ahead, or what was around the bend in the road. When the uneasy feeling would not go away, he found more often than not that the enemy was lying in ambush ahead. Using this sixth sense, he was able to avoid being taken by surprise on many occasions. Many times he would change their course, or avoid a certain road, only to find out later that other Japanese units who had gone in after them had been ambushed and decimated. By keeping the One Point, he could even handle sudden surprises. Without it, he realized, most people did not even notice when they were in danger.

By learning to relax and keep One Point, he was able to find considerable peace of mind, even leisure time, despite their very desperate circumstances. He again took up his habit of writing and decided to compose poetry in the classical Chinese style. He would write a collection of poems and send them to Japan to a teacher with whom he had studied since his school days, Katô Hosogai, for corrections and advice. Hosogai Sensei was a man reminiscent of the Zen priest Ryôkan. He had a spirit as free as the wind and had always taken a special liking to Tohei. Tohei's father wrote back that Hosogai Sensei had since died, but that in his place the well-known writer and literary critic Sohô Tokutomi had offered to check his poetry. Although this was a very rare opportunity Tohei declined it, saying that a three year period of mourning was needed to show respect for his former teacher. He felt that it was not right to suddenly switch to another teacher, just because his own teacher had died. He sent his deepest respects to Tokutomi Sensei along with his refusal. But instead of resentment, Tokutomi Sensei expressed great admiration for a man who had the spiritual strength to continue to write poetry in the face of death, saying that such an individual would surely remain out of harm's way.

On August 15, 1945, Japan was facing disastrous defeat. Tohei's unit was deep in central China, so they did not even hear about Japan's surrender until a month after it happened. They had thought it odd that the daily air attacks of the United States Air Force had suddenly stopped. When the official announcement finally came, nearly everyone collapsed from exhaustion, grown men crying like children.

In August of the following year he was finally able to return to Japan. He was deeply moved to see how his parents' hair had turned gray during the two and a half years of his absence.

Though he gained many important insights into the nature of Ki through his wartime experience, he never felt that it was necessary to undergo such an ordeal to understand Ki. His youth happened to coincide with a time when his country was at war, and he found that through his training he was able to survive it. These experiences were later articulated in terms of Ki principles, which he realized could help anyone to reverse the tide of bad luck and find a safe passage through danger or misfortune.

The confusion and devastation in Japan in the aftermath of the war caused a serious decline in the standard of living. The Tohei family had owned a large number of animals: 100 pigs, 50 sheep, 2 goats, a cow, a horse, 100 chickens, and 20,000 carp; but these had all been sold, due to the scarcity of food during the war. Much of the pre-war private property was confiscated and redistributed by the new government. Formerly large landowners, the Tohei family was now left with only a few fields and the house. Not only did he not have much to work with, but he had practically no farming experience. He found that the work tired him very quickly. After tilling just a single row of ground he was ready for a rest. He noticed that older farmers could not only work hard tilling the soil from morning to night, but that when they would swing their tools to dig or cut, they would accomplish more in one stroke than he would in several. It was not long before he recognized that their secret was to stay relaxed and to hold the tool lightly. As soon as he started doing this himself he no longer had problems with fatigue. Nevertheless, successful farming involves far more than just digging. Tohei eventually decided to give up farming, as he had virtually no practical experience with it, and in any case it seemed to hold little future for him.

Needing to earn a living, he decided to try his hand at business. His father had just come back from Osaka, intrigued by a study he had read about on the possiblity of manufacturing charcoal from pulp. The research was being pursued by Dr. Gorô Kanô, head of a scientific research institute, and it seemed to have promise. There were large amounts of sawdust near the Tohei home, and his father plunged into the project with enthusiasm, even inviting Dr. Kanô to the home.

However, his father was as quick to abandon projects as he was to start them. His next project was working on the research and production of activated carbon which is used in the filtration of alcohol. But this too was an unfamiliar field, and he found it did not go well. They had difficulty producing high-quality charcoal. The business met with a series of setbacks. There were post-war restrictions on the use of electricity. Once the employees decided to go on strike and shut down production. Eventually he ran out of money, and was only growing deeper in debt by the day.

Tohei seemed to see no way out of the worsening situation. He thought he could count on the help of the people he worked with, assuming that if he trusted other people, they would reciprocate. But he found that when the money grew scarce, many of his so-called friends and associates abandoned him, leaving him with only three employees in the end. It was then that he concluded that his calling did not lie in business after all. He dissolved the company and released his employees, assuming the entire debt himself. With great effort, he eventually paid it back.

Chapter 2: Development of the Teachings

Discovery of Mind and Body Unification

After the war, while still farming for a living, Tohei of course also resumed his practice of Aikido and *misogi*. He went to Iwama in Ibaraki Prefecture, where Ueshiba Sensei had set up a temporary dôjô during the war to avoid the air raids. Tohei would pack rice on his bicycle, enough to stay at the dôjô for a week of practice at a time. Ueshiba told him that he was now many times stronger than before the war, and immediately promoted him to sixth dan. Ueshiba's techniques had reached an even fuller level of maturity, but there was still something unfathomable about them. Why could he do it so smoothly, when all of his students tried to wrestle their way through? This difference bothered Tohei, because he could not understand it, and Ueshiba himself never explained it.

At that time he was introduced to Tempû Nakamura Sensei, and the Tempûkai at Gokokuji Temple, in Otowa, Tokyo. Tempû Nakamura had served in the Japanese wars with China and Russia as a youth, acting as a military detective, something between a spy and a Green Beret, and penetrated deep into the continent. His nickname was Man-Cutting Tempû, and he had been quite a frightening figure. But years before he had contracted a nearly fatal case of whooping cough, known as "galloping horse" tuberculosis. Nakamura had gone to the United States of America to seek treatment, been cured, and then stayed on to earn a Medical Degree from Columbia University. But despite his "cure," he continued to cough up blood. So he went to India, into unexplored territory, seeking a complete cure in Yoga. He studied from a Yoga master and became perhaps the first Japanese to bring Yoga to Japan. He started preaching in the streets about the great hidden power of man, but eventually gained such reputation that he could count among his followers the likes of Admiral Tôgô, Prime Minister Hara, the heads of corporations like Matsushita Electric, Hitachi, Nomura Securities, and even John D. Rockefeller III. He taught what might be known in the West as the power of positive thinking and he himself had a tremendous power to move others with his words.

Nakamura Sensei's fundamental premise was that the mind and body were inseparable, like a continuously running current. He said that the mind was like the source of a stream, feeding the body, which was like its downstream currents. Once you realize this, he maintained, you naturally see the importance of always maintaining a positive mind under any circumstance.

Nakamura Sensei talked constantly of mind and body unification and it was these simple words, that the mind leads the body, which helped Tohei realize the secret of Ueshiba's movements. Because he could lead the opponent's mind, he could easily control the body. His students on the other hand, would try to force their opponent's body to move, and so would naturally meet resistance.

Tohei realized that before you could lead an opponent's mind, you had to be able first to control your own, and the secret to self-control was mind and body unification. Without being able to control your own mind and body, you had no hope of understanding or leading the mind of another.

The word Aikido means "the way to union with Ki." This is another way of saying the way to harmony with the universe. This then was the secret of Ueshiba's exhilarating techniques. Tohei realized that this goal could never be achieved simply by trying to blend with the movements of a single opponent. In order to achieve union with Ki, it was essential first to unify the mind and body which the universe had given you. Anyone who could not first integrate himself had no hope of becoming one with the universe.

Tohei reevaluated all of the Aikido arts which he had been taught, thinking of them in terms of mind and body coordination. Though this was not the way Ueshiba taught, it seemed to be what he himself did. Ueshiba's Aikido techniques were flawless from the point of view of mind and body coordination, but his teaching was vague and mystical, and often contradictory. From that time on, Tohei paid very close attention to what he did, and largely ignored what he said. Eventually Tohei became able to easily lead and throw men much larger than himself.

In September of 1959, at the age of thirty-nine, Tohei published his first book on Aikido from Kôdansha Publishing Company. In the foreword, Tempû Nakamura wrote a personal endorsement about the author: "Mr. Tohei has realized that the essence of the martial arts is not technique, which is no more than a branch, but the mind itself. Since his graduation from Keio Gijuku University, he enrolled in the Tempûkai, and was exceptional among the many students the founder has seen over dozens of years. He has thoroughly researched the practical applications of mind and body unification, making almost super-human efforts, achieving the highest degree of enlightenment into the essence of the martial arts, and working constantly to teach it to the world."

Introducing Aikido to the West

He decided to follow the way which the universe directed him in, and went back to train with Ueshiba Sensei in Iwama. Soon it became incredibly clear what it was that he should do. He determined that he must spread the principles of Ki and Aikido to the world. He met a Japanese-American from Hawaii, Kyôtô Fujioka, who later became a Japanese language teacher at Hawaii University. Fujioka was impressed with the teaching that the mind leads the body, so he invited Tohei to come to Hawaii to teach young people. After Fujioka returned to Hawaii he looked everywhere for a sponsor and eventually found one in the Nishikai, a health-oriented organization founded by and based on the teachings of Dr. Katsuzô Nishi. The Nishikai had members on all of the islands of Hawaii.

Tohei made his first trip to Hawaii in 1953. He boarded the President Liner ship from Yokohama Harbor in February of 1953 and set out across the Pacific. Many people came to see him off. Among the well-wishers were his mother's uncle, Chôzô Takamatsu, the rear admiral of the Genkai Navy. The old navy man warned Tohei with a very solemn expression, saying: "Some foreigners are like ogres or bears. Don't make the mistake of engaging in any competition with them. They'll kill you." Tohei wondered what kind of big men might be awaiting him. Having set out to introduce Aikido to the West, he felt a bit like the Peach Boy in the Japanese fairy tale, heading out to slay the demon.

The Nishikai had set up challenges for him to compete with professional wrestlers, often for money, the proceeds of which were to go to building a dôjô. Of course Tohei did not go to Hawaii seeking to engage in competition, but rather to teach the way of non-dissension through Aikido. He agreed to participate in these matches only if he was challenged by someone else, and did not initiate any challenge himself. He told himself that he would treat any challengers like a piece of smoldering cinder that happened to land on his clothing and simply brush them off.

He had no particular plan for gathering students in the beginning, except to show any wrestlers and black belt martial artists who came how easily they could be thrown. Many of the martial artists were so surprised that they signed up for lessons on the spot. But no challengers seemed to come from among the professional wrestlers. Finally the vice president of the Nishikai, Dr. Kurisaki said that Aikido was too refined an art to be put up for entertainment, and he withdrew the offer.

One time, however, Tohei was asked to give an Aikido demonstration between matches at a professional wrestling competition being held at a civic center. He offered to throw anyone who wanted to try, but got no takers. The wrestlers had little to gain from such an offer and much to lose. No one would be impressed or surprised if a large American wrestler overcame a small Japanese man, but it could be very embarrassing if Tohei threw one of them to the ground.

Eventually, one man volunteered, Wally Tsutsumi, a large wrestler who had just recently become Tohei's student. At first the crowd rooted for Tohei, since he was by far the smaller of the two, but after he threw the wrestler more than ten times, the crowd shifted its support to Wally. Crowds can be very fickle.

The next person to step forth from the crowd was a large Portugese man, who was confident that he could easily bend Tohei's extended arm. Holding Tohei's arm with both hands, he strained to bend it until he grew red in the face, could not move it an inch. All the while Tohei was smiling, as if he hardly felt any pressure at all. The Portugese wrestler grew angry and tried to sweep Tohei's right leg out from under him. At that moment, Tohei stepped in with his outstretched arm, throwing the large man on his back. The announcer told the cheering crowd that this was called extending Ki. Later, Tohei found out that there had been a $500 prize offered to anyone who could bend Mr. Tohei's arm. After that the expression "Extend Ki" came into popular use in Hawaii.

In the beginning, during his first visits to Hawaii, people were very suspicious about the whole idea of Ki. Tohei's reputation preceded him, but people somehow expected a much larger man and doubted that what they had heard about him could really be true. The Nishikai arranged a demonstration at the Shôbukan, in front of about thirty people, in which each opponent was a fourth or fifth dan in Judo or Kendo, or a professional wrestler. He threw or held each of them down quite easily and every one of them signed up to be his student on the spot.

A week later he gave a lecture-demonstration at the Kawananakowa school gymnasium, in front of 1,000 people. He was nervous but regained his composure by concentrating on One Point. He recalled how in his school days he had been frightened by the sight of a firefly in a graveyard and was deeply moved and surprised that he could now be calm in front of as many people as this.

Even though Japanese *samurai* films commonly feature scenes with multiple attackers, this is found more commonly in the movies than in the martial arts. Up until 1953 when he went to Hawaii, Tohei himself had never done Aikido against more than one opponent at a time, and nearly everyone he practiced with had always been around his own size. In Hawaii Dr. Kurisaki commented that in watching Tohei do Aikido techniques, he always seemed to move aside when he threw his opponent. Tohei replied that if he stayed in one place, his two arms and legs would become tied up with his opponent, and he would not be able to handle another attacker. Dr. Kurisaki asked if it were then possible to handle multiple attackers using Aikido. Tohei replied that it must be possible, if you maintained mind and body coordination. Dr. Kurisaki wasted no time and immediately asked for a demonstration. Surprised, and not quite sure of what he had gotten himself into, Tohei agreed to give it a try. Dr. Kurisaki immediately gathered seven large men, each one of them ranking higher than fourth dan in Judo, and even brought out a 16-mm camera to record it on film. Tohei tried to get out of it, saying that his Aikido was still not yet mature and that he did not want to hurt anyone. But this was no deterrent, as his opponents were all experts at throwing and being thrown. Seeming to have no choice in the matter, he at last agreed to the match. The seven large men circled him and slowly approached, then on Dr. Kurisaki's signal, leaped at him at once.

Tohei moved like mad, throwing and evading, until finally someone gave the signal to stop. Thinking he had terribly embarrassed himself, he was surprised to hear a great applause. Later, when he saw the film of the multiple attackers, he himself was surprised at how smooth it looked. Once he figured out the secret of how to lead another person's Ki, he was able to handle multiple attackers with more mental calm. Eventually, wherever he taught he was asked to do demonstrations of Aikido against five or six attackers and this became one of the trademarks of his teaching style. Sometimes the mats were not well secured to the floor and by the end of the demonstration they would be spread out all over the place. Close inspection of the films taken at such times however, reveals that the mats only moved when the attackers stepped on them or fell. Whenever Tohei stepped on the mat it stayed in place.

In May 1953 the All American Judo Tournament, sponsored by the AAU, was held at San Jose State College in California. People came from all over America, Mexico, and Canada. Dr. Kurisaki was president of the Hawaiian Black Belt Holder's Society, as well as vice president of the Hawaii Nishikai. He brought four participants from Hawaii and suggested that Aikido be introduced at the Judo tournament. There were close to 2,000 spectators in the gymnasium. Tohei gave the demonstration between matches, easily throwing as many as three Judo players coming one after another. The audience was quite surprised at the power of this new martial art, which must have looked to them like no more than simple dance steps. On returning to his hotel, Tohei found a message for him from a reporter, who said that the demonstration had been so wonderful, but was over with so quickly that he had had no time to take pictures or notes. Could Mr. Tohei please do it again the following day?

The next day was the last day of the tournament, and Tohei again demonstrated Aikido techniques against three partners, during a thirty minute intermission. There was great applause, after which Dr. Kurisaki told the audience something that excited them very much, but which Tohei could not quite understand. Suddenly, five Judo wrestlers appeared at the edge of the mats. Dr. Kurisaki said that they were not used to hitting or kicking, so Tohei was not allowed to strike or hurt them, but that the five men were permitted to hit, kick, or bite, and would attack Tohei all at the same time, coming from different directions. One large black man began uttering strange cries before his attack and suddenly grabbed Tohei around the waist. Tohei whirled around, throwing his attacker to the ground, apparently so hard that he was not able to get up for a while. Later Dr. Kurisaki commented how strange it was that Tohei had been smiling throughout the whole time. Tohei replied however, that even though it was unintentional, he had a habit of smiling when he was in trouble.

Dr. Kurisaki went back to Hawaii proclaiming that Judo was nothing, that high ranking Judo players who attacked Tohei fell like leaves from a tree. Naturally this angered the

Judo people, and many complained to him directly. Tohei explained that each art had its merits and that a student of one martial art should not criticize the others. The mountain did not criticize the river for being lowly, nor did the river criticize the mountain for sitting still. But many of the Judo people would not listen, still upset by the damage done to their reputations. As many of Tohei's early students were old men, women, and children, rumors spread that Aikido was only for weak and non-athletic people.

This rumor however, proved groundless when the chief of the Hilo Police on Hawaii Island ordered his force of twenty-five men to study Aikido from Tohei. The minimum height required to join the force was five feet nine inches. Tohei himself was only five feet four inches. Many of the men on the force were giants in comparison and he felt like he was at the bottom of a valley, always looking up to his students. He spoke to them through an interpreter, but no one seemed to be paying any attention. Despite his instructions, they stood in place without moving a muscle, arms folded. Most of the men had hairy chests, and wore old running clothes. Obviously, none of them wanted to be there. Tohei broke off the lecture, saying that it was time to start practice. He went down the line and threw each one of them, before they had a chance to unfold their arms or comprehend what was happening. This changed the atmosphere completely and suddenly everyone got very serious about practice. No one crossed their arms anymore, and each man paid close attention. The Japanese-Americans who were watching through the windows were delighted as many of them had experienced police harassment after the war. They hoped that through this, there would be an improvement in the policemens' attitude toward people of Japanese descent.

Tohei had a harder time getting started on Maui Island, but with the help of Mr. Seiichi Tabata of Lahaina, he was able to start a class. Then Shinichi Suzuki, who later became a major on the Maui Police Force, talked the chief of police into starting a class. All members of the force under the rank of captain were instructed to attend. There were fifty students in the morning class and another fifty in the afternoon. This class did a lot to increase the popularity of Aikido, as well as validate its effectiveness as a martial art.

One day the policemen were all standing around Tohei in a circle; none of them sat in the formal *seiza* posture. There was so much else to teach that Tohei did not dwell on etiquette. Some of them ignored even Western rules of etiquette, doing anything they could to challenge or disprove his teachings about Ki. One policeman named Morina tried to sneak up behind and attack Tohei, but was thrown to the ground so hard he could not get up for a while. Later at dinner, Suzuki asked if Tohei could sense an attacker which he could not see, because he had apparently looked behind himself just before the attack occurred. Suzuki had said nothing to warn Tohei, because he was curious what would happen. Tohei said that there was no mystery involved. Every police force has four or five mischievous types and that he always looks at their faces beforehand to see if anyone is up to anything. Morina was one such and Tohei had simply determined not to let him stand behind him. When he began to sneak around behind, it was obvious that he was up to something. Suzuki said that this sixth sense was exactly what policemen needed in dangerous situations. This he knew well from his twenty years as a policeman.

Tohei gave an Aikido demonstration once in a gymnasium on Kauai Island, assisted by several Judo wrestlers and his student, Wally Tsutsumi. One Japanese-American policeman named Matsuda had studied an old Japanese martial art and was jealous of Tohei's presence, as he himself had always wanted to instruct the Kauai Police. Matsuda frequently attacked Tohei without warning, but Tohei always threw him. Once after the demonstration, when the audience was still clapping, Matsuda sneaked up behind and leaped on Tohei's back, both arms around his neck and legs around his thighs. Tohei immediately bowed forward, which ordinarily would have thrown him overhead, except that his legs were hanging on tight. Tohei bowed again, this time dumping Mr. Matsuda on his head, and rendering him unconscious for a moment. The audience applauded even more, and after that Matsuda became a very polite and helpful student.

At first the Honolulu Police were not allowed to practice Aikido. A Judo teacher had reported to the chief of the Honolulu Police Force during a demonstration, that Aikido was too dangerous for them to practice. But an incident occurred which changed the police chief's attitude. A year and a half before, a young man named Mateas had escaped from prison with a friend, just after beginning a sixty-year sentence. Pretending to be sick, he had pulled a knife on the guard and easily escaped. After a year and a half he was finally apprehended. The Hawaii Hochi Newspaper featured an editorial which said that if the Honolulu Police had been allowed to study Aikido like the police on the other islands, they would have easily been able to handle a knife attack. This was in 1954, and just before Tohei was to return to Japan after one of his annual visits. The Judo instructor was scolded for having advised them against studying Aikido. The chief of police, Dan Liu and his assistant chief Tarbel took private lessons from Tohei when he returned in 1955, and recommended that their men study with him. This was the beginning of Aikido lessons for the Honolulu Police Department.

In addition to his reputation for being able to throw multiple attackers, Tohei became well-known for his uncanny ability to sense an attacker coming from behind. He taught that you must always move forward and never turn your back on an opponent. Since he obviously had no eyes in the back of his head, the only way to explain his ability to move out of the way in time was that he must be able to feel the attacker's Ki. But during a teaching tour to Boston, a famous local lawyer, Lane Rose, told everyone there that Tohei did indeed have eyes in the back of his head and could see as clearly behind as in front. Tohei of course denied it, but Rose insisted it must be true, because he knew a policeman on the Boston Suburban Police Force who personally witnessed Tohei's ability to see behind his back. Though he did not know any policemen in Boston, after some discussion Tohei realized that it must have been a man he had met in Hawaii years before.

In Maui there had been a large man who had strong doubts about the whole idea of Ki and once tried to put Tohei to the test by suddenly attacking him from behind. Tohei had somehow sensed it, grabbed his right arm and thrown him a considerable distance. The man had apologized and seemed very impressed with what had happened. When this man graduated from college, he went to work as a policeman in Boston. He told people there that Tohei could throw you just by looking at you and that he could see everything behind him even without looking. Actually, anyone with a little genuine experience in the martial arts has experienced this kind of awareness to some extent. It is the kind of sixth sense about danger and safe distances that birds and animals have. What is unusual is the degree to which Tohei developed and sustained it, even in daily life.

On Maui, Tohei had been introduced to the chief of police by Mr. Shinichi Suzuki, who also worked on the force. Suzuki used to come to the hotel to get Tohei before training. One day, though it was still early, they heard a disturbance coming from another part of the hotel. The hotel manager came running up to ask them for help, saying that two large foreigners had been drinking heavily and had started fighting in the basement bar. As a policeman, Suzuki tried to interfere, but the two men were so caught up in their fight they did not seem even to notice him.

Tohei immediately cleared the tables and chairs, and began cheering the two fighters on. Rather than trying to stop them, he actually encouraged them to have at it! The unexpected attention from the outside made them self-conscious, and his penetrating voice, which obviously meant business, brought the fight to an immediate halt. The two brawlers suddenly realized they were no match for this strong looking policemen, to say nothing of his calm counterpart! The wide space around them brought them to their senses and they left the bar quietly. Tohei called this an application of Ki awareness. In twenty years working as a policemen, Suzuki experienced many dangerous situations, including being shot at and attacked from behind. Whenever this happened, he always made use of Ki awareness to maintain good judgment and minimize risk.

Tohei's ten day seminars in Hawaii drew 114 participants the first year, 217 the next, and 419 the next. When he taught mainly Aikido, he could only gather 50 or 60 students, but when he began emphasizing Ki, he easily gathered 300 to 450 students per seminar. After Hawaii, he taught in many states throughout the United States: Oregon, California, Nevada, Washington, Arizona, Colorado, Illinois, Wisconsin, Indiana, Ohio, New York, New Jersey, Connecticut, Massachusetts, Washington D.C., Pennsylvania, Georgia, North Carolina, and Florida. Not only were the seminars well attended, but many of the places he visited formed active dôjôs, and have continued to teach Ki principles and Aikido with Ki ever since.

Tohei was the first person to introduce Aikido outside of Japan and he received considerable media coverage, partly due to his winning presence and effective teaching style. He first went to Hawaii, and then later all together to twenty-one American states, plus Guam, the Phillipines, and New Zealand, as well as Europe, teaching Ki and Aikido and starting new dôjôs around the world. Later he sent his own students to America to teach. Aikido even gained renewed popularity in Japan, due to the tremendous interest overseas. On January 15, 1969, he received from Ueshiba Sensei the rank of tenth dan, the highest Aikido rank available.

Breaking away from Tradition

But just three months later, to the deep regret of his many students, Ueshiba Sensei passed away at the age of eighty-four. Even though Tohei was the chief instructor of the Aikido organization as appointed by Ueshiba, out of respect for his teacher Tohei recommended and saw to it that Ueshiba's only son, Kisshomaru be elected as the director of the Aikikai. This was the only government recognized Aikido organization at the time, accredited by the Ministry of Education.

In time it became clear however, that Kisshomaru's interpretation and approach to the practice of Aikido was entirely different from his own. Kisshomaru taught that Aikido was a way of harmonizing with the Ki of other people through Aikido arts, while Tohei taught it as a way of harmonizing with the Ki of the universe, through mind and body coordination.

When Kisshomaru demanded that Tohei's picture be removed from the dôjôs in Hawaii and America, the dôjôs which Tohei had founded, he decided to leave the Aikikai, after twenty years as its director and chief instructor. He resigned from the Aikikai in 1974, at the age of fifty-five.

Before he left the Aikikai, where he had spent thirty years of his life, the second head-master, Kisshomaru Ueshiba forced him to make the following promises whenever he taught Ki development. No Aikido techniques or names may be used in the classes. The Aikido headquarters, name or funds may not be used. No Aikido students may be invited to attend his Ki classes.

Morihei Ueshiba himself had fully mastered Ki and its applications in the arts of Aikido. But he never taught it as such. Perhaps he was not capable of teaching it, or perhaps he believed that the only way to do so was to show it. But after his teacher died, Tohei felt that unless the Ki principles were more clearly articulated and taught in a more practical manner, they would gradually be forgotten. Therefore, in 1974 he started a new organization to teach those who wanted to learn Aikido with Mind and Body Coordination (Shin Shin Tôitsu Aikido).

Foundation and Growth of the Ki Society International

Tohei started the Ki Society International (Ki no Kenkyûkai) with just six members, his closest students at the time. When the number of Ki Society members increased to several hundred, the Aikikai started to put pressure on them, asking various of Tohei's student-instructors to quit. Therefore he formally separated in 1974. The chief instructor of the Aikikai quitting to form his own independent organization caused quite a bit of consternation among long time practicioners overseas. Tohei was the best known and best traveled teacher and he had a great popular following. Some people felt that they were better off sticking with the established organization, particularly if they had achieved a certain rank and status in it. Among them were those who felt strongly that loyalty to the founder of Aikido should be transferred to his son on the master's death. Tohei gave central emphasis to the teaching of Ki Principles, or Mind and Body Coordination, and its application to Aikido. The Aikikai did not teach Ki as such, claiming that it was something which could only be understood over time by practicing Aikido techniques.

In a sense, the Aikikai approach was the more traditional Japanese style: observe, re-peat, learn by doing, and expect to spend a great deal of time at it. Tohei's method was a radical departure from this, partly an outgrowth of his own character, and partly a response to his extensive experience teaching overseas. When he went to America, he encountered something that was almost unheard of in Japan: everyone wanted to know why and how it worked, and they constantly plied him with questions and challenges. Unfortunately, many people would be satisfied with intellectual answers, and were not motivated to gain a physical understanding of the art. Japanese, on the other hand, tended to work very hard at practice, but rarely questioned why or how, and therefore would often end up following a teacher down a blind alley. Tohei concluded that the best approach was a combination of the two, asking to understand why, and then practicing until you understand it with your body. This approach had a great appeal overseas, particularly with Tohei's emphasis on the application of Ki principles to daily life. The majority of the dôjôs overseas followed Tohei and joined the Ki Society, although the Aikikai and several other splinter organizations have continued to thrive since. Particularly the dôjôs in Hawaii, over thirty in all, trusted and followed Tohei from the start. In fact, now that they were part of a new and struggling organization, they trained even harder. Every year Tohei went to Hawaii to teach, eventually gathering over 1,000 members at a single seminar. Even third generation Japanese-Hawaiians, who could not read Japanese any better than the average American, came to study with Tohei to gain an understanding of Ki.

On October 19, 1977, the Ki Society received official accreditation status from the Japanese government, through the Ministry of Health. This was not for Aikido itself, but rather based on the stated purpose and ideal of the Ki Society: to help people develop their latent and inborn strength through mind and body coordination, to prevent illness, maintain health, and lead a full life.

In 1978, Tohei received a Certificate of Appreciation from the Upper and Lower House of the State Government of Hawaii, at which they asked him to shake hands with every member present. In that same year he went to Europe for the first time and held training seminars in England, Belgium, Italy, France, and Germany. In time Ki Society dôjôs were opened in Sweden, Holland, Spain, Finland, and Australia, and continue to branch out in other parts of the world as well. He himself was surprised at the large attendance and great enthusiasm of the participants. Through this he realized how right he had been in the path he had chosen.

In October of 1990, the Ki Society held the official opening for the new world headquarters training center. The new Ki Society Headquarters campus complex is located in Tochigi Prefecture, north of Tokyo, Japan. This Headquarters, known as Ki no Sato, described in detail in Chapter 14, is the crowning achievement of Tohei's lifetime of devoted effort. Through Ki no Sato and its outreach programs, people from around the world can directly benefit from Tohei's own remarkable experience.

Creating Strength from Weakness

Obviously, to do all of these things, Koichi Tohei possessed an unusual amount of energy and talent. It would seem that he also had abundant physical health, however this was not the case. Throughout his life, he experienced his own fair share of illness and temporary disability. But in each case, he used the experience as an opportunity to further develop and test his Ki. Adversity is said to contain the seeds of success, but whether or not they grow depends on how they are cultivated. In any event, the following episodes illustrate how difficulties can strengthen a person.

Experiences with Illness

Pleurisy

Tohei's bout with pleurisy as a youth has already been described. However, there are several points about it which are worthy of mention, in the context of how he turned adversity into strength. He was extremely weak as a child. When his mother was pregnant, before he was born, she suffered a bout of pneumonia which was nearly fatal. She managed to survive and gave birth, but she always had the nagging suspicion that the illness had left a permanent mark on her son, and always treated him as frail.

One of life's ironies is that the more apprehensive you are about a person's health, the more likely that person is to grow sick. He was always the first person to catch whatever was going around in his village. Due to illnesses of one sort or another, he missed a third of his schooling in the first and second years of primary school.

Tohei's father had been a strong Judo player since college and probably felt that his son was pitifully weak, so he enrolled him in Judo training from the age of nine. Thanks to this training, he was able to strengthen himself to the point where he no longer caught colds. But while attending an intensive Judo training camp as a student, he injured his chest on the left side by being thrown very hard by one of the larger senior students. After that he found that every evening the pain would return quite sharply and took nearly an hour to go away each time, which caused him a lot of concern.

His father came to visit from their home in the country and took him to the Keio Medical Center to have the problem looked at. He was diagnosed as having pleurisy and was hospitalized the following day. Tohei was discharged seventeen days later with a warning from the director of the hospital, saying that his body was as fragile as a cracked teacup and that the next major shock to his body could be the last. He was told not to raise his left arm too high over his head, to avoid any blow to the chest, and not to raise his voice, for even this could put pressure on his chest. That meant that he could hardly do anything at all. The doctor's advice was extremely negative and almost impossible to follow, and it carried very serious repercussions.

He returned home for a period of rest, but was unable to do much more than take short walks. If he but kicked a stone he felt pressure on his chest and ran home to take his temperature. If he moved his left arm too suddenly, he would quickly pull it back to protect his chest. He became so negative that after a month he had a relapse of the disease, with a fever of nearly forty degrees C, which lasted for a week. He had actually proved the principle that the mind leads the body, by leading himself headlong into a serious illness.

Tohei had to drop out of school for a year, but even when he resumed his studies the following year, he spent much of his free time just resting. He reached the point where he felt as though such a restricted life was not worth living. A lesser person might have committed suicide. But he chose life, and even at the risk of fatal injury, trained himself to become stronger through Zen meditation and *misogi*. This training made him stronger in mind, body, and spirit, and showed him the importance of mental attitude to health.

Spinal Hernia

During Tohei's many visits to Hawaii, his students often came to greet or welcome him wherever he was staying. A favorite and frequent gift was a bottle of the region's finest local whiskey. On one occasion, his students started coming in the morning and kept coming all day, each new group insisting on a toast. Though the students came and went, Tohei was present at each toast and by evening had consumed a large quantity of alcohol. Thinking that the toilet was at the end of the corridor on the right hand side, he left the room and made his way down the darkly lit hallway. However the toilet was actually on the left, so when he took a wrong turn he stepped on to a steep staircase, lost his balance and fell all the way to the bottom. Somehow he unconsciously managed to avoid a direct blow to the spine, but the torque of the fall on his spine dislocated a vertebra and he was unable to move.

They sent for a doctor immediately and he was rushed to the hospital, where they took X rays. To relocate the vertebrae, he had to lie face down suspended between two tables, with his chest on one and legs on the other. They said that using an anesthetic would make it difficult to get the bone to fall back into place and would take even longer for it to heal, so they performed the whole procedure without any pain medication. It took two doctors to help push the vertebra into place. As painful as it was, the bone did slip back into place and in time healed of itself.

He was ordered to wear a cast for three months and a corset for another three months, which would have kept him in the hospital for half a year. Although the accident was his own fault, he determined that there must be something that he could gain from the experience, something that he was to learn from it. Being bedridden during most of that time, he spent many hours doing Ki breathing. Because his body was rigidly enclosed in a cast, the only thing that he could do was to breathe, think, and move his hands. Of course he was totally off of alcohol, so his head was relatively clear. He decided to use the time productively and during that period in the hospital wrote a book called, *Aikido in Daily Life,* later revised as *Ki in Daily Life* (Tokyo: Ki no Kenkyûkai, 1978). This book became a bestseller and brought thousands of new students into the Ki Society.

Despite the doctor's forecast of six months recovery time, thanks to the curative effects of Ki breathing, he was out of the cast in two months and out of the corset in one. He left the hospital and a group of astonished doctors, just three months after the accident. Because his visa was to expire in another three months, he went back to Japan and began getting himself back into condition, beginning with long distance running. But before the visa had expired, he was back teaching in America. In the years following he spent two months of each year teaching in various states in America and in the Philippines.

The doctors had recommended that he wear the corset at least for a year and avoid strenuous exercise for the rest of his life; which he found unnecessary. Though he taught Aikido to people in America much larger than himself, he never had any problem performing Aikido techniques. He was confident in the strength and stability of his legs and hips, but having injured his back, there was for a time an uneasy feeling that it might still be weak under strain. It was during this time that he learned how to lead an opponent's Ki freely, without receiving the physical pressure of the attack anywhere in his body. Being unable for a time to rely on the purely physical strength of the body, he was able to discover how to rely on Ki principles alone.

Peptic Ulcer

Tohei once spent four months teaching Aikido in New York City. Noticing that he was fond of whiskey, one of his students told him that it was not a good idea to drink a glass of whiskey on an empty stomach before dinner every night. He said that it made a better after-dinner drink and that some other drink would be better before the meal, like a martini.

It was summer, so the sun went down after nine o'clock in the evening. Aikido practice would begin around seven, when it was still light outside. After class all of the instructors and students would go out to eat. Following his student's advice, Tohei grew fond of having a cocktail made with vodka just before the meal. Between conversation with students and before-dinner drinks, sometimes he would end up skipping the meal altogether. After continuing this custom for some time, he noticed that his stomach was not quite right. After New York, he spent two months teaching in Chicago, one month in San Francisco, and then moved on to teach in Los Angeles, all the while continuing the drinking habit that he begun in New York. Now after more than six months of this, his stomach really began to trouble him. The pain was persistent, so every night he gave himself abdominal Kiatsu, a healing method which he had developed by pressing lightly on the tissue and sending Ki from the fingertips. This gradually eased the pain, but his bowel movements were like coal tar and the problem did not go away.

One of his students in Los Angeles was a physician, so he asked him to have a look at his stomach. X rays revealed that Tohei had a peptic ulcer the size of a fifty cent coin and two smaller sized ulcers on his duodenum. The doctor was seriously worried about the possibility of stomach cancer and said that Tohei should have an operation at once. Tohei refused, saying that an operation was not necessary. The doctor said that if the condition did not improve within a month, he would have to insist on an operation. Tohei agreed to this and to follow the doctor's strict orders against alcohol and for a proper diet.

During that month Tohei followed the dietary regimen to the letter. Aikido practice began just two days later and none of his students seemed to notice that he had an ulcer. He gave himself Kiatsu morning and night, during which his stomach belched perhaps two or three hundred times, and after which his chest and abdomen would feel much relief. Of course, he also continued to practice Ki breathing as much as possible everyday. After a month passed he went in for another X ray. The ulcers had all but disappeared. The doctor was totally astonished, for he could hardly even identify where they had been.

The ulcer was a problem of his own making and a result of his own excesses. But it caused him to feel even greater responsibility about what he was to teach in later years as the founder of the Ki Society. For a teacher with the responsibility of teaching people how to practice Ki principles and maintain their health, it would be a tragic contradiction if he were to die prematurely of problems related to heavy drinking. This would be a great disservice to those he had taught.

In addition, these illnesses helped him discover the powerful curative effects of Kiatsu therapy and Ki breathing, and how they help restore the life-force that is naturally ours.

Stroke

Late in 1988, at the age of sixty-eight years old, Tohei had begun to feel an unusual degree of fatigue, which was certainly unlike himself. Everyone was taken by surprise one afternoon when he was unable to stand up or move, having evidently suffered a stroke. He was immediately hospitalized, and since he had full consciousness, determined that he would devote at least three hours per day to Ki breathing. He also received Kiatsu therapy everyday from the top instructors whom he himself had trained over many years. Within three weeks he was apparently fully recovered. Even so, he determined to continue with his three-hour-per-day regimen, to prevent any recurrence and ensure that he could live long enough to fulfill his calling in life, that of spreading Ki principles to the world. His doctors were quite astonished at his recovery, particularly considering his age, and the fact that the position of the blood clot in his brain had come very close to paralyzing him. He publicly explained what had happened at a speech which he gave at the Nihon Seimeikan in Tokyo, at the first Jissenkai Taikai on February 5, 1989; not only to show that he had fully recovered, but in an effort to help others who suffered from physical or health impairments to understand the tremendous healing power of Ki.

Spinal Disk Operation

Tohei had seriously injured his back in an accident in Hawaii during the early 1950s. He not only recovered from it in half of the time that the doctors predicted, but also wrote a best-selling book from his hospital bed, *Ki in Daily Life*. His back did not give him any serious trouble until he was in his sixties, in the early 1980s, when he began to limp and favor one leg. Because he never complained or talked about it, only his closest students were aware of the pain and numbness which was beginning to bother his lower back. Somehow he was always able to treat the pain with Kiatsu, but it seemed to be getting worse, not better.

Finally, at the age of seventy, just several months before the opening ceremony of the new Ki Society Headquarters campus in his home in Tochigi, he had his back problem diagnosed. His doctor said that several of his lumbar vertebral disks had been virtually worn away, possibly a result of the intense and forceful training of his youth, and that it was a miracle that he could even walk at all. The doctor ordered him to have it operated on immediately, and to have artificial discs inserted in-between the vertebra. Without the operation, he said, Tohei would soon be in a wheelchair. Tohei was told there was a 10 percent risk of dying with such a serious operation, which he interpreted as a 90 percent chance of living, saying that he was certain to remain living until the day he died. With the operation there was a good chance that the artificial disks would become integrated into his bone tissue and could last another ten to fifteen years, but that this would take one full year and he was absolutely to do no Aikido or hard exercise during that time. His operation took place in June of 1990. Of course, he wasted no time in the hospital, having plenty of time on his hands, he did many hours of Ki breathing and received Kiatsu therapy several hours a day. He was told to begin rehabilitation after three weeks of total rest. To learn to walk again he was to take thirty steps the first day and increase the number gradually by five steps per day after that. His first day of rehabilitation he walked thirty steps, the next day 400, and the third day he took 1,000 steps. After that he began moving about with a cane. Within a few months he felt no more pain or numbness and could easily walk about with a cane. The doctor was so impressed by Tohei's swift recovery, that he gave him permission to do Aikido by February of 1991, just eight months after the operation, and recorded it on video tape to show at an international doctor's convention. Apparently the speed and degree of Tohei's recovery was so remarkable that it had to be seen to be believed and it gained international attention in medical circles.

Lessons Learned

Tohei was often criticized by outsiders for his excessive drinking, thinking that it was unbefitting a person who was teaching a philosophy and discipline of health. Those who knew and drank with him however, saw in his drinking a more human side, one which could enjoy life and still remain in control of himself. In fact he had an amazing capacity to drink, at one time imbibing four large bottles of *sake* at one sitting, each containing 1.8 liters of strong Japanese wine, and he walked home. Some of the tough policemen and martial artists in Hawaii thought they could outdrink him, even if they could not defeat him in the dôjô. But no one could keep up with him, and he was never late for early morning practice. However, some of his students got the wrong idea, and became heavy drinkers themselves, somehow expecting that Ki would prevent them from any of its negative effects. Yet Tohei's own experiences with illness were nearly all attributed to excessive drinking, which he claims is the one major error of his life, and the one thing which he encourages his students not to imitate. Still all in all, no one can acuse him of having been an alcoholic, because he was able to quit whenever he needed or decided to, and it never interfered with his performance or teaching ability. Western readers should also remember that in Japan heavy drinking carries little or no social stigma, and is very much a part of the night life of people who hold respected and responsible positions during the day.

While Tohei focused heavily on Aikido arts in his early career, his purpose was simply to show otherwise disbelieving people the power of Ki. Later, however, he realized that people were placing more emphasis on Aikido than on Ki in daily life. This was like ignoring the roots for the sake of the branches. So he began to emphasize more and more the application of Ki to health, which is itself the root of all else that we do.

Portrait of Tohei Sensei by Koretoshi Maruyama

Born on January 20 in 1920, Tohei Sensei was raised in the Tochigi Prefecture of Japan. When enrolled in studies at the Keio University Preparatory School, he became very ill. This illness inspired him to heal himself, through intensive training in Zen, *misogi,* Mind and Body Unification, and meditation beneath a waterfall. During World War II he was sent to China and given a position of command. He learned the true meaning of calming the mind at the One Point in an environment where slackening of Ki for even a single moment could cost one's life. It was here also, without medicine and far from medical care, that he learned how to send Ki through the fingertips and heal, with what he later came to call Kiatsu Therapy.

It was on September 16, 1971 that he founded the Ki Society, realizing the importance and need to teach mind and body unification to people around the world. He is not only the founder of the Ki Society, but also the author of many books on Ki development.

After some years of considerable effort and preparation, he was able to gain official recognition and accreditation for the Ki Society from the Japanese government, in October of 1976.

> A man whose spirit is equal to any,
> careless in nothing.
> Resolute and unflinching.
> A man who can encourage others.

How to describe such a man—In another age, he might have been called heroic, valiant. Though frail and weak in his youth, by his own efforts he strengthened himself. In time he transformed himself and his vigor penetrated to his heart and soul and bones.

Late at night, after Aikido practice he would take us drinking. Rarely did we return before 3 A.M. Yet for most of my life, I cannot recall his being late for early morning practice even once.

He was implored by the chief of police in Hawaii to teach Aikido to officers on all of the islands. The tough reputation of the Hawaiian Police Force notwithstanding, on the mat he led them about like children. Thinking they could outdrink him, the officers challenged Tohei Sensei off the mat as well. Again, he was the only one left standing. And he walked home. . . .

To the age of fifty he trained and strengthened himself. As he puts it: "I teach how to walk the big road of the universe, and how to maintain one's health. If I drink too much, maybe I'll die too young, and my students will have much trouble to follow me. After fifty years old, I decided no more than three glasses at one time." —Of course, some glasses are bigger than others.

Demanding of himself, or so he appears to others. But he laughs it off, "Hard discipline?! Nothing hard! You only need to change the subconscious mind. Very easy!" Twenty years a smoker. One day he decided to quit. And that was it.

When he goes to bed at night, he decides what time he wants to get up, as if setting a subconscious alarm clock. Precise to the minute, he jumps up wide-eyed and alert and begins the day. Whatever you decide you want to do, he says, follow through on it.

You need perseverance to lead others. No matter how clumsy a person, no matter how slow, if only they have motivation to learn, he never gives up on them. If one teaching method fails he has another, and another. . . .

"There is a way to lead any person. If they still can't do it, there is something missing from the way of teaching. If the student can't do it, the teacher must feel shame." And Tohei Sensei is an outstanding teacher.

A man of empathy and strong emotions. But somehow different from others. His emotion does not sway his judgment. He can scold without reserve, because he does it for the other person's benefit. Who would not tremble under those thick eyebrows and that penetrating gaze, with a voice like thunder? But of course he is not really angry. We just are not accustomed to having our subconscious mind spoken to so directly.

Nor are we ready for the wonderful smile which follows it. Like the warm sun which is there when the typhoon passes, his smile is captivating. An instant friend to small children.

Scrupulously honest. White lies and secrets hold no credence with this man. Showing off, boasting, bragging, all of these are pure counterfeit, and buy as much in the end. Real honesty is facing up to the universe and its truths. Our daily life itself is a dialogue with nature and its principles. Even in the heat and noise of the city, we can live with dignity and harmony.

Do not distort or waste your Ki. There is no time for anxiety or neurosis. Instead, replenish the Ki that you have squandered. In a word, you are better off with a good night's rest.

And then there is Tohei Sensei's teaching itself. Tohei Sensei was drafted and sent to China during World War II. Under a rain of bullets he discovered the vital importance of Ki. He believed that as long as he extended Ki, bullets would never find him. It was a belief on which he literally bet his life to test.

When the war ended, his return was noble. Not one of the eighty men in his charge was killed. His belief was for more than just himself. No situation is hopeless when your mind is positive. Tohei Sensei cannot be put into a pinch, because he has firm control over himself. He always finds a way, because he always seeks one.

Though Japan was devastated by the war and beset by a long list of problems, he always accepted as a given that the fundamentals of the universe remain unchanged.

Many people in the world today complain about their lack of ability. But the real problem is that they have not discovered the abilities that even now they possess. We speak of the tip of the iceberg. The massive ice chunks that float in the Antarctic Ocean are 90 percent invisible, below the surface. Our abilities as human beings are no different.

When you truly coordinate mind and body you are no longer limited to the visible part of the iceberg, it is all available to you. Tohei Sensei teaches us that this is the real meaning of human ability and talent.

However, it has always been assumed that because mind and body coordination is so very difficult, its fruits must be for the very few. And still fewer have been able to show others how to do what they themselves may have learned.

Yet Koichi Tohei is one who did. Not stopping at realizing the essential unity of mind and body, he showed others how to learn it. He articulated the four basic principles of mind and body unification, and even gave us a way to test it with certainty. His method of Ki testing enables anyone to clearly see the state of another person's mind through the body, as well as develop and deepen the state of mind and body unity at the same time.

Four universally valid principles and a way to verify them, anytime, anyplace. This is an achievement which is perhaps unequalled, and one whose magnitude will only increase with time.

In whatever he has done, he first considers how to help others. What the world needs, what other people lack, from morning to night, throughout his life he has deepened and clarified the way of Ki. The word Ki has come into common parlance in many languages of the world today. The one who did most to spread its use was Koichi Tohei.

Those who have met him in person have recognized the way of Ki. Those who know him feel both deep respect and genuine affection. Someone said it quietly, "A truly great man emerges once in a thousand years."

58

Portraits of the Master

Fig. 1. Tohei at the age of twenty-three (left), at the time of his graduation from Keio Gijuku University (1943).

Fig. 2. Tohei had already received his eighth dan in Aikido by the age of thirty-two, from his teacher, Morihei Ueshiba (1952).

Fig. 3. Tohei on his first trip to Hawaii at the age of thirty-three, where he performed traditional Japanese dance (1953).

Fig. 4. Portrait of Tohei around 1953.

Fig. 5. After Tohei was invited to teach Aikido in Hawaii, he later escorted Ueshiba Sensei. Here Tohei (right) appears with his teacher (center) and the State Governor (left).

Fig. 6. Certificate of tenth dan in Aikido, given to Koichi Tohei and marked as the first of that rank given, bearing the signature and seal of Morihei Ueshiba, dated January 15, 1969.

Fig. 7. Portrait of Tohei at the age of fifty-six, taken for the fifth anniversary of the founding of the Ki Society.

Fig. 8. Character for Ki, painted in the early days of the Ki Society. Every officially registered dôjô receives a hand-painted original like this one, as well as a portrait photograph of Tohei Sensei.

Fig. 9. The Four Basic Principles of Mind and Body Unification, developed by Tohei and written here in his own brushwork.

Fig. 10. Portrait of Tohei at the age of seventy, taken for the opening of the new Ki no Sato Headquarters (1990).

PART II

How to Experience and Develop Ki in Daily Life

Experience is the worst teacher;
it gives the test before presenting the lesson.
—Vernon Law

Learning from Experience

After establishing the Ki Society, Tohei began telling his students that they need not follow the path that he himself did in order to understand mind and body unification. Instead they should follow the principles which were the essence of what he had learned from his remarkable experiences. He in fact made significant changes in all of the disciplines and techniques, discarding many practices which he considered misleading and greatly simplifying the rest in order to make them more practical for daily living. To reinforce the differences he also assigned new names and definitions to each part of the curriculum. These changes grew more and more distinct as time went on, until it evolved into a discipline which was entirely different from Zen, *misogi,* or even the original Aikido. He called this new discpline "The Way of Mind and Body Unification," and its application in Aikido, "Aikido with Mind and Body Coordination," or simply Ki-Aikido.

Still no small number of his students suspected that he got where he did precisely because he had studied Judo, Zen, *misogi*, and even hand-to-hand combat. Strangely, none of those who attempted these disciplines could seem to find what Tohei did, nor could they easily reconcile what was being taught in those disciplines with the Ki principles which Tohei was now teaching. Even Ki-Aikido was different from other styles of Aikido being taught, including the one which he himself had learned from Master Ueshiba.

Tohei acknowledged that anyone who followed those disciplines or repeated those experiences with the same degree of dedication and will-power would arrive at the same result. But this was no easy task. The average student dropped out or did not practice nearly as hard as Tohei himself did. Few people pursue any discipline deeply enough to grasp its real essence, and even fewer attempt to apply what they have learned in real life. Many of the old ways are fraught with fundamental errors, or are too closely tied to the era and the culture in which they were developed. Furthermore, Tohei could not recommend anyone to have a wartime experience, for there is no guarantee of coming out of it alive. A modern battlefield is very unforgiving of mistakes. Tohei spent his life paring what he learned from experience down to the essence and attempting to organize it into a teachable way that works for anyone, in any culture and any time. This was based on the conviction that the way of the universe was wide enough for anyone to walk, not just a select few.

The essential teachings of that way are contained in the four basic principles which Ko-ichi Tohei discovered for mind and body unification. They will be explained in detail in this chapter.

Four Basic Principles for Mind and Body Unification:
1. **Calm and focus the mind at the One Point in the lower abdomen.**
2. **Completely release all stress from the body.**
3. **Let the weight of every part of the body settle at its lowest point.**
4. **Extend Ki.**

How to Experience and Test Mind and Body Unification

Since it is impossible to see the mind directly, traditional disciplines have relied on techniques which abuse or punish the body in order to wake up or focus the mind. In Zen meditation, a senior monk may hit you with a flexible stick if your posture slumps. During the chanting practice at the Ichikûkai, senior students slapped your back very hard to "encourage" you to exhale more completely. The problem with these methods is that unless the senior student is very advanced indeed, it can easily degenerate into old schoolmaster brutality. Tohei said that physically striking a student only interferes with his progress, so he completely dropped these practices when he taught meditation and breathing methods. There is no need to physically abuse someone to instill discipline, for the only genuine discipline is self-discipline.

But without a physical means of testing oneself and others, there is no way to be sure whether or not you have mind and body unification. This is a field which is fraught with the danger of self-deception. Perhaps the best example of this is the macho man who lords it over other people most of the time, but when faced with a real problem tucks his tail and slinks away. People like to believe that they are strong, capable, and confident, but they frequently forget to ask themselves on what their strength is based.

To help you get a taste of your potential strength, try the following experiment. Lightly touch the tips of your thumb and forefinger in an "O.K." gesture. There is no need to force them together, just think of your fingers as forming an iron ring. Ask another person to insert both forefingers into this ring, and try to pull it apart. Ask him to pull gradually at first. Try to absorb, rather than resist their force. You will find that your two fingers appear to be many times stronger than the other person's two arms. At this point, your partner may attempt to suddenly jerk your fingers apart, or twist them at different angles. In the beginning you should ask the person to pull gradually, but with as much force as he likes. With practice you can maintain the iron ring against a very strong man.

Now try the test again, this time using the strength of your fingers to resist your partner's two arms. There is no contest; arms win, hands down. The important thing to draw from this test is the difference in strength and staying power using Ki compared to relying on physical strength alone. You may not realize that you used Ki, but you have demonstrated that the mind can integrate and strengthen the body, without using any particular force.

The power that we ordinarily use, a combination of our physical strength, knowledge, experience, and abilities, is obviously quite limited. With training you may be able to double or triple this power, but soon age and youthful competition begin to take their toll. Tohei refers to this power as the small, visible segment of an iceberg. Below the surface is a vast potential which is in fact the whole iceberg itself. If we are able to tap into even a portion of this potential, then we can increase our life power many fold. The unseen portion is the mind, and when we unify the mind and body, then for the first time we can make full use of Ki. This is not as difficult as people assume, if you follow the four basic principles for mind and body unification. But how do you know if you have followed them correctly?

Tohei's most original and ingenious invention was a method he called *Ki Testing,* a simple technique which makes it immediately clear not only whether or not a person has mind and body unified, but also the degree to which the person is unified. This method has no precedent in East or West, in modern or ancient times. Certainly many people in various cultures throughout history were able to achieve mind and body coordination. To them we owe the works of genius and invention, as well as the deeds of courage and strength which from time to time brighten the human race. But no one has ever before been able to devise a clear way of teaching it to others. The way which Tohei developed consists of using Ki testing to help the student experience mind and body unification through the four principles.

A Ki test is a way of measuring the strength, stability, and balance of the body under steadily applied physical pressure. It is not a contest or demonstration of power, but rather a means of comparing how the body changes when applying or losing one of the four basic principles. To fulfill its purpose, you should always compare the "right" way with the "wrong" way, using the same amount of force, applied in the same way. The Ki test then acts as a form of biofeedback, letting you know immediately whether or not you have got it and gradually helping you learn how to keep it. It is not a game to see whether or not you can lift, upset, or move the other person. The best way to avoid falling into this error is to try to see not how much force, but how little force is required to move the person when he does it wrong. Then use the same amount of force to test them in the same way when he does it right. There are dozens of Ki tests in the curriculum and a few of the basic ones are described in this chapter. The important thing however is not how many tests you know, but whether or not you perform them with a proper understanding of their purpose.

The Ki testing methods are an effective and non-aggressive way of determining a person's mind and body condition. Mind and body have totally different properties, but they are ultimately part of the same continuum. In this sense they are essentially one. However, this oneness is a matter of integration, not equality. The body has shape, texture, color, odor, and is subject to the laws of the physical world. The mind is formless, free, and imaginative, in no way the same as the physical body. How such unlike entities can be fully integrated is hard to fathom intellectually, but very easy to experience and apply. In fact, in your better moments you do it quite naturally. The advantage of the Ki test is that it provides a mirror to show the condition of the mind through the body. One might say that the body is the visible aspect of the mind, while the mind is the subtle aspect of the body. Once you learn in this way to "see the mind," you can unify mind and body even without doing a Ki test. In order to ensure that people use the method properly, Tohei developed a set of guidelines for Ki testing.

Five Principles for Ki Testing

1. Not a test of strength but a test of whether or not the mind moves.
When we think of putting something to the test, we imagine applying stress to see if it can survive without breaking or losing form. In Ki testing, we test the body to see if the mind moves, or is disturbed, when the body is subjected to controlled physical pressure. Since the mind is intangible, how is it possible to see if it moves? You cannot look at your face directly, but you can easily see it in a mirror. Although the image in the mirror is not your face, it offers a clear reflection of it. By looking at the image in the mirror, we get a reasonably good idea of what we look like. In the same way, using the Ki test, through the movement of the body we can see the movement of the mind.

A word which frequently appears in the martial arts is *fudôshin*, or "immovable mind." It refers to a state of mental clarity and physical integration in which you are capable of using your full potential. This is what the Ki test is designed to measure. If your mind is distracted and your body tense, then mind and body operate with very poor integration. What Tohei discovered was that in this state, the body is very easily upset. The reverse is also true. When the mind and body are unified, the body is centered, relaxed, calm, and very strong.

If you use too much physical force to test a person, then he can pass your test without following Ki principles. Anyone with a little experience in Judo, Karate, or wrestling learns how to resist a physical force by subtly flexing the muscles in only part of the body and maintaining a low, stable posture. If the incoming force is totally concentrated at one spot, it does not penetrate beyond the surface. However, if you pretend to test at one spot and then suddenly test at another, most people will move. An experienced martial artist can resist such a test by simply shifting his resistance subtly and swiftly to meet each new angle of pressure. In this case the mind has still moved, only not in a very obvious way. This is trickery, not mind and body unification. If you can pass the test by moving your mind, subtly shifting your weight, or in any way bracing yourself against the test, all it shows is that your partner is not using Ki to test you. A real Ki test cuts right through all of the resistance and easily moves a person who is not practicing the principles.

A genuine Ki test is done with a totally relaxed arm. Rather than straining to break the surface muscular tension, you move your Ki through the person, as if dipping your hand into water. The pressure is applied smoothly and steadily, with the fingertips or hand. One of two things happen. If mind and body are unified, the person remains completely unmoved in the same posture, without receiving any of your Ki or pressure. If the Ki principles are ignored, deliberately violated, or carelessly applied, then the person moves, loses his balance, or even falls down.

By the time the fingertips touch the body, the Ki has already penetrated deep below the surface, and moved the partner's mind. Therefore, any attempt to resist, however subtle, proves totally ineffective. Because the tester is not shoving or pushing with any apparent force or leverage, it greatly confounds the person who is unable to resist it. A good student will want to learn how to pass the test by properly applying the Ki principles, for this is the only way to truly maintain an immovable mind and body. A poor student may complain that the testing method was not correct, or make up some other excuse to hide their own immaturity.

One thing should be understood however. The purpose of Ki training is to develop a mind which *will not* move, not a mind which *cannot* move. It is self-control that we are after, not stubbornness. After all, if a dump truck is heading right for you, you would be wise to move out of the way. How do you know when it is appropriate to move and when to stay still? Use common sense. If the oncoming force presents some danger, or threatens to collide violently with your body, it is best to move out of the way. If the force is possible to absorb without moving, then you need not move. Gradually with Ki training you learn to sense the difference. You also learn how to move when you must, without losing mind and body coordination or physical balance.

2. Give instruction appropriate to the level of the student.
In school, students sometimes try to guess which items will be on a test. If they guess correctly, they can earn good marks on the test, without having to study very many things. Therefore a smart teacher will test them on the unexpected. The only way to pass such a test is to study everything. A real Ki test is like this, for it reveals what you really know, not just what you want to show off that you know.

On the other hand, unless the difficulty of the test is appropriate to the level of the student, no learning occurs. An elementary school student cannot learn anything by taking a test in calculus, nor can a university student learn much from a test in simple addition. The Ki tests are actually graded into a series of levels, testing different degrees of mind and body unification. Because of the number of Ki tests and the difficulty in performing them, there is not space to explain them in detail here, except in general terms. The beginning level (*shokyû*) Ki test is done with mild and steady pressure, just enough to show the difference when you do and do not follow the Ki principles. The intermediate level (*chûkyû*) Ki test usually involves a feint or hesitation, followed by a beginning level test, which is usually disturbing enough to make a beginner move or react in an obvious way. The advanced level (*jôkyû*) Ki test involves testing at different angles, with more Ki and less hesitation, or by deliberately trying to disturb the mind before testing. There are an additional three levels beyond this, which test the student's mind and body unification in more subtle ways, ultimately including observation of behavior in daily life.

The main difference between the beginner and the advanced student is the degree to which he or she can sustain the state of mind and body unification. A beginner can usually extend Ki long enough to pass the test, but easily loses it the next moment. With practice, the student learns how to keep extending Ki over time and under pressure. The advanced student is able to extend Ki more or less in most situations in daily life. But this is still many, many steps away from the Ki master, who rarely, if ever loses it, and is able to apply it in a wide variety of circumstances. The fastest way for a student to advance is to share what he has learned with others. The ultimate measure then of a Ki master, is the degree to which he has helped others learn how to coordinate mind and body.

3. Test in order to teach, not in order to contest.
The Ki test is a teaching tool, not a strength contest. Oddly, some people think that being physically stronger than another makes one a better person. One student in America asked Tohei if the purpose of Ki testing was to learn how not to move. He asked him what he would do if a car came at him as he crossed the street. There is a world of difference between saying, "I cannot move," and saying "I will not move." The Ki test helps you verify whether or not you are unified, that is to say that you have enough integrity and control to move or not, as you choose. It does not mean that you do not move under any circumstance. If the force applied is very great, or if it is dangerous to remain on that spot, of course you move out of the way. But even though you move, you do so as a unit, without losing mind and body coordination.

If you are truly coordinated, you can move rapidly any time you choose, even if you are held up at gun point. Obviously, no one can outrun a bullet once it leaves the gun barrel. But there is more time than you think between the moment the man decides to pull the trigger, and the response of his finger to do so. If you have mind and body unified, your mind is clear enough to pick up on his intention to shoot before the finger pulls the trigger, and you literally have time to move aside and apply an Aikido technique before he can shoot you. Needless to say, this should not be practiced with a real gun, because you might not have mind and body as unified as you think.

People who have practiced a martial art or related discipline for many years often believe that they have achieved a deep state of mind and body unification. However, unless one has been really tested, there is no way of knowing for sure. Tohei once met a Zen priest who asked to be tested while sitting in the meditation position. Because of his long years of training, the priest expected to easily pass; but when Tohei lightly pushed on his shoulder, the man fell over on his back and stayed there, with his legs still folded, like a Buddha statue that had fallen on its side. Even though he completely failed the Ki test, he still insisted that he had an immovable mind, because his body was in the same rigid posture as when he had been sitting. The body only moves if the mind is disturbed. This priest simply did not want to believe that he was wrong. Tohei later compared him to the small Daruma dolls which are so popular in Japan. Shaped like a pear and weighted on the bottom, they are easily tipped over, but roll right back. Tohei said that since the founder of Zen was called Daruma, this man was probably doing his best to follow what he had been taught, except that he forgot to roll back. His insistence that the mind did not move even though the body fell over is a good example of mind and body separation.

On one occasion, a Japanese Aikido instructor who had achieved the high rank of eighth dan in another Aikido style traveled to America to teach the art. He happened to visit one of the Ki Society dôjôs which Tohei had founded in Phoenix, Arizona. As a visiting instructor, the students invited him to teach a class. The first exercise the man taught was *Kokyû Dôsa*, in which partners face each other in the *seiza* position, legs folded under and sitting on the heels, one partner holding the extended wrists of the other. He tried to throw one student after another, but found that he could not budge any of the black belts. Nor was he able to throw any of the white belts, including a young woman who had only recently started taking classes. The visiting instructor was confused and surprised that everyone seemed so strong. They explained that they were not particularly strong, they were just holding with Ki. The eighth-dan instructor had never had any trouble throwing his own students, because they had been taught to resist with physical strength, and he knew how to throw them using tricks of leverage. But these same tricks were useless against a person who had mind and body unified.

The Zen priest resisted with his mind, while the Aikido instructor resisted with his body. The immovable mind is strong without resisting. The purpose of the Ki test is to teach how to attain this state, not how to resist.

4. *Learn by testing others.*

There are actually two ways to do a Ki test, one physical, one visual. An experienced instructor can see without testing if a person is unified or not. But no one likes to take someone else's word for it. People like to be shown, rather than take something on faith. This is why Tohei developed a physical Ki test.

However, with a little experience it is possible to learn to see it without having to physically test a person. This actually has wider applications, if you see accurately. This sense is partly intuitive and is greatly enhanced by learning yourself what it means to be unified. But it is also a matter of knowing what to look for. As explained later in this chapter, a unified posture is one which is lifted and "floating," rather than heavy and sagging. Try raising one hand to shoulder height, arm parallel to the floor. This should be done as a single movement, but if you look closely, you will see that most people actually make two movements: one to raise the arm and a second to adjust its position. A movement done with mind and body coordinated is clean and distinct. When the arm is raised it stops cleanly, that is without dropping down or settling in at the end. The reason for the extra movement is that the body was not relaxed or centered to begin with, so in effect the arm misses the target and tries to get it back.

The same thing can be applied to any posture, even without an overt movement. Most people find it very difficult to simply sit or stand in the correct posture. Usually they shift around, or assume what is known as a *kamae*, or stance. Though it may seem strong when tested in one direction, it is usually very weak when tested in an unexpected direction. The effect is one of leaning on a door which you thought was securely latched, only to find it open suddenly. Even when there is no obvious physical stance, people often essentially do the same thing in their minds. This is commonly known by such terms as bracing yourself, keeping a stiff upper lip, hardening yourself, or holding fast. Pressing down or resisting mentally is the equivalent of the extra and unnecessary movement in the arm. In either case, when you see it you know that the person has lost mind and body unification. Not surprisingly, you will reach the same conclusion if you test them physically.

5. The test merely points the way, and is not an end in itself.
How then, did Tohei discover the method of Ki testing? He claims that it was a natural result of wanting to know the truth and show it to others. Tohei is a born teacher, and has no patience with things which are false. He also had a habit from his youth of putting theories to the test, considering real life to be the ultimate testing ground. Many of the things which he studied as a young man had long and well-established traditions. But they were taught in such vague and haphazard ways that only the most dedicated students had a prayer of understanding them. Many people who mastered the martial, performing or healing arts had little idea themselves of what they knew, and still less idea of how to teach it to others. Or they guarded their secrets so closely that only one or two followers could be thoroughly trained in a lifetime. As a result, many fine traditions have only maintained their vitality for a generation or two.

A metaphor for truth commonly used in Zen is the moon, because of its round shape and bright white color. Zen describes its own teachings as nothing more than a finger pointing to the moon. The finger is useful to help you find the moon, but once you have found it, there is no need to keep looking at the finger. Tohei uses the same metaphor for Ki testing, saying that the test is a means of understanding Ki, not an end in itself.

The Ki test is one of the least understood elements of Tohei's teaching, yet one of the most important. This is why it is presented here first. It so easily turns into a contest in which the tester does everything he can to move his partner. Remember however, that there are certain parts of the body which move when tested, no matter how well unified a person may be. For example, hair, ears, the tip of the nose, the skin, and so on. Yet in each case, these are parts of the body which cannot be consciously moved or controlled without moving the rest of the body. Any part which is subject to your conscious control should remain unmoved when tested. When correctly applied to a person who is unified, a Ki test hardly feels like a test at all, because the tester is pushing on the part of the body which is immovable. If the same test is applied to a person without mind and body unified, the test seems incredibly strong and irresistible. A person who does not understand the purpose of the Ki test will be tempted to twist, stretch, or find tricky angles which can create an impression of movement. If someone tests you in this way, be sure to explain the correct way of performing the test.

In Japanese there are many words to describe our natural or original state. *Ari no mama* refers to "things as they are." *Shizen tai* means a natural posture. But this is very difficult to achieve or maintain in practice. Blame it on modern urban life, centuries of bad karma, or the human condition, but somehow human beings have a habit of always standing on guard or mentally resisting. The stress which this causes in turn becomes the source of endless personal, social, and health problems. Ki testing, when applied with the following principles, can help you to regain your natural state of mind and body integration.

There are only four basic principles to remember. Each one describes the same thing from a different point of view. However, you cannot climb a mountain by more than one path at a time, even though separate roads might ultimately lead to the same summit. If you properly maintain one of them, you automatically have the other three. But if you lose one of them, you also lose the other three. These four principles are sufficient for a lifetime of Ki training. There are times when one will make more sense than another, but you can never fully exhaust them. Each time you come back to them, they will reveal new layers of meaning. In order to ensure that his students retained a proper understanding of each principle, Tohei developed five criteria to go with each of the basic principles. These are described below, along with simple Ki tests which you can perform to better grasp their meaning.

Correct Attitude Comes from Correct Posture

Usually translated as "posture," the Japanese word *shisei* can be used to mean attitude as well as physical posture. The literal meaning of the word is, "a form with energy," suggesting the body infused with vitality. In the original Japanese, all of the sets of five criteria which Tohei developed to explain the four basic Ki principles end in the word *shisei*. The English word *posture* does not sufficiently convey the Japanese meaning, so it has been dropped from the translation. However, it should be noted that each criteria below refers to both mind and body, even when one may be emphasized over the other.

•*Rule No. 1*
Calm and focus the mind at the One Point in the lower abdomen—Keep One Point.

1. Center on the point in the lower abdomen where you cannot put tension.
Martial artists frequently refer to the importance of the *hara,* or lower abdomen, as a source of power and stability. The problem with this concept is that it is not specific enough to teach anyone who does not already know what it means. If a person wanted to go to a certain platform in Tokyo station, you would not draw them a map showing only how to get to the greater Tokyo metropolitan area. *Hara* refers to an area, rather than a point. It is in the ball park, but it is not home plate.

There are several practical ways of identifying precisely where the One Point is located. When you are standing or sitting erect in the correct posture, the One Point is the infinitely small point in the lower abdomen, located on the front surface of the body, on the top center of the pubic bone at the height of the two hip joints. It is the lowest part of the torso, where the abdomen curves under into the groin. It is the only part of the lower abdomen at which you cannot put muscular tension or move independently, without physically moving your hips. If you study an anatomy chart, you will find that many muscle fibers radiate from this point in all directions. Because it is at the center of this radius, it cannot itself move or store tension. Try to locate this point on your body with your forefinger. If you can flex or move it without moving your hips, then your finger is too high. When you find the proper point, which is immovable and impossible to flex, instead of trying to put tension there focus your mind on it. If you do not know how to focus your mind on it, simply touch it with your finger and say aloud the word "One Point." In teaching this to another person, you are better off explaining how to find it rather than feeling around to find the other person's One Point yourself. Otherwise they will almost certainly lose it!

While your mind is focused on this point, have a partner stand at your side, and push gradually but firmly on the center of your chest. The fingertips of the testing hand should be parallel to the floor, with the thumb pointing down. You will find that this posture is surprisingly stable, even though you make no particular effort to push back. Be sure that you are being tested properly, for the results are less clear if your partner shoves or straight-arms you using more body weight than Ki. If the test is given suddenly, or at an odd angle, or with the fingers all pointing up, then it easily generates into a contest, and has no meaning as a Ki test.

To really see how strong this posture is you should compare it with one in which you do not keep One Point. To make the comparison crystal clear, try the same test while focusing on or touching the top of your head. See how little force is needed to push you back, then ask your partner to use the same amount of force again, this time focusing on the One Point. Without the Ki test it is difficult to know whether or not you have truly unified mind and body, but with a little practice you can learn to keep One Point with or without the test. When you lose it or become upset, you can get it back anytime just by correcting your posture and saying the word "One Point," aloud or to yourself.

2. Let your body weight fall on your One Point, not your legs or feet.
The One Point is also the center of gravity on which the weight of the upper body falls. This is easier to understand when standing than sitting, so next try standing tall with weight on the balls of your feet. Bring your heels as high as you can off the ground. If you have trouble keeping your balance, try relaxing your upper body more and standing taller. In this posture, the weight of your upper body falls naturally on the One Point, and the weight of your entire body falls directly beneath it, on the center of the line connecting the balls of your feet.

The Ki test for this posture is to have your partner try to lift your leg straight up at the ankle, without twisting or leaning against you. You will find that the leg feels deeply rooted to the ground, even though you make no particular effort to push down. Next lower your heels gently to the ground, until they just lightly touch, being careful to maintain the same lifted posture in every other respect. If you are not careful, your weight will shift back on your heels imperceptibly, your lower back will sag, and the weight of your body will fall on your legs and feet rather than your One Point. This is the correct standing posture, and when you test the ankle should feel just as rooted as before.

To compare it with the incorrect posture, deliberately let your weight shift back on your heels, letting your legs feel heavy. Now the ankle should be easily lifted, even if you lean your entire body weight on the leg being tested. Once again try the Ki test with the correct posture, again asking for the same amount of force as was required to lift your ankle before. You will find that you are far more stable and calm when you keep One Point.

3. Your breathing is calm and subtle.
While we may be able to accept that mind and body are one in theory, it is easier to experience in terms of our breathing. When the mind is calm and concentrated, the breathing also becomes calm and steady. If a person is emotional or upset, his breathing reflects it immediately. When your mind is calmly focused on a task, your breathing naturally becomes

very quiet. If concentration is so acute that you can literally hear a pin drop, then breathing is almost certain to be inaudible.

In the past, when samurai dueled with real swords, keen observers were said to be able to predict the outcome of the match by watching the breathing of each contestant. The one whose mind was unsettled showed it by audible breathing, which was even more obvious in the rise and fall of the chest and shoulders. One who fought thus in anger or fear was at a terrible disadvantage against an opponent whose mind was calm and clear, and hence whose breathing was calm and subtle. The term *suki,* meaning opening or flaw, was apparently derived from the idea of *sû-ki,* or "inhaling Ki." You can easily exert strength when you exhale or hold your breath. But it is almost impossible to move or generate power at the moment that you inhale. Therefore the moment considered ideal for striking down an opponent was the moment of inhalation, and the samurai trained themselves to conceal their breathing from their opponents. Interestingly, this same technique can be used in conversation. If the other person is talking on and on without letting you get a word in, calm your mind at the One Point and deliver your remarks precisely at the moment that the other person inhales. You will find that it is not so difficult to get a word in if you use the proper timing, because it is difficult for the other person to speak while inhaling.

Calm breathing is not the same as holding or conserving your breath. Rather it is a state of mental and physical composure in which your breathing is so natural and smooth that you are unconscious of it. Nor is it obvious to others. This is the natural state of your breathing when you calm and focus the mind at the One Point.

You can repeat both of the Ki tests explained above, comparing the results when your breathing is smooth with when it is rough. This is not the same as Ki breathing, which is explained in the next chapter. Still it is a useful criterion for checking your own state of mind and body unification.

4. You can accept whatever happens without losing your composure.
The location of the One Point described above only really applies to the postures of standing, sitting, or walking. Whenever you lean forward or back, or bend the body out of this standard posture, the One Point tends to shift out of the body, acting much like the sliding counterweight which was used on the old-fashioned balance-type scales.

When you are involved in rapid or vigorous movement, it is impossible to consciously follow the precise location of your center of gravity, nor is it necessary. It is easier to think of the One Point as a starting point for any posture or movement, not unlike the starter switch in your car. You must turn the key to get the engine started, but once it is running it goes by itself. Continuing to turn the key while the engine is running only damages the mechanism. Use the One Point to correct your posture before you enter into an activity, and you will be able to keep it naturally. If you lose it, you merely need pause and get it back again in the same way. Thinking about the One Point is not the same as keeping it, and in fact tends to interfere with your concentration on the task at hand.

The important thing to remember about the One Point is that it is not a physical or fixed anatomical point, but rather a point of mental focus. This will be covered in more detail in the next chapter under the topic of Ki meditation. When you maintain One Point you have a greater capacity to perceive things as they are, to understand what needs to be done, and to accept change without losing your composure. Tohei describes the One Point as a magic pot, into which whatever you put disappears, including anger, fear, and any other negative emotion that we tend to carry about with us. In other words, it acts like a disposal which keeps your mind clear of needless debris and able to function in the present. This is a very useful thing to know. Because there is only One Point to remember, you have no real excuse for forgetting. Still, we all need occasional reminding and the Ki test is the best way to remind yourself. An increased capacity to absorb the force of a Ki test is an indicator of an increased capacity to handle stress. If you try to physically resist the test you lose your One Point and fall over. With Ki training you learn to absorb and dissipate rather than resist the stresses that you encounter in daily life.

5. Therefore you can do your best at any time.
The first four criteria describe ways you can check yourself to make sure that you have One Point. The fifth guideline begins with the word "therefore," because it refers to the results of keeping One Point. People often give up trying before they succeed. They may believe that they have done their best and still failed. In fact, if they did not act with One Point, they could not have used more than a small fraction of their potential ability. Psychologists know human beings possess unlimited potential, but have no clear idea of how to develop it. The secret is to keep One Point first, and then do your best. Once you gain experience in this process, you will find it much easier to do your best, and success itself tends to develop poise, courage, and confidence. Mind and body unification is the foundation of a successful life.

The obstacles which hold us back are often partly of our own making. A simple exercise demonstrates this concept clearly. Sit in a chair and keep One Point. Have your partner test you as before, but this time try to stand up and walk forward. You will find that it is easy to brush aside even a considerable amount of external resistance. If you do it correctly, you will move like a ship through water, and may feel as if you are not really being tested. Try it again without One Point, and you will see how easily you can be stopped. Whenever we encounter an obstacle without having mind and body unified, inertia wins out. You never know if you can do something until you try, but to really do your best you should try with mind and body coordinated. This works for mental obstacles as well as for physical ones.

You might wonder if there is a danger in this of growing too confident, or attempting something foolhardy. If your mind is truly calm, you develop a sixth sense for danger and a realistic perception of possibilities. The One Point allows you to do your best, which is much greater than you think, but it does not give you supernatural powers.

You Are Stronger When You Are Relaxed

A person suffering from stress finds it very difficult to relax completely, even when sleeping. Relaxation is almost universally considered to be a good thing, but it is frequently misunderstood. Most people spend their lives alternating between states of excessive tension and excessive relaxation, both conditions a result of mind and body separation. Stress is not so much due to external pressures as to our overreacting to pressure with excessive tension, or shrinking from it in slackness. Real relaxation is a dynamic state, not one of limp placidity.

People commonly assume that tightening up is strong, and slackening is weak. However, Ki testing reveals that both extremes are weak. Rather than shifting back and forth, always trying to slacken over-tight muscles, it is best to understand relaxation in terms of mind and body unification.

•*Rule No. 2*
Completely release all stress from the body—Relax Completely.

1. Each part of your body settles in its most natural position.
Most people are aware that they carry around an excess burden of tension in their bodies, but do not know how to shake it off. It may accumulate in the neck and shoulders, lower back, or joints, but it serves absolutely no useful purpose whatsoever. The most common cause of this tension is stress, which gradually upsets the mind and weakens the body. Another source of muscular tension is inefficient and excessive use of some part of the body in performing a repetitive task. In either case, when stress becomes chronic, the body develops a defensive form of "body armor," which diminishes personal appearance as well as performance. Despite the number of psychiatrists in the phone book, the number of tranquilizers sold, and the booming recreation industry, few people really know how to relax.

Ironically, learning to relax is not as difficult as it seems. When you are tense, it is very difficult to move rapidly. The reverse is also true in that if you can move rapidly, you must be unconsciously relaxed. By standing in the correct posture described above and rapidly shaking your wrists, you can easily shake off any excess tension. For this exercise to have a lasting effect you must relax your body completely. This is easy to do if you shake your wrists properly.

Let your arms hang at your side and begin shaking the wrists in a rapid up-and-down motion at their natural height, below the belt line. Continue this for a few moments, then let them quietly come to rest at their original position. The fingertips rapidly alternate pointing in and down. This motion should look like you are shaking water off of your hands, not as if you are trying to flap your wings. Furthermore, to relax the whole body, the vibration should be strong enough to cause your heels to rise and fall slightly each time you shake your wrists. It also helps to keep your elbows and knees somewhat loose, but when your wrists come to rest, your posture should be the same natural one with which you started. If you do it incorrectly, you will end in a posture which neither feels nor looks natural. The hands should end in the same position, neither held out to the side nor sagging when they stop.

As soon as the wrist motion stops, have your partner hold one of your wrists with one hand and try to lift the arm straight up toward your shoulder. Just as with the ankle test described above, you will find that the wrist does not budge. Nor does the shoulder move, whether the wrist is lifted or pulled straight down. Not only the ankle and wrist, but each part of the body has settled at its natural position. The posture is not only comfortable, but alert and ready to move in any direction.

Shaking the wrists rapidly helps bring the body weight on the balls of the feet, because the vibration brings the heels off of the floor. In effect, you have used a physical means of achieving the same result that you get when you keep One Point. Therefore you should get the same results from each of the Ki tests that you have already done. This exercise should be done frequently, because tension accumulates unconsciously throughout the day. With practice you will find that you can remain relaxed under pressure, without needing to carry around excess burdens or needless worries.

2. You relax positively, without collapsing or losing power.
The common approach to getting rid of stress is to try to escape from it, by reducing or

increasing the amount of stimulation and activity. When the tension is localized, people may try to let the tense muscles grow limp, or to massage the stiffness out. The problem is that none of these approaches have more than a temporary or illusory effect. Everyone knows that they should relax. But they either do not know how to relax, or assume that relaxation is a weak and limp state that is inappropriate for daily life. Nothing could be farther from the truth.

Try to stand like a marionette, with the arms dangling limply at your sides. True, this posture may feel relaxed, but it cannot pass any of the Ki tests. Yet this is most often the state we assume when we try to unwind. Japanese businessmen are often accused of working too hard. They seem unable to relax, even when on vacation. Because stress is taking its toll on their health, the Japanese government is encouraging them to imitate Westerners, to take longer vacations, and to unwind when they are off the job. What they do not realize is that any fool can relax while sunbathing at the beach. It takes a mature person to be able to relax under pressure.

Beginners sometimes try to pass the wrist test by stiffening the arm to resist with tension. This only works if you are tested with strength in kind. A real Ki test will break the balance of any posture which is not completely relaxed.

3. Your sense of presence makes you look bigger than you actually are.
The world of the silver screen is often described as larger than life. Not only in the movies, but even stage actors and actresses appear larger than they actually are, particularly when they are relaxed and at ease with their roles. Similarly, the person who stands out in a group is not always physically the largest one there.

If you embarrass yourself in front of others you feel very small. Not surprisingly, when this happens you are also very tense. Looking big is not a matter of posing, acting big, or puffing yourself out. Rather, it is a matter of presence. The easiest way to gain a sense of stage presence, even in your daily affairs, is to learn how to relax completely. This implies that you also have the correct posture.

When Tohei taught in America, people usually asked him to pose for a group picture at the end of the training. Although a stocky man, he was usually the shortest person in the group, and physically dwarfed by some of the larger men. The fact that many of the participants did not realize this until they stood side-by-side with him for the photograph is a good illustration of how you look larger than you are when you are completely relaxed.

4. You are strong enough to be relaxed.
When you are relaxed, you are neither vulnerable nor weak. You can demonstrate this with a simple exercise. Stand in the correct posture and shake your wrists vigorously as explained above. This time have your partner grab your right wrist with his right hand and attempt to hold it in place. If you try to forcibly lift it by colliding with his strength, you will need a great deal of effort. However, if you remain relaxed, and casually reach up to scratch your ear your partner will find it almost impossible to hold your wrist down. Be sure to maintain the correct posture. If this is done correctly it requires no sense of effort.

Sometimes it is easier to gain a perspective on human behavior by watching people interact who are ten, twenty, or thirty years younger than you are. The social games and manipulations of young teenagers, while deadly serious to themselves, seem quite transparent and unnecessary to adults. Yet some adults, both male and female, maintain this immature attitude in believing that aggressive behavior is stronger than relaxed behavior.

This is so common in business, that some people act as if the only way to get to the top is to step on others. This may achieve some temporary advantage, but rarely succeeds in the end. If you truly want to gain the respect of other people, then you must learn how to be strong through relaxation.

5. Therefore you have an attitude of non-dissension.
If you relax completely and correctly according to the four criteria above, then you naturally develop an attitude of non-confrontation. This comes from the dual realization that a fighting mind is doomed to fail, and that tension only diminishes your strength. The Ki test is only one example of this. The more tense you are, the more you limit your possibilities. If you are relaxed, you are open and aware. This gives you the flexibility to respond, and the courage to face change.

   While keeping One Point was a principle for the mind, relaxing completely is a principle for the body. Each one expresses the same thing, but in the languages of different media. Do not try to practice both principles simultaneously; just realize that each approach leads to the same result. You may find that one works for you more easily than another, but this too, changes according to circumstances. The remaining principles work in the same way.

A Calm Mind Is Not Easily Disturbed

True calmness is found in the midst, not in the absence of activity. A top finds equilibrium when it is spinning most rapidly, in a state of living calmness. When it stops and comes to rest, this is a state of dead calmness. Everything in the universe is in a state of constant motion: the earth, our heartbeat, time itself. Any attempt to resist or escape this motion is futile, and only results in a loss of balance, both mental and physical.

   Yet when people seek tranquility and rest, they usually try to escape from activity, rather than learning to find calmness in action. This is why vacations always seem too short and time seems to fly or drag depending on our mood. The more you try to organize things around yourself, the more upset you become when things do not go your way. When the mind is upset, it is always out of joint with people and circumstances around it, because it is too rigid to adapt and move with them. On the other hand, if you too readily compromise and give into the demands of others, then you lose all initiative in life. The easiest way to remain calm and self-possessed when busy is to learn how to keep weight underside.

•Rule No. 3
Let the weight of every part of the body settle at its lowest point
—Keep Weight Underside.

1. You maintain the most comfortable posture.
Like relaxing completely, keeping weight underside is also a principle for the body. One reason that people find Ki practice difficult is that they assume it involves constant vigilance, or arduous postures that are difficult to learn. However, because mind and body unification is actually our original and most natural condition, it should be both comfortable and easy to maintain.

The most common mistake people make in trying to be natural is to assume that whatever is easy and effortless must be natural. This is an attitude of laziness, and ignores the fact that unless you correct your bad habits you can never truly be natural. In hearing that the weight must be underside, the tendency is to try to push down to achieve the right effect. In fact, this produces the opposite effect, just as holding a cork underwater violates its natural buoyancy.

A towel hanging on a laundry line follows the laws of nature by coming to rest at its most natural state. It does not hang in a crooked or crimped way, nor does it stretch rigidly toward the ground. Yet if you watch the way in which most peoples's arms hang at their side, you get the distinct impression that the arm is not hanging relaxed in a natural state. This is easy enough to verify through a Ki test, but very difficult to achieve in practice. While standing with mind and body unified, hold your arm high above your head and let it fall naturally to its original position at your side. You may find it very difficult to let the arm return to the original position without having to make a slight adjustment at the end of the movement. This adjustment is a sign that your weight is improperly placed. A posture which is truly comfortable is not only easy to assume without need for adjustment, but easy to maintain for a long period of time without looking or feeling unnatural.

Watch people at a party, and you will notice that though they are supposed to be at their leisure, hardly anyone seems comfortable with any posture for more than a few moments. People are constantly shifting around, and do not know quite what to do with their arms and legs. Because the weight of every part of the body does not fall at its lowest point, a considerable amount of effort is required to hold themselves up and shift the tension from one place to another. If it were not somehow tragic it would be comical.

By relaxing completely you naturally assume the most comfortable posture. The important thing to remember is that this is not an artificially constructed pose, but a posture which both looks and feels comfortable.

2. Your body feels light and does not sag.

While standing with mind and body unified, try raising one hand to shoulder height, arm parallel to the floor. Have your partner lightly grasp your arm from below with one hand, between your elbow and shoulder, and try to lift it straight up. He may use as much force as he likes, but should apply it gradually and steadily. If your arm comes up it means that your weight is upperside. It may seem natural that something as light as an arm could be easily lifted. However, consider what happens when you attempt to lift a table by one of its legs. If you can tilt it, you can easily lift a rather heavy table; but if you have to keep the table level, you will be unable to lift even a small and relatively light table. Most people, when lifting their arm as described, at the same time unconsciously shift their weight back onto their heels. This is like the tilted table, and is very easy to lift. However, if you can lift your arm without disturbing the natural weight distribution with which you started, then you become like the level table, very hard to lift.

This is only difficult if you try to put your weight underside or let your arm sag slightly after you lift it. Raise it in one swift and clean motion to shoulder height and just let it stay there. There is no need to put the weight underside because it is already naturally there. If you raise the arm without changing the other aspects of your posture, then your partner feels as if he is trying to lift your entire body, not just your arm.

Two forces operate on your physical body. Gravity pulls it down toward the center of the earth and the centrifugal force of the earth's spinning tends to pull it away. Gravity is the stronger, or we would be flung out into space. But it is not strong enough to flatten us to the ground, so the most natural position is one which is buoyant, not rooted. Yet this buoyancy is not a condition of weightlessness. When the mind and body are unified, the body actually becomes very hard to lift.

You can experiment with this by asking your partner to try to lift your body, putting his hands under your armpits and lifting straight up. If you resist or carry your weight upperside, you will be more easily lifted. If you unify mind and body, your body feels as though it weighs a ton, even though there has obviously been no change in your weight. This exercise is known as "the unraisable body," and it became one of Tohei's trademarks as he taught around the world. A very strong or determined partner can sometimes lift you even if you try to unify mind and body. There are ways of preventing this which are taught in the Ki Society curriculum, however basically the secret is to maintain the Ki principles without being disturbed. It also helps to stand erect, and to "ground" the incoming Ki by lightly touching your partner's arms with your hands.

3. Your Ki is fully extended.

When you have one Ki principle you automatically maintain the others. When you lose one, you lose them all. Therefore, when your weight is underside you naturally have strong Ki. Like a bubbling spring, the force of your Ki pushes aside outside influences which are weaker. This means that you are less susceptible to irritating behavior in other people, which would otherwise get under your skin. An amusing way to test this is to see how ticklish you are with and without mind and body unified.

Stand with both arms stretched out at shoulder height, leaving your armpits and ribs exposed. Have your partner attempt to tickle you there, to see if you can maintain the correct posture and a straight face. Anyone who is reasonably ticklish to begin with will fall apart before even being touched, from the sheer torture of anticipation. What they do not realize is that by unconsciously pressing down in self-defense, they have actually forced the weight up, weakening their Ki and making them even more susceptible to being tickled. The secret to passing this test is simple. Rather than pressing down, even in your mind, stand as tall as you can, like a stork stretching its wings. While you may not be totally immune, you will find that you remain in control. You will gain a better understanding of what it means to extend Ki by reading the next set of five principles.

4. You are flexible and can adapt to changing circumstances.

Keeping weight underside was defined as a principle for the body, because it is easier to grasp in physical terms. However, as mind and body are essentially one, it also has the aspect of mental calmness. When you are calm enough to let events take their course, to let people be themselves, and to relax in the face of pressure, then you become extraordinarily adaptable. The person who is able to take change in his stride is much stronger than the one who is upset by it.

One of the reasons for rigidity in human thought and behavior is that people make a habit of carrying their weight upperside, and so become very insecure about change. Every new piece of information or different way of doing things becomes a threat. Yet we live in a world which is diverse and constantly changing. To pretend otherwise is simply to live ostrich like, with one's head in the sand. Like the bamboo, unless we are flexible enough to bend, then eventually we shall break. Learning to keep weight underside is the best way to learn to make friends with change.

5. Therefore you perceive everything clearly.

The reason that the calm, still surface of a lake reflects things so clearly is that the movement of the waves on its surface is imperceptibly small. The rougher the surface, the choppier the waves, the more distorted becomes the reflection. Similarly, when the weight is underside the mind is also calm, resulting in very acute perception. This clarity is based on natural reflection however, not hyper-alertness. By nature, our senses are selective. We shut out far more than we take in, otherwise our brains would be overwhelmed with meaningless information.

The mind which is calm and composed does not necessarily take in more information. Instead it processes it better, alerting us to what we need to know, giving us insights into useful possibilities, and leaving us a better sense of reality. The majority of information is processed unconsciously, or organized when we sleep. The conscious mind operates better when it is free to concentrate on the task at hand. Perception is one aspect of intelligence. When the mind is clear it not only focuses, like a good camera, but records the information clearly in memory, and organizes it in such a way that we can make good judgments and learn from experience. All of these are natural human abilities, but they work so much more effectively when the mind and body are unified. To paraphrase an old Chinese saying, when the mind is absent, we look without seeing, listen without hearing, and speak without understanding. The mental aspect of weight underside is presence of mind.

A Positive Mind Speaks and Acts Positively

The word "Ki" is commonly used in the Japanese language. It appears in word compounds such as *yûki* (courage), *genki* (health), and *kimochi* (feeling). While it makes intuitive sense in Japanese, the term "extend Ki" did not exist in English until Tohei coined it. While it remains a very useful shorthand for those who have experienced and know how to use Ki, it can be misleading to someone who hears it for the first time. Therefore Tohei explains that extending Ki means having a positive mind. The power of positive thinking is not a new idea, however most people misunderstand what kind of power this is and how to attain it.

We all know that wishing does not make something so. But it is also true that life tends to give us what we expect and look for. Two people can have the same experience, and one walk away from it with a positive impression, the other negative. We may not be able to control all that happens to us, but we have the final say on how we interpret and respond to it. The reason that people have difficulty exercising this control is that they try to achieve it without first unifying mind and body. This is like trying to drive a car without turning on the engine, it simply does not work.

If you want to develop a positive mind, you should begin by determining to use only positive words. If you cannot say anything good about something, you need not lie or pretend, just remain silent about it. When you coordinate mind and body, you will find it easier to think, speak, and act positively. The reverse is also true, in that losing mind and body coordination can make a person very negative. To keep yourself positive, you can check yourself against the following criteria.

•*Rule No. 4*
Extend Ki.

1. You are not overly conscious of your body.

Like relaxation, extending Ki is a natural state. However, people tend to assume that Ki is a special or supernatural energy, and sometimes behave in very strange ways to try to attain it. In ancient India and China, it was commonly believed that only by assuming contorted postures, or imitating the movements of animals, could one develop strong Ki. It is true that assuming such postures can give one unusual experiences, sometimes accompanied by illusions of great strength. But few of these special poses are stable enough to pass a Ki test, suggesting that they might actually weaken, rather than strengthen Ki.

If a hose is turned on and allowed to flow unimpeded, no excessive stress is applied at any part of the hose. However, if you step on or sharply bend the hose, the restriction causes the water pressure to build up at that point. This is essentially what happens when you violate any of the Ki principles, tensing your body or raising your weight upperside. The pressure that this puts on your blood vessels and organs gives you a physical sensation that something unusual is happening. This is not extending Ki, but restricting it. If you do it too much you will make yourself sick, which is why many of the ancient Indian and Chinese "Ki" exercises were taught with the warning that they should be practiced in mild doses. If an exercise produces a negative result, perhaps it is better not to practice it in the first place.

When you are in good health you rarely think of your body. Only when something is wrong do you focus on parts of your body. Our senses are designed to keep us aware of and involved in the external environment. Only when something is wrong do they alert us of the inside of our bodies. The only time you are aware of your teeth, stomach, or joints is when they hurt. The body is designed to function naturally, freeing us to attend to more important matters. Breathing, digestion, blood circulation, and metabolism all take care of themselves, without need for conscious assistance.

When we are relaxed we can forget and enjoy ourselves. But when social pressures or mental insecurities overtake us, we become miserably self-conscious. This is also a state of cutting or restricting Ki. In order to extend Ki you must let it go, not hold it in. Fresh air comes in through an open window, while entrapped air quickly becomes stale. Therefore, extending Ki is a state in which you are not overly conscious of your body.

Another of Tohei's teaching trademarks is what he calls the "unbendable arm." The arm is held out at shoulder height, as if it were a fire hose with water extending from it. This is a metaphor for extending Ki. Your partner attempts to bend your arm at the elbow toward your shoulder, by applying strength and leverage with one hand under the wrist, and the other hand on top of the middle of the arm. As long as you maintain this mental image, your partner will find it nearly impossible to bend your arm. The moment that you think of the water being turned off, the arm is easily bent.

This is an easy exercise to do, and a convincing demonstration of the power of Ki. However, to ensure that you are doing it properly, you should check yourself against the criteria for extending Ki. It is possible to maintain a relatively unbendable arm by thrusting out a stiff arm. But a rigid arm cannot be held so for very long, and is only strong as long as you think of nothing else. The moment you move your body, or try to remember what you had for breakfast, your arm will be bent. Because a stiff elbow is unnatural, it makes you overly conscious of your arm and therefore you cannot really extend Ki. After vigorously shaking the wrists as you did to relax completely, raise the arm to shoulder height just as it is, without trying to reach further or stretch the arm. Because the elbow is naturally bent and the arm totally relaxed, you may think that it can easily be bent. However, when you relax completely you naturally extend Ki. The arm is just as strong as before. Tohei teaches his students to mentally extend Ki, not to physically extend the arm. When you do this exercise properly, you will be surprised at how strong and effortless it really is. No matter how strong your opponent is, you can remain relaxed, smile, or even carry on a conversation, all the while maintaining an unbendable arm.

All you need to do is to think that Ki is extending. If you do not know how to think it, say it aloud. If it still is not clear to you, instead use a positive statement such as, "I can do it," or "I like you!" You will find the arm is much stronger and more relaxed when you use positive words. Repeat the same test saying that Ki is weak, or utter a negative statement such as, "I cannot do it," or "I don't like you."

The reason for saying these words aloud is that it is impossible to say a word without first thinking it. When you remain silent, neither you nor your partner really has a clear idea of whether you are thinking positively or negatively. A positive mind always expresses itself in positive speech. Words have power, and if you repeat them often enough they seek an outlet in action. If you want to avoid negative circumstances you should stop using negative speech, and make a habit of expressing yourself in positive thought and action.

2. You make full use of centrifugal force in your movements.
To get an idea of the difference between moving with and without Ki extended, try the following experiment. Stand in the unified posture, holding a ball or small object lightly in your hand. First be sure that the object will not hit anything or anybody around you, then swing the hand up to shoulder height as before, letting go of the object at the top of the swing. Do not consciously try to throw the object, just let it fly out along the path naturally dictated by centrifugal force. You will be surprised at how far and forcefully it travels, despite the fact that you did not consciously throw it. This is a natural consequence of extending Ki.

Now try it again, but this time grip the object very tightly, and do not let go of it until your arm completely stops. Obviously, it will fall dead to the ground, directly beneath your hand. This is what happens when you move without extending Ki. Of course it is also possible to extend Ki and move without letting go of the object, otherwise we would not be able to hold onto anything.

Because all of the parts of your body are attached, there is no danger of anything coming loose. Instead, when you move with Ki extended, the "centrifuge" action of your motions keeps the body from becoming cramped, and helps improve the blood circulation. However, it is important that you move in a coordinated way when you extend Ki, for if you do collide with an object, you do so with a tremendous amount of force. Perhaps you have had the experience of bumping into something unexpectedly while walking through a dark room. Thinking that nothing is there you walk ahead naturally extending Ki, until you meet an object which is more solid than you are and come to a grinding halt.

Ki is energy, and movements done with Ki should be energetic. The same thing applies to your voice. When you speak with Ki extended, your voice is clear and words distinct. When you cut Ki, you mumble and mince words.

3. You have soft eyes and a poised manner.

The smaller the muscle fibers, the easier it is to store tension without being consciously aware of it. The best example of this is the muscles in the eyes and face. No other part of the body so clearly reveals the state of the mind as the eyes, so much so that they are considered windows to the soul itself. Eyestrain, as well as "hard" eyes which come from tension, is a result of using the eyes improperly. The eyes are designed to reflect and absorb light, not to grasp it. When the eyes are relaxed, they face forward, in the same direction as the face. When they are tense, they easily shift up and down or to the side. Moving the eyes at sharply different angles from the face causes eye fatigue and creates the impression that you are trying to hide something. A relaxed eye has a wider field of vision, so it does not need to shift around to see. If you want to look at something off to the side, it is easier to turn your head.

Many people in the martial arts develop hard eyes, not always out of cruelty, but because they believe that they are extending power from their eyes. Staring at a person with hard eyes is a good way to get into a fight. But as we have seen, real strength comes from relaxation, so the eyes too must be soft and kind.

Famous portrait paintings have the curious feature that the eyes seem to follow the viewer as he walks in front of it. This is the one feature that cannot be reproduced in a copy, no matter how skilled the technique, because it is a result of the original painter's broad vision. The same applies for photographs, and the portrait of Tohei which hangs in every Ki Society dôjô is a remarkable example of this remarkable feature. No matter where you stand in the room, he seems to be looking right at you.

A simple exercise can show you how much more perceptive the eye is when it is relaxed. Stand and face a partner, both hands held out palm down at stomach height. Ask your partner to place his palms under yours facing up, wait for a few moments, and then try to slap the top of your hands before you can pull them away. If you look at your partner's face calmly, with soft eyes, you can almost read his mind as to when he will try to slap your hands. If you stare at his eyes or at his hands, you may see it coming, but you will not be able to move your hands quickly enough to avoid getting slapped. You can also try reversing roles, to see if you can use soft eyes to catch your partner cold.

The same thing applies to conversations with other people. Do not stare at a person's eyes. Nor should you avoid their glance. Instead, simply look calmly at the area around the eyes and nose, taking in the whole body if possible. It will appear that you are looking right at the other person, but it will not look aggressive. You can also do this when you have your picture taken. Do not stare directly at the lens, or your expression will look rigid. The flash may even bounce directly off of your eye, causing your eyes to look red and wolf-like in the photograph. Instead, look just above, below, or to the side of the lens, and you will appear to be looking at the camera with soft eyes and a poised manner.

4. You show composure in your posture.

Thinking of Ki as energy, some people assume that it must be wild and frenzied, like a hard-rock concert. Some cults practice going into a trance, or move the body in uninhibited and agitated ways. Certainly this is a kind of energy, but it is not Ki. Just as excess tension results in slackness, extreme excitement results in collapse. Ki energy is very steady and self-sustaining. Although it is strong enough to exert considerable centrifugal force, to project the voice, or throw an attacker, the person extending Ki has no particular feeling of doing anything special. He or she is simply acting in accordance with natural principles.

Because the mind is calm and the body relaxed, there is no feeling of supernatural powers or unusual energy flowing in the body.

This is only a mystery to one who has never experienced a Ki test. After you experience true mind and body coordination, the errors of the other approaches become obvious and even comical. Note that in any art form, the deeper the level of mastery, the more natural the form and expression. An immature artist is filled with agitation and special posturing, all in an effort to express an energy they really do not yet understand. The highest purpose of art is to express Ki, that is to show the beauty of natural form, not the ugliness of artifice.

5. Therefore you are bright and easygoing.

A person who extends Ki is naturally positive and full of energy, relaxed and calm, and therefore very easy to be with. But this does not mean that one must lose the qualities of other human emotions. Even the bright blue sky is clouded over on occasion, and nature has many seasonal expressions. However, nature is always dynamic. The spirit of a person who extends Ki a good deal of the time is well expressed in an old Japanese saying: "At a smile, small children draw near. At a frown, wild animals flee."

Plus attracts plus, minus attracts minus. Like-minded people tend to flock together. When you yourself are positive, you draw many positive people to you. If your friends and associates are too negative, you should reflect on yourself.

Our behavior always has roots in our speech and thought. At first it is hard to believe that something so easy as thinking that Ki is extending could unify your mind and body. This doubt is based on lack of experience, which can be remedied by frequently repeating the Ki tests. With practice, mind and body unification become second nature. When you lose it you feel uncomfortable, as if you have forgotten to brush your teeth or wash your face. When this happens you become more and more interested in Ki development, because you recognize what a valuable tool it is for self-improvement.

Chapter *5:* Ki Development through Mind and Body Unification

Learning How to Extend Ki

We have seen how through Ki testing we can gain a direct physical understanding of mind and body unification, which is a prerequisite to being able to develop and use Ki. If done correctly as described, then each of the Ki tests above should be easy to perform. Yet things which come easily tend to go just as easily, and Ki is no exception. Under the highly controlled conditions described above, almost anyone can learn how to keep One Point, relax completely, keep weight underside, and extend Ki. Doing so in your daily life is another matter.

The reason for this is that most of our behavior is based on subconscious habit. Conscious understanding is not usually sufficient to change behavior, as anyone trying to diet or give up smoking can tell you. Furthermore, our conditioning is not just a matter of personal habit. We also receive the influence of thousands of years of history, of our culture, and of our genetic heritage. These things cannot be changed overnight. However, Ki itself is very strong, a universal energy. It can easily overcome such relative influences. But this is only possible if applied continuously in daily life.

No one can suddenly extend Ki all of the time. It takes time to learn how. If you correctly apply the principles and practice regularly under the guidance of a competent and qualified instructor, you can make significant progress in a matter of months and years. If you are satisfied with merely knowing about it, then Ki principles will have little effect on your life one way or the other. If you deliberately practice in a way counter to Ki principles, then you will never attain it in a lifetime of effort. As Tohei frequently says, right effort brings right results; wrong effort brings wrong results; no effort brings no results.

In order to help people practice and teach Ki principles, Tohei developed a Ki curriculum which could be followed by anyone, regardless of whether or not they practiced Aikido. There is not space in this book to describe how to do most of the exercises. Specific Ki development exercises are described in detail in several of the books which Tohei has written in English, which are listed in the appendix, under references for further study. These exercises are also a regular part of the training offered at Ki Society affiliated schools. What is covered here is a description of what the various types of Ki training are like, the rationale behind them, and some suggestions on how to practice.

The basic Ki development curriculum is divided into four programs. Ki unification methods are an extension of the Ki tests described in the previous chapter, showing how to maintain mind and body unity in a wide variety of postures. Ki exercise methods involve learning how to move and exercise the body without losing your balance or mind and body unity. Ki breathing methods teach how to practice whole body breathing, which not only promotes health but mental calmness as well. Ki meditation methods help to deepen the state of mind and body unity at a deep subconscious level, to fully integrate what you have learned in the other methods.

Ki Unification Methods Develop an Immovable Mind and Body

Training in mind and body unification is really nothing more than an intensive course in the four basic principles and Ki testing, which were described in detail in the previous chapter. Far from being limited to the basic standing or sitting posture, Ki tests can be applied to nearly every posture and simple movement found in daily life. This includes walking, various ways of sitting, bending forward or back, leaning against something, lying down, moving the arms, turning the head, even speaking. The tests are graded at different levels, so that once you have mastered mind and body unification at the basic level, you are immediately presented with a new challenge.

Mind and body unification is an essential prerequisite to understanding and applying Ki in daily life. Ki testing helps you to build a proper foundation by teaching you how to develop *fudôshin*, immovable mind, and its natural consequence, *fudôtai*, or immovable body. As difficult as this is, it is relatively easy to maintain when you deliberately assume a fixed posture. However, *fudôshin* is easily lost as soon as you move or change to another position. When first beginning Ki training, the exercises seem so easy to perform that it is easy to grow overconfident. After a little training in Ki unification, you soon realize that easy come is also easy go.

There are two reasons why the immovable mind is so easily lost. The first is that while you may be close, you may not quite have it. A plant that has barely taken root can still be torn loose by the slightest force. You may be able to coordinate mind and body for an instant, only to lose it as soon as you feel the pressure of the test. In fact, it takes some years of practice for the roots to take hold. The second reason is that human beings are slaves of habit, and whatever your conscious intention, most of your behavior is automatic and ingrained. The older you are, the more this tends to be the case, particularly if you have not made efforts to correct your bad habits while you were young. The feedback from Ki testing can change your subconscious habits and help you learn to maintain mind and body unification in any posture.

For example, if you hear a sudden loud noise, rather than raising your shoulders in surprise, you learn how to absorb the sound into your One Point, which leaves you calm and undisturbed. You do not spook as easily. If you must speak before a large group, instead of physically shrinking from it, you learn to assume the unified posture in which you will look and do your best. When working with your hands, instead of thinking about something else or rushing through the task, you check yourself to see that your posture and movements are relaxed and centered.

By testing the stability of your body in various postures, you soon learn that the One Point is not a fixed point on your body, but rather a center of gravity which sometimes shifts out of your body. The location of the One Point described in the previous chapter really only applies when you are standing, walking, sitting in the *seiza* position, or sitting erect in a chair. When you sit cross-legged, the pelvis shifts to a different angle, so that the One Point must be thought of as lower, even on the floor, if you want to maintain stability. If you raise your arms high overhead, the One Point also shifts down to compensate. Whenever you bend forward or lean back, the One Point shifts slightly forward like a counterbalance to help you remain stable. Other subtle shifts occur when you lean on an object, but usually the One Point moves down or forward, never back or inside the body.

Though rather difficult to describe, each of these shifts can easily be verified through Ki testing. Stand in the basic unified posture, and point to the One Point in your lower abdomen. Keeping your mind on this point, bend forward as if to tie your shoelaces, and have your partner try to lift one of your wrists toward your shoulder. For most people the wrist will come up very easily, because they tend to shift the weight forward without dropping the center of gravity, thereby losing mind and body unity. The lower abdomen is simply too high a center of gravity for this forward leaning posture.

Now try the test again, this time focusing your mind at your fingertips, which is where the One Point has shifted. Your partner will find the wrist very difficult to lift, even though you make no particular effort to push back. The knees should bend slightly, so that the arms can hang straight down from the shoulders. The primary difference in each test is where you focus the mind. Other Ki tests can be performed on a variety of postures commonly assumed in daily life. What is important in the end is not theory, but what you can do to correct your own personal habits. It is very difficult to be objective in correcting oneself. To make rapid progress in Ki development, you should practice with a partner, under the guidance of a teacher.

Fudôshin is an old concept in Oriental thought. It can be found in Chinese and Japanese Zen. Tohei was first exposed to the idea as a youth in reading the Chinese classic, *Saikontan*. Later, he tried to attain it through Rinzai-sect Zen meditation and *kôan* practice. Although he passed many tests in the Zen temple, he found it difficult to maintain that state of mind amidst the trials of daily life. Convinced that he could face death calmly, he found himself a different person when death actually came to call. Eventually through his experiences in the war, he gained some practical understanding of *fudôshin*, which he later articulated in terms of the four basic principles for unifying mind and body. In time he used these principles to teach others how to be unmoved in the face of trouble and how to adapt to change, by maintaining an immovable mind and body under any circumstance.

Ki Exercise Methods Coordinate Mind and Body in Movement

Tohei first learned Judo from his father and then Aikido from Morihei Ueshiba. As interesting and worthwhile as these martial arts were, to the average person they were an irrelevant and esoteric pursuit, an item of only passing interest. These traditions had grown out of the classical medieval martial arts of Japan. They had developed over time, from secret fighting methods into sports and semi-spiritual disciplines. Furthermore, the martial arts could not be used in daily life, except for self-defense, which seemed to Tohei to be a seriously limited use of Ki. He quickly realized that to spread Ki principles, he needed something far less exclusive, that could be practiced by anyone, anywhere.

At first he tried to teach mind and body coordination through the techniques of Aikido. He found that his students were able to coordinate mind and body in movement while he was present to teach and correct them, but as soon as he left, no one could agree on exactly what he had taught. Many of the movements were simply too complicated to be remembered for more than a short period of time.

At first he developed Aiki exercises, which were the movements of the Aikido throws practiced without a partner, and tested for mind and body unification. This made it considerably easier to teach and remember. If the exercises were performed correctly, the student would maintain mind and body unification, even after moving through the exercise. No matter how hard a partner tried to resist, the same movements would work very well in executing the Aikido technique on which they were based. These were not warm-up exercises, but full Ki exercises in their own right, and a very useful tool for teaching Aikido. However, these movements made little sense to those of Tohei's students who had no experience with Aikido, or to those who were more interested in Ki itself than in its application in the marital arts.

On the other hand, Tohei found that while students of Aikido could coordinate mind and body in movement, the average person lost it very easily. Somehow people had a habit of moving the body without the full concentration of the mind. The faster or more complex the movement, the more mind and body seemed to come apart. At this point he made an ingenious and original discovery. If a person made the same movement twice in a row, it was much easier to unify mind and body, almost as if the mind caught up with the body on the second movement. In Aikido, he taught that the mind leads the body, so physical movements were usually initiated and led by the mind. People who had difficulty coordinating mind and body did just the opposite, moving the body first and then trying to settle the mind. Yet when the same movement was repeated twice, even a beginner could pass the Ki tests, whether or not he concentrated on Ki principles! Moving twice seemed to unconsciously coordinate mind and body. The Ki test helped convince people that this way was more unified, and helped them experience what extending Ki felt like. While he retained and continued to refine the Aiki exercises for his Aikido students, Tohei also developed a set of Ki exercises for health, which were simple enough to be performed by anyone, not just the very young and athletic. He synthesized these Ki health exercises into a three minute routine, based on the movements of daily life, rather than only of Aikido techniques.

To understand how the principle of moving twice works, it is best to experience it through a Ki test. When we are too busy we become careless in our movements, and therefore lose mind and body coordination. One example of this is answering the telephone. Stand up and go through the motions of answering a telephone, asking your partner to try to lift your elbow at the moment you "hold the receiver" to your ear. The timing is important, because the sudden motion of raising the arm tends to pull your weight upperside. If your partner waits too long you may be able to pass the test, but most people lose it if tested the moment they say, "Hello." Answering the phone represents an unavoidable and unexpected interruption in what we are doing. If this disturbance catches us off guard, then we will be unprepared to deal with whatever the caller brings us.

Now try making the same unhurried motion twice, being sure to lower your arm back to the starting point before beginning the second motion. Each movement takes approximately one second to perform. Again have your partner test under the elbow, this time at the end of the second arm movement. You will find that it is much easier to pass the test, whether you try to coordinate mind and body or not.

As a practical matter, you cannot pick up the receiver twice to answer the phone. In fact, most movements of daily life must be done correctly the first time. The reason for practicing doing the same movement twice is that it allows you to experience calmness which is not upset by careless movement. Once you know what it feels like, it is easier to recognize and reproduce. The Ki exercise trains your body to naturally move in this way, without needing to think about it every time.

The secret to achieving the same effect in a single movement is to maintain the same rhythm, but do the first count in your mind, then raise your hand on the second count. One executive tried this at his office, making sure to send strong Ki to each caller before picking up the receiver. Whenever he remembered to do this he handled each call smoothly and pleasantly. Because the first mental count only took a second, his movements were perfectly natural, and no one ever suspected that he was practicing Ki development at the office. But when he occasionally forgot and picked up the receiver first, he always found a problem waiting on the other end of the line. Most of our problems increase or diminish in size according to our readiness to deal with them.

The three minute Ki health exercise which Tohei developed is performed standing up, and involves swinging the arms and twisting the trunk, side to side, left and right, front to back, and so on. There is also a sequence for the neck, knees, and arms. Every movement is performed twice on each side, in two sets of eight counts. The sequence is described below, not in an effort to show how it is done, but to give a rough idea of what it looks like. Readers wanting to learn the exercise should seek instruction from a qualified teacher.

Tohei-style Ki Exercise for Health

1. Twisting the trunk by swinging the arms.
2. Bending the trunk to the side.
3. Bending forward and back.
4. Shoulder blade exercise.
5. Bending the neck to the side.
6. Bending the neck forward and back.
7. Turning the head to the side.
8. Knee bending exercise.
9. Knee stretching exercise.
10. Arm swinging exercise, each side in turn.
11. Arm swinging exercise, both arms together.
12. Arm swinging exercise, with knee bends.
    (End by shaking wrists.)

Common knowledge has it that before you exercise you should try to stretch your muscles. Most people who play sports go through a series of warm-up exercises which involve stretching the muscles. However, if this is done without mind and body coordination, it is counterproductive. The feeling of stretching that you get in the muscle may actually come from contracting it under tension, so that the muscles get shorter instead of longer. You can prove this to yourself by standing an easy arm's length away from a wall, and touching the wall lightly at shoulder height with a lightly closed fist. Then, being careful not to lean toward the wall or move the shoulder forward, try to punch the wall "Karate" style, stretching the muscles as hard as you can. You will find that your punch falls several inches short. Instead of stretching, you have actually contracted and made your arm shorter. If you remain relaxed you can even punch with several inches to spare, like a boxer. Therefore, Ki exercise is done with complete relaxation, so that you do not try to stretch any set of muscles in particular. Though you do not feel any strain on your muscles, actually they are extended to their maximum length, just as when you easily touched the wall with a relaxed arm.

In order to ensure that people practiced Ki exercises correctly, as he did for the Ki principles, Tohei developed a set of criteria for Ki exercise. They are listed here for reference, but they can only really be understood in terms of actually practicing and testing the various Ki exercises, something which is beyond the scope of this book, but is covered in Tohei's books, which are listed in the appendix.

Principles for Ki Exercise:
1. **Movements center on and begin from the One Point in the lower abdomen.**
2. **Ki is fully extended in each movement.**
3. **Move freely and easily.**
4. **Do not feel any tension in the muscles.**
5. **Show and feel a clear sense of rhythm in your movements.**

Ki Breathing Methods Promote Whole Body Breathing

Many centenarians have been interviewed as to the secret of their long life. People want to know what special diet or health methods they followed to help them live longer than the average life span. But in most cases, interviews revealed that these people followed no special health method at all. In fact, a surprising number of them had bad habits like smoking or drinking, which are usually considered to shorten life. When pressed for their secret, it turned out to be a simple one: not to worry about things, and to live within natural limits.

Even more surprising is that it is not unusual for the founder of a so-called health method to die of natural causes several decades earlier than the average life span. And the ones who do manage to live a long life often do not practice the very method they so earnestly promoted in their youth. This has been true from jogging, to Yoga, to health food diets.

With all of the well-placed concern over environmental pollution, there is an increased interest in clear air, clean water, and natural food to maintain health. No one can dispute that these things are better than their opposites. But we should not assume that these things alone will prevent illness. In Hawaii, even though the air is fresh and the climate ideal, many people suffer from asthma. On the other hand, while the air in Tokyo is not very clean, there are many people who live there well past the age of 100. As important as it is, air quality alone is no guarantee of health. On the other hand, breathing itself is another matter.

Everyone knows how important breathing is. You can live without food for a month, without water for a few days, but without air for only a few minutes. Since ancient times there have been numerous methods of breathing taught for health and spiritual development, in both East and West. Before practicing such a method, there are several things which you should consider. First, find out whether or not the method is based on the actual process of respiration, that is whole body, not just lung breathing. Secondly, see if it is possible to practice it without losing mind and body unification. Thirdly, be sure that it in fact improves health and has no harmful side effects. Many methods popular today do not meet these criteria, so you should investigate them carefully before undertaking any regular practice. The various methods can be divided into four major types.

The first method recommends that you inhale through the mouth and exhale through the nose. This method was taught by Ueshiba Sensei, and is based on the idea of trying to gather Ki inside and conserve it by holding it in. Unfortunately, it produces the opposite effect, because it violates the principle of relaxing completely. The second type recommends that you both inhale and exhale through the mouth. This is good way to catch a cold and weaken your respiratory system. The third method involves both inhaling and exhaling through the nose. This is the method taught in Zen meditation, usually combined with counting the breaths to help focus the mind. There is nothing wrong with this method, if it is practiced with mind and body unification.

The fourth method is to inhale through the nose and exhale through the mouth. This is usually taught in combination with some form of "abdominal" breathing, moving the abdomen in as you exhale or out as you inhale. One method, known as the Okada method, after its founder Mokichi Okada, teaches to move the abdomen in the opposite way. Most forms of abdominal breathing emphasize extending the abdomen out with each inhalation and drawing it in as you exhale. The Okada method taught just the opposite, sucking in the stomach as you inhale, and pushing it out as you exhale. Tohei learned of this method in his youth from a book, and briefly practiced it. However, Okada Sensei died of a stroke in his late forties, not a very good endorsement for a teacher of a health method. When Tohei learned this, he stopped practicing it. Okada's students claimed that he died because he gave away all of his life energy helping other people, a doubtful rationalization. If you really extend Ki to others, the universe gives you back more than you gave. In either case, you lose mind and body coordination because you end up putting strength into your lower abdomen, which causes you to lose One Point. Even though you breathe very deeply, as long as you coordinate mind and body the abdomen does not move in or out. The process of respiration occurs anyway, whether or not you move your abdomen; and putting unneeded strength into the body only restricts the full delivery of oxygen to all of the capillaries.

A fifth method hardly deserves mention, but the ancient Chinese said that a wise man breathes through his heels. That is an impossibility of course, but even taken as an analogy, it is misleading. According to where the weight of the body falls, the correct place should be the balls of the feet, not the heels.

In fact, breathing does not occur in the lungs, abdomen or the feet, but in the whole body. Respiration is considered to have three phases. External breathing is what we usually think of as breathing, that is the exchange of oxygen and carbon dioxide which takes place in the lungs. But it does not stop there. Internal respiration occurs all over the body at the cellular level, through the bloodstream. In addition to this there is skin respiration. In the early days of the circus, some performers suffocated by painting their whole body surface, thereby preventing respiration through the skin. Third degree burns covering more than 15 percent of the surface area of the skin can pose a serious threat to life, for the same reason.

Respiration through the skin is very important, for the skin is the membrane which separates the internal and external world, and therefore acts as passageway for Ki. The flow of Ki is traditionally represented in acupuncture as following channels or meridians along the surface of the skin, somehow connecting the vital organs of the body. But it is more accurate to say that Ki flows in and out of the body through the skin. If the circulation is good, Ki is always fresh, like air circulating through a room with open windows. This helps to maintain good skin tone and quality, an important sign of health. If the Ki circulation is restricted through tension or improper living habits, then the skin quality suffers, and the face lacks color. An easy way to visualize the process is to think of putting your hands into some fresh water, and tightly sealing off a small amount of it. In time, being stagnant that water would grow stale. However, if you were to cup the water lightly, with open fingers, allowing it to circulate freely, then it would remain fresh. Our bodies contain and circulate Ki, but only when we are totally relaxed. This is one reason why sleep is so refreshing. The best way to improve the circulation of Ki is through whole body breathing, a process which Tohei calls Ki breathing.

Whole body breathing helps clean the blood, through the process of complete "combustion," or metabolism of food and wastes in the body. Waste products are also removed through the skin. Omnivores and vegetarian animals like horses and cows perspire. Human beings also perspire, so that the pores of the skin remain able to breathe. Some people brag that they do not sweat, but this is an unnatural and dangerous sign. Dogs, cats, and other carnivores do not perspire. Instead they cool themselves by panting with the tongue hanging out. However, we are not built that way. For human beings it is natural to perspire, not pant. The combination of external, internal, and skin respiration is called whole body breathing. This is a natural process, and cannot be forced as is taught in some breathing methods. One of the most common misunderstandings is to assume that whole body breathing is breathing while moving the whole body. Some breathing methods teach movement in various unusual postures, imitating the movements of animals, which presumably "circulates" Ki around the body. When animals imitate human movements, the result is comical circus material. Animals in captivity do not live as long as they might in the wild. The same can be said for human beings which imitate the movements of animals. What nature designed for one of its creatures does not necessarily fit the others. Furthermore few animals live as long as human beings, so why imitate a creature with a shorter life span?

In addition to its importance for health, breathing has long been recognized as the link between mind and body. When the mind is calm, so is breathing. The reverse is also true; so if you learn to calm your breathing, you can also calm the mind. In fact, Ki breathing is considered a powerful method of unifying mind and body. When performed correctly, whole body breathing allows you to completely relax, no matter how much pressure you are under.

There is no greater pressure than the threat of being killed, which Tohei first experienced during the war in China. To help maintain his mental and physical equilibrium, he disciplined himself to practice 200 deep breaths every day. But he found it very difficult to practice the way he had been taught at the Ichikûkai, particularly while marching with heavy loads and the constant threat of danger. During his training at the Ichikûkai, he noticed that there was one old woman named Kaneda, who seemed to exhale very softly and smoothly during the breathing exercises. Because everyone else produced very forceful and audible exhalations, Tohei assumed that the old woman was simply too old and weak to keep up. But when he went off to war and determined to practice it 200 times a day, he found that the old woman had been right after all. Her way was the only one possible to apply in daily life, particularly under pressure. Gradually he learned to practice breathing in long, smooth, and barely audible breaths. When Tohei returned to the Ichikûkai after the war, the old woman smiled and commented that his breathing technique had improved. Tohei later developed a method based on this which he called Ki breathing. He also modified many of the other *misogi* practices to make them safer and free from error.

According to an old Zen story, a teacher asked his student what he wanted more than anything else in life. The student replied that he sought the truth. On hearing this, his teacher thrust the student's head into a nearby tub of water, nearly drowning him. When he finally allowed the student to come up for air, it was clear to both of them what the student really wanted more than anything else in life. Even knowing how important breathing is, there are people who complain that they have no time to practice breathing exercises. No matter how busy you are, you always carry your mind and body with you wherever you go. You also continue breathing as long as you live. What could be a more fundamental part of our life and existence? If you have a health problem, or suffer from a lack of Ki, you should not expect a doctor or government health program to help you. You will wait a long time, and be greatly disappointed in the end. Ultimately, you yourself are the one who must take responsibility for your health, and the most practical thing you can do about it is to practice Ki breathing on a daily basis. Here is how.

To properly perform Ki breathing, it is essential first to coordinate mind and body and relax completely. While it can be done sitting upright in a chair, it is easier to unify mind and body in the *seiza* posture, sitting on your ankles with legs tucked under. Kneel on the floor, if you like on top of a firm but comfortable cushion, or thick carpet. First raise your hips so that you are standing on your knees, and release the tension in your upper body by lightly swinging the arms side to side in front of your body. Then slowly lower your hips, as if sitting deep in a chair. Sit between your heels, with one big toe crossed over the other, the right one on top of the left. You should sit so lightly that your upper body is relaxed, and your lower back is erect. Sit so that the weight of the upper body falls on the One Point. Though you are sitting erect, it should look as if you have a slightly forward lean, like riding on horseback. The posture should be comfortable enough to maintain, and stable enough to pass a Ki test. To prevent your lower back from sagging, imagine sitting on a thin sheet of paper without tearing it.

Lowering the hips gently in this fashion may make you feel as if there is still residual tension in the shoulders. To be sure that the upper body is completely relaxed, once again gently swing the arms and lightly place the hands palms down on the thighs, halfway between the knees and the One Point. The effect that you want to achieve is complete relaxation, while still maintaining a feeling of height and stability. In this position, the body is extremely stable. Whether pushed at the shoulder, or lifted at the forearm or knee, the body should feel as immovable as a heavy rock. Now that you are sitting in *seiza* with mind and body unified, you are ready to begin practicing Ki breathing. If your legs are too stiff to maintain this posture without discomfort, then you may practice sitting cross-legged, or in a chair, but be sure that the lower back supports your upper body and does not sag.

Let the jaw and throat open, and exhale slowly to produce a voiceless, but barely audible sound of "Hah . . . ," with the breath. Breath out as long as you can make a sound, without moving the head or upper body. To expel the lung's capacity of 3,000 to 4,000 cubic centimeters takes only about six or seven seconds. Even though the air in the lungs is expelled rather quickly, the blood vessels which line the lungs continue to bring carbon dioxide and other waste products to the lungs for some time. There are perhaps tens of thousands of cubic centimeters of air dissolved in the bloodstream. It takes approximatedly twenty-two seconds for the blood to travel once around the body. With practice, it should be possible to exhale with a continuous sound for about twenty-five seconds, or more. But do not force yourself to try to meet this standard. The average person typically breathes out no more than a second or two. In the beginning, any improvement is worthwhile. If you are comfortable, then you will be more likely to continue practicing, and that way can gradually approach the goal of twenty-five seconds.

You cannot make a sound unless air passes through your windpipe. If you exhale silently, then you cannot be sure whether you are really exhaling, or cheating by taking in small gulps of air as you go. Once the sound has faded away or stopped and you think you have exhaled virtually all of the air you can, lean the upper body forward slightly (about 10 degrees), and you will find yourself able to exhale the small amount of air remaining.

While maintaining the slightly forward position, next close your mouth and inhale slowly from the tip of the nose, as if smelling a fragrant flower. You may or may not be able to produce a sound at first. In any case, the sound should be barely audible and never forced. Do not try to fill the lungs, but rather imagine that you are slowly filling the whole body like a container, starting from the feet and gradually coming up to the head. The reason for concentrating on sending the breath down to the feet is that it helps take your mind off of the lungs and chest, which easily tense up and shorten the breath if you try to fill them. If you try to fill only the lungs, you will reach capacity in six or seven seconds. Inhaling slowly allows the air in the lungs to be steadily absorbed into the bloodstream, and greatly increases your capacity. With practice you will be able to inhale for approximately twenty-five seconds.

Remain in the forward leaning position until you feel as though you have inhaled to capacity, then calmly return the upper body to the original position, directing the breath toward the back of the head. This will allow you to take in a little more breath at the end of the cycle. Now you are ready to begin the next breath cycle with the sound of "Hah. . . ," as described above. Because inhalation is more difficult than exhalation, you may wish at first to practice only exhaling in this way, and then taking a comfortable inhalation quickly to start again. Once you become comfortable with a long exhalation, then you can work on extending the inhalation as well.

The secret to sustaining a long breath is to maintain good posture, that is to keep the chest expanded throughout, without letting it collapse as you exhale. Be careful not to let the shoulders sag as you exhale, or come up as you inhale. The air should seep out slowly, not all at once. This is the way a singer breathes, and the reason why a singer can exhale almost continuously for minutes on end, without ever getting out of breath. The ordinary person breathes out only for a few seconds with each breath, and as many as sixteen to twenty times per minute. With Ki breathing, you reduce this rate to one or two breaths per minute. This is not only good for health, but it actually extends life. Long breath means long life; short breath brings on an early death.

If you practice Ki breathing faithfully everyday for thirty to sixty minutes, your body will always be filled with a fresh supply of oxygen, which will be delivered to all parts of the body where it is needed. This facilitates a more complete metabolism of the foods that you eat, and helps the body rid itself of carbon dioxide and other waste products of metabolism. In other words, it helps you to maintain your life-force and immune system at an optimal level. The time alloted for Ki breathing may be divided into fifteen minute sessions. You may even do it while waiting for a friend or listening to music, provided that you first unify mind and body. It is not recommended however, that you practice while involved in a task that requires physical activity or mental concentration. It is also best to practice in a place where the air is fresh.

Ki energy is what protects our health and sustains life. As long as it is strong, we need not worry about health. Ki breathing is a superb method for strengthening the life-force. People who are reasonably healthy tend to assume that they have no need to practice. But daily practice when you are healthy will develop reserves of strength that will help you when you get sick, or as your body ages. If you wait until some illness strikes, you may find that you lack the energy to practice.

For a person who has already become sick, or is unable to sit up, it is perfectly acceptable to do Ki breathing while lying down, face up. In this position there is no need to move the head or body at the end of the exhalation. Just exhale and inhale as far as possible, without moving the body, using the same imagery described above. Ki breathing will so speed the recovery process that the doctor will be surprised.

The body naturally produces toxins just in the process of moving about. It is natural to want to wash away the dirt of the day's work before going to sleep. If you are going to wash the outside of the body, it makes even more sense to wash the body from inside as well. The bloodstream and body tissues are daily charged with the natural wastes and by-products of metabolizing the food that you have eaten. If you practice Ki breathing before you go to sleep, you rid the body of these unwanted substances, and recharge it with a fresh supply of oxygen, as well as ensure an efficient delivery of nutrients to all parts of the body. It is only natural then, that you should wake up clearheaded and refreshed, full of energy for the new day.

Ki breathing also deepens the state of mind and body unification, which is easy to verify with a Ki test. You will find that even without thinking about the Ki principles, while you are practicing Ki breathing you are naturally more stable. To help his students practice breathing in accordance with Ki principles, Tohei developed the following criteria for Ki breathing.

Principles for Ki Breathing:
1. **Exhale gradually, with purpose and control.**
2. **Exhale with a distinct, but barely audible sound.**
3. **At the end of the breath, Ki continues infinitely like a fading note.**
4. **Inhale from the tip of the nose until the body is saturated with breath.**
5. **After inhaling, calm the mind infinitely at the One Point.**

Ki Meditation Methods Strengthen the Power of the Will

In the West the word *meditation* usually suggests thought, in the form of contemplation, analysis, or consideration. In Eastern tradition meditation more often suggests absence of thought, as in reflection, tranquility, or pure awareness. Even within the many sects of Buddhism you find different approaches to meditation, some emphasizing mental activity, some mental passivity. Meditation is supposed to benefit the mind on many levels, improving concentration, perception, judgment, and intuition at first, and ultimately leading to higher levels of consciousness, culminating in a state of oneness with the universe.

Yet even while proclaiming these benefits, many schools teach methods which run counter to the principles of mind and body unification. Some types of meditation actually teach mind and body separation, usually by ignoring bodily needs and trying to achieve so-called "out-of-the-body experiences." The dangers of such approaches will be dealt with later under the topic of misconceptions about Ki.

Not surprisingly, Ki meditation is based on the principles of mind and body unification, particularly Keep One Point and Extend Ki. While Ki unification teaches how to unify mind and body, Ki exercise teaches how to maintain mind and body coordination in movement. If this were all that were needed, then people could develop strong Ki in a short time through Aikido practice alone. Unfortunately, that is not the case. Many people practice

Aikido for years without making substantial progress in Ki development. Something more is needed to thoroughly integrate mind and body at a deep physical and subconscious level: Ki breathing and Ki meditation. While the ultimate goal is the same, Ki breathing approaches it through the body and Ki meditation through the mind.

Ki meditation can be practiced in the *seiza* position, cross-legged, or sitting erect in a chair, as long as you have a unified posture. The palms rest comfortably on the thighs. By focusing on the One Point your body becomes very stable against a Ki test, at least for the moment. Even without consciously changing the posture, most people tend to lose it in less than a minute's time. After testing the person once, calmly wait more than ten seconds and test again. Most people will move when tested the second time. The tendency is even more obvious if you ask the person to close their eyes. But unless you can maintain mind and body unification while sitting still, how can you practice Ki meditation?

When the body is forced to sit still, then the mind tends to become very restless. The nature of the mind is to move, and any attempt to stop that movement only agitates it further. If waves roughen the surface of a lake, nothing can be reflected clearly. Only when the surface is calm can it accurately reflect whatever passes overhead. A lake may be as still as glass, but it is never as solid. Even when it is calm, water always has the potential of generating waves. Our mind works in the same way, as long as we live. The secret of Ki meditation is not to try to stop the waves of the mind, but rather to reduce them to infinitely small, imperceptible ripples.

As an abstract idea, this may be hard to grasp, but in practice it is not so difficult. Sit in a unified posture and gently close your eyes. It is important to close the eyes gently, for if you shut them tightly, then unconsciously you put tension into your face and upper body, thereby violating the principle of Relax Completely. Blinking is a natural phenomenon which helps clean and relax the eyes. But it should not require any force. People who blink frequently, tightening their face in an exaggerated way each time they blink, cut their Ki every time they close their eyes. This is a sign of nervous fatigue and weak Ki extension, and may forewarn of a physical or nervous breakdown. People who blink frequently are hard to photograph. When the picture comes out, they always seem to have their eyes shut. You can easily verify what effect shutting the eyes has by performing a Ki test at the moment the eyes close. If you close the eyes forcefully then you fall over when tested. If you close the eyes gently, then your mind and body unification remains undisturbed.

Some forms of meditation teach to concentrate on a point in the center of the forehead. This is where the forebrain is located and, is considered by some to be an important energy center in the body. Certainly, any part of the body with a heavy concentration of nerves is an important energy center. The forehead is also a very vulnerable place. A light tap with a hammer to the forehead is enough to kill a strong animal. But just because it is important, does not mean that it is a place to focus the mind. If you concentrate your mind on your forehead, you will be unable to pass even the easiest of Ki tests. Ancient texts of meditation teach to put the tip of the nose straight above the navel. This may have been correct for the individual who wrote the text, but it may not work for a person with a large nose or stomach. It is certainly not correct for a pregnant woman! Tohei found a far better way to describe it, saying that you should put the forehead over the One Point, then focus your mind in the lower abdomen.

Rather than trying to hold your mind at a fixed point in the lower abdomen, think of the One Point as a point of mental focus. To help you find your center, let your upper body sway from side to side like a metronome, making each movement smaller by half than the one before. It only takes three or four motions before the movement is too small to be obvious, or even visible. Even so, continue to move mentally, each movement becoming smaller and faster than the one before, and never stopping or reaching zero. After a few seconds the movement is too small to see or feel, but continue to pursue it, knowing that it never stops. The effect is something like that of watching the fading vibration of a tuning fork. Even after the sound is gone, the ears remain alert. If you focus on your center in this way, then you can still pass the Ki test, even after a minute of silence. Focusing the mind on the One Point helps achieve a real, but temporary state of mind and body unity. In order to maintain the One Point, it must be a point of continuing mental focus, not a stopping point. The only way to do this is to think of the One Point as a focal point for the center of the universe.

It is fairly easy to image infinite space above, or even beyond the horizon. What is difficult to visualize is the fact that space is also infinite below us. Because the ground serves as a stationary reference point, we tend to assume that it is not moving, even though we know that the earth is turning on its axis, as well as flying through space. Even our galaxy is in motion, so the sun is no more the center of our movement than the earth. What is the center of our solar system, if everything in it is moving, and the universe itself has no known edge?

The easiest way to visualize the One Point as the center of the universe is to think of the universe as a sphere with an infinite radius and no circumference, in which every point in space is the center. Rather than thinking of the One Point as resting on the ground, it is more realistic to imagine that it is floating and suspended in vast space. This "floating feeling" also helps you to maintain the correct posture, even if your legs get tired. While you may not be able to imagine a limitless sphere shrinking by half, you may be able to think of a fading vibration, like the tuning fork, focusing on the One Point. Some forms of Buddhist meditation begin with a small bell or gong to help focus the mind on the fading note. The important thing is that the mind focuses on the One Point, and remains alert as a result.

Once you grasp the feeling of the rapidly reducing vibration, which Tohei refers to as, "half, half, half...," then you can more easily find it without needing to physically sway side to side. The problem is that while this may last for a minute or so, eventually the mind loses interest in something too small to perceive. As soon as the mind fixes on a point you lose mind and body unity. The same thing happens to people who think they have achieved enlightenment. As soon as you think you know, you lose your inquiring beginner's mind and stop learning. How then to keep the mind fresh?

In Ki breathing, we alternate long exhalations with long inhalations. Similarly, in Ki meditation you can alternate contraction with expansion. Focusing on the One Point is called contractive meditation. Extending Ki out from the One Point is called expansive meditation. It works in much the same way, Ki radiating out in all directions toward the limitless edges of the universe. Expanding out and doubling in size, very quickly its dimensions become hard to imagine, like a rocket leaving the atmosphere. We know that even though we cannot see it, the rocket continues on its course. All we can do is to let it go and remain calmly at the center. But as with contractive meditation, soon the mind loses interest in that which it cannot perceive. When this happens, you begin again focusing on the One Point with contractive meditation. By alternating keeping One Point with extending Ki every minute or so, you keep the mind moving but focused.

We never breathe the same air twice. Nor should we meditate by drawing the same Ki in and out. Once it fades from view, let it go. At first you feel as though it is your personal Ki expanding and contracting. But after some minutes you focus less on your body and more on the feeling of centering. Eventually you will be able to sense the motion of Ki, not just in and out, but circulating freely, like the wind. This is a very natural and comfortable state of mind, a higher degree of integration of mind and body.

Eastern religions such as Zen and Taoism have various words for this state: the experience of nothingness, the flow of the Tao, being one with the universe. In any case, it is important not to stop or limit the mind.

If you have trouble understanding or practicing Ki meditation, go back and review the criteria for keeping One Point and for extending Ki. You can always tell if you are on the right track by having a partner test you. The important thing is to make a habit of spending some minutes each day in Ki meditation. When done correctly it is very pleasant and refreshing, so you should have no trouble finding twenty or thirty minutes to practice. Like Ki breathing, daily practice is essential. A good time to practice is before going to sleep at night, because this attunes the subconscious mind to its roots, and helps you relax completely when you sleep. A troubled mind is not only unsettled, it is also extremely undisciplined. If you wait until you are seriously troubled, you may find that you are unable to even sit still, much less practice Ki meditation.

It is possible to resist, but not to stop movement and change. The more you resist, the more you lose your balance. Violating the basic principles of mind and body unification makes you weak and unhappy. The more self-centered we are, the more self-conscious, and the more we act as if the world revolved around us. With Ki meditation you learn to gradually let go of this selfish view, and gain a more universal perspective. People who try to rely exclusively on themselves always meet their limit, sooner or later. People who seem strong and self-reliant can be surprisingly weak with a change of circumstances. Even if you live on an island and grow your own vegetables, you must rely on the rainfall, sunshine, and air. In a sense we are totally dependent on the universe for our life and existence. In Ki meditation we rely totally on the universe, not on the ground, or our own limited strength.

The attitude of leaving everything up to the universe is sometimes called faith. However, there is a significant difference between faith with mind and body unified, and faith without. Confidence in universal principles is intelligent; simply hoping that things will turn out well is blind faith. We tend to think of will-power in terms of self-reliance, the ability to get things done. But this definition is incomplete. If that were all there was to it, every dictator and hardened criminal on the face of the earth could be said to have strong will-power. A person may insist on maintaining a habit that is killing them, even if he or she has been well warned. This is called attachment, not strong will-power. What then is will-power?

Tohei uses the words *Ki no ishi-hô*, literally "Ki method for strengthening the will-power," to describe Ki meditation. But he also defines will-power in a specific way. Will-power is the source within the mind which enables us to act correctly and accomplish the right thing. But this too requires qualification, for the notion of what is right varies widely from culture to culture. Morality is a very relative thing. A hero in one era could be a scoundrel in another. When one generation attempts to impose its values on another, there is no easy resolution. In the end, it is difficult to say who is right. Therefore, Tohei also defines "right" in a very specific way. That which is in accordance with universal principles may be considered to be right. Because the universe is infinite, it must have an infinite number of principles. To keep it manageable, we can start with what we are sure of, such as the four basic principles of mind and body unification. People everywhere can agree that it is better to be concentrated than scattered, relaxed than tense, calm than upset, and positive than negative. Therefore, to paraphrase the definition given for will-power, it is the source of the mind which allows us to act in accordance with Ki principles.

Ki meditation is a practical method of developing a mind with a strong will-power. Such a mind, acting in accordance with universal principles, is naturally concentrated, perceptive, and intelligent. It judges well and has the capacity to act correctly and courageously.

In the beginning we assume that it is our own personal effort that is responsible for our progress. As we mature, we realize that this is the smallest of factors. Our progress is determined far more by our willingness to learn from the universe, our good fortune in being alive and healthy enough to understand, and by our teachers who show us the way. The posture of Ki meditation is based on Ki principles, so it is naturally stable and strong. These qualities are summed up in the following criteria which Tohei developed for Ki meditation.

Principles for Ki Meditation:
1. **You maintain a posture of mastery.**
2. **You have a sense of freedom.**
3. **You create an atmosphere of harmony.**
4. **You are vividly aware of the spirit of life in all things.**
5. **Therefore you can feel the movement of Ki in the universe.**

Changing the Subconscious Mind

By now it should be obvious that any reference to the mind also implies the body. As we have seen, the body is the visible aspect of the mind and the mind is the subtle aspect of the body. Both exist on a continuum, each one a different manifestation of our whole living self. While the self has many individual characteristics, it ultimately has its roots in the universe, both physically through the natural world, and mentally through the collective unconscious. We are unique individuals, but we are all connected, like branches to a tree.

There is no need to subjugate our individuality, for this is as much a part of ourselves as our common ground. In fact, the more you unify your mind and body, the more you develop the unique talents and characteristics which make up your personality. Governments which try to force people into a mold, or insist that everyone be alike, are doomed to fall apart because they ignore the one basic truth: that we are all unique individuals. Likewise, when individualism degenerates into selfishness then chaos results, because people forget the other basic truth: that we are all interdependent. The best way to achieve a balanced development is to train the subconscious mind thoroughly in the principles and practice of mind and body unification.

The basic methods for doing this have already been described. However, human beings are largely slaves of habit. You may know what should be done, but somehow be unable to bring yourself to do it. Or you may find that you can coordinate mind and body when you consciously practice it, but tend to lose it when you become busy with daily affairs. Psychologists say that more than 90 percent of our behavior is based on habit. Many of our perceptions, thoughts and actions are patterned after what we have done in the past, more than what is appropriate for the present. This is not always a bad thing, because it frees our conscious mind to focus on something other than how to perform simple motions. Problems occur when we develop bad habits that work against us. Fortunately, we have the capacity to learn, that is to retrain ourselves to form good habits. The most important part of Ki training involves learning how to correct bad habits and form good ones. At first everything seems awkward and unfamiliar. You know you are making progress when you can do unconsciously today something which required deliberate effort yesterday. This frees your conscious mind to concentrate on the next level of development. When you thoroughly train your subconscious mind to be unified in mind and body, then you will apply Ki in your daily life naturally, without needing to think about it.

If you would like to achieve this state sooner than later, if you want to truly make it your own, then you should take positive steps to change your subconscious mind. There are several practical ways to do this, none of which require much time or effort.

The first way is to become thoroughly familiar with the Ki principles and criteria described above. Do not just memorize the words, but use them to check yourself frequently in daily life. Take one set of criteria at a time, write them down somewhere where you can easily refer to them, and do so. Each principle describes mind and body unification from a different angle, so you need not feel that you are limiting yourself. Work on the five criteria for keeping One Point the first week, for relaxing completely the second, keeping weight underside the third, and extending Ki the last week of the month. Writing them down and saying them aloud will speak more directly to your subconscious mind than just reading about them. Using them as criteria to correct your posture in daily life is an even more powerful suggestion. Your subconscious mind tends to believe what you do more than what you think or say, so practice what you preach.

The best way to retrain the subconscious mind is to engage in daily Ki practice, preferably in a group setting at a Ki dôjô. If this is not possible, then you can arrange to practice with family and friends in your home. At least you should practice yourself. Try to find one hour a day, even if you must divide it into two or three sessions, and devote that time to Ki testing, Ki exercise, Ki breathing, and Ki meditation. You may prefer to make more time, or to concentrate on one type of training over another. Ultimately, each method has the same goal, but you should become familiar with all of them, otherwise you may end up deluding yourself. If you can do one method correctly, you can do them all. If one method is difficult for you, then you really have not understood the others either.

There is another method, which Tohei learned from Tempû Nakamura, which involves using a mirror for self-suggestion. This is a very powerful technique for changing your subconscious mind, and is often overlooked. We spend roughly a third of our lives in sleep. Because we are not conscious, we assume that there is no way to train ourselves during sleep. But we can make good use of the minutes before sleep which set the tone for the mind for the rest of the night. Rather than just collapsing into bed, spend a few minutes unifying mind and body through Ki breathing or Ki meditation. Then stand in front of a mirror and think or say aloud to yourself a few words which state positively how you want to become. This suggestion can be framed as a statement about yourself, your values, your skills, your life condition, or anything that you can do something about, but it should be stated positively. For example, instead of saying, "I will try not to smoke cigarettes," phrase the suggestion as, "I don't like cigarettes." Instead of saying, "I will try to have more self-control," phrase it more positively as, "I have a strong will-power." Anything that you would like to improve about yourself, any habit you would like to correct, any suggestion for character improvement is appropriate. Send strong Ki to yourself in the mirror for about thirty seconds as you say this, and then go right to bed without doing anything else. When you wake up, this thought will still be on your mind, as it was all through the night. You can repeat it first thing when you rise. Before going to sleep, phrase your suggestion as a command for the future: "You will. . . ." On arising, state it as a fact of the present: "I am. . . ." In this way you will find that the suggestions gain momentum.

You may be tempted to try more than one suggestion at a time, but this only weakens the power of the process. Work on one thing at a time, and keep doing it until you are satisfied that you have corrected it in your daily life. Then work on the next thing. The stronger you become, the less time it takes to correct a bad habit. Even a very stubborn habit can be corrected within six months if you persist. Most habits take less time and as your Ki develops you will gain the ability to correct a habit simply by making a decision to do so. No one is perfect. We all make mistakes and form bad habits. In most cases, if you correct a bad habit, you can free yourself from its influence, even though it has plagued you for many years. What is most damaging is to persist stubbornly in self-destructive behavior, without making any effort to improve.

Many people in the world try to control or influence others, without being able to control themselves. Parents and teachers who say one thing to children while doing something else themselves will never gain the respect of youth. It is easy to admire and follow a person who is unified in mind and body, and continually strives to become a better person. You will find that as you gain better self-control, you automatically gain the ability to influence and lead others. This is where Ki training really becomes interesting, in its applications to your daily and professional life.

Chapter 6: Applications of Ki in Daily and Professional Life

Applying Ki to Business

If you extend Ki you will succeed in business, though not always only in the limited sense of earning large profits. Many factors enter into business success, including such intangibles as good fortune, timing, and serendipity. However, no one can count on these things alone completely. Often the chance comes to the one who can recognize and take it. Ki training makes you much more likely to succeed in business, as well as make a profit, simply because it gives you the energy to put good ideas into practice. It is really no secret how to succeed in business; despite the claims that universities make about their M.B.A. programs. In fact, the one who succeeds in business is not necessarily the best educated, but rather the one who makes a habit of doing what should be done. This may seem oversimplified, but so few people actually do what they are supposed to, that when someone actually does, he or she stands out from the crowd and soon earns peoples' trust.

It is almost impossible to succeed in business without investing in your people, in your ideas, and in your equipment. This requires doing more than what is minimally required to get by, and usually implies borrowing money. Being in debt carries a negative connotation only if you are being hounded by creditors who really consider you to be a worthless scoundrel, but cannot fully write you off until you give them back the money you owe. But if you have the energy, ideas, and background to have earned peoples' trust, banks will bend over backward to lend you money. Most successful businessmen continually make use of other peoples' money, but they keep it moving in such a way that they can always give back more than they take. This obviously requires experience and knowledge of your field, as well as good time management, human relations skills, and old-fashioned hard work. However, other things being equal, the businessman who extends Ki will be more successful, because he has the energy to put his resources to their fullest use. Most people just let their resources lie, and devote no more than a small fraction of themselves to their jobs, somehow expecting that they have a right to be paid regardless of what they contribute. Even if such a person inherits a fortune, he will easily squander it in a lifetime. Hence the old saying: "From rags, to riches, to rags again."

Thomas Edison said that genius is 1 percent inspiration and 99 percent perspiration. Intelligence helps a person to become successful, but without the tremendous energy needed to carry out the work it cannot be of much use. The world is full of good ideas, but people who can put them into action are rare indeed. To be successful you must take initiative. Followers never come out ahead. The most productive members of any enterprise always have more initiative than the ones who are just along for the ride. Their motivation and enthusiasm is not a result of higher pay or special privileges, but is rather a basic element of their character. They tend to enjoy what they do and therefore do it well. Unconsciously, they may have grasped something of the art of coordinating mind and body in their work.

It is easy to extend Ki when you are having fun. People can ski all weekend or play cards all night, and never get tired. But if the same person has to make an unpleasant phone call at work, or take care of a tiresome task, suddenly he finds it hard to lift a finger. As long as you are thus controlled by your likes and dislikes, you will never be able to sustain enough energy to be truly successful in your field. You must learn how to extend Ki whether or not you particularly enjoy the task which you must do. Unifying mind and body alone will considerably lighten any load and may even make a job more interesting.

Having a goal ahead will help enormously in overcoming the burdens of the moment. You cannot be motivated in the abstract. Your energy must be directed toward something that you value, something you want to achieve or acquire. If you cannot find any such elements in your work, perhaps it is time to think of changing jobs or profession. But you should remember that if your motivation in changing jobs is to escape an unpleasant situation, you will most likely exchange one set of problems for another. Move toward something good, not just away from something bad. At the very least, you can learn to enjoy the challenge of learning how to coordinate mind and body under pressure.

Gradually, as you learn how to extend positive Ki, your circumstances will develop in such a way as to enable you to enjoy your work and do your best. Like most aspects of Ki training, this is a matter of habit and daily practice. To help people learn how to focus Ki on their work, Tohei developed five principles. They are fairly straightforward, but very powerful if actually put into practice.

For Office Work:
1. **Take initiative to find work without waiting to be told.**
2. **Make a habit of taking notes to organize and improve your work.**
3. **Do not postpone something that you can do now.**
4. **Before going to sleep, plan the next day's work.**
5. **Make a habit of reviewing your notes first thing in the morning.**

There is probably no more important job to the lifeblood of a company than sales. Most other jobs, from maintenance to administration, consume income while performing more or less necessary tasks. Only sales activity generates income. This is why salesmen are so highly paid and why their incomes are usually tied to commissions. A salesman needs more than just hard work to succeed. Creativity, communications skills, follow-through, and an ability to sense customer or client needs are as important as effort, if not more.

Despite its potentially high rewards, there is hardly a more discouraging job than sales. The results of your work come out in cold figures at the end of every month. Regardless of how many hours you put in, your income, and perhaps even your job security depend on selling at or beyond a quota which was set by someone other than yourself. Almost no customer wants to talk to a salesman, even if he is a paid buyer. The salesman is usually perceived as a nuisance, interrupting whatever more important thing the person was doing at the time. A salesman's pitch is often canned, and therefore suspect. People today are so overwhelmed with advertising messages that they tend to shut them all out as unwanted intrusions. Rejections greatly outnumber sales in almost any field. Sales is not for the fainthearted.

Mr. Katsuhiro Enoshita is a Ki Society member who graduated from Keio University in the early 1980s. After graduation he went to work as a salesman for a large company which sold pre-built homes in the Tokyo area. The price of real estate in Tokyo is so high that homes are extremely difficult to sell. Since the buying decision often has to be made jointly by a married couple, Mr. Enoshita was told to make his calls after seven o'clock in the evening, when both the husband and wife were more likely to be home. Tired after a day's work, few people were in the mood to talk to a salesman, particularly when he

103

showed up during dinner, as was often the case. He frequently had to make repeat calls, and was so persistent that one customer greeted him with a bucket of cold water in the face. Mr. Enoshita had been a dedicated Aikido student, but when he joined the company, he found he had no free time for practice. So he determined to apply Ki principles as much as he could in his work instead.

He decided to try two simple things. First, no matter how he felt personally, he would tell himself that he liked the people he was going to see. This made him more positive about each sales call. Human relations is much like a mirror. If you smile, people smile back. If you grimace, people grimace back. By being positive about his work, customers tended to be more receptive. The second thing he did was to memorize Tohei's Ki Saying regarding Aikido, "The Way to Union with Ki," and to repeat it to himself before each sales call. It reads as follows:

"The absolute universe is One. We call this Ki. Our life and our body are born of the Ki of the universe. We study thoroughly the principles of the universe and practice them. We are one with the universe. There is no need to despond, no need to fear. The way we follow is the way of the universe, which no difficulty or hardship can hinder. Let us have the courage to say with Confucius, 'If I have a clear conscience and a calm spirit, I dare to face an enemy of ten thousand men.' "

While still in his twenties, Mr. Enoshita became the number one salesman in his company, and the Shinjuku branch of the firm where he worked led every branch in the entire corporation. All of the older salesman came to regard this young man as the one to learn from. What many salesmen fail to realize is that part of the reason that they meet so much resistance lies within themselves. If your self-image is poor, it is reflected in your posture, in the way you walk and talk. A poor first impression can defeat a person before he gets started. Good salesmen are so rare that when you meet one, it almost makes you want to buy something. Enthusiasm is contagious, particularly when it is not forced, and when the salesmen genuinely seems to be on your side. Books on salesmenship present this common truth of human relations in various ways, but it is very difficult to put into practice without first unifying mind and body. Tohei developed the following guidelines to help salesmen apply Ki in their work.

For Sales:
1. **Know the value of what you are trying to sell.**
2. **Approach your customer or client with positive Ki.**
3. **Focus on customer benefits, not whether or not they buy.**
4. **Always provide responsible after-sale service.**
5. **Even when you do not make a sale, always leave a positive impression.**

As the world grows increasingly independent, corporations are expected to be socially responsible, environmentally concerned, and above all, fair to their employees. At the same time, a manager must keep the company financially healthy and growing. This is an enormous task, if you consider it to be the sole work of one individual. However, if that individual can orchestrate the efforts and resources of many other people, the job is more than doable. Many hands make light work, if they work together.

An age-old problem in business is how to motivate people. From customers to employees, the more cooperation and support you get, the more successful your business will be. One of the key principles of Ki is that the mind leads the body. Unless you can lead a person's mind, you will never be able to gain willing cooperation. No one likes to be forced or pressured into doing things. No matter what you say to someone, your message is always perceived and evaluated in terms of the way you say it. Most people can tell the difference between a person who is genuinely trying to help them, and someone who is trying to deceive or manipulate them. Unifying mind and body sharpens this sense, and therefore gives you a great advantage in human relations.

Even so, managers must do more than simply motivate. They must make decisions, not always popular ones, which will serve the long-term benefits of the company and its employees. They must always learn to see the particular in terms of the whole picture. This is not easy, because that picture is constantly changing. Furthermore, most of the picture is invisible, and must be guessed at intelligently using information, data, opinions, and past experience. Caught between conflicting demands, ambiguous information, and enormous responsibility, it is a rare person who can remain relaxed and positive. Yet as Ki principles demonstrate, unless you are relaxed you cannot possibly do your best. Certainly, management requires knowledge, skills, and experience; but without Ki, none of these resources can be put to effective use. Even if a person can manage successfully without unifying mind and body, the job will probably takes its toll on the manager's health or family life. If you want to learn how to manage well and still develop yourself as a human being, you would do well to study the guidelines which Tohei developed for managers.

Whether a person leads a family, a corporation, or a country, the greatest disservice he can do is to be blind to the welfare of the people the leader is responsible for. Too often society is vexed by the proverbial case of the blind leading the blind. Shortsightedness is most often expressed in aggressive striving for selfish or short-term personal gain. However, experience shows that such an approach usually ends up backfiring. Tohei says that profit is like water: the more you try to gather it to yourself, the more it runs away from you; the more you push it away the more it returns to you. Wealth is not a bad thing, any more than air or food. Moreover, it tends to increase when it is shared with others. A good manager stays alert for opportunities to reinvest profits in employee development and to the benefit of society.

For Management:
1. **First become a positive person yourself.**
2. **Do not work for selfish gain, but see how your work benefits others.**
3. **Be calm enough to be aware of larger trends in society and the world.**
4. **Always make efforts to help your employees grow and develop.**
5. **Return your profits and benefits to society in some way.**

Of all the things that men are known to fear, public speaking stands high on the list. Being forced to stand up and talk before a group is enough to transform a perfectly normal person into a miserable coward. It can drive a self-conscious person into a state of paralysis. None of this need happen if you know how to unify mind and body. Relaxed, calm, and positive, you should be able to easily get your message across without undue stress.

One of Tohei's students had a particular problem speaking before a group, but was unable to avoid it in his work. When he learned about calming the mind at the One Point, he determined to do so the next time he had to speak before a group. Soon the opportunity came to deliver a talk on his company's new product, to an important group of clients. Before he stood up and went forward, he thought of nothing but keeping One Point. Unfortunately, when he began his talk, he mumbled something to the effect of, "Today, I am going to talk about the One Point." Through this embarrassing experience, he learned that thinking about One Point is not the same as keeping it. This also illustrates how difficult it is to try to apply Ki principles at the last minute, rather than making them a habit in daily life.

One of the reasons that people get nervous speaking in public is that they focus more on the fact that they have to face a large group of people under the spotlight, than on the contents and presentation of what they want to say. In so doing, they collapse under the apparent scrutiny of all the members of the audience, as if they were greatly outnumbered by a mortal enemy. Most audiences want a speaker to succeed, partly to avoid the vicarious embarrassment of failure, but also because they want to enjoy the time they have invested. If you assume that you are speaking to a gathering of good friends, that alone will make the task much easier. You can reduce the pressure even further by directing your remarks to various individuals seated throughout the auditorium, rather than to the group as an abstract entity. As long as you select people in each quadrant of the auditorium, you will look as if you are addressing the group as a whole. Tohei himself is a remarkably good public speaker, always taking in the whole group in his gaze, but occasionally meeting the eyes of individuals, as if it were a conversation between the two of them.

Of all of the skills needed in business, public speaking probably heads the list. If you cannot present your ideas in public, then you will be forced to accept other peoples' ideas, whether you like them or not. A polished presentation does not necessarily make a good one, because people instinctively distrust glib and fast talkers. Sincerity, personality, and enthusiasm are far more important to good communication.

Listening audiences have notoriously poor memories. Somehow when you are in a group, the responsibility for listening, understanding, and reacting becomes greatly diluted compared to a face-to-face conversation. Teachers are constantly astonished to find that even though they think they have made a point perfectly clear, none of the students in fact understood it. People who teach or lecture for many years gradually lose confidence in the capacity of the human brain to understand verbal information. Good teachers learn to get it across in other ways. A good speaker will present one or two points well, from a variety of perspectives. If you try to say too much, you so dilute your message that you end up losing the audience altogether.

A poor speaker wastes the listeners' time by being disorganized, mumbling, or by distracting the audience from the message with annoying mannerisms and poor presentation. A good speaker has something to say, says it well, and is remembered long after the talk. Good teachers naturally extend Ki when they speak. We can emulate them by keeping in mind the principles which Tohei developed for speaking before a group.

For Public Speaking:
1. **Begin with a strong and clear introduction.**
2. **Write down the key points of your talk and keep them in mind.**
3. **Extend Ki from your whole body when you speak.**
4. **Speak slowly and punctuate your remarks.**
5. **Always conclude with a positive story.**

The principles described for successful application of Ki in business are nothing new. You can find them in one form or another in many of the best-selling books on time management, sales, leadership, and public speaking. In some cases, they are just concise expressions of common sense. What is puzzling is how uncommon they are in the working world which we know. People with the best intentions fail to follow through in practice. One of the fundamental reasons for this is that without mind and body coordination, no one can really find the energy needed to apply these principles consistently enough to achieve success in their career.

The Ki to Winning in Professional Sports

Other things being equal, if you extend Ki you will always win in sports. An untrained person cannot defeat a well-trained sports player using Ki alone. But if competitors are reasonably closely matched in training, technique, and experience, the one who extends more Ki will be the winner. Well-trained professionals and amateurs do extend Ki to a certain degree, especially when they are in good form. But they do so unconsciously and without any real control or understanding of how they do it, or how to get it back when they lose it. If an athlete can consciously extend Ki, then he or she has an incredible advantage over a competitor who does not. There is no substitute for training in sports, but Ki ensures that your training is used to best advantage.

Even Olympic champions are only a few seconds or meters beyond the average person in their performance. All of that intensive training may double or even triple your strength, but is not likely to do more. With Ki training you learn to magnify your performance many, many times beyond that. If a professional sports player learns how to coordinate mind and body, he can easily outdistance any competitor who does not.

A dance teacher remarked that once a performance got underway things usually went well, but the first step on stage was the most anxious. This is because she forgot that the mind moves the body. Anytime you try to do something without first extending Ki, you will feel anxious and uncertain. Determine first that you can, then go ahead and do it.

In Ki exercise, we first learn to coordinate mind and body by doing each movement twice. On the first movement the body usually goes ahead of the mind out of habit. But when that movement is repeated, the mind is more committed to it, so you naturally unify mind and body. Sports demand quick responses. Seldom is there enough time to repeat a movement twice. However, if you have trained yourself to be coordinated in movement, then you are more likely to be unified in every movement you make. When this happens unconsciously, there is no need to move twice. This helps explain the effectiveness of image training in sports. By replaying the moves over and over in their minds, players can perform them more smoothly. Whether they realize or not, they are using one application of mind and body coordination. The problem is that most people who coach using image training do not understand the correct method of relaxation, nor do they know how to coach the athlete to use Ki in movement. Under these circumstances image training works in spite of the coaching, not because of it. The safest way to practice is to thoroughly learn Ki principles, then apply them to your practice.

Tohei's most extensive experience in the professional sports world was in the world of baseball. By 1953, Hiroshi Arakawa had played for the Daimai Orions ball team (now, Lotte) for eight years without showing any special ability. His batting average was only 0.251. From 1959 to 1960 he came to Tohei's dôjô almost daily, and even earned a first degree black belt in Aikido. He must have sensed intuitively that there should be some way to apply Aikido to baseball, not the techniques per se, but what Tohei called Ki and mind and body coordination. When he became team manager, Arakawa brought many young players to Tohei for special instruction. The first one was Mr. Kihachi Enomoto, who had joined the Orions in 1955, but whose batting average had dropped to the 0.200s. Tohei immediately understood why, when he heard the pitifully weak sound of Enomoto's swing as it cut the air. Tohei applied Ki tests to Enomoto's shoulder, elbow, and bat, but wherever he pushed, Enomoto lost his balance. He then taught him the four principles of mind and body unification and how to initiate the swing from One Point. Most batters swung from the hips, which was too high to generate any real power, and caused them to shrink away from the ball. Tohei taught Enomoto how to swing from a lower center, and step into the swing. When he did this, his swing made an entirely different sound, one which Arakawa immediately recognized as the right one. By 1960 Enomoto was batting 0.344, and doing very well. The media gave him the reputation of being a baseball player who sat in Zen meditation on the bench, never suspecting that he was really practicing co-ordination of mind and body. Later Arakawa brought other players to Tohei: Takao Katsuragi, Takeo Daigo, Haruki Mihira, and Shôichi Ono, each of whom learned the same method. The media took notice that Arakawa had some secret technique, and termed it the "missile" hitting method.

Arakawa had an excellent eye for talent, even when he was working as an outfielder for the Daimai Orions. One player he discovered was still a boy at a junior high school in the Sumida Ward of Tokyo. His name was Sadaharu Oh. Though Taiwanese-born, Oh had as-sumed Japanese citizenship. After graduating from junior high school, Oh went on to Waseda Vocational High School, planning to become an electrical engineer. But Arakawa guided him instead into professional baseball. On graduating from high school, Oh joined the Yomiuri Giants, and Arakawa immediately became his coach. The character used to write Oh's name means "King," so he had a reputation to live up to. The first year his bat-ting record was 0.161, the second year with great effort he batted 0.270, the third year dropped down to 0.253, and earned the unpleasant nickname of the "three-swing King." The Giants even began to regret having taken him on. It was that year, at the end of 1961, that Arakawa retired from the Orions and went to work as a coach for the Giants. One of the players, Mr. Tatsurô Hirooka, recommended to team manager Tetsuharu Kawakami that Arakawa be made batting coach. Hirooka had been only one year junior to Arakawa at Waseda University, so he knew him well. The next year in 1962, Oh brought up his aver-age to 0.280 under the pressure of Arakawa's severe quota: to hit twenty home runs. As part of his program to make Oh succeed, he brought him to Tohei for special instruction.

Arakawa said that Oh had exceptional potential, but somehow could not manage to live up to it. At first, even though Tohei taught him the four principles, Oh could not produce more than a weak sound with his swing. Tohei noticed that though his starting posture was good, Oh had a bad habit of driving his right leg into the ground when he hit (Oh was a left-handed hitter). This put tension into his legs and made him lose mind and body coordi-nation when he swung the bat. Arakawa was aware of the problem, but thought that it was an ingrained habit and assumed nothing could be done about it. When Oh raised his leg, he tended to raise his weight upperside at the same time. Tohei told Arakawa that any habit which is acquired can be changed, and then taught Oh how to keep his weight underside, even when he raised one leg off the ground.

Eventually Oh became able to stand unified and balanced on one leg for as long as fifteen minutes. Arakawa trained him daily in this method, checking his posture with the Ki tests that he had learned from Tohei. In time, Oh became famous for this one-legged, or "flamingo" stance. At first, Arakawa worried if it was all right to practice in such an unconventional way. Tohei asked him if there was any rule against it, and he could not think of any. On July 1, 1962, in the Taiyô match, this stance was put to the test in the field. The day before as second batter, Oh had swung three strikes. So this day, Arakawa ordered him out first, and told him to use the one-legged stance which Tohei had taught him. His first time up he got on base, but his second time up he hit a right-field grandslam home run. That year Oh hit thirty-eight home runs, and earned the nickname "King." His batting average was 0.272, and his number of hits was well over Arakawa's quota.

By July of 1976, Oh's home run record was one short of 700, which would then set a new record, a first in Japan. The suspense was high, as baseball fans all over Japan watched the Giants play each night. No pitcher wanted to be the one that helped Oh make that record. Good pitchers tried their best to strike him out; pitchers who lacked self-confidence simply walked him. Starting on July 3, and running for three weeks in succession, Oh ran into a slump. He simply could not produce the fine sound which his bat usually made when it cut the air or hit the ball. When he was in good form, the games got rained out. The eyes of the entire nation upon him nearly all of the time, he became exhausted, playing in fields from the northern to the southern tip of Japan.

Why could he not hit? Under pressure, he had forgotten how to extend Ki. Tohei had worked with Oh closely, using Ki tests in a variety of postures, to the point where Oh perfected his trademark "flamingo" hitting stance. Tohei had just returned from a long teaching tour in America. He heard about Oh's slump, and watching it on television, realized that Oh had forgotten a significant thing that he had taught him. Watching Oh warm up in the batter's box, Tohei noticed he was gripping the bat too tightly. This made his body tense and unable to extend Ki. Tohei learned later that by that time, Oh could not sleep at night, and had nearly forgotten what food tasted like.

The next day Tohei called Oh's home at noon, knowing that he slept all morning to rest up for the game. He asked Oh why he was gripping the bat so tightly. Apparently, Oh himself had been totally unaware that he had been doing so, nor had his manager mentioned anything about it. Tohei recommended that he sit in Ki meditation for thirty minutes, focusing his mind on the One Point and releasing all stress from his body. These were all things which he had been taught before, but had forgotten under the pressure of the circumstances. Tohei also gave him a bit of good psychological advice. Rather than thinking that he was one hit away from 700, he should think he was 101 hits away from 800.

That day, Oh left the house smiling. That night, in the famous Taiyô match, with the bases loaded and against the first pitch from pitcher Tatsuo Uzawa, Oh hit his 700th home run, deep into the right center-field grandstands. And he continued to hit well. On October 11 of the same year, he broke Babe Ruth's home run record with 715 runs. The next year on September 3, he broke Hank Aaron's record with 756 runs and became the world's top hitter. Even fourteen years later in 1990, on national television he was still attributing his success directly to Tohei's continued coaching in mind and body unification.

Tohei's teachings had significant effects on what were to become common practices in baseball. Before Sadaharu Oh, no one in Japan hit by standing on one leg and stepping into the swing. Oh had a habit of doing this, and Tohei encouraged him to go ahead and lift the leg high, while testing him to be sure that he still had One Point. After special training with Tohei, Oh was able to surpass world-class home run records, which brought him great popularity and fame. Now many professional players, as well as school children all over

Japan imitate his one-legged stance, though they usually imitate form and forget substance.

Hirooka was the man who recommended that Arakawa be made batting coach. He had followed Oh's career closely, particularly his difficulties, saying that if a talented boy made that much effort and still failed, there must be no God. But Oh's effort succeeded. In his best condition, he could suspend several children from his arm while standing on one leg, and still not lose his balance. Many players since have tried to imitate his stance, thinking it must be the secret of his success, but no one has been able to come close. The key to Oh's success was not standing on one leg, but hitting from One Point.

Hirooka himself was a very intelligent but skeptical person, and therefore very hard to persuade. At first he was quite doubtful about the whole idea of applying Ki to baseball, but gradually became convinced when he saw it work so well in the field. Eventually Hirooka went to work for the Seibu Lions as team manager. During this time, he brought many young players to Tohei for Ki training. They were all strong professional athletes, and had trained their bodies with weights and heavy exercise. No one knew what to make of Tohei at first. They were unable to budge this man of fifty, no matter how hard they pushed, yet Tohei could easily move each of them, apparently without even using any strength. Eventually they each became convinced that a unified mind and body was stronger. Because each player's progress was so dramatic, Hirooka assumed that Tohei was giving them special training designed for professional ball players. Actually, Tohei taught the same things as he did to other people, just as he always had. The difference was that because these professional players worked very hard to apply it, they naturally made dramatic progress. Among the players which Hirooka brought to Tohei were Kôichi Tabuchi, Hiromichi Ishige, Kôji Akiyama, Eiji Kanamori, Takuji Ohta, and an American player named Terry White. The Seibu Lions had previously had a poor record, dragging along for a number of years in a row. Hirooka asked Tohei if he could train them to win the series within a few years. Tohei said that if they applied Ki principles correctly, they would win it that season. They not only won that year, but for several years in a row after that, throughout the entire time which Tohei continued to help coach the team. The year that Tohei stopped teaching them they lost their first place standing.

Different personalities responded differently to Tohei's teachings. Enomoto and Oh were very open-minded and hard working. Hirooka was skeptical, but trained hard once he saw the value of it. Shigeo Nagashima was another popular player with the Yomiuri Giants. Nagashima was very insightful and grasped Ki principles instinctively. He was also a natural-born fighter with a very positive spirit, famous for the "Sayonara" home run upset hit against pitcher Minoru Murayama of the Hanshin Tigers, during the Tenran match in 1959. Nagashima to this day supports Tohei's teaching, considering it very close to his own philosophy of life.

Not all of Tohei's baseball students were batters. Suguru Egawa was a pitcher with the Yomiuri Giants. While still a student in the Sakushin Gakuin High School baseball division, Egawa was throwing so poorly that nearly anyone could hit his pitches. His manager Yamamoto was a student of Tohei's, and came to ask for help. Tohei's advice was to hold the ball lightly enough to be completely relaxed, but firmly enough that the left hand could not pull the ball out of the right hand, nor should another person be able to pull it out, even with great effort. Many professional coaches advise not to grip the ball too tightly, but they have no means of checking the grip, such as a Ki test. Tohei said that if he held the ball in this way, each pitch would have strong Ki and be very hard to hit. Egawa's pitches eventually earned the nickname of the "hard" fast ball. His high school won the Eastern Japan League Series, and went to national competition at Kôshien. High school baseball is followed with great enthusiasm in Japan, and always gains national television coverage. Egawa became a very popular player as a result of his excellent pitching, yet few people suspected that what they were really drawn to was an outstanding expression of Ki in sports.

Baseball was not the only sport in which Tohei played a significant role behind the scenes. Tohei also taught Ki principles to a number of Sumo champions. Sumo is an ancient Japanese sport, with ties to the Imperial court. Sumo wrestlers are known for their enormous size, low center of gravity, imperturbable faces, and sense of grand style. What few people realize is that it takes a long time to gain these qualities and many young men drop out at the lower levels. The competition and pressure are perhaps unmatched, a kind of Olympic sport with ceremony. Each match begins with great formality, but is generally over in a few moments. Wrestlers enter a large elevated circular area called the *dohyô*, a ring marked by a very heavy rope, half buried in the earthen floor. These mammoth wrestlers face off with a mere seventy centimeters (twenty-eight inches) of space between them and wait for the referee to start the match. The bout ends when one of the wrestlers is pushed out of the ring, or caused to touch the floor with any part of his body above the knee.

A Sumo wrestler from Tokyo's Higashi Murayama, Mr. Kuniyoshi Kurosegawa entered the Isegahama Stable at age fifteen. He trained for ten years without once entering the Jûryô, or second-highest class in the Sumo ranks. As the oldest member of the stable, nearly twenty-five years old, he himself and the people around him assumed that his professional career was nearing its end. He had a reputation in the Sumo world of being a weakling. His father had died while he was still a boy, and Kurosegawa was well-known for his devotion to his mother. His mother brought him to Ki Society, thinking that it might be his last chance to make his name. At first he did not want to come, thinking it was some kind of religion. But when he arrived, he was surprised at the confidence which Tohei showed in him. Tohei told Kurosegawa that Yokozuna, or Grand Champion, was only attainable by a small few, but that with Ki training at least he could expect to go to the Sanyaku rank, one of the three positions just below the Grand Champion. Sumo wrestlers must compete through three ranks in the step division (dan), then they enter the second rank (Maku-shita, or "below the curtain"), next they become first rank division contenders (Jûryô), after which a small number climb to the first rank division (Maku-uchi), which progresses from Senior Wrestlers (Maegashira) to Pre-Champions (Komusubi) to Junior Champions (Sekiwake) to Champions (Ozeki), and finally the top rank of all, Grand Champion (Yokozuna). To a discouraged man who was near retirement and had never even been a first rank division contender, the idea of being a Champion in the top three ranks seemed no more than a pipe dream. In fact, at the time he thought that Tohei must be crazy. But Tohei then explained how the strength that we ordinarily use is no more than the tip of the iceberg. No matter how much we try to develop it, it can only take us so far. If he wanted to develop his true potential strength, he would have to learn how to unify mind and body.

Kurosegawa was 183 centimeters (6 feet) tall and weighed 132 kilograms (290 pounds), the size of a small bear. In the dôjô, Tohei matched Kurosegawa against many of his students, none of whom weighed more than 60 to 70 kilograms (130 to 150 pounds.). Using simple Ki tests (not Sumo wrestling techniques), every one of Tohei's students could move or throw Kurosegawa, but the Sumo giant could not budge anyone. Tohei himself, then at age of sixty, could easily throw Kurosegawa, even when he charged with full strength. Kurosegawa exclaimed that all of Tohei's students must be above the Jûryô rank, but Tohei explained that they would be no match for a Sumo wrestler who had learned how to unify mind and body.

One of the things which Tohei taught Kurosegawa was to only think of going forward. He said that was no need to try to unbalance or throw his opponent with a technique, as all he needed to do to win was to push the opponent out of the ring. Between tournaments he always came to Tohei's dôjô for intensive Ki training. He was a very open and serious young man, who did his best to apply what he had been taught in the ring. Soon he started winning. Kurosegawa was rather clumsy at technique, but eventually developed a reputation of being as immovable as a rock. A number of people who lost to Kurosegawa began to doubt their own abilities, and one or two retired, thinking that if they lost to such a weakling, they must be nearly finished themselves. In the May 1976 Tournament, he at last entered the Jûryô rank and earned considerable respect. In the May 1978 Tournament he entered Maku-uchi and twice became Komusubi. In just two years, Kurosegawa had entered the Sanyaku rank as a Pre-Champion, just as Tohei had promised. People who knew Sumo said it was a miracle. But Tohei said that any Sumo wrestler who used Ki principles and trained in the same way could do as well or better.

At the time Kurosegawa began his instruction, it was common for the Sumo wrestlers to crouch low, but to keep their hands off of the ground in a ready position. Although there are no weight classes in Sumo, and frequently a wrestler must face a man much larger than himself, still there is an advantage in being the first one to push. They would wait in the ready position and collide headlong, each trying to push the other out of the ring. Kurosegawa was unable to resist this headlong push, so Tohei showed him how to become more stable with One Point and helped him develop a strategy of lightly touching the fists on the floor as he crouched, and then coming up from a low angle to uproot his opponent. With this approach he became very successful and now it is commonly imitated in the Sumo world, although without the fantastic results that Kurosegawa achieved when he coordinated mind and body. In both sports and the martial arts, while physical strength, leverage, timing, and technique may help, none of these alone is a match for a unified mind and body which is similarly trained.

Tohei also had the opportunity to teach amateur Sumo wrestlers. In 1955, when Tohei was teaching policemen in Honolulu, Hawaii, one of his sincerest students was a man named Larry Mehau. Larry had the build of a Sumo wrestler and at the time was studying wrestling from a professional wrestler named Rikidôzan, a former Japanese Sumo wrestler who later converted to professional wrestling. Larry was not only strong, he knew how to use Ki. A former Yokozuna Grand Champion from Japan, named Azumafuji, had retired from Sumo to become a professional wrestler in Hawaii. When he was matched against Larry Mehau, perhaps he was overconfident in facing an amatuer, but Larry pushed the Yokozuna out of the ring three times.

Larry was said to be the strongest man in Hawaii. He practiced Judo as well as Sumo and believed he had nothing to fear from a small Japanese martial artist. Though he later became one of the most enthusiastic of Tohei's students, at first he thought that Ki and Aikido were fake, watching demonstrations with arms folded. He mocked Tohei in front of his teacher Rikidôzan, who then told him that Tohei was for real and that Larry should learn from him. Mr. Hirata, a fifth dan in Judo, introduced him to Tohei and Tohei accepted him immediately as his student. Larry assumed that Tohei's willingness was based on his fear of Larry's teacher. Tohei told him that at first, he had gotten a negative impression about Larry, because his eyes were very negative and condescending, but now he realized that his expression was based on honest doubt. Larry later became a trusted and loyal student of Tohei's and went on to win Hawaiian Judo and Sumo championships.

A few years later, another Yokozuna in Japan named Kashiwado trained with a group of amateurs from Hawaii who had come to Japan to learn Sumo. The Grand Champion threw them one after another. No matter how big or strong an amateur was, none were any match for a Yokozuna. Then Larry stepped up, fully determined to do his best. Kashiwado expected him to be just like the rest, but Larry pushed him all the way back to the wall. Literally taken aback, Kashiwado asked Larry who his teacher was. He said Koichi Tohei.

Hawaii has produced Sumo wrestlers who have become champions in Japanese professional competition. The most famous of these is Daigoro Takamiyama, who acquired the nickname of "Jesse." As a youth in Hawaii, he had spent six months in the hospital after breaking both legs in a truck accident, and was never able to make a sports team until senior high school. When he came to Japan at the age of nineteen, experts predicted that he would never make the grade. Nevertheless, he worked hard and performed well, becoming famous for his consecutive wins. Knowing of Jesse's reputation, Tohei called him when he was in Hawaii and taught him Ki principles personally twice. Just after that, at the 1972 Nagoya Tournament, Takamiyama dramatically achieved a new rank, becoming the only foreign born Sumo wrestler ever to win a major Japanese tournament, with thirteen wins to two losses. Eventually he ended up holding one of the top two ranks below Ozeki for a total of twenty-six times. After his retirement, he frequently appeared in Japanese commercials because of his winning smile and massive size (198.5 kilograms, or 438 pounds). There may have been more to his success than just Ki training, but it is significant that he recognized the value of Tohei's teaching, and used it to achieve his greatest success.

Another Sumo great who benefited from Tohei's teachings was Chiyonofuji, who retired in 1991, after accumulating 1,045 victories and 31 championships over a career lasting twenty-one years. He was relatively small for a Sumo wrestler, weighing only 126 kilograms (278 pounds), but had a reputation for his fierce expression, which earned him the nickname of "Wolf." Part of the price he paid for his phenomenal achievements was a string of injuries. He dislocated his left shoulder nine times and his right shoulder twice. Part of what allowed him to make such spectacular comebacks was the fact that he received Kiatsu therapy from Tohei Sensei. During one Kiatsu session he commented to Tohei about something he had read in a book somewhere, on how it was important to have soft eyes and a composed manner. Before he could finish his sentence however, he himself realized that he had read it in one of Tohei Sensei's own books!

Just as certain countries seem to excel in particular sports, others always seem to be in the lower ranks. Japan is not noted for its performance in rugby or in American football. In foreign competition, a Japanese team usually looks out of place, like a high school team competing against professional players.

In 1989, thanks to an introduction from Mr. Tatsurô Hirooka, Tohei had an opportunity to teach Ki principles to a Japanese rugby team, particularly to their forward, Toshiyuki Hayashi. He taught them that one is stronger when one is relaxed and showed them how to apply it on the playing field. On May 28, 1989, in Tokyo at the Chichibu no Miya Rugby Field, the Japanese rugby team competed against a team from Scotland, which was the strongest of eight in the league. Ever since 1971, when Japan was invited to compete in England, the Japanese team had never won a match. On this their twenty-eighth match, with 20,000 spectators watching, the Japanese defeated the Scottish team in a remarkable upset, one which they have been unable to repeat since playing against the teams of Europe, Australia, and New Zealand. In this game, the Japanese were especially praised for their tackling, which had always been considered their weakest point against foreign teams. Tohei had taught them that if they were relaxed, any oncoming force would be returned in kind. Forward Hayashi absorbed this secret in just two days of special training. Even the coach of the Scottish team praised the Japanese team's tackling ability.

In every case in which Tohei has coached professional sports players they have performed many times beyond their former abilities. Some of the corporate baseball teams which he has coached have set new records and enjoyed winning streaks for the first time in their history. But much depends on the follow-up and support of the team manager. The Ki principles work, but they work better if there is a dedicated commitment to put them into practice.

Naturally, one of the things which a competitive sports player tries to develop is strength. Many students of Ki wrongly assume that they should not use strength at all, but rather take a passive attitude. Instead Tohei teaches how to use strength most effectively, not how to lose it. An American football player once asked Tohei how it was possible to avoid being tackled and still hold on to the ball. He could do one or the other, but not both at the same time. Tohei showed him how by staying relaxed, he could bounce his opponent away at the moment of collision with a strong and explosive extension of Ki. This is not possible if the body is tense. When Tohei did a Ki demonstration for a group of weight lifters in Las Vegas, at first they were very skeptical, not believing that it was possible to lift weights with a relaxed body. Tohei taught them that the heavier the object, the lighter they must hold it. The weight lifters were proud of their own strength and some refused to accept what they saw in the Ki tests. But while publically claiming it was a trick, one or two men privately apologized to Tohei, saying that after all, he was right. Relaxing completely allows the muscles to operate in unison, just at the moment they are needed.

This is not a matter of avoiding using strength, but rather learning to use it most effectively. A person who is tense most of the time is unable to exert real strength when he needs it. There have been many documented cases of ordinary people who have exerted incredible strength in a crisis, a single person lifting a car which pinned a child, or carrying a piano out of a burning home. When the crisis had passed, they were unable to budge the object. This is a good example of using the strength of the whole iceberg, not just the visible tip. The problem is that people do not know how to tap into or control it.

Another element considered important in sports is control, or skilled execution of technique. One of the most demanding examples of this is found in golf. Not only must the golfer adjust to ever changing weather and landscapes, but the slightest deviation in the angle of the stroke can cause the ball to go many meters off course. When he was in Hawaii, Tohei taught the former teacher of professional golfer Jack Nicholaus, Mr. John Roberts, who at the time was seventy-five years old, at the Waiarai Country Club, the second oldest golf course in Hawaii. This club had once been so exclusive that it refused membership to Japanese-Americans, but that rule had recently been lifted. The difficulty of putting, Mr. Roberts said, was learning to move the upper or left hand straight, without letting the lower or right hand knock the ball off course. Mr. Roberts could putt from three meters, but not from five or six. As the distance increases, people tend to use too much force with the right hand. Tohei first taught him how to unify mind and body in the standing position, and while holding the club. Then he offered the following advice on how to hit the ball. Instead of concentrating on the arm movements, Tohei suggested that he focus on moving the body from the One Point. This lent the extra power needed, but ensured that the ball traveled on a straight line. With this advice, Mr. Roberts then sank the last three out of four attempts, all from a distance of six meters.

On another occasion Tohei helped amateur golfers sink putts from distances of six or seven meters, even though Tohei himself had never played the game and did not even know the rules. This was done by correcting their posture at various parts of the swing, using Ki tests. He made no attempt to teach golfing technique.

People say that mistakes in sports come from trying too hard. Psychologists have even invented a name for it: the so-called "Law of Reversed Effort," claiming that the harder you try, the more you tend to fail. But this is confusing, because it suggests that it is better to try not to try, or to make no effort at all. Without effort there is no learning or progress, but it must be correct effort, based on mind and body coordination. One of Tohei's favorite axioms is that correct efforts produce correct results, wrong efforts produce wrong results.

Sports and new forms of exercise enjoy an unparalleled popularity today. This is fine, as long as the movements fit natural principles. If they do not, you had better not practice them. A true Ki exercise makes you stronger, no matter how often you practice it. Some breathing exercises developed in India and China are taught with great caution. Students are warned not to practice them more than a few times per sitting, because the exercises can lead to physical or mental imbalance. But any exercise that entails such risk must have something wrong with it, and is best avoided in the first place. Ki breathing has no dangerous or negative side effects. You can practice it as much as you like.

Similarly, any sport which unnaturally strains or misuses one part of the body cannot be good for health. The whole body benefits from exercise, not just isolated parts of the body. This is why walking and swimming are still considered to be among the best of exercises. Golf is no answer, for it uses only one side of the body. If people walked the course it might be good exercise, but instead they ride in golf carts and defeat the purpose. It used to be that people would get plenty of exercise just cleaning the house and working with their hands. Now daily life has become so convenient that people let the house get dirty and set time aside entirely for the purpose of exercise. A sedentary person who suddenly forces himself into a too rigorous program can get injured in the process. Jogging, for example, can be very dangerous, for it puts an unaccustomed demand on the heart muscles. Doctors in Japan now warn that people with heart trouble should not practice aerobics. People should remember that the man who started the aerobics and jogging for health movement, James Fixx, died of heart failure while jogging, while still in his fifties. A long a brisk walk is a far better form of exercise. It uses the whole body and you can stop anytime before you overdo it.

Ironically, many people who take up aerobic dancing for health end up with injuries. People choose aerobics because they think that they can lose weight over a short time, and enjoy moving their body to music. The biggest danger of aerobics is that the movements are done in time to fast music, while constantly changing directions. As the mind has no time to catch up with the busy body, the person becomes more and more divided, until the body is truly weak and vulnerable to injury. Do not assume that merely because you get out of breath and work up a sweat that you have done something good for your body. Looking at the instructors, students assume that aerobics will help them become young and beautiful, but most of the instructors were that way already before they took up aerobics. A young body can withstand a fair degree of abuse, but the same movements can be dangerous to a person unaccustomed to hard exercise. The only kind of exercise that really is good for health is that which is performed with mind and body coordinated.

Sports are supposed to be good for health. But there is a therapeutic specialty called *sports medicine*, which deals entirely with the vast range of injuries which can occur in sports. Some of these injuries stay with people for life, like the familiar "football knee," or "tennis elbow." Most of them can be prevented, if you train with mind and body coordinated.

But just because of its limitations and excesses, sports should not be given a bad name. Some people even consider themselves above competitve sports, thinking that non-dissension is on a "higher plane." Competitive sports can take on an ugly cast, resulting in violence and the willingness to do anything to win. Sometimes even the fans commit violence over a game, as has often happened in international rugby competitions. However, this is generally considered to be poor sportsmanship and is more often the exception than the rule. Most of the excesses of sports could be avoided if people practiced them with mind and body unified, and emphasized self-improvement rather than winning.

Ki in the Performing Arts

Japanese rock gardens are famous for their austere and tranquil beauty. The gardens are designed so that they can be enjoyed from a variety of angles, but some angles are also deliberately hidden from view. This is to suggest that we never know the fullest extent of a landscape, or of anything else in life. The largest portion of each rock is also buried below the surface, not only for stability, but to suggest that the garden's residing power is mostly hidden. These artistic devises have profound symbolic meaning in terms of Ki as well, as Tohei so often points out in his analogy of the tip of the iceberg.

People in any field attain mind and body coordination when they are at their best. Artists are no exception. But it is rare artist who can sustain or control that condition, much less teach it to others. Some works of artistic genius come about almost by luck, accident, or a rare combination of the right conditions. This leads creative people to describe the state of mind in which they work as a trance, or inspiration. Artists frequently shun any planned approach to their work, fearing that conscious effort might interfere. In fact, a haphazard approach to anything is no better than hit or miss. It is not effort which interferes with creativity, but lack of mind and body coordination. If an artist already has both talent and training, there is no reason why it should not be available on call. The secret is to learn how to infuse the work with Ki. An artist who can do this on a regular basis need not suffer the insults of low status or the miseries of poverty. If an artist is in need of inspiration, Ki principles offer a precise way to get it back anytime, anyplace.

As part of their training, calligraphers copy master works to develop brush technique and refine their aesthetic sense, much as artists in the West copy master drawings. A Japanese calligraphy teacher once asked Tohei to teach him how to put Ki into his brush strokes. The teacher found that he could paint what seemed a reasonable likeness of a master work if viewed up close, but that when viewed from a distance, the difference between the original and the copy was obvious. Tohei told him that the major difference was that the master work had Ki and the copy did not. The way to put Ki into the brush strokes was not simply to imitate the form, but to not cut Ki at any point in the process: while grinding ink, selecting the brush, spreading the paper, concentrating on the form, or holding the brush between strokes. He also advised him to hold the brush lightly, so that his body would remain relaxed. With this advice, the calligraphy teacher not only gained better control, but actually won prizes in competitions as a result.

Ki can also be applied to music. There is an accomplished performer of the transverse wooden flute in Japan, known as Master Hyakunosuke Fukuhara. This flute master happened to sit next to Tohei at a dinner party, and asked him how to put Ki into his music. He knew when he had it, but could not seem to control it, particularly on a concert stage. His audiences may not have always been aware of the difference, but he knew it and it bothered him deeply. Tohei asked to him assume the posture that he normally did when he was playing. Without saying a word, Tohei immediately gave him a Ki test and he was as solid as a rock. Tohei told him that he apparently already knew how to extend Ki. The man expressed disbelief, asking if that was all there was to it. Tohei suddenly tested him again and this time he fell over easily. Tohei then explained that when he could pass the test in daily life as well as when he played the flute, then he would really earn the title of Master.

One of Tohei's students had taken up the *shakuhachi,* or bamboo flute. He somehow got the idea that his flute practice could easily substitute for Ki breathing, so he had not been practicing Ki breathing since he started flute lessons. He had only been taking lessons for three months however, when he heard the story about Master Fukuhara. It was not surprising then, that even though he assumed the posture he did when he practiced the *shakuhachi,* he was unable to pass a Ki test. There is a considerable difference between a beginner and a master. Conventional wisdom has it that it takes one year even to learn to produce a sound from the *shakuhachi,* three years to move the head properly, and eight years to produce music that is emotionally rich. An art form may be a marvelous way to express Ki energy, but it is no substitute for Ki training. Tohei often reminds his students of Aikido that they should practice Ki breathing everyday, saying that Aikido techniques alone are not enough to develop Ki.

A professional singer once asked for Tohei's advice on how to sing high notes. She said that when she got nervous on stage, her high notes became very shrill. When someone told her that she sounded like a chicken being strangled, she started to lose confidence. Tohei told her that she should be careful not to let her One Point come up as she tried to reach for high notes. By relaxing and keeping the One Point low, she became able to produce beautiful tones, well into the high soprano range.

Tohei taught Ki principles to Jazz pianist Joe Bushkin during the 1950s. Musicians are very sensitive people, and performing musicians are constantly under pressure. Bushkin became so nervous before performances that he had to smoke heavily to calm his nerves. Tohei taught him how to do Ki breathing, and told him that he should do it whenever he felt the urge to smoke, since it was impossible to smoke while exhaling. Through this method, Bushkin learned how to relax under pressure. By unifying mind and body, he also learned how to strike the piano keys with the weight underside in the fingers, which helped produce clear and definitive sounds. Bushkin fans thought that it was just good music. How many of them realized that it was also good Ki?

What Children Really Want from Parents and Teachers

Until the age of eleven or twelve, children spend more time with their parents than with any other adult. As role models during this formative period, parents have a major impact on how the child develops. Even more than from their teachers, children absorb many things unconsciously from their parents, including how to walk, talk, and breathe. A child of seven or eight may have bad habits, but habits are relatively easy to correct when the child is still young. By the time a child gets to high school, parents, teachers, and indeed society itself may have a real problem on their hands. You can blow out a match with a single breath, but once the flames spread, even an entire fire department may have trouble keeping the damage under control.

In large cities around the world, people are troubled with confused and delinquent youth. Young people absorb countless influences from the media which they cannot digest, and can easily be swayed by them in their lifestyles. There is no use expecting the school to train the children, as many teachers have already given up. Nor should parents rest easily just because their child gets decent marks in school. Academic performance alone has never been a reliable indicator of balanced human development. Parents who assume that all is going as well as it says on the report card may be in for a real surprise someday.

While the child is still at its parents' side, that is the time to teach clearly what is right and wrong. If a child learns how to control himself, then when he gets older, he or she will naturally think and act correctly. If children have strong Ki, then parents can turn them loose with peace of mind.

Naturally parents want to please their children. But they should not think that buying whatever a child wants is an expression of love. What children want is full parental attention and care, not just new toys. Spoiled children have neither self-control nor consideration of others. The world is not an easy place to live in. Even if a child gets along well in school, this is no guarantee that he will be able to survive in society.

Since his first visit to Hawaii in 1953, Tohei started children's classes, some dôjôs listing 200 to 300 children as members. Patterned after this, children's Ki and Aikido classes were started in many parts of the United States, usually meeting once per week. Parents felt that a Ki dôjô was one place where they need not worry about their kids. Tohei usually recommended that one or both parents train with their children. One class in Hawaii contained about fifty children. Not all of the mothers attended. Some of the smaller kids came in car pools, while the older ones came on their own. There was a boy of twelve whose mother never came. One day she asked him what he learned at Aikido. He told her they learned that relaxation was the strongest way. She told her son that was the stupidest thing she had ever heard, saying he should realize that it was much stronger to resist. The boy could not convince his mother, until her neighbor showed her that her son was right. The mother felt ashamed of herself for not trying to understand her son better.

Through training in sports or martial arts, some people can develop very strong bodies. But this is no guarantee that they will develop strong characters or be good people. Athletes sometimes commit crimes. Large men are sometimes timid. Training the body alone is not enough. The mind and body must be trained as a whole.

People assume that you must struggle to survive and get ahead, but not everything in the world works that way. Many things work better by cooperation. What kind of a world would it be if husbands and wives, parents and children competed to get ahead of each other? Even if you can win out over others, can you win out over yourself? In children's classes they were taught that Aikido is based on the spirit of non-dissension. Students learned how to move correctly and lead rather than force others.

Young people are not persuaded by simply being told that something is so. You have to show them. Aikido does this, step by step, movement by movement, not just in theory. Each of the exercises has a deeper meaning which can be applied in daily life. But for a child to really absorb this meaning, it is immensely helpful if the parents practice together with the child.

A old Greek tale tells of an upper class woman who approached a philosopher, asking him when she should begin educating her child. The philosopher asked how old the child was. When she replied that her child was three years old, he told her that it was already three years too late. Probably aware of this story, Charles Darwin gave the same answer to a woman who asked him the same question. In Japan, people usually say that education begins in the womb, with the mother's lifestyle and environment. For people whose children are already of school age, it is better to be late than to never start. In either case, there is no time like the present.

For children, Ki practice begins in the home. Adults may choose to practice on their own, but you cannot expect as much of a small child. First you must stimulate their interest. This is not as difficult as it may seem. Help them to enjoy Ki training as a form of play. Children love to play, and will readily learn if given a chance to enjoy it. Teach them in the context of their interests. Most games and toys have ready Ki applications, if you look for them. Children are deeply impressed by strength and good form. They show no interest in abstract lectures by teachers, but they never tire of baseball players or rock musicians. With Ki you can show them how to be stronger and how to look good, and you will have their rapt attention. Be sure to compliment and praise the child. They will reevaluate their own idea of themselves through your genuine interest in their growth.

If you teach a child that the mind leads the body, that whatever thought is held in the mind immediately appears in the body, then you do them a favor for life. They will realize early on that they must hold only positive thoughts. With early success they will gain confidence in themselves that will help them face the many problems of growing up. There is a famous saying in Japanese which emphasizes the importance of positive action and attitude.

> For most things in life, if you try you succeed.
> If you don't, you fail.
> The people who couldn't do
> are usually the ones who didn't try.

Though many children are bored with school, almost all of them want to be strong and well-accepted by their peers. As long as that is the primary concern on their mind, they will never be able to concentrate on their studies. Many parents brought their children to Tohei for advice on this point. He first asked the children if they liked to study. The answer was usually no. Then he asked them if they wanted to become strong. The answer was usually yes. He told them that they did not have to study, but if they wanted to become strong, they must follow his advice. Having gotten their attention, he proceeded to teach them how to unify mind and body by maintaining the correct posture. He said that in class, they need not particularly pay attention to the teacher, but they must maintain the correct posture and just pretend to pay attention, in order to stay out of trouble. One teacher, surprised by a child's sudden change in posture, asked the parents if they were practicing Spartan education at home. But in time, the child's change in posture resulted in a change in attitude. By unifying mind and body, the child naturally became more receptive to what the teacher was saying, understood it better, and even found it interesting. More than one child went from the bottom to the top of the class through this approach.

Children are very active creatures. It is very easy to lose or forget the One Point in movement, so it is particularly important to learn how to keep One Point while young. A Japanese proverb says that when you enjoy something you tend to become good at it. All kids have subjects they like and subjects they dislike. It is easy to extend Ki when you like something, but it takes training to extend Ki when you do not. Children must form the habit early of using the mind in a positive way. If a child must read a book which he does not like, he should sit in Ki meditation for five or ten minutes before picking up the book. This will focus the mind, and help the child to extend Ki naturally to the contents of the book. If you read something without interest, you can read for pages without absorbing a thing. By extending Ki as you read, you will understand it better, remember it more easily, and maybe even develop an interest in it.

This is not only useful for study, it can help prevent accidents. Japanese children, when they leave the house, have a custom of calling out loudly that they are leaving, and will be back soon! Children who leave the house grumbling complaints, or without saying a word are not really safe to go out in traffic. An unfocused mind has very poor reflexes. At the dinner table, children should be taught to focus fully on what they are eating. This will not only help them appreciate and enjoy their food, but it will improve their digestion as well. Children who eat absentmindedly while reading, or who complain as they eat, often suffer from digestive problems.

Children enjoy challenges. Give them a chance to prove what they know. Teach them a Ki exercise, and test them to be sure they have understood it. Then send them on an errand, telling them that you will test them again when they return. If they are successful, you can praise and reward them. You can also feel easy knowing that they are safer leaving the house with Ki extended.

A parent who tests a child often in daily life, and praises him when he does well, gives the child a feeling of security, because it shows that the parent really wants the best for him. With a little ingenuity, Ki tests can be applied to nearly any movement in daily life. A child who learns to pass Ki tests given even when not expected will develop a strong spirit of self-reliance, and will not be careless in small things. Children develop quickly with their parent's support. By teaching self-reliance in little ways, as a natural part of daily life, you can gradually help develop a self-sufficient individual.

The support of parents at home is very important, but if possible the child should train and play with other children at a Ki Society dôjô. It is all the better if the parents can participate in the Ki classes, for it will give them a strong common ground to grow together. Most parents are not so much interested in seeing their children become strong martial artists, as in their developing a strong and good character. The instructor should give the same emphasis in teaching a children's class. Tohei gives the following advice for instructors of children's Ki and Aikido classes.

The child must enjoy coming to the dôjô. It is a child's nature to want to run about freely. This may be possible in the country, but in a crowded urban environment the home is too small and the street too dangerous, so many children are deprived of a chance to really play. When they are young, they are always told to do this, or not to do that. By the time they gain some independence, it is not surprising they want to run wild. Children should be given the opportunity to let off steam in the dôjô, to run around and make noise, as long as they do not injure themselves. In the beginning, it is more important that they have fun than that they practice the techniques correctly.

Children should be scolded positively, not negatively. What seems like a small choice of words to an adult, can have a big effect on a child's subconscious mind. Choose your words carefully, and make them positive. Know a child's strengths and weaknesses. Do not just teach techniques, but try to understand the child's character. Talk to the parents. Children will not listen to abstract advice or theories, but if you build on their strengths and try to correct their weaknesses through the techniques and exercises, then they will improve naturally. Try to select and teach Ki exercises which are appropriate to the child's needs and problems.

Help children learn to get along with each other in group activities. An only child may tend to think that the world revolves around himself. Try to get the older kids to help the younger ones, and teach all of the children to respect individual differences.

Aikido can help children overcome many fears, such as fear of losing balance, falling, rapid or complex movements, bigger kids. But as a discipline it requires an atmosphere of respect. Teach correct manners and etiquette. When you give the kids time to run about, let them run freely. But when it is time to be calm, insist upon it. It is also important to bow properly when entering and leaving the dôjô, and to the teacher for instruction. After running wild, it is very easy for children to become excited and lose their manners. Line them up and test them one at a time. The first four or five will fall over, but seeing this, the ones who are tested after will try very hard to coordinate mind and body properly. The first few inevitably ask to be tested again to show that they can get it right. In this way, children learn a balance of freedom and self-discipline. Above all, children need to have the difference between the right and wrong way clearly pointed out, and to be trusted to want to do the right way when shown how. Tohei developed the following principles for parents and instructors to help children develop strong Ki.

For Raising Children:
1. **Be resourceful in letting them play and enjoy what they learn.**
2. **Never allow them to injure themselves or make serious mistakes.**
3. **Always relate each exercise to their growth, and use positive words.**
4. **Make it perfectly clear what behavior is good and what is bad.**
5. **When they misbehave, scold them firmly but with a positive attitude.**

Aikido: The Way to Union with Ki

The founder of the martial art of Aikido was Morihei Ueshiba (1883–1969). His teaching career spanned fifty years, during which he taught tens of thousands of students, and trained some four generations of high-ranking teachers in the inner aspects of his art. Tohei was one of the members of the second generation of these teachers. Beginning his training with Ueshiba in 1939, he received his fifth-dan rank from Ueshiba when he was drafted into the army in the early 1940s, his eighth dan in 1952, ninth dan in 1960, and the rank of tenth dan on January 15, 1969, just a few months before Master Ueshiba's death. The certificate, certified by the Master's seal and signature, shows that this was the first tenth-dan rank which Ueshiba issued, and it is the highest one available. From his first trip to Hawaii in 1953, and for many years after serving as the chief instructor at the Aikikai, Tohei was a mainstay of the art, and the primary instructor responsible for spreading Aikido overseas.

However, his attempts to introduce Ki principles into the Aikikai curriculum met with much resistance. In September of 1971 he founded the Ki Society (Ki no Kenkyûkai), in an effort to spread Ki teachings independently. However, strained relations with the Master Ueshiba's son Kisshomaru and other Aikikai teachers led him to the decision to resign from the Aikikai, on May 1, 1974. Later that month he sent a form letter in both Japanese and English to dôjô heads throughout Japan and overseas, explaining his reasons for the separation, and announcing that he was now teaching Shin Shin Tôitsu Aikido, or the art of Aikido with Mind and Body Unification, based on Ki principles. Most people overseas called it Ki-Aikido. As most of the instructors at the time were his own students of some years, the split put many people in a predicament. Those who had known Tohei for years, and basically considered him to be their teacher, followed him without hesitation, and joined the Ki Society. Others with divided loyalties remained in the Aikikai, while the loyalists refused to even recognize Tohei as a teacher of Aikido. Tohei was not the only one to split off from the original organization. There are now a number of Aikido organizations, each following their own interpretation, and each with international memberships. Tohei never considered himself as representing one school or style of the art of Aikido. Rather, he considered Ki-Aikido to be merely one application of Ki principles, a means of understanding Ki, and not an end in itself. There are many opinions on both sides as to whether Tohei was right or wrong. However, as we have seen from his biography, he viewed his life in a larger context than just Aikido. Still, to truly comprehend what Tohei developed, it is essential to understand how he viewed and taught Aikido.

Tohei changed or eliminated over half of the Aikido arts which he learned from Ueshiba Sensei, because he found that they would not work against the strong men he encountered in America, who would not only hold on in earnest, but often in difficult and unconventional ways. Japanese students were more likely to fall down whether actually thrown or not, out of a desire not to challenge the teacher, or because they thought it was what they were supposed to do. American students were more likely to try to put the teacher to the test. Unlike other martial arts, Aikido has no competitions, so it is very difficult to know if a technique would work if one was really attacked. The men who Tohei taught when he first went to Hawaii were not only many times bigger and stronger than the average Japanese, but many were skilled wrestlers, Judo experts, or experienced policemen, and most were highly doubtful about the whole idea of Ki. Everyone wanted to put Tohei to the test.

Ueshiba himself had beautiful Aikido arts and very strong Ki, but he was unable to teach Ki to others. His explanations were so vague and mystical that they were impossible to follow, as can be verified by reading any of his writings, most of which have English translations. For example, he explained that his body was immovable because certain gods entered it on clouds of purple smoke. This led to ridiculous misunderstandings, as when in the mid 1970s, several American students who heard about the purple smoke interpreted it to mean that Ueshiba was a marijuana smoker! Ueshiba himself held his students very lightly and was completely relaxed, and therefore had strong Ki. But the reason that he gave for this in his later years was that his body was old and his arms too weak to hold otherwise. His students asked him then how he could hold them down without seeming to use any force. He explained simply that he held his opponents with spirit, which forced each person to form his own interpretation of what his teacher meant. Ueshiba never taught Ki principles as such. He did make vague references to what he called, *Ki-musubi* (binding-Ki), or how Ki must enter the head from Heaven, but no one ever understood or knew what to do with this advice. Ueshiba explained Aikido in terms of blending with the opponent, never in terms of extending Ki. He explained it in terms of the "Principle of Ten": saying that if attacked with a power of eight, you must meet it with a power of two; if attacked with a power of six, you must meet it with a power of four. This response might be possible if faced with only a single attacker doing a prescribed technique; but what kind of equation would allow you to deal with multiple attackers coming from different directions, doing any attack they felt like? These and other contradictions bothered Tohei as he encountered real life challenges outside of the dôjô and during his teaching tours in America.

But Tohei was also disturbed about the growing tendency to mystify Aikido, and treat Ki as if it were some kind of supernatural power. After Ueshiba's death, many rumors spread about his so-called magic powers, including an alleged ability to catch bullets in his teeth, or to teleport his body over great distances. There was never any verification or proof of course, only second- and third-hand stories, and none of Ueshiba's students could do these things. In any event, how could one ever practice such feats?

Although Tohei never had any doubt of his teacher's ability to use Aikido effectively, in his public demonstrations Ueshiba Sensei never threw anyone other than his own students. He never accepted challenges from people he did not know, although he claimed it could be done and no doubt could have done it. But Tohei successfully did accept challenges from strong and capable opponents, over and over again. This produced a considerable difference in teaching style and philosophy. Readers should not draw from this the idea that other styles of Aikido are not effective. As a martial art, almost any style of Aikido contains techniques which can be extremely effective for self-defense and can even cause serious injury to an attacker who is unprepared. The questions to ask are whether the training helps you to develop mind and body unification, and whether or not it works in a nonartificial situation. It is relatively easy to throw a partner who is taught to take a fall, or to hold in such a way that the technique is easy to apply. Tohei's own experience led him early on to shun such an approach, and to create exercises which developed Ki and could be applied in daily life.

People develop an exaggerated idea of what is possible from watching marital arts movies. No matter how many techniques you know, or how fast your reflexes, how can you defend yourself against a machine gun, or an atom bomb? The purpose of Aikido is not to learn how to fight, but rather how to coordinate mind and body and develop a positive mind. Then you can live your life to the fullest and develop the energy to find your way out of any bind.

It is commonly assumed that the more self-defense techniques you know, the better you will be able to defend yourself. However, not even a thousand techniques will serve you if you panic and become tense. If you learn how to extend Ki correctly, there is no need to practice Aikido for ten or fifteen years to be able to use it. Even a relative beginner can make a basic technique work effectively, if he or she gives the proper emphasis to Ki development. Up to *shodan,* or the first degree of black belt, learning Aikido is mostly a matter of technique. Any fool can achieve *shodan* with enough practice. Beyond that, Aikido training is mostly a matter of refining your Ki and character. Unfortunately, many people drop out or stagnate when they achieve black belt, because they are unwilling or unable to change themselves. Others continue to practice techniques, but never gain the respect that their rank would indicate, because they fail to develop themselves. The first degree of black belt (*shodan*) in Aikido is like a high school diploma; the second degree (*nidan*) like a college degree, with further degrees representing further amounts of graduate education. It is better to have a rank than not to have one, but having a rank and living up to it are two different things. Like a diploma, a rank in Aikido may just mean that you put in your time and learned a few things. The real test is in how you meet the demands of daily life off campus, where a diploma may neither be a guarantee nor even a predictor of success. Just as there are Ph. D. holders pumping gas, there are black belts in the martial arts who off of the mat only make use of a fraction of their potential.

An interesting paradox found in the martial arts is that the better you become at the art, the less you need to use it. Even without knowing a martial art, the average person is very unlikely to be attacked. This is especially true if you extend strong Ki in daily life. Tohei himself never had to use Aikido once on the street, for no one ever attacked him, even though he frequented dangerous parts of Tokyo and large Western cities at night. One time he attempted to save a woman who was screaming for help as three men tried to wrestle her down. But when he got there he realized that it was the men who needed help, for the woman was having an epileptic fit, and was so wild that she was becoming dangerous to herself. Tohei had to use Kiatsu on her neck and shoulders to calm her down.

On several occasions Tohei was approached by people in bars looking for a fight, but they never found one. He stayed calm, smiled, and asked them to sit down and have a drink. If you yourself do not have a fighting mind, it is very difficult for an opponent to pick a fight with you. If you do get into a fight, it shows that your Aikido is still immature. On the other hand, if anyone did attack Tohei in earnest, they would truly be taking their lives into their own hands, as it would be difficult to survive being thrown in earnest. People are afraid to relax under pressure, thinking that it will make them weak. Actually, the opposite is true. The more important the event, the more need there is to relax. A boxer becomes most effective after he starts to get tired. Then he can relax and throw a real punch.

The idea that relaxation is weak is not the only misconception found in the martial arts world. Many people approach the martial arts as a sport, and try to develop big muscles or fast reflexes. You may be able to rely on strength and reflexes when you are young, but these are the fleeting privileges of youth. A person who trains the body alone and fails to develop strong Ki will find his martial arts career cut short in his thirties or forties, just as happens with players of professional sports. However, if you base your training on Ki and mind and body coordination, you can practice Aikido effectively throughout your whole life. Newcomers are often surprised to see that older dôjô members in their fifties and sixties, who have trained for many years, are often stronger and more skilled than young students in their twenties.

A number of times, while teaching in America, Tohei found his seminars attended by individuals who had very severe looking expressions and hard eyes. They resembled the *yakuza,* or Japanese mafia in their physical appearance, but behaved like nice people who wanted to learn. He later realized that their hard facial expressions were a result of their belief that such eyes were required to practice the martial arts. It was not they themselves, but their teachers who were to blame for this misunderstanding, for soft eyes and a gentle manner are in fact much stronger.

The less effective schools of the sword concentrate on the technique and grip. More advanced schools teach to concentrate on the tip of the sword, or even the opponent's eyes. But to be truly effective, you must not look at any part, particularly the opponent's eyes or weapon, or you will give all of the initiative to your opponent. The best way to hold the sword is to calm the mind like a mirror, so that it reflects your opponent's every thought and movement. By holding the sword lightly and calming the mind at the One Point, you will always be able to protect yourself and wield the sword effectively, even if you do not know any sword techniques per se. No matter what devious move an opponent makes to try to cut you, you will strike first if you stay in the center and hold the sword with Ki.

In sports such as Judo and wrestling, most mat pins are done with the partner lying face up, the person on top then winning a point. This will earn points in a contest, but it is very dangerous in a real fight. You may be able to hold down a single opponent, but if your opponent is face up with arms free, he can just as easily hold you down as well. How then would you get up if you had to deal with a few of his friends? Aikido is a martial art, not a sport. Therefore, all Aikido mat pins have the opponent facing down, with his arms and joints locked. In this way, your opponent is unable to move until you let go, but you can get up and move any time you like.

Tohei was primarily interested in using Aikido as a way of teaching Ki, not the other way around. It is impossible to use Ki effectively if you do not coordinate mind and body. Coordination means moving as a unit, not trying to do opposite things at the same time. You can draw a circle with your left hand and then draw a square with your right, but not at the same time. Aikido techniques are similar, in that they require the coordinated movement of each of the limbs. If just one arm or leg tries to move out of concert with the others Aikido techniques lose all of their power.

When a technique does not work properly, it does not do any good to complain about the way you were attacked, or to set conditions on how your opponent should hold. You must correct yourself if you want to make any real progress in Aikido.

Master Ueshiba used to hold very lightly, saying that he was too old to hold with strength. But he taught his students to hold with physical power. Gripping tightly actually makes a person much easier to throw, because tension tends to lock the joints and makes them easy to manipulate. Tohei watched his teacher closely and followed what he did, not what he said. For some reason Ueshiba criticized Tohei for this, saying that he should use more physical strength, as he was still young. Unable to contradict his teacher directly, Tohei invented the excuse that he was too drunk from the night before to hold with physical power. This light way of holding with Ki quickly made Tohei one of the hardest people to move using traditional techniques. However, it not only worked for Tohei, but for all of his students as well, whose Aikido became stronger the more they practiced Ki. If you hold an opponent with Ki, in a relaxed but penetrating manner, your grip is sensitive enough to read your opponent's every movement. Because you do not apply pressure at any point in particular, whenever he tries to move forcefully he collides with your Ki. If he tries to muscle his way out, he will find it very difficult to move at all, and possibly painful.

Tohei was once praised at an Aikido seminar at a university in America by a professor, for teaching them a practical application of economics: how to get a maximum return on a minimum investment. While some traditionalists complained that Tohei was reducing the number of techniques or oversimplifying them, in fact he was distilling their essence. Not only in Aikido, but in any art form, the higher the level of mastery, the easier it looks. Technical virtuosos may impress beginners with their complex movements and acrobatic skills, but they are no match for someone who has grasped the essence. In a sense, the less you do the more happens. This does not mean being passive, but to master fundamentals and use no more effort than is necessary.

This was clearly reflected in the curriculum which Tohei later developed for Ki-Aikido. Based on Ki principles and using Ki tests for feedback and instruction, students learn first how to sit, bow, and walk properly. No matter how many techniques you know, if you cannot do these things properly, you are not really prepared to take an examination. At the same time, if you can really perform daily life actions without losing mind and body coordination, then Aikido techniques can be learned relatively quickly. In order to help students learn Aikido with Ki, and to avoid falling into the many errors that can occur without it, Tohei developed five principles for Aikido with Mind and Body Coordination.

For Ki-Aikido:
1. **Ki is extending.**
2. **Know your opponent's mind.**
3. **Respect your opponent's Ki.**
4. **Put yourself in your opponent's place.**
5. **Lead with confidence.**

These are best understood in the context of an Aikido technique, which is beyond the scope of this book to describe. Appropriate references on Ki-Aikido are listed in the appendix. However, Aikido principles can be understood by thinking of them in the following terms. The first principle, *Ki is extending,* means that you must begin with mind and body unified. The way you can tell whether or not you have it is to ask your partner to test you. Usually, this is done by exerting pressure from the hold itself, or from the direction of the initial attack. If you can pass the Ki tests, you are ready for the second principle. *Know your opponent's mind* means that you must be aware of how your opponent is attacking you. If he is attacking with strength he may be relatively easy to throw, but if he too is unified in mind and body, then you must follow the five principles. The way that you know how you are being held is to test your opponent back, usually done from the hold or position of the attack. If you find that you cannot move your oppponent with a Ki test, then you are ready for the third principle. *Respect your opponent's Ki* means that you must not collide with it or try to force the technique to work. You have already verified that you cannot move your opponent or escape from his hold using a Ki test. Therefore, to respect his Ki you do not test it, that is you do not move the parts of your body over which your opponent has control. This does not mean that you are frozen stiff, but rather that you are relaxed enough to feel what you can and cannot do, and do not try to force the technique against your opponent's Ki or strength. Up to this point, you still have not moved. You have been tested, you have tested your opponent, you have verified that you cannot force your way free and therefore you do not try to do so. Then you are ready for the fourth principle. *Put yourself in your opponent's place* means to execute the technique skillfully enough that you do not collide with your opponent, and that you end up in a position in which you are facing the same direction, and therefore are now behind him in a position to lead. In effect, you have turned the tables on him. This may be done by entering (*irimi*) or by turning (*tenkan*), but there is always a way of moving the arms and legs that allows you to move without colliding. This way is the Aikido technique itself (*waza*), and these arts take some months or years to learn how to perform well. Once you are in position, you are ready for the fifth and final principle. *Lead with confidence* means to go ahead and execute the throw while maintaining mind and body coordination. Whereas before you found that you could not move without colliding, having followed the first four principles, you now find that you can easily move, and your opponent cannot resist you using either Ki or strength. At this point, your opponent is obliged to go with the technique, not to help you, but to protect himself from getting injured. The fall which he takes is called *ukemi*.

Once you have learned how to do the fundamental movements accurately and with mind and body unified, then you can practice the technique more smoothly, without breaking it down into steps and testing. This process can be refined to the point where you begin the technique at the moment his Ki moves, and throw your opponent very vigorously, sometimes hardly even touching him. The danger of training without first breaking it into steps is that all too easily, both partners become accustomed to the movements, and tend to cooperate without really attacking or really throwing. Because it looks and feels as if you are throwing, you have no idea how ineffective it would be against a less cooperative opponent. People have a tendency to get sloppy when they speed up. If you never test yourself on fundamentals, and try to skip ahead to the higher levels, you will find yourself unable to call upon the technique when you need it.

Aikido is a highly refined martial art, born in the twentieth century, based on the principle of non-dissension and representing the essential goal of the martial arts. All of the techniques of Aikido are based on unification of mind and body. Any art which imitates the form of the technique without mind and body unification cannot be called true Ki-Aikido. The practice of Aikido involves no competition. Through the Aikido arts, we can see the depth of mind and body unification. Performing the Aiki exercises without a partner teaches a person how to maintain mind and body coordination in movement. Techniques performed with a partner reveal whether the person's mind and body are correctly coordinated or not. Learning to perform a number of techniques continuously without stopping teaches how to sustain mind and body coordination throughout the movements of our daily life.

Aikido is a superb martial art, but its founder, Morihei Ueshiba, while demonstrating mind and body coordination in his Aikido movements, failed to explain it in his words. Shin Shin Tôitsu Aikido is designed to teach this essence in clear terms, so that anyone may practice it.

In an age of nuclear proliferation and ready availability of automatic weapons, what role do the martial arts (*budô*) have anymore? Most of the martial arts as practiced in their present form emphasize competition. Gradually and without notice, they cultivate in their practitioners a fighting mind. But the character for *Bu* in *Budô* means to stop the spear, that is not to fight. To cultivate the principle of non-dissension we practice the martial arts. However, as the martial arts have become more and more influenced by sports and competition, this spirit has gradually given way to techniques for fighting and winning.

The correct approach to Aikido is to thoroughly master the principle of non-dissension by practicing each movement in accord with the principles of the universe, not just to win out over an opponent, but to learn to control your self. Most people assume that non-dissension means the avoidance of violence, as in non-resistance, or by looking the other way. This is a negative interpretation of the principle. The positive view is that under whatever circumstances, the mind remains undisturbed and the body is capable of responding appropriately even if attacked.

We live in a world measured in relative terms, and tend to assume that one must struggle and compete to survive. But we forget that beneath all of this is the unchanging principle of unity of the universe. To one who lives this principle there is no need to struggle and fight. Aikido arts are based on this principle, and if you maintain mind and body coordination, then you are able to see and lead your opponent's movements, even under attack. If you lead the mind, the body will gladly follow. Since it is useless to attack, it is better to avoid fighting. This is the positive view.

But unless you can control yourself, it is impossible to lead another. When you unify mind and body you avail yourself of the great power that is originally yours, that of the whole iceberg, not just the visible part above the surface. War in the modern era is a frightening prospect, and must be avoided at all costs. The way to practice non-dissension and lead the rest of the world to peace is to show that you are too strong to attack, without needing to rely on the threat of nuclear weapons.

It is not the purpose of this book to explain how to do the exercises and techniques of Aikido. To learn these you must attend classes at a dôjô. A list of books and Ki Society dôjô centers for various countries is provided in the appendix. However, it may be useful to know that the exercises Tohei developed for teaching Aikido also help develop mind and body coordination, and have practical psychological implications for daily life. Naturally, as physical exercise they develop joint flexibility and strength, as well as improve circulation and Ki flow. Because they exercise the body ambidextrously and move in many directions and angles, Aikido techniques are an excellent means of maintaining health. Specific exercises are also useful for developing assurance, decisiveness, concentration, calmness, balance, centering, and the spirit of being able to get out of any bind or setback.

It is hard for some people to understand why Aikido does not engage in competitions. Sports are played to win. People enjoy the competition, players are supposed to follow the rules, and there is little or no risk of life in playing the game. Players are allowed to retake a play if a foul occurs. However, in real *Budô* you are in earnest; deadly serious, for a moment's carelessness can result in injury or loss of life. In the modern age, most societies have laws which do not permit the use of *Budô* to take life or cause injury. Like policemen, martial artists are usually required to use maximum restraint, even if they are attacked. However, it is always possible to make full use of the spirit of *Budô* in living our life in earnest, by facing all of its changes and challenges with our fullest ability and power. Studying a martial art in this sense is far more interesting than just for self-defense, or to win competitions.

On the other hand, self-protection is a critical part of any martial art. The key concept for self-defense in Aikido is *ma-ai*: maintaining a distance at which your opponent must make a major body movement to deliver an attack. At this distance, any serious strike involves a simultaneous loss of balance and power. This distance is also one in which your opponent's entire body lies in your field of vision. If you maintain *ma-ai*, you neither feel nor occasion a sense of threat. *Ma-ai* is essential in any martial art. The eye is a lens, and if you stand at the proper distance, you can see your opponent's entire body while looking straight ahead, and your eyes easily reflect any movement which he attempts. If you stand too close, just as with a camera, you cannot take in the whole. You must not look at the striking hand or weapon, nor stare at the opponent's eyes. Some martial artists develop a bad habit of staring at other people with hard and dominating eyes. If you stare at another person, say in a job interview, you will look like a trouble maker; one who is likely to sabotage the company's interests. Instead, Tohei teaches to look calmly at the area around the other person's nose and eyes. No matter how strong the other person may appear, you will notice that like everyone else, he has only two nostrils, and after all is not such a big threat. Many martial artists are strong from the front, but weak from the sides or rear. If you maintain *ma-ai* you are strong from any angle, which can be verified in the dôjô by Ki testing.

The basic attacks used in Aikido involve grabbing a partner by one or both wrists, striking or punching to the face or chest, grabbing a partner's body or arms, and simple kicks. With practice, the techniques can be applied to more than one attacker, even as many as five attacking at once, as Tohei so often demonstrated in his tours overseas. Advanced techniques also make use of a wooden knife, sword, or staff to attack.

Aikido techniques are broadly divided into *irimi* techniques, that is entering, leading and returning your opponent's Ki without colliding; and *tenkan* techniques, in which you join, lead, and turn your opponent's Ki away from you in a circular motion. You may either pin an opponent face down to the ground after breaking his balance, using one of half-a-dozen joint manipulations. Although some of these can be quite painful, the pain is momentary, and if applied properly causes no damage. These techniques can actually help to limber the joints. In any case, joint immobilizations are so effective that it is foolish to try to resist.

The majority of Aikido techniques are throws, which cause a person to roll back or forward, using a technique called *ukemi*, which allows you to protect your body by taking an efficient and safe fall when thrown, without losing mind and body unification. The attacker is called *uke* and his role is to test and develop his partner's state of mind and body unification by attacking in the strongest way, without himself losing mind and body unification. The person who is attacked and applies the Aikido techniques is called *nage* and his role is to lead and throw his opponent's body at the moment it breaks *ma-ai* with an attack, without ever losing mind and body coordination. In the beginning techniques are taught in a step-by-step manner, emphasizing accuracy and correct posture, almost like printed handwriting. Gradually students learn how to perform these movements more smoothly, in what might be considered a cursive style. The movements are broken down for the purpose of teaching and mastering fundamentals, but Aikido is actually practiced in the fluid style.

Aikido can be performed equally effectively by men and women, because it does not depend on physical strength or size. It is literally possible for a small woman to throw a large football player or wrestler using Aikido, if she is proficient enough to maintain mind and body coordination throughout the technique. If she loses confidence or tries to use strength, the outcome is what you would otherwise expect. People who see Aikido for the first time assume that the partners are cooperating, doing a kind of dance, rather than a real self-defense technique. This may be the case if the people are not training properly, but need not be so. Still, like anything worthwhile, it may take some years of training to get to the point where you can properly do Aikido techniques consistently and effectively. A great deal depends on the quality of instruction which you receive and your degree of commitment to the art. Students are also constantly reminded that the goal of training is not just to become strong in Aikido, but to learn how to use Ki in daily life, and this you start doing from your first day of practice.

Once a year in Tokyo, Ki Society students gather from all over Japan to engage in what is called the Taigi Competition, which usually draws an audience of several hundred people. Non-members sometimes react negatively to the idea of competition in an art which is supposed to emphasize non-dissension. However, in the Taigi Competition, partners do not compete against each other as in a sports competition, but rather against other pairs of partners performing the same prescribed set of Aikido arts. In this sense the Taigi Competition is more like the Olympics, or a performing arts competition, in that contestants are judged on their degree of coordination or skill of performance.

The criteria used in the Taigi Competition are three: technique, unity of mind and body (*fudôshin*), and rhythm. A prescribed set of six or more throws must be performed in the correct sequence without mistakes, timed to a prescribed number of seconds, plus or minus two seconds. As many as twelve throws must be executed within less than a minute's time, while using as much space as possible, yet without any sense of hurry. There is no room for hesitation or error. *Fudôshin* is measured in terms of how well the *nage* is able to throw without losing balance or mind and body unification, and still keep Ki clearly extended before, during, and after the throw. Even if the techniques are performed correctly and with strong Ki, they must show a sense of rhythm, which is measured in terms of fluidity, graceful movement, and stage presence. There are other criteria, involving the timing of the bow, entry and exit, and use of the eyes. When the competition is very close, other factors may enter, how long or hard the student has trained, whether they are ready for a promotion, and so on. As in the Olympics, medals are awarded to the top contestants. The *nage* of the team winning a gold medal receives a promotion of one rank of black belt. Silver and bronze medal winners receive a certificate of recognition along with their medal. Contestants compete with people in the same age range and rank, different groups performing different Taigi. Small children perform simple arts, while black belts of the second and third dan perform complicated weapons sequences.

Weapons training, using a wooden knife, sword, or staff, involves learning how to disarm an attacker, as well as how to use the weapon, and there are prescribed routines for both sword and staff which are as beautiful as they are powerful. The major challenge of weapons work is learning how to hold and use the weapon in such a way that it becomes filled with Ki, a natural extension of your body. There are several practical advantages to this training. When held properly, it is almost impossible for an opponent to strike you or even get close, without being struck first. This does not depend on fast reflexes or special technique. Simply by holding the sword or stick in a triangular stance your entire body is hidden behind and protected by the tip of the weapon. No matter how your opponent tries to go around it, he must cover a much greater distance to go around your weapon than you need to reach his body by entering in a straight line.

However, this is not simply a matter of mechanics. The weapon must be held very lightly, yet so full of Ki that it cannot be knocked aside without almost instantly flipping back to the center line, as if held in place by a strong elastic cord. Nor can the weapon be pulled or pushed out of your hands, for it operates as a unified extension of your own body. Tohei learned very little in the way of sword technique from his teacher Ueshiba Sensei. Of course he often saw techniques demonstrated, but rarely with any explanation at all. Tohei is a master at wielding the sword and staff, but virtually all of his training in it was self-training. Most of that involved holding the weapon in the correct posture and calming the mind until it reflected everything around it with mirror-like precision. He usually spent between thirty minutes to one hour everyday, standing imperceptibly still with wooden sword drawn, facing a tree. Then he would practice simple cuts and movements, always in a state of deep mind and body coordination. He eventually developed an ability to wield the wooden sword with incredible lightning speed and power. This he often demonstrated by cleanly splitting a green bamboo branch, often as thick as the sword itself. This was all the more remarkable because the bamboo would be suspended between holes cut in two pieces of rice paper, precariously held at the top of the hole by a knife which had been inserted blade up. The weight of the bamboo was almost enough to tear through the hole by itself, yet Tohei could split the pole in two pieces without tearing either hole open any further. The bamboo would split on impact, and the two tips of the pole would lift forming a "V" shape, so that the ends could fall out of the hole rather than tear through it. Not only was Tohei able to do this repeatedly, but many of his students could do it. Even some beginners could do it thefirst time with his coaching. He explained that the purpose of the demonstration was not just to cut bamboo, but to show people how many things which they considered impossible or beyond them were in fact easy if they would first unify mind and body.

Because sword and stick work is rather advanced practice, no techniques are described here, but for reference, the principles for weapons training which Tohei developed are as follows.

For Training with the Wooden Sword:
1. **Hold the sword lightly.**
2. **The tip of the sword must be calm and steady.**
3. **Make use of the weight of the sword.**
4. **Do not slacken your Ki.**
5. **Cut first with the mind.**

For Training with the Wooden Staff:
1. **Hold the stick lightly.**
2. **Control the stick with the rear hand.**
3. **Manipulate the stick freely.**
4. **When changing the position of the stick, one hand must always have hold.**
5. **The line traced by the stick is never broken.**

Of these principles the most important is to hold lightly. People assume that to control something you must grip it very tightly. Books on golf, tennis, and baseball technique devote a lot of space to the grip, suggesting that this is what people have the most trouble with. But if you hold too tightly, or in an unnatural way, then unknowingly you also put tension into your arms and shoulders, thereby losing mind and body coordination. This seriously limits your ability to put centrifugal force into the swing, and makes your body movements awkward as well. Considering what a good golfer or batter can do to a ball, the use of the wooden sword in a focused cut toward the head or upper body is nothing to take lightly. It requires very strong Ki extension and skillful timing, but it is possible to take a knife, sword or stick away from a person wielding it in earnest.

In Hawaii, Tohei also instructed policemen in how to take away a pistol held at close range. From this, rumors started that he could move faster than a bullet, but no one alive can do that. What he did was to read the movement of his opponent's mind and step aside before the trigger was pulled, taking the weapon away before the opponent knew what happened. One of Tohei's advanced students, a police officer, actually did this successfully against an attacker with a real gun.

A brief note is in order about the uniform worn in Aikido practice. Beginners wear a light but sturdy white jacket and loose fitting pants, with a long wide band belt tied about the waist. Black belts wear in addition a long black skirt called a *hakama*, which is pleated and split like loose trousers. The *hakama* is securely tied below the belt and has a firm upright backing in the rear, at belt level. The design of the *hakama* suggests both the calm low center and the upright lower back so essential to a unified posture. The *hakama* helps you keep One Point and lends a feeling of stability. It also keeps the jacket from becoming disarrayed, despite vigorous movement and rolls. Its tall pyramid-like shape largely hides the feet, which makes it easier to stay calm. Public speakers achieve something of the same effect by standing behind a podium. Lastly, by folding and taking care of *hakama* properly, you learn to keep your mind orderly and calm.

In Aikido, students are permitted to wear a black *hakama* only after they reach the rank of black belt. Before that, everyone wears loose fitting trousers. The *hakama* is not only a sign of rank, it helps lend stability and grace to the movements. In his later years, Ueshiba Sensei wore a white *hakama*, which in the Shinto religion is a sign of greatly elevated spiritual status. Tohei himself never wore a white *hakama* because he did not care for the exclusive or religious associations. However, during one seminar in Europe, he encountered an Aikido group in which all of the students were wearing white *hakama*. He thought it must be a religious gathering, until someone explained that in that school, white belts wore white *hakama*, and black belts wore black *hakama*, apparently a local variation on custom. Some traditions are better off left alone.

In Japan, people wear a white belt for every rank until they achieve black belt. In Judo, sometimes a very advanced teacher is distinguished by wearing a red belt. One young woman from America appeared in a Japanese dôjô wearing a red belt and surprised everyone on the mat. Later she explained that where she came from, red was the lowest rank. In Japan, colored belts are only issued to children, as a motivation to keep them interested.

Of course practice in the dôjô is done barefoot. Shoes and slippers are left outside, always lined up in rows facing outward. This reflects an orderly state of mind and originally had the practical benefit of allowing people to make a quick exit in an emergency. This practice was once given great emphasis in Japan in daily life. During the eighteenth century, one Zen aspirant decided that it was not worth training at a certain temple because he found the sandals were in disarray. A thief in the same period was very successful because he made a practice of only robbing houses in which the sandals were not carefully lined up. He was caught the first time he ignored his own rule. This is also a good habit for children at home, because it teaches them to take care in little things and to keep their living environment neat and orderly.

Along with this goes an almost fanatical obsession with cleanliness. Not only the *uchideshi*, but even the higher ranking instructors are expected to pitch in and give the dôjô a thorough cleaning both before and after a major training event. Teamwork may be a matter of obligation, but it is impressive nevertheless. Neglect or carelessness in the cleaning of part of the dôjô or dormitory facilities is not treated lightly. Students are expected to keep their practice uniforms clean, and any neglect of personal hygiene is viewed with disgust. Not only is this a healthy practice, it also serves as a way to help polish the spirit. Some of the wooden floors in Zen temples are so well-polished by hundreds of years of daily cleaning, that they actually reflect images.

How to Get the Most of Ki Training

Much of what can be said of Aikido training also applies directly to Ki training itself. One of the most remarkable things about Ki development is that people make vastly different rates of progress for the same amount of time devoted to the art. In his many years of teaching Ki to people of all ages and in many countries, Tohei recognized patterns in what made some people progress rapidly and others simply tread water or even sink. One thing which he made very clear however, was that there was no way to tell by first impressions whether or not a person would make a good student. More often than not, people who were athletically inclined and picked everything up quickly tended after a few months to get bored and quit, never having made any significant progress. Others who seemed clumsy and slow to catch on sometimes exhibited an extraordinary tenacity and eventually ended up improving their character and physical appearance altogether. What could also be said about Ki development is that there is no standing still. You are either progressing or regressing, and those who go at it halfheartedly are left behind very quickly. Some people are attracted to Ki development at first, because they think they can use parts of it to enhance another discipline or philosophy which they believe in. This rarely works however, for Ki development must be taken as a whole. Take it or leave it, but do not try to nibble at it, for it does not mix with philosophies or practices based on fundamentally contradictory ideas. To get the most out of Ki training, there are certain attitudes and habits which are worth cultivating early on. These will ensure that you not only make rapid progress, but do not take a wrong turn along the way.

Ultimately, you are the one responsible for your own development. Abraham Lincoln said that after the age of forty, a man must be responsible for his own face. What we start with is not nearly so important as what we finish with. One man attending a Ki lecture asked Tohei a peculiar question. He said that he could not decide if the lecture fee of ¥5,000 was reasonable or expensive. Tohei replied that if he applied what he learned there in his daily life, it was a fantastic bargain; but that if he did nothing with what he learned, he was wasting his money.

Tohei sends Ki constantly to his students, as if their health, success, and welfare were a reflection on him. He often scolds his closest students quite firmly for what seem to outsiders like small transgressions, but this is done for the student's benefit and is directed to the behavior, not to the person. He tells his students that they must not become negative when they are scolded. Those who took the grilling personally were often those who were unable to change or admit a mistake. Over the years a number of advanced students have quit the Ki Society, trying to take what they learned and form their own approach to teaching Ki, altering the Ki principles, or even inventing their own. They justified themselves saying that, after all that is what Tohei himself did. But most have found after a few years they did not take as much with them as they believed they had at the time. When a person stops learning he does not stay still, but actually begins to slide backward. When this habit continues for many years, it is very difficult to come back again.

Ki training is not difficult if you stick to fundamentals. People usually assume that it must be very difficult to unify mind and body, thinking of them as separate and incompatible entities. But when you realize that they are simply two inseparable aspects of yourself, a unified posture is nothing unusual at all. Many Zen stories reinforce this concept. One Zen master said that Zen was nothing more than your everyday mind. Another said that enlightenment was no different than your usual state, only it felt as if you were an inch off of the ground. This suggests not a wild or excited state, but rather the "floating" feeling of mind and body unification. Just as waves on water calm down naturally if you leave them alone, and cannot be forced flat, the best way to calm your mind is to let it find its natural state of calmness.

Computers and robots are commonplace in our daily life. While they make some tasks easier, no computer can ever improve the human spirit. This takes self-discipline and effort. The only difference between a beginner and an advanced student is the degree to which they are able to sustain mind and body unification in their daily life. When a beginner truly practices Ki principles, even for a moment, he is as unified as an advanced person, except that he tends to lose it more easily. Try to seek more depth from the Ki principles, not just learn more techniques.

In Japanese ink painting, they say that you must become a bamboo if you want to paint it. This is not to be taken literally of course, but means that you must first unify mind and body before you paint the bamboo. When the mind is calm, then it reflects all things clearly, and is capable of using Ki freely. If you forget your unity with the universe, you have nothing to rely on in a crisis but your own small self. And that is a meager package in the face of the problems which we see everyday on the evening news.

A successful student of Ki is one who is able to maintain a beginner's mind, no matter how many years he has practiced, or how many times he has done an exercise. It is careless to assume just because you could do something before, that you can do it again. Each time you do something, apply yourself to it fully, with an open mind. Do not practice in order to become strong; practice in order to instill the correct principles into your body. A person who says he is strong is not dependable. Gloating over past triumphs is not true strength. It just means that the person has not yet met someone stronger than himself. True strength means knowing your own weaknesses and training to overcome them. People wash their faces everyday, but usually forget to cleanse their minds.

In learning anything new, as soon as you begin to make progress it starts to get demanding. If you give up when you meet difficulties in training and try to seek less challenging methods, all you do is stagnate or regress. The reason that training is difficult is that it runs counter to what is in the subconsious mind. If you can change the contents of the subconscious mind through gradual and consistent practice, then training itself becomes easy and natural. Beginners often marvel at how advanced students can get up early, practice Aikido for hours, and still have time and energy to work a full day. However, to those who have done it for years it is just a natural part of their daily routine.

People who have gained a great deal of intellectual knowledge about Ki from books often find Ki training to be a frustrating process. It is easy to convince yourself that you understand something which you have read about, but difficult to face yourself when you find you cannot do it. Even though you may learn something of practical value in your first lesson, real progress in Ki training takes years. A beginner is someone who has trained less than ten years, which includes most first and second dan black belts. Tohei himself admits that it takes ten to fifteen years to thoroughly train an *uchi-deshi* and that is training full time, with virtually no vacations! Obviously, the average student, working much less intensively in a far less ideal training environment, should take much longer to achieve the same level. This is enough to discourage the most hardened idealist, unless you remind yourself that any degree of mind and body coordination is better than none. Even if you do not become a master of Aikido, you may well learn something which will improve, or even save your life. Beginners should remember that real progress is not measured by rank, but by how well you apply Ki in your daily life. For this, there is no rank and no limit on how far you can go.

Even with the best of intentions, it is sometimes difficult to find practical ways to work Ki training into a busy schedule. A haphazard approach is unsatisfying at best and naturally people want to get the most from the time and money that they invest in it. Like any major task you undertake, you should think things through before you take action. If an architect tried to build a building without a plan, he may realize too late that he forgot to put in a toilet.

There is not physically enough time in the day to do all of the forms of Ki training available in the curriculum. However, if you have your priorities in order and can get good personal feedback on your progress, then you can make good use of your training time. With experience, you can use image training to review many of the Aikido arts that you learn. Obviously, physical practice is preferred, but if you cannot go through them clearly in your mind, then you probably are not being very thoughtful in your practice either. People often ask Tohei how they can continue Ki training when they are away from the dôjô. But more often than not, they are not fully training even when they come to the dôjô. Frequently students ask questions which are fully covered in his books, even though they have read the books before. A good book is worth repeated readings, even to the point of memorization. Even if you underline passages which impress you at the moment, you will find that entirely different passages stand out as significant when you read it again several months later. Tohei once received a lengthy letter from a student overseas, containing page after page of detailed questions. Although he was in the habit of personally answering every letter he got, this one would have taken weeks to write a full answer to. Instead he wrote back a simple reply, saying that the answer to each of the man's questions could be found in his books, so please reread them. The man wrote back embarrassed, saying that on rereading the books, he found the answer to each question was clearly spelled out.

The most important thing in Ki training is not learning new techniques, but correcting your bad habits. You must not think that being just a little wrong is O.K. Error only compounds itself if you practice without correcting bad habits. When you objectively see your own faults, you are not so ready to criticize others. If you overlook your own shortcomings, the faults of others dominate your thoughts. Most people are very easy on themselves and hard on others. The best way is to reflect on yourself, and be forgiving of others.

The beginning of practice is a very important time. Not only does it set the tone for the class, but that is the time when the instructor introduces the themes and objectives of that day's practice. If you are late for practice, you will be late in life as well. When you are late you waste other people's time as well as your own. If you are late to an important event, you cannot use heavy traffic as an excuse, as you must be responsible to be there on time. If you are going somewhere the first time, find out beforehand how long it takes.

The end of practice is also important, in that it contains the summary and essence of the day's learning. People have a tendency to wind down toward the end of something, but you must not cut Ki as you near the finish. Just before you reach the goal is where you tend to tire out. Extend Ki as if your goal was still far off, then you will be able to reach it. A Japanese proverb says that you should consider the first ninety-nine miles as halfway to a hundred.

The principles and practice of Ki are interesting enough to attract almost anyone's attention at first. But unless you seek knowledge and applications of Ki on your own, you may find yourself bored in time hearing the same stories or going through the same exercises. If you think you have heard it before, ask yourself if you know it well enough to be able to do it or teach it yourself. In all that Tohei has taught, he has only given us hints. We ourselves must make efforts to find out how to apply it in our daily lives.

One excellent form of learning is called *kengaku*, which means to learn by observing others. Originally in the traditional arts *kengaku* was not permitted, for fear that people would steal trade secrets. Nowadays there is little danger of this, as few people are skilled enough to learn much from observing or imitating alone. Everybody wants to do his own style, in other words, few people are willing to face themselves enough to change their own habits.

You never know if you can do something until you try. If you decide to try something, assume that you can do it, and say so aloud. In most cases, you will find that you are successful. If you try and fail, you can say "I could not," which is fundamentally different from the attitude which says "I cannot," from the start. If you cannot bring yourself to say something positive, say nothing at all, because minus words produce minus results. Some people mistakenly put themselves down, assuming that they are being humble. Real humility is not negative speech. Instead you should say that you are still immature, which implies that you will someday be mature. Even if you fail, do not forget your gratitude to the universe for being allowed a second try. As long as you live you always have a second or third chance.

Real confidence is not self-confidence, which is based on relative strength, but confidence in the principles of the universe, which are based on absolute strength. In Japanese, a person speaking with confidence is said to be blowing a conch shell, much like in English we say a person is tooting his own horn. This is actually a good thing. Aiming high is not the same thing as empty boasting. A salesman who says he is going to sell double his quota will not be blamed if he only ends up exceeding it by 30 percent. On the other hand, we should not claim that we will do something if we have no intention of following through in action. That is merely bluffing. And of course the man who claims he can jump over a building is not confident, just crazy. Do not ever assume that you know your limits, or that you cannot do something without trying. This is self-defeating, based more on conceit than self-knowledge.

If we focus on the branches and leaves of a person's success, the roots are easily forgotten. The root of success are always found in mind and body coordination. The older you get, the more obvious this becomes. Finally, you should not engage in Ki training just for your own benefit. Try to become a person who lives to help and benefit others, and your own needs will take care of themselves.

The Art of Teaching Ki Principles

A book on Koichi Tohei's life and teachings would not be complete without examining his own philosophy of teaching. Tohei himself is a master teacher, and claims that only by teaching others can you learn yourself. Many readers may already be involved in Ki training or teaching and therefore may use this philosophy as a guide to evaluating and becoming an effective teacher. George Bernard Shaw expressed an all too common view of teachers when he said that, "He who can, does. He who cannot, teaches." Tohei's view is precisely the opposite, as he says, "I understand means I can do."

When Koichi Tohei first went to Hawaii, he encountered various difficulties in communication before he learned to speak English fluently. One newspaper got his name wrong, reporting that a seminar in Aikido was being taught by Toichi Kohei, which was a bit like calling Bill Smith, Smill Bith. Misspelling a foreign name is perhaps understandable, but once he was puzzled when a certain student insisted on calling him "*Seito* Tohei." In Japanese, *seito* means student, so he tried to tell him that he was the Sensei, not the student. When the man wrote it down, Tohei realized that what the student had been calling him was, "Saint" Tohei, after which Tohei told him he had better just call him Sensei.

Although in the early days he was best known as an Aikido teacher, he insists that he only used Aikido as a means of convincing unbelievers about the power of Ki. Buddhist doctrine has it that in early eras, men had faith on simply hearing the truth. As time went on, they needed to be shown the truth through artistic imagery and religious art in order to believe it. Then as men became more materialistic they wanted proof and believed nothing without evidence. Tohei says if people want evidence, give it to them. There is nothing wrong with asking questions, as long as it is based on a desire to know the truth.

Tohei refers to what he does as Ki development, because the teaching is always evolving and maturing. This means that students of Ki must also develop and mature, but many people become stuck along the way, complaining that things used to be better in the old days. This attitude is evidence that the person's progress has been halted. The basic Ki principles themselves never change, as they are universal. But the means of teaching and practicing them will and must change to suit the changing environment and people who come to learn. During the 1970s the martial arts were very popular, but in the 1980s they went out of fashion. To the degree that you emphasize Aikido over Ki, you will have trouble finding students. If you teach Ki through Aikido and other Ki development methods, then you will never have trouble gathering students, because Ki principles are always relevant in any culture and any era.

One of the fastest ways to earn a student's respect is to practice what you preach. People teach a lot of good things in this world, but how many actually live what they teach? A hypocrite is one who speaks falsely and does not act with full mind and body unification. This has no value in real life. The vast majority of people are well meaning, but lack the initiative to make things happen on their own. A good teacher must blaze a path for those who are not likely to do so for themselves. One of the difficulties of teaching Ki principles is that, even though they work in practice, many of them go against long-standing habits and beliefs. It is hard to convince a person who has been fighting all of his life that relaxation is stronger. But many of the things we take for granted now as laws of nature were once considered absurd assertions at best, if not outright heresy. The world looks flat and stationary, but it is not. Scientists once believed that the human heart would burst if the body traveled at speeds over sixty miles per hour, and physicists once taught in the best university classrooms that it was impossible to exceed the speed of sound. When the sound barrier was in fact broken, they found that different laws come into play, and require a different way of operating the airplane. It is the same way with mind and body coordination. Until you experience and apply Ki principles, it is hard to believe how relaxation could be so strong, or how changing your thoughts could make your body any different. Because Ki is an unfamiliar concept to many people, it is best to help them experience it, rather than try to explain or argue about its merits.

After you help a person experience mind and body unification, it is very important to praise them for what they have done. The Japanese say that even a pig will climb a tree if you praise it. You should seek out other people's good points and help them to develop, rather than criticize and put them down. This is the real meaning of education. Everything and everyone has unique qualities and value. The purpose of education is to bring this potential into reality.

Encouraging a student is not difficult. All you need to do is to send Ki to the person, search for and focus on his or her positive qualities. Then the student will naturally want to improve and will make great efforts to only show you his best side. On one occasion, unbeknownst to Tohei, a drug dealer wanted by the police came to train at a Ki seminar. Tohei never had a clue about his background, until a narcotics officer attending the same seminar arrested him after practice, because the man had never shown Tohei his bad side.

Just as people need encouragement to grow into good habits, they also need discipline to grow out of bad ones. Young people must be pushed to work hard, respond, and perform, otherwise they grow into weak adults. A person's character comes out in his Aikido technique. Bad character habits appear in the form of hurried, forced, or overly abbreviated techniques, carelessness, frustration, and the whole list of ways by which we make life difficult for ourselves and others. Up to a point, as we correct our technique, we also improve our character and correct our bad habits.

The fact that two people are of the same rank in no way means that they are on the same level, in or out of the dôjô. The instructor must sometimes scold a student, particularly when the student develops an attitude which obstructs learning. No one likes to be scolded, and to prevent the student's taking it personally, you must treat each student equally. Criticize the behavior, not the personality. When a student makes a mistake Tohei always says, "Something wrong," not "You are wrong."

As the students advance, the instructor has a responsibility to advance as well. This requires patience and perspective on the learning process. In scolding children, remember how you acted at that age, then advise them accordingly. If you made the same mistakes when you were young, tell them so, and explain how it produced bad results. Then you will gain their attention and respect. No child takes a parent or teacher seriously who acts as if they are perfect, or gives hypocritical advice. Think of children as essentially good, and whenever you have to criticize, try to find something to praise in them at the same time. Constant criticism gradually drives a person into a negative state of mind.

In Japanese, if a child is ridiculed by a parent or teacher, he says "Don't make a fool of me!" This is actually what the adult is doing, if he continues to scold with negative words. Children need to be scolded to learn what is right, but there is a world of difference between calling a child stupid, and saying that because he is a good boy, he should not do stupid things. If you always scold positively, then the child will naturally choose the right way as he grows older. Mutual respect is the best way to prevent or heal a generation gap.

The greatest artists do not necessarily make the greatest teachers. In fact, performing and teaching are entirely different skills. The problem with the words of most of the world's best performers is that they are usually too vague for a beginner to make any sense of. They make sense to a person who already knows how, but leave everyone else confused. The famous Japanese conductor in America, Seiji Ozawa, said that to perform your best, you should not be too relaxed or too tense, but something in-between. This may be true, but it is not very specific. Sadaharu Oh was able to break world hitting records by applying Ki principles to baseball, but when he retired from play and became team manager, he was not able to teach anyone a fraction of what he himself knew. A company's top salesman is often the worst choice for sales manager.

One of the dangers of vague instruction is that it can be interpreted so many different ways. It conveys the impression that what is being taught is basically arbitrary, or a matter of personal style and preference. Many of the rules of etiquette in Japan come from the Ogasawara School. Ogasawara was an accomplished martial artist, particularly in the art of Japanese archery. His teaching was no mere school of manners, it was based on creating a posture without opening or flaw, a posture which was not easily subject to attack. Many rules were developed for every aspect of deportment in daily life.

Rules were accepted more readily in the past, because tradition carried its own weight. However, in an effort to keep up with modern life, modern Japanese teachers of etiquette have begun making arbitrary changes in the Ogasawara rules and forms, claiming that individuality is more important than traditional form. Some teachers make changes simply to distinguish their own school from the one down the street. It is true that modern people are not inclined to follow rules for behavior, nor should they necessarily do so. But it is irresponsible to make changes arbitrarily, without understanding the original reasons for the rules and forms.

For example, until not so long ago, it used to be considered very rude in Japan to eat while walking. These days young people do it without thinking, and most have not a clue of the original reasons for this rule. The martial arts emphasize concentration on what you are doing, for both aesthetic and practical reasons. Not only is it much harder to appreciate the taste of food as you walk about town, but you are also much more vulnerable to attack while you are eating.

Bowing is an old Japanese custom, particularly emphasized in the martial arts. Bowing is still as common a greeting as shaking hands in the West, but few modern Japanese have any idea of how to bow properly. Ogasawara taught that to bow from a standing postition, one should bend the knees, and cover the kneecaps with thefingers. This is not only more comfortable, but far more stable than bowing with the knees straight. Modern department stores in Japan nearly all ignore this traditional custom, and teach their shopping clerks to bow with stiff knees. The question of fashion aside, the traditional method passes the Ki test, the contemporary style does not. Similarly, Ogasawara taught that in bowing from a kneeling position, the hands should touch the mat very lightly, as if there was a thin sheet of paper directly beneath them. This is another way of saying relax completely and let the weight naturally come underside. However, today when people put their hands on the floor to bow, they usually put their full upper body weight on their palms, which puts tension in the arms and shoulders. This is not only bad form, it is also a posture in which you are very vulnerable to attack, because you cannot move quickly when you are leaning on your arms. On hearing such explanations, many young Japanese say that such things may have been important to the samurai in medieval Japan, but surely are irrelevant to modern life. What they overlook is that mind and body unification is never irrelevant.

Even Tohei himself claims that there is no need to memorize endless rules of behavior. There was recently a best-seller on etiquette in Japan which gave detailed advice on nearly every aspect of business behavior and social relations. Much of the advice was common sense, and most of the things in the book were things which were taught in Japanese homes and schools in the past. Tohei's comment was that although it was hard to argue with what the author said, if you seriously tried to follow all of his advice, you would be a nervous wreck.

If you maintain mind and body coordination you naturally follow most of the rules of etiquette and maintain an unassailable form. Tohei once attended a formal tea ceremony, where a great deal of attention is paid to the refinements of protocol and manners. It takes years of training to learn all of the rules. Most people thereforefind it very hard to relax, for fear of doing things the wrong way. Tohei told the tea master beforehand that he was not familiar with the proper rules for behavior during a tea ceremony, but the teacher said just to relax and be himself. Later the teacher complimented Tohei for his excellent mastery of tea ceremony etiquette.

In fact, the current headmasters of both the Edo Senke School of tea ceremony and the Komparu School of the Noh drama spoke at the opening ceremony of the new Ki Society Headquarters, each saying that they considered what Tohei taught to be the essence of their own art. They even added that he made it much easier to understand than their own teachers ever had. The genius of Tohei's way is that it helps people to experience and discover, rather just giving them rules to follow.

No one was ever made worse off by coordinating mind and body. It is one of the few things in this world which has no negative side effects. But unless it is clearly presented, it can be confusing. Do not try to teach or practice more than one Ki principle at a time. You can only ascend a mountain by one road at a time, even though different roads may lead to the summit from different directions. Needless confusion results from trying to pursue two or more principles simultaneously. In effect, you end up losing them both. Get one and you have them all. Lose one and you have nothing. If you find it difficult to understand or practice one principle, you can try to achieve it using another, as long as you focus on one at a time. This is extremely important in teaching. If you tell a person to put his mind in his lower abdomen, relax all of his muscles, think of the bottom of his arm, and send his Ki out to the end of the universe, without letting you bend his arm, you create an impossible task. A student may have trouble relaxing, but find it easy to think of the One Point. The teacher must understand all of the principles, but for the beginner it is enough to understand one. There is no situation for which at least one principle will not work for someone. The important thing is helping the student to experience and then apply the principle.

Ki principles can easily be applied to games and sports, which makes an otherwise abstract phenomenon quite tangible. A person who is not interested in philosophy or Aikido may be interested in lowering his golf score. It is quite possible to teach golf and tennis professionals how to play their sport with Ki, but you should not try to demonstrate yourself unless you already have considerable skill in the sport. A good coach does not have to be a good player. Performance in sports requires practice. Concentrate on showing the other person how to do better what he or she already does well. If you try to compete or show off when you do not know what you are doing, you will quickly lose your audience.

It is also important to remember that you will never teach a person by stepping on his pride. When demonstrating and teaching Ki in America, Tohei never used his own students, but would always choose the largest and strongest looking man in the group. Without realizing it at the time, he once picked a man who had been a world class boxing champion. However, he always let the other person pick him up or bend his arm the first time and complimented him on his superior strength. When he would ask the man to try again, he would find himself unable to budge Tohei an inch. Then Tohei would explain how it worked and teach the other person how to do it. This way he never embarrassed anyone or made him look weak. A strong wrestler could always save face by telling his friends that after all, he *was* able to lift Tohei the first time, even if he could not figure out what happened the second.

Teachers of Ki principles should also avoid the tendency of thinking that they belong to a privileged elite. Anyone who becomes strong tends to think that his way is better. People who follow another way are very sensitive to this subtle form of arrogance and easily pick up subconscious attitudes in a gesture or tone of voice. Taking pride in your own way is not necessarily a bad thing, unless it blinds you to the strength of another. It is very foolish to think lightly of another person, just because they are small in size, or have practiced another martial art. Occasionally you meet someone trained in another martial art or sport who has learned how to extend strong Ki, and may possess a wide repertoire of techniques. If you let down your guard by thinking they cannot be any real match for you, you may be in for a surprise. The best way to meet a challenge from someone of a different discipline is not to compare which is better, but to show the person how to apply Ki principles in his own discipline. People at the higher levels of any art tend to have a grasp of Ki, even if they do not recognize, describe, or teach it as such. If you show a person how to improve at what he does, he will naturally be grateful. An open-minded person will appreciate that Ki principles have more to offer than meets the eye.

Tohei frequently quotes a famous naval officer of World War II, Isoroku Yamamoto, who in fact had been opposed to the war from the beginning, knowing that there was no hope of Japan ever winning it. Like Tohei's approach, Yamamoto's philosophy of education was simple and practical: "First explain how to do it, show how it is done, have the student do it, then praise him for trying. Otherwise how can you expect him to learn?" The important thing is that your teaching must enable the other person to do as well as to know. The old proverb says: give a man a fish and you feed him for a day; teach a man to fish and you feed him for a lifetime. It takes tremendous energy to teach another person, so you yourself must be strong, healthy, and unified in mind and body before you can truly help others.

The difference between the instructor and the student is not one of knowledge but responsibility. You can learn all of the knowledge that you need about Ki practice in a few months of lessons, but it takes years to fully understand or apply it. The instructor is responsible for seeing that students learn how to practice Ki, not just hear about it. Some instructors complain that people today do not want to get up early or train in Ki and Aikido. However, in any country and any era, if people think there is something to be gained, they will go out of their way to get it. If you hold Ki classes and no one comes, then you only have yourself to blame. If you teach what you know to ten people, you have the power of ten. If you keep it to yourself, you risk losing even the power of one. You should not complain about having so few students, or say that people are not interested in learning Ki. This is really an admission that you have not tried very hard to teach. There are a lot of people in the world, and even a small fraction of them makes for a large number of people.

While small classes allow for two-way communication, large groups are not easy to address. Always consider what you can give the audience that will benefit them in their daily life. There are some groups of people who have no interest at first in hearing about Ki principles. Tohei many times lectured to groups of prisoners and school children, who in both cases were forced to attend the lecture against their will. He realized that they were not inclined to listen or learn if he lectured to them as students. Instead, he found a way to get their attention. Captive groups were very attentive whenever he began his talk by criticizing their guards, teachers, or parents. He told school groups that although the faculty complained about lack of student interest in learning, most of the teachers themselves had very bad posture. He then explained that anyone in a position to lead others must first correct himself. This approach always got and kept their attention and made it very easy to lead into the teaching part of the lecture.

Some people become nervous when talking to a large audience. Do not think that you must face an audience of hundreds of people. Look at and speak directly to individuals in different parts of the auditorium and everyone will feel as if you are speaking to them personally. In talking to a large group about Ki, it is not possible to go around and personally test each person. On the other hand, if you speak too much in theoretical terms, you will lose most of the audience. The best way is to determine beforehand what you want them to gain, what single useful idea or technique you want them to take home, and concentrate entirely on that. Every member of the audience should be able to remember your lecture in terms of its single underlying theme.

Ki instructors can feel very confident about what they teach because it is both rational and practical. Even though he frequently talks about the universe, Tohei describes himself as more of a scientist than a mystic. The fundamental difference between Western science and Oriental philosophy is that scientific knowledge is cumulative and empirical, while philosophy is subjective and intuitive. Oriental thought contains much that is good, but also much that is just plain nonsense, with no way to verify its claims. To a certain degree belief has power. This explains the curative effect of some placebos and folk medicines. However, you cannot feed an empty stomach with words or pictures of food. This is the limitation of Oriental thought. Most people assume that Ki is a part of Oriental philosophy, but Tohei teaches it as a science: knowledge which can be verified, repeated, tested, and applied.

On the other hand, conventional science tends to limit itself to the obvious, that which can be easily measured and observed. This overlooks many things which are quite subtle and hard to measure, yet nevertheless very real, such as the human mind, feelings, art, ideas, culture, and language. Words have power. You may think that there is no harm in uttering negative words or complaints, but the Ki test reveals that negative words have an immediate and detrimental effect on your mind and body. Truly, thoughts and words are things, so we must learn to take responsibility for what we say.

Ki training may be scientific, but it is guided by principles. You cannot ignore the four basic principles if you want to teach Ki. One of Tohei's students became the chief instructor in Europe. As an experiment, he tried for a time to teach Ki without any mention of the four basic principles. After two years of trying different ways to explain it to different groups, he concluded that Ki could not be taught without them.

On the other hand, basic principles are also self-evident. There is nothing esoteric about universal truth, for the universe always reveals itself plainly to us. Many Zen priests are incapable of teaching without quoting from the Buddhist sutras. This should not be necessary. Truth requires no authority because it is its own authority. Tohei holds no secrets in teaching Ki, insisting on teaching all that he knows. This keeps his teaching fresh, because he is always open to learning more. If you hold something back, you soon find that you have stopped learning yourself. One candle can light many, without diminishing its own flame.

One person can lead a horse to water, but even ten people cannot make it drink. Not everyone needs to become a Ki master, but for human survival, people in positions of responsibility, school teachers, managers, politicians, should have an understanding of Ki. Some people have a limited capacity for understanding, and ultimately it is not your responsibility to make them understand. However, you should never give up on them because people do change, and you should always give everyone an equal opportunity to learn. You are responsible to give everyone an opportunity to understand and encourage them to practice, but the final responsibility for Ki development lies with the student. If a person does not practice as he was taught, then he has only himself to blame for his lack of progress.

Common Misconceptions about Ki

Although the word Ki has existed in the Chinese and Japanese language for centuries, it was virtually unknown in the West until Tohei introduced it in Hawaii in 1953. People seemed to prefer the word Ki to any English equivalent, and it soon came into popular use. Other groups soon recognized its convenience in explaining many concepts and phenomena in the martial and healing arts based on Oriental philosophy. Some groups claimed that Ki came from China originally and had a 3,000 year tradition behind it. Tohei's response to this claim was that the Chinese character for the word Ki may have come from China, but Ki itself was universal, and was not the exclusive property of any culture. Soon, many groups began using the word Ki, or claiming that it was the same thing that they had always called by another name, such as *Qi, Chi, Prana*, Life-force, or Spirit, each citing sources more ancient than the other for their authority. Tohei's response to this was that many of these ancient traditions were born in eras in which people knew little about the human body, much less the universe itself, and that antiquity alone was no guarantee of validity. In any event, it was more valuable to look at the assumptions behind the words, and what people actually did to experience or apply that which they were calling Ki. Then any differences or similarities would become obvious, regardless of similarities in terminology. There is a proverb in Japanese which warns that many things which appear alike are in fact fundamentally different. Sugar and salt may look almost the same, but their taste is very different. Not only can we not rely on appearances, but it is very difficult to describe the difference to someone who has not actually tasted it.

Tohei has found over the years that many students are confused by other things which they have read or heard about Ki, many of which are different from or even contradictory to what Tohei himself teaches. You cannot be successful in any discipline if you constantly doubt and contradict yourself. Rather than trying to force fit things which are not compatible, he advises his students to clearly understand the differences and then make a choice.

It is not within the scope of this book to examine each of the many different ideas about Ki, both ancient and new. However, it is appropriate here to give examples of how Tohei has responded to people who have approached him with different ideas on the subject.

Some of the most instructive lessons have been when people found out more what Ki was not, than what it was. The remainder of this chapter looks at some of the bizarre, humorous, and sadly common misconceptions that people have about Ki.

The Ghost in the Machine

One of the most common misconceptions about Ki stem from a mistranslation, assuming that Ki means spirit. There is a long tradition in the West of thinking of the body as a vehicle for the spirit, a kind of "ghost in a machine." This notion is not unique to the West however, for the belief in reincarnation has long been strong in the Orient. Tohei teaches that the mind and body are essentially one, existing on a single continuum, which itself has roots in the universe. Thinking of Ki as spirit and the body as matter is already wrong, because it assumes a fundamental separation of mind and body.

Tohei was often asked about life after death, or about spirits and other phenomena beyond our senses. He usually replied that he did not know about life after death, but would find out when he got there, and in any event would carry on as usual. People who think too much about death are often only half alive. Both life and death require total committment. As to spirits, he does not deny that they exist, but says that they do not appear or bother you if your Ki is strong. A place may or may not actually be haunted; whether or not it haunts you is the point.

Others have told him that they were worried over what they would do if they got killed. What could they do? If you live your life to the fullest, developing your latent abilities and helping others without ceasing, then you can die with peace of mind. People who think only of themselves are like the living dead, constantly thinking about death until it approaches. Then they really panic. Tohei advises that while you are alive, think only of living. After you die you have plenty of time to think about dying.

Tohei himself rejects the conventional idea of reincarnation, because it assumes that the mind or spirit inhabits the body like a vehicle, and hops from one body to the next every fifty to seventy years. Our bodies are constantly changing, and death is the biggest change of all. At this point our Ki returns to the universe. But nothing ever disappears completely, so all that we are and do continues in some form, though what we cannot say. There are people who, after narrowly escaping death on an operating table, claim to have actually died and come back to tell about it. Oddly enough, no human being ever actually dead, buried or cremated has ever come back to tell about it. There may be life after death, but no one can know this for certain without actually dying.

While some people claim to have died and come back, others claim to have had an out-of-the-body experience while still alive. They claim that this is possible, using as "evidence," the fact that amputees still feel a phantom arm or leg long after it has been removed. But doctors have found that stimulating certain areas of the brain can produce predictably similar experiences. Subjective experience is thin evidence for claims of spirit travel. Whatever there is for us after death, it is almost certainly nothing like anything living human beings imagine. It is more important to ask how to make the most of life as we know it, and how to leave the world a better place than we found it. If you want to overcome your fear of death, or ensure that your life has meaning after death, you should live your life to the fullest and do your best to improve life for as many people as you can.

Archaic Thinking in New Forms

Students of the martial arts, or of Oriental healing and meditative arts often assume that they are pursuing one of many equally valid roads up the same mountain, leading to the same summit. Each discipline, they reason, is suited to different people, based on different backgrounds or interests, so which path you take is really a matter of personal preference or style. If a person believes this, it is natural to assume that Ki must be the same thing as *Qi, Chi, Prana,* the "Force," or any of a dozen other names in popular use.

Yet this assumption overlooks one significant fact: that most of the disciplines and philosophies which lay claim to this terminology were developed in an era in which nearly everyone believed that the earth was flat, motionless, and the center of the universe, in a word, finite.

The finite view of the universe, and of man, is essentially self-centered. It is based on the way things appear, not on the way they are. Originally people believed that the earth was both stationary and flat, and the stars and heavenly bodies moved around it. Nowadays hardly anyone believes in such a theory, although apparently there is a Flat Earth Society in England, which claims that photos of the earth taken from space were faked in a photographic laboratory. Galileo was persecuted and arrested by the church in the seventeenth century for teaching otherwise, and it was not until late in the twentieth century that the Roman Catholic Church formally pardoned Galileo for his sins. The finite view has ruled our philosophical, religious, and political thinking for centuries. In its context many familiar ideas make sense: nationalism, survival of the fittest, conquering nature, heaven and hell, ups and downs. Yet increasingly, we are beginning to recognize that not only is the universe infinite, but that everything is interconnected and constantly changing. We will examine this idea in more detail in Part III, but here we will look at the implications of the finite view of Ki.

One of the most common postures assumed in the martial arts is the low "fighting" stance. This stance is based on the assumption that you are more stable if you stay low to the ground. Actually, though you may feel more stable when you are crouched down, in fact you are probably too tense to move rapidly. The low stance is based on the wrong idea that the earth is solid and immobile. Its effectiveness in competition depends partly on your opponent doing the same thing. A good fighter stands tall and relaxed and is capable of making very rapid movements. You can tell a martial artist is on the wrong path if he takes a low stance. One group of Karate students got into an argument with some rugby players. The Karate students dropped into a low stance, but the rugby boys just plowed them down and thoroughly pounded them.

The Ki tests used in Ki and Aikido training show that the most stable posture is one which is relaxed and "floating," not tense or rigid. The desire to hug the ground only causes you to lose your balance when tested. Yet this tendency is more subtly ingrained than we realize. Even if you do not obviously crouch down, the same thing happens when you merely press down mentally, or even hold your breath. Some martial artists practice movements in slow motion, working against an imaginary opponent, thinking that they will be able to use them in fast motion if needed. In fact, by moving slowly and at the same speed, you tend to press down and kill the sense of rhythm. If you never practice with an opponent, you may not be as strong as you think if you were really attacked.

The low stance does look strong, particularly if the hands and feet are locked in a ready position to strike, or if the person is holding a weapon. In fact, it is much weaker than it looks. Tohei was able to throw much larger attackers who challenged him, partly because they always favored the low stance, and he never did. Tohei once received a challenge from a man who was skilled with a dangerous weapon, the *nunchaku*, which consists of two forearm length hardwood sticks connected by a chain. The *nunchaku* can be wielded like a whip or a staff and is dangerously unpredictable. The man began swinging the sticks in afigure 8 motion, cutting the air with a menacing sound, and started slowly approaching. There was no way to do any Aikido techniques, and the sticks moved too rapidly to try to block or intercept, so Tohei did the unexpected. He gave one *Kiai*, a penetrating shout focusing breath and Ki in the voice. The other man lost control of the *nunchaku*, hitting himself in the head. Tohei did something similar with boxers who crouched low and tried to jab at him. Instead of trying to take control of their hands, he just pawed them down with both hands, moving irresistably toward their center. By directing his strong Ki and rapidly moving arms right at his opponents, he found their centers virtually unprotected.

The idea of trying to maintain a low center of gravity by pushing downward is not only found in the martial arts, but in various forms of Oriental meditation. In Japan, neurotic people are advised not to practice Zen meditation, because it often aggravates their nervous condition. Why? Trying to repress thoughts or force the mind to calm down can be very aggravating, largely because it makes it almost impossible to unify mind and body.

According to the *Zazengi*, a classic Chinese Zen meditation text, students should sit with back erect, ears held directly over the shoulders and the nose directly over the navel, putting strength in the pit of the stomach, and holding the lips tight against teeth. When Tohei studied Zen meditation, he was given these instructions and tried to follow them faithfully. But he found sitting in this way, that tension would gradually spread through his chest and he would develop a painful stomach, stiff shoulders, and a headache. After sitting this way for many hours, at work he would get tired very quickly and in the dôjô he could not throw very well. In other words, he found it useless in daily life.

Tohei's teacher, Tempû Nakamura, learned many types of Yoga breathing and meditation exercises in India. Tohei asked him once when he practiced them. His teacher replied that he never took time to practice them as such, but did them naturally all of the time. In effect, what he meant was that he had stopped doing those exercises which were unnatural. One of these was called the *Kumbahaka Method*, which he taught for calming the mind. It involved tightening the anus, putting strength into the lower abdomen, softening the solar plexus, and letting the shoulders drop down. This was actually an exaggerated and awkward way of explaining a very natural posture, and his teacher never did it in the way he explained. The problem with many of the ancient methods from India and China is that they use exaggerated expressions to describe what should be natural postures. The result is a caricature of nature, not an expression of it.

A superstition is a false belief, based on a wrong idea of the universe. Not surprisingly, no small part of the so-called "wisdom of the East" is laced with superstition. This is not to denigrate the founders or generations of followers of Buddhism, Hinduism, or Taoism, which contain much of valuable reference for modern man, but rather to suggest that we should not swallow everything that comes under these labels whole. Many of the errors which occurred in these approaches were the result of ignorance or confusion, not by the founders, but by some of their interpreters.

Superstitions sometimes serve a useful function. Belief is a powerful force, and if it is used positively it can motivate far better than material reward or rational persuasion. Relying on an astrologer's advice may help a person who is otherwise hopelessly confused, by making some sense of life's events. Many of the New Age disciplines are based on someone's experience and contain grains of truth. There are people who seem to possess psychic ability and may be sensitive to energies which are not obvious to our five senses. The problem is that intuition is not always reliable. Superstition has a dark side, based on fear. Medieval maps of the world showed the oceans teeming with sea monsters. Eye-witnesses claim to have seen them. Even today, there are people who swear to have boarded alien space ships or communicated with spirits of the dead. Though no one can say for certain that this did not happen, no one yet has proved for certain that it did happen either. Subjective experience, human memory and perception are simply too unreliable a base on which to build a living philosophy. Tohei says that such phenomena may be very real to the person who experiences them, but they never occur to one who has strong Ki. In other words, Ki frees the mind from the dark side of superstition and allows a person much greater control over his or her own life. What concerns us here is which superstitions should be disregarded as unhelpful in the study of Ki.

Taoism began as a philosophy of oneness with nature, but soon degenerated into occult magic and quackery. Several of the formulas written in ancient China for elixirs of long life are not only poisonous, some of them are explosive! They were also very expensive; only the wealthy could afford to take them. Traces of mercury have been detected in some of the ancient corpses of wealthy people. Seeking eternal life, they purchased a shortcut to the grave.

It is commonly believed in Chinese traditional medicine that eating various parts of animals will give a person additional powers related to that part of his own anatomy. This partly explains the widespread use of aphrodisiacs and the incredible variety of items which appear on a Chinese menu. For example, it is believed that if you eat the eyes of a tiger, your own eyesight will become more acute. Other body parts are claimed to increase your Ki power. Unfortunately, this has led recently to a huge black market for increasingly rare and endangered species, which makes the already doubtful practice even harder to justify. This is one example of why we should not follow ancient practices, simply because they made reference to Ki thousands of years ago.

Use of the word Ki has become very popular, and now everyone seems to be promoting their own particular interpretation of it. When Tohei went to Hawaii in 1953, few in the West had ever heard of Ki, nor did anyone teach it as such. Five years later, in 1958, an organization was founded in Hawaii to promote the Chinese art of *Qi* circulation. This group claimed that Ki came from China and that its teaching had a 3,000 year history (this was later modified to 5,000 years as claims grew more earnest). But during the Cultural Revolution in China, no one was even permitted to talk about such things. Furthermore, the ancient Chinese interpretation of *Qi* is very different from Tohei's own approach. The Chinese originally thought of Ki as something like a great wind which circulated from one side of the (finite) universe to the other. When it was with you, it was a good time to engage in business, travel, or social activities. When it flowed elsewhere, it was best to avoid such things and wait for the tide to turn. The human body was considered to be a reflection of this process on a smaller scale and great efforts were made to match human behavior, diet, and exercise to these universal currents. Because the whole system was too complicated for the average person to follow, specialists evolved who could supposedly divine fortunes, diagnose and cure diseases, as well as predict the future. Those who specialized in health developed exercises and therapies designed to hold Ki inside the body, or to manipulate its circulation to affect different organs. Practitioners claim that they can actually feel this energy accumulating in their bodies, and make great efforts to hold it inside and not let it escape, exactly the opposite of what Tohei calls extending Ki. Many of the ancient ideas about Ki are still commonly accepted inside and outside of the Chinese community. What few people realize however, is that medical doctors in China have discovered that people who practice ancient *Qi* circulation methods very seriously for a number of years are often subject to chronic listlessness and fatigue. This should be a sign that something is wrong in the method.

Look closely at the definitions and interpretations given by each school teaching Ki and examine well their methods and the results which follow from them, and you will clearly see the difference between Tohei's approach to Ki and any of the others.

Supernatural Self-deception

P.T. Barnum said that there is a sucker born every minute. Human beings seem to have a weakness for anything out of the ordinary, often believing the most outrageous things on the slightest of evidence. They say that if a dog bites a man it never makes the news, but if a man bites a dog all of the papers will cover it. A Japanese doctor recently wrote a book which claimed to expose the false assumptions which underlay traditional wisdom about diet and health. Japanese have long considered the salted plum to be good for health. But this doctor performed an experiment in which he fed fifty salt plums a day to mice, each one as big as a mouse's brain. Not surprisingly, the mice came under severe stress from massive doses of salt, if they survived at all. From this dubious experiment he concluded that salt plums were not good for health.

Much of what is promoted as "Ki" today under the guise of supernatural powers is really nothing more than deception. Japanese television helped create a "Ki boom" by doing special programs on just such things, claiming that any unusual or unexplainable phenomena was a matter of Ki, or supernatural powers. Later, many of these were exposed as nothing more than dime-store magic tricks, but the media gave far more coverage to the deception than to its debunking.

A real martial artist takes great care with the details of daily life, and is very sensitive to the environment and other people. A fake martial artist tends to show off his power or make displays of unusual "powers" or abilities to impress others. The difference between the Ki artist and the con artist is that the Ki artist uses Ki, while the con artist uses deception or tricks.

Some feats demonstrated by martial artists and magicians have simple physical explanations, most of which can be found in how-to manuals for stage magicians. Once you understand the trick involved, it loses most of its power to impress you. A Japanese martial artist once demonstrated walking up a ladder barefoot, which had steel swords (blade up) for rungs. Apparently, with tough feet this is possible, as long as you step straight down on the blade and do not slip. Swords cut much better by slicing than by chopping. Another man tried to imitate this feat without understanding it and ended up cutting deep slices into the soles of his feet when he slipped.

There was a demonstration held on Japanese television in which a group of Karate black belts reduced a country house which had been constructed on stage to splinters in a matter of minutes, using only their bare hands and feet. This was particularly impressive, because Japanese traditional construction uses interlocking joints instead of nails, and is generally firm enough to resist earthquakes. What none of the audience or even the announcer realized however, was that before the show assistants had cut joints in every major piece of wood, so that even a bunch of school children could have knocked it down. Such feats may have entertainment value and often require a great deal of skill or practice to fool the audience, but they should not be thought of as demonstrations of Ki. A good magician never reveals his tricks, but an honest one also never claims that he is using supernatural powers, or doing things which he alone can do.

Once Tohei attended with one of his students a demonstration of hypnotism, which was being given in a Las Vegas Hotel. The hypnotist asked for volunteers from the audience. Tohei's student was determined to reveal the man as a fake and was the first to volunteer to go up on stage. The hypnotist asked each of the volunteers to close their eyes, fold their hands together, and hold their forefingers an inch or two apart. They were instructed to imagine that there was a wooden matchstick between their fingertips which prevented them from touching, no matter how hard they tried. Tohei's student thought he would prove the whole thing a fake, so he touched his fingertips together right away.

With that, however, the hypnotist asked him to step down from the stage, saying that this little experiment indicated that he was not very susceptible to hypnosis. Those who had followed the instructions remained on the stage, but were told in front of the large audience that hypnosis did not work on people with mental illness or low intelligence. Naturally, all of them cooperated to the letter.

The hypnotist wanted to demonstrate how he could control the subject's subconscious mind through suggestion, after putting him into a trance. In this trance state, a subject can sometimes exhibit remarkable strength or endurance, simply based on the power of belief. Tohei's student was furious at having lost his chance to discredit the hypnotist. However, Tohei told him that instead of trying to make others look bad, he should learn how easy it is to do many of the same things by oneself while fully awake, simply by coordinating mind and body. Hypnotists sometimes demonstrate an exercise called the "human bridge," in which a person in a trance is made to believe that his prone body is as rigid as iron. When the subject is laid across two chairs several feet apart, he can sustain the weight of two or three adults sitting on the unsupported part of his body, without any apparent strain. Yet Tohei has frequently taught this exercise even to children, without using hypnosis, simply by extending Ki. He calls it the unbendable body.

There is a story that says Tohei once demonstrated how he could stick a nail in his forearm without drawing blood, something which was witnessed by more than a few people. But he himself claims it was no nail, rather a hypodermic needle, and he did it for Tempû Nakamura Sensei once just to demonstrate how if you relaxed when you got an injection, the needle puncture would draw no blood. The needle only hurts on entry and withdrawal, because the nerves which report pain to your brain are concentrated in and below the skin. Anyone can do the same, he claims, but it is not necessary to imitate this sort of thing. Besides, stories tend to become exaggerated over time. The needle becomes a nail, five attackers become ten. His own teacher Ueshiba became the subject of endless tall tales, suggesting that he could disappear or teleport his body freely between countries. Unfortunately, in his old age, Ueshiba did little to deny or discourage such rumors and there still is a handful of people who believe them, even though there is no way to verify them and still less of a way to repeat them.

At a seminar in Los Angeles, Tohei found a Karate teacher staring at an ink bottle very intently. He asked him what he was doing, and the Karate teacher replied that he was trying to move the ink bottle with his Ki. He asked if Tohei Sensei could do it himself, and if so, could he please see it done. Tohei said that indeed he could and would be happy to demonstrate it. He then picked up the ink bottle with his hand and moved it to the other side of the table. The Karate teacher complained that he had used his hand. Tohei said that no, his Ki had used his hand. If he had no need for his body, what use was there in staying alive? Ki moves the body, but the body moves the object.

There is a well-known teacher in the so-called popular "Ki" movement in Japan, who has written many books and frequently appears in the media. This man specializes in demonstrations in which he throws multiple attackers high into the air, from a distance of several meters. Not only do the attackers never get close to him, but they seem to be propelled through the air by an invisible force, a force which he calls Ki. Interestingly, he only uses his closest students in these demonstrations, saying that beginners are not sensitive enough to Ki to feel its force. New students are not allowed to work with the teacher directly and are often told when they do not fall down on signal, that their Ki is too weak to feel his power and that they need more training. Once this man was challenged to a match by a Karate Sensei. The "Ki" teacher declined however, saying that he was teaching Ki for health, not as a martial art. The Karate man commented that he had often heard people talk about how Ki made them feel as strong as tigers, but found that they always lost in competition.

When Tohei used Ki to throw multiple attackers, he also physically touched them. Furthermore, he accepted any challenge which came to him, even though it was from martial arts experts whom he had never met, and who were eager to prove him wrong. Many people have tried to imitate what they thought Tohei did. Their tricks may fool a few people, but in the end they really only fool themselves. What value is there in deceiving others, or in using special tricks to destroy objects as a means of impressing people? People who do such demonstrations of supernatural power often show how they can break things. Even a child can break something, but it is very difficult to create orfix something broken. If they really have the power that they claim, why do not they use it to help people really in need?

While some people seek outward demonstrations of the supernatural, a far greater number seem to be interested in unusual "spiritual" experiences. Many of these people are extremely idealistic and drift from one teacher to the next in search of what they think Ki should be. Over the years, many have knocked on the Ki Society's doors and some have even enrolled in training, but none have lasted more than a short time. Inevitably, they move on. Idealists drift from one teacher to another, always disappointed, because their own internal standards for behavior are totally unrealistic for any human being. Ironically, they rarely apply the same rigid standards to themselves, but easily criticize the behavior of a teacher whom they expect to be perfect. Though Tohei never bothered himself with the opinions of such people, he was at times criticized by them for his heavy drinking. They seemed unable to accept that a man teaching health principles could drink alcohol. His willingness to eat whatever was served him troubled many vegetarians. His relaxed manner and sense of humor bothered the purists in the martial arts traditions, who thought that a dôjô was no place for laughter. His often funny and sarcastic remarks about mistaken interpretations of Ki principles were sometimes taken as personal affronts by the people who had other ideas about Ki.

What bothered these idealists most was his ready display of emotions. Somehow they considered that to become angry, show joy or sympathy was a sign of losing composure.

In fact, though Tohei scolded his closest students often, his voice carrying an unmistakable authority, he never showed any sign of tension or irritation, and never remained angry. Somehow his anger was all the more effective because he was completely relaxed and used strong Ki. Among his live-in students *(uchi-deshi)*, one could be said to be doing very well if he were never scolded for the same thing twice. Although Tohei often seemed impatient with the *uchi-deshi* that lived and trained with him everyday, he showed endless patience and encouragement to beginners and ordinary students.

Most people who came to know and respect Tohei Sensei however, felt that these displays of emotion were a welcome sign of his humanity. The fact that he could drink, dance, and sing with the rest of the students after practice made him all the more popular. In fact, in Hawaii, he was considered such a good social dancer that he was often asked to teach others, and even gave remarkably skillful and funny demonstrations of hula dancing at parties.

A surprising number of people who practice the so-called New Age disciplines are in fact extremely idealistic and rigid in their thinking. Tohei has always rejected the cult mentality, or any claims that truth is the esoteric and exclusive right of a small few. Any human being who wishes to lead others must himself have a wealth of life experience. If a person is rigid and self-righteous, claiming to have no vices and showing disdain for others, in time no one will take him seriously. Being too pure is almost as dangerous as being too corrupt. No one is perfect, but the measure of a person's maturity lies in their dedication to self-improvement and their commitment to helping others.

One of the Oriental disciplines which attracted many Westerners was Zen Buddhism. Tohei himself was influenced by Zen, as were most of the martial arts. However, as it was popularized in the West, it became a very different thing. Around 1967, when popular interest in Zen was extremely high, Tohei visited San Francisco. Zen books and teachers were highly regarded in the hippie community and many people assumed that Tohei was a Zen teacher. Zen concepts are extremely difficult to translate, and are seldom understood even by modern Japanese or Chinese. One of the fundamental concepts in Zen is that of *Mu*, a word meaning "not," but variously translated as "nothingness," "void," "emptiness," or even "enlightenment." A term widely interpreted by Zen writers, particularly Daisetsu T. Suzuki, was *munen musô*, meaning "no-mind, no-thought." Tohei found one young man practicing Zen meditation on the street. Curious about his blank look, Tohei waved his hand in front of the man's face, but got no reaction. When Tohei tried to take his picture, the man suddenly demanded a modeling fee of 50 cents. Tohei later remarked to Professor Suzuki that he had unintentionally helped to create the hippie movement in America. Tohei taught how to calm the waves of the mind to infinitely imperceptible ripples, but never to stop or make a blank state. Wherever he taught in America, he had to emphasize to Zen enthusiasts that there was a difference between "Think nothing" and "Do not think anything," between "Do nothing" and "Do not do anything."

Zen priests in the old days achieved deep levels of understanding because they used to sit in *zazen* for many hours a day. Modern priests and young monks spend relatively short periods of time in meditation. It is possible to practice something incorrectly for a short while and think you are doing it right. But if you continue doing something wrong for long periods at a time, any unnatural posture or forced movement becomes impossible to sustain. At this point, you are faced with a dilemma. You can correct your posture so that you can continue, or you can continue your mistakes but shorten your practice period so they do not affect you as much.

One contemporary Japanese Zen priest, who is also a prolific writer about Zen, claims that when he got enlightenment (*satori*) he was so elated that he ran barefoot three times around the pond. When asked what enlightenment was like, he said it was the state at which plus and minus cancel out at zero. With these few words he showed how little he had actually understood. Tohei was often asked if he had achieved enlightenment. He always answered that he did not know, and then explained that enlightenment was not something that you get or list on your resume anyway. Real truth is not found by trying to stop the mind at zero, but by calming it to infinitely imperceptible ripples. The moment you think you have it, you have already lost it.

Tohei has never had any fondness for cult religions and is very vocal in his opinions of them. A man involved in one such group approached Tohei, asking him to interpret a strange experience he had had, in which he heard a voice from above a pine tree saying, "I will give you the universe. Be confident!" Tohei asked him whether he would obey the voice if it told him to stick his head in the toilet. He then explained that being one with the universe meant to be natural, not to have visions and hear voices from the sky.

Among the students who attended Tohei's many Ki and Aikido seminars in the United States were people who had also practiced other disciplines, ranging from Yoga, to Zen, to Transcendental Meditation. Modern people tend to be rather lazy and seek shortcuts to enlightenment, or philosophies which justify rather than challenge their existing way of life. One woman had practiced a popular form of meditation in which you try to separate your spirit from your body in order to practice what they call soul travel. This was supposed to lead to spiritual enlightenment after eight years. She had practiced this form of meditation faithfully for nearly ten years, but had gotten nothing but confusion. She was quite bewildered by Tohei's teaching of mind and body unification and had a great deal of trouble doing even the simplest of the exercises. It was almost as if she did not believe, or would not even try them. Tohei told her that since she was the only one who could not do it, she should reflect on the reasons why, saying that if she continued to practice mind and body separation, she may find one day that she cannot unify mind and body, even if she wants to. This brought her to her senses and she began to practice very sincerely.

On one occasion overseas, Tohei noticed strange animal cries coming from another room in the large athletic complex where they were holding their training. He was curious and tried to get a look, but the door was locked. One of his students told him that it was a cult religion which he had formerly been a member of and which non-members were not permitted to observe. The purpose of the religion was to return to nature and each person was assigned an animal type, which presumably they most resembled. Some members acted like monkeys, trying to climb the walls. Others slithered along the floor like snakes and still others walked slowly around the room on all fours, trying to imitate the King of the jungle. These exercises were supposed to remove your civilized inhibitions and help you to relax. But the ex-member said all it did was to give people exaggerated hang-ups.

Tohei once tried to go to a seance out of curiosity, but his students told him not to, for if anyone saw him there, they might think it was part of Ki training. Some so-called spiritual seers claim to be able to foresee the future, or read into people's private lives. However, their predictions are usually vague enough that they can claim later to have been right about some things, even though they missed the details. When occasionally they seem to have been right, people make a big fuss, but on the more frequent occasions when they were totally wrong, no one pays any attention. More often than not, people choose to believe what they want to believe. This is called self-deception and it has no place in Ki training.

Even when a person is sincere about Ki development, certain problems can arise from misunderstanding the four basic principles of mind and body unification. Therefore, it is as important to know what they are not, as to know what they are. Two things determine your progress in Ki training: direction (what you do), and effort (how much you do). Actually, you cannot separate direction and effort. When Tohei says, "Right effort produces right results," he means that effort should be made in the right direction. The following anecdotes should help you to ensure that you are making right efforts with regard to Ki training.

Concentration versus Attachment

Do you know the difference between concentration and attachment? Though quite the same to the untrained eye, there is a world of difference between focusing Ki and losing yourself in something. A person may become so involved in a movie, that he completely forgets about everything else. But when the lights come on, he realizes that his pocket has been picked. This is not concentration, it is attachment. A mother may assume that her child is deep in concentration if he does not answer when his name is called, but actually this just proves that his mind and body are separated. Real concentration is not narrow-minded or fanatical, but rather a natural state in which a calm mind clearly reflects everything around it.

Ki principles do not work if you fail to apply them correctly. One woman commented that walking with One Point allowed her to walk without getting tired, but she found that she was unable to do her shopping. She was afraid to look left or right, for fear that she would forget her One Point. There is no need to be so stiff. Ki extends naturally, whichever direction you look. Thinking about the One Point is not the same thing as keeping it. If you do it correctly, it should enhance your performance in daily life, not inhibit it.

Another woman found that after two hours of Ki meditation, she became so anxious and uncertain that she had to stop. She claimed to be following the instructions in Tohei's books, but she had missed one vital criterion. Instead of thinking of the One Point as the center of the universe, she thought of herself as the center of the universe. Thinking of nothing but yourself is a surefire prescription for neurosis. When Tohei explained that the One Point was at the center of the universe, one student in New York said that he did not want to be at the center of the universe, because that place was only for the Buddha. Evidently he was studying a form of Japanese Buddhism which taught that the center of the universe was a fixed location.

One man tried to practice Ki breathing while lying down, to overcome his chronic insomnia. He even received special instruction on how to do so from one of Tohei's top instructors. But the man found it harder to sleep than ever. He said that he was following the instructions carefully and even showed Tohei his notes, which were basically correct. But when Tohei asked him to show him how he did it, he exhaled with a wheezing noise that would have kept the person in the next room awake. He said that he tried it all night long, but only found himself more tired and tense in the morning. Even though he had properly written down to exhale with a soft, barely audible sound, without realizing it he was putting so much tension in his throat that it made a loud and rasping sound. This is a case of the fault being with the learner's careless attitude, not the teacher or the teaching.

In the old days, Japanese craftsmen were rarely taught anything. They were expected to learn by observing and doing. This requires real concentration. Nowadays people have trouble learning, even when you spell it out for them in great detail. We should not forget that the ultimate responsibility for learning is with the student.

Students in school who do not like to study need not be forced to do so. If you teach them how to sit with a strong and unified posture, unconsciously they will absorb most of what the teacher has to say. If they understand it, they will naturally become interested and perform well. If they perform well, they will enjoy their studies. But we should also remember that good grades in school is a poor predictor of success later in life. To succeed in life you need strong Ki.

Karate people are fond of demonstrating what they call "hard" Ki, in which they break boards with their bare hands. Breaking boards is possible if you harden the hands and concentrate the muscular force at a point. It may make an impressive demonstration, but if you do it regularly, you are almost certain to have joint problems later in life. Many martial artists are disillusioned when they reach the age of forty or fifty and find that they are partly crippled from long years of abusing their bodies. If you practice correctly, you should be able to keep practicing into old age. Aikido, some people claim, is "soft" Ki, which deflects or turns a force away instead of breaking through it. This is the wrong understanding. There is only one Ki, though it may be extended strongly or weakly. One student asked Tohei to explain the difference between hard and soft Ki. Tohei asked him in return if he could explain the difference between fat and skinny Ki, saying that Ki was the same for everyone.

People who spend a lot of time concentrating tend to have hard eyes, which are a result more of tension than of mental focus. When you see a person claiming to use Ki who is staring with hard or transfixed eyes, then you know he is a fake. The eyes are designed to reflect, not to stare. A tour guide in Hokkaido, the northern island of Japan, advises people on what to do if they encounter a bear while walking in the woods. She says that you should stare at the bear's eyes, for bears were afraid of the human gaze. On hearing this, Tohei called it a perfect prescription for suicide, saying that the bear would certainly feel threatened and attack. The best thing to do, he said, was to look unconcerned and stay calm. The same thing would apply if you encountered a dangerous person. Real concentration is a matter of centered awareness, not narrow-minded focus.

Relaxation versus Losing Power

Do you know the difference between relaxation and losing power? Many people misunderstand the idea of the power of relaxation. People who are relaxed appear confident. But where does this confidence come from? Some martial artists, like the famed swordsman Musashi, trained themselves based on the idea of total self-reliance. If you have strength and talent, this can take you rather far compared to the average person, but your personal power means nothing in the eyes of the universe. Others, like Tohei's teacher Morihei Ueshiba, trained based on the idea of total faith, relying on gods and mystical powers. This too, can take a person rather far if genuine, but is hard to regain if lost, and almost impossible to teach. The real power of Ki lies at the intersection of self-reliance and faith. You must do your utmost and make serious efforts if you want to learn Ki. But after that, you must also leave the results up to the universe, recognizing that all you can do is your best, and knowing that the rest will take care of itself. Self-reliance alone tends to result in delusions of grandeur, while faith unquestioned tends to be blind. Real confidence is not self-confidence, but confidence in universal principles.

There is a difference between being natural and being selfish. Ki training should not isolate you socially, but actually help integrate you into daily life. There are Taoist stories of so-called masters who became hermits, so isolated that they would wash their ears if they heard any profane speech from another person. Some so-called spiritual seekers became so oblivious to other people that they showed no manners, sleeping naked in public and never bathing regardless of how other people felt, saying that it was natural. Ultimately, this is a matter of extreme selfishness and unwillingness to develop as a human being. The word for human being in Japanese *ningen*, is written with two characters, meaning "person-interval," suggesting that a real human being exists in relationship, not in isolation.

Relaxation is not idleness. Taking it easy is not same as relaxing completely, for it may inconvenience others. Middle-aged shoppers out for a leisurely afternoon are seldom aware of how they block the sidewalks, or interfere with traffic. Tohei says many of them have such poor posture, that they resemble a family of ducks more closely than a group of people. Professional models should also learn how to walk more naturally. Many of them have extremely stiff shoulders from posturing all day long. Looking relaxed and being relaxed are not necessarily the same.

A prominent Japanese magazine recently featured an article on how Japanese do not know how to relax. The cover showed two men at the pool side, a Japanese with a tense expression working on a laptop computer, and a Westerner with a wide grin wearing sunglasses and a straw hat, laying back with a drink in hand. The implication was that Japanese should learn to relax like Westerners do. What few people realize however, is that slackness can be just as stressful as tension. Real relaxation is a matter of releasing stress, not of losing power.

Living Calmness versus Dead Calmness

Do you know the difference between living calmness and dead calmness? Some methods of hypnosis teach people to imagine parts of the body growing very heavy as an aid to mental calmness. This may help a person to fall asleep, but they will wake up with a heavy feeling, having filled their subconscious mind with that thought. Feeling heavy is not the same as having the weight underside. Real mental calmness can only be achieved by having a feeling of buoyancy in the whole body. When you are healthy in mind and body, you feel light and free. If you have a problem, you feel heavy.

Many people in the traditional Japanese martial and cultural arts sit straight and move slowly, but in fact can be pushed over quite easily. Those in the past who had it, somehow figured it out on their own. Today many people just imitate the outer form without understanding. In martial arts movies, trained actors and stunt men use a variety of tricks to both ensure their own safety and convince the viewing audience that they are really fighting. Actually the whole thing is staged. The more complicated and convoluted the fighting, the more choreography is involved. In real life none of this could possibly work. A real fight is over very quickly, and is largely decided before it begins. There are exceptions, however, in the better martial arts movies. Some actors have a strong background in the Kabuki theater, where they naturally absorb much of the basic feeling of mind and body coordination. Even though it appears to be staged, it is possible for a single person to take on multiple attackers. When done well, it almost looks like a dance. The only difference is that it would be impossible to choreograph.

If you are really calm, you can use your head in a crisis. If you just pretend to be calm, you may act inappropriately, by reflex. Some of the things taught in self-defense classes are almost certain to backfire. In Hawaii, a policeman who was held up at gun point tried to surprise his assailant by throwing a lighter in his face. The man was so surprised, that he pulled the trigger and killed the policeman by mistake. The policeman was not trained to get out of the line of fire. If you ask your partner to strike you in a certain predetermined way, anyone can learn to respond with the proper technique. If you know which questions the teacher will ask, anyone can pass the test. You must train so that you can deal with any attack, any question. Real calmness is capable of action, while dead calmness is forced to react, or suffer in silence.

Plus Mind versus Minus Mind

Do you know the difference between a plus mind and a minus mind? Businessmen are encouraged to be positive and motivated in their work. However, in practice it often turns out with less than happy results. In the world of Japanese business, being motivated often means being aggressive, ignoring your family, and behaving like a soldier in the army. The problem is that many of the generation who sincerely worked in this way burned out, and ended up having no energy and few friends. Now Japan wants to try to imitate the West by taking long vacations and by being less productive. Both ways are wrong. If you truly extend Ki you have more energy while expending less effort. Naturally you should be more relaxed and more productive.

People often assume that an extroverted personality extends more Ki than an introverted one. Yet is it not strange how some people who love to gossip suddenly shut up when asked to speak before an audience? Being extroverted is a personality tendency. It does not mean that you necessarily have strong Ki. The same can be said for displays of courage. Because Tohei was able to successfully respond to so many surprise attacks and challenges from his students on the Hawaii Police Force, they asked him if he was in fact afraid of nothing. He said that to be afraid of nothing was to invite disaster; that there were many things he was afraid of, but just chose to avoid times, places, and people who were dangerous. Any martial artist who claims to be fearless might think twice about how he would defend himself against a machine gun or atomic weapon. Extending Ki is not the same as being reckless.

The priniciple of non-dissension is a very important one in Aikido. But it does not mean that we should always compromise. One student of Tohei's, who is also a lawyer, was asked to mediate a difficult conflict between two disputing parties. No matter how they tried, they kept ending up in an argument and could not arrive at any solution. One of the parties hired the lawyer to represent him. After just one meeting, the lawyer came back with a contract in his hand that was more than his client had hoped to get. He asked the lawyer how he possibly managed to arrange it. The lawyer replied that all he did was to speak ill of his client and gain the other man's sympathy. He was able to resolve the dispute without conflict and without compromise.

People commonly assume that extending Ki must be some special state of mind, only accessible through esoteric training. However, when we are doing something we truly enjoy, we are nearly always coordinated in mind and body. People may ski all weekend or play cards all night long without getting tired. But the same person may feel suddenly fatigued when he has to take care of an unpleasant task at work, even if it is only a phone call. The problem is how to control our selves. It is easy to relax or be positive when we enjoy something, but we have to do many things in life that are not so pleasant. One measure of the maturity of a man is his ability to do his best, even if circumstances are working against him. Enlightenment is not some extraordinary or mystical state of mind, but just a deep state of mind and body unity. This is nothing more than 100 percent concentration, whether at work or at play, what Tohei calls extending Ki.

A plus mind is not a neutral one. People complain that they cannot understand why bad things happen to them, since they did not do anything bad to deserve it. On the other hand, they may not have done anything good either. Even if no one is watching, the universe itself keeps perfect accounts. You may not be able to rely on banks built by men, which are subject to human error and failure, but you can always rely on the universe. This is the real meaning of *intoku*, or doing good in secret without seeking reward. If you persist in doing good, you will always find what you need to accomplish your goals.

Tohei's definite way of expressing himself and occasionally sarcastic remarks about other disciplines sometimes convey an impression that he thinks other ways are wrong. However, he himself says that he never claims that Zen or Yoga or any other way is wrong. He says that wrong Zen is wrong, but not Zen itself. He acknowledges that there are many great people in each of these disciplines, as well as in ordinary daily life, who live Ki principles without consciously practicing them. However, few of them have been able to express them well, or teach them to others. The universe hides nothing. Its truths are always plainly there for everyone to see, only most people shut their eyes to it and try to distort it with their own limited views.

Tohei's main concern is to avoid the confusion produced by wrong ideas, and to help the vast majority of people who could benefit by Ki principles, if they were only aware of them. There was a story recently in a Japanese paper of an old man who died of starvation, living in a low rent apartment, with only the minimum things needed to get by in life. The media was going to use the story to draw attention to the plight of the elderly, when they found that he had millions of yen in cash stashed away in his mattress. Most of us are like this, having an endless supply of Ki available from the universe, but going through our whole life without using it.

Our real power is not in the visible tip of the iceberg, but rather in the part below the surface that we cannot see. Everyone knows that they have a mind or spirit, but few know how to use it. If you think of yourself as being nothing more than your physical body, then you may suffer someday from a nervous breakdown trying to protect it. People may think that mind and body unification is a nice idea, but assume that it is too difficult to be practical. Trying to separate mind and body is irresponsible, like running away from a crisis to let someone else solve your problems. The reason that it is difficult is that people do not know how to concentrate without becoming attached, relax without losing power, remain calm without being dull, or be positive without being aggressive. Therefore they spend their lives going back and forth between extremes, growing more and more confused the older they get. Perhaps by gaining a correct understanding of Ki principles and how to study them, people can learn to improve their lives in a practical way.

Living Long and Well

A early Roman philosopher wrote that life is not merely living, but living in health. Like so many things of value, we tend not to appreciate good health until we lose it. We take clean air for granted until it is polluted or taxed, rarely pausing to reflect that we could not live without it. Just as a fish swims in water without being aware of its existence, we live in an ocean of Ki, and only seem to realize its importance when our supply is cut off. In Japanese, the word *genki* means health, literally, "source of Ki." To maintain good health, or to restore it when it is lost, we need to understand what it is that makes us healthy or sick.

Health is a natural state, the organism functioning as it is supposed to. When something goes wrong, we experience sickness. If we remove the causes of sickness, then we shall be healthy again, as long as we live. Technically speaking, it is the immune system which protects us from harmful influences in the environment. Approximately 90 percent of the bacteria in the air is kept from entering our body by the skin, 9 percent is flushed out in sweat and other body fluids, and the 1 percent which do enter the body are controlled by the immune system. Although there are many types of antibodies and other immunological agents which make up the immune system, there are probably 100 times as many known bacteria; yet ordinarily our immune system works to protect us. Why then, do people get sick? When the immune system weakens, it loses coordination or even goes on strike and refuses to work. Then we get sick. What prevents this from happening and keeps us healthy is our life-force, or Ki.

Relaxation is the real key to health. Doctors generally agree that more than 80 percent of the illnesses which plague modern man are preventable, and most of them are stress-induced. The easiest time to relax completely is when you are asleep. Because we spend up to a third of our lives in sleep, it is very important that we learn how to relax completely during this time. Sleep is very important for health, because that is the only time in which we truly relax completely and receive a fresh supply of Ki from the universe. However, depth of sleep is more important than the number of hours which you sleep. Tohei was always known for his ability to sleep deeply for short periods, almost anywhere. As he often proved when he was in the army, he could sleep despite any disturbance, but would always wake up in time if necessary. Both Napoleon and Edison had the same ability, and each was able to make very effective use of his waking hours as a result.

It is wrong to try to relax by escaping from stress. Not only is this impossible to do, but a stress-free environment can actually shorten your life, as has been proved in experiments with animals. Continuous, unrelenting stress however, can injure your health. Just like a bow which is never unstrung, the body under constant stress becomes fatigued and weak. On the other hand, a bow which is never strung is also useless and weak. The best way is to alternate stress and release, which is the natural cycle of working and resting.

If you coordinate mind and body during the day, you have positive dreams at night, such as chasing away the enemy or being popular with the opposite sex. If you forget to coordinate mind and body during the day, your sleep will tend to be fitful and restless, and you will be more likely to have nightmares. The problem is that people take the stress of the job home with them. Some people even take it to bed, to the point where they cannot even get a decent night's sleep, no matter how many hours they get.

The best way to prevent this is to unify mind and body through Ki breathing or meditation before you go to sleep at night. If your mind is preoccupied with problems at work or home, it will be very difficult to relax. In Japan, they say that a troubled or sick person usually has a hot head and cold feet. A person who is free of anxiety has a cool head and warm feet, and can sleep like a baby. You may not be able to think your troubles away, but you can at least learn to forget about them when you rest. It is much easier to do this if you concentrate on mentally directing the blood to your feet. This literally takes your mind off of your problems and allows you to sleep on it, whatever it is. Tohei developed the following guidelines to help people learn how to sleep deeply and peacefully.

For Sleeping Deeply:
1. **Always unify mind and body before you go to sleep.**
2. **Believe that the mind controls the body.**
3. **Calm and collect your thoughts before you go to bed.**
4. **Maintain a cool head and warm feet.**
5. **Use your mind to direct the blood to your feet.**

Correct posture is another important prerequisite for good health. The right posture is the most natural one. It should be so comfortable that you can sustain it all day long, amidst your daily busy routine. If you have a habit of standing with poor posture, you will soon develop fallen arches and flat feet. This condition is not limited to your feet. The same thing happens when you sit down on a chair. If you sit with a slumped lower back, the area of your buttocks in contact with the chair spreads out to the sides, and the muscles supporting your hips become lazy. In Japan, Sumo wrestlers have a custom of making hand prints in red ink and then signing them with a brush, as a gift to a shop which they patronize. The hand prints are not only very large, but surprisingly little of the surface of the palm and fingers actually touches the paper, even though a great deal of pressure is applied to make the print. Young people these days try to make hand prints, but the impression usually shows flat palms. Nearly every part of the hand touches, which is a sign of how weak their arms have become. Correct posture is a lifted, not a flattened state.

Wearing shoes all of the time is not good for health. Japanese never wear shoes in the house, which gives the feet a chance to exercise and remain strong. Formerly, Japanese people used to wear sandals or wooden clogs instead of shoes. This was a very good custom, for it kept the feet strong and the posture good. For modern people who are unable to adopt this custom, it is a good idea to spend sometime walking barefoot, take long walks, or engage in some active sport.

Tohei has spend much of his life teaching people how to maintain their health through Ki principles. He found with experience, however, that someone who is already sick is usually not interested in hearing about Ki principles. They suffer from a lack of Ki, and therefore need direct assistance in the form of Kiatsu therapy, as well as instruction in how to maintain the correct posture and how to do Ki breathing. In Japanese, there is a distinction made between *yamai*, which is a sickness or injury of the body, and *byôki*, which is sickness coming from weak Ki. If Ki is weak, it can be made strong.

Sick people are often anxious, particularly when the cause of a problem is unknown.

Many problems draw their power from anonymity. A prank phone call is far more threatening if you do not know who the caller is on the other end of the line. Helping a person realize why they are sick and that they *can* do something about it, does a great deal to restore confidence.

There are people however, who enjoy being sick. Hypochondriacs unconsciously prefer being sick, because it gives them lots of attention. Do not think you are helping such a person by showing sympathy for his or her negative remarks. If the person refuses to make any effort to improve, or meets all of your advice with a "Yes, but . . . " attitude, then you should explain clearly about the difference between a positive and negative attitude toward health, and help them realize that they must make a choice. If a person is genuinely weak or sick, you can protect them by sending them strong Ki. The most direct way to do this is through Kiatsu therapy.

We all have this healing power, but it is not the supernatural or fantastic miracle described in some books. Anyone can learn to do Kiatsu, but its effectiveness depends on the depth of your mind and body unification. Problems of shoulder stiffness or whiplash injury often take as long as six months to heal if you go to a hospital or get ordinary treatment, but can be healed in just a few treatments with Kiatsu. There is a whole category of such illnesses, which are only covered by Japanese health insurance for a period of six months; otherwise people with chronic problems would draw insurance claims for their aches and pains throughout their whole lives! These days modern medicine is very good at diagnosing disease, much better than it is at treating it. The problem is that some diseases, like neurosis, do not show up on the X-ray film.

It used to be that grandchildren in Japan would massage the tired shoulders of their grandparents; but these days even young school kids get stiff shoulders, and often it is the grandparents who must massage the young peoples' shoulders. Shoulder stiffness is not considered a disease itself, but it can have very serious consequences. The neck and shoulders contain many vital nerves and blood vessels, which if restricted or distorted by tension, can actually interfere with brain function. This explains some crimes of insanity, such as when a man kills the entire family living next door, saying that their incessant piano playing got on his nerves. People who easily become hysteric usually have very stiff necks, to the degree that their nervous systems do not reflect reality. If your nerves report a stimulus of one as one, then your nervous system is functioning properly. But when a stimulus of one is reported to your brain as one hundred, then you are driven to irrational and destructive behavior.

Health is the most basic condition of life. Without it you cannot be productive, you cannot truly enjoy anything, no matter how much money you have. You can purchase health care, but you cannot buy health itself. People spend a lot of money on health and exercise aids, but usually these devices end up collecting dust in the closet. Health is the foundation of a good life. It is upon this base that we build happiness and prosperity. Though health is universally desired, why is it so difficult for many to maintain it? Most people will admit to having some health problem, even people who appear to be in perfect health. The problem may not warrant the formal attention of a doctor, or it may be a minor annoyance which refuses to respond to medical attention. A great many people in this position have simply resigned themselves to live with the inconvenience. This is understandable in the case of the elderly, in whom the vigor of youth has faded. But increasingly today, even young school children are beginning to exhibit signs of stress and physical breakdown.

One of the biggest problems facing society today is that of an aging population. Because so few people train their mind and body together, the result in old age is either a sharp mind with a broken-down body, or a reasonably healthy body, with a mind that is so senile it does not even recognize friends and family members. Once a person is in this state, we must do the best we can to take care of them, but it is very difficult to reverse the damage of decades of neglect. A match flame is easy to put out, but a forest fire may take weeks. Prevention is the best medicine.

Japanese people living during the early Heian period (around A.D. 800) had an average life span of only thirty-five years. This was attributed to the famine, disease, fires, and natural disasters which plagued that period. In time the expected life span increased to fifty years. Today with advances in medicine, culture, and freedom from the curse of war, the Japanese people enjoy the highest average life span in the world: seventy-three years for men and eighty years for women. However, we need to approach these happy statistics with caution. Those people who have reached eighty or ninety years of age were all born during the Meiji period (1868–1912). They were raised on a simple diet, endured hardship and poverty, and were made strong through trial by fire. They were born in an era in which people walked most of the time, ate little meat or fat, and generally were expected to maintain good posture in daily life. It is doubtful that people born since World War II will live as long, given their present lifestyles. Even if they do, they may suffer from mental or physical disabilities in late middle age. Medicine can extend life years, but it cannot extend life power. If we want to enjoy long life, we must be healthy in mind and body. When our time is up, then we can then say thank you to all who have helped us along the way, and bid everyone a cheerful farewell. The children of contemporary Japan, as well as those of many other industrialized nations, accustomed to luxury, weaned on soft instant foods, and lacking the discipline or interest to train themselves, are not as likely to live as long as their great grandparents. The child who suffers from stiff shoulders, stomach problems, and curvature of the spine before he even graduates from elementary school may find his later years must be artificially extended, if he can afford full medical support. We have to ask ourselves, how many of these people will end up old in years, but bedridden? How many may end up too mentally decayed to recognize their relatives or even feed themselves? And what will happen to the cost of health care for such a generation?

A complete definition of long life should include the capacity to work, to be of some use to others, and to make some positive contribution to the world. Hardy in old age, able to help take care of the grandchildren while the young people go out to work, giving more than they take, and saying a cheerful farewell when it is all over; this should be the model of long life that we seek. Happiness never results from the selfish pursuit of pleasure. In the end, greed and avarice always consume the one they serve. The more your actions benefit those around you, the more you find that you have to accomplish in your life, and the greater others will value your existence. Happiness consists of forgetting the pettiness of the small self.

Senility is a tragedy to the victim and a tremendous burden to the victim's family. Like an infant, a senile person thinks only of himself and requires constant attention. One of the physical causes of senility is a chronic deficiency of oxygen in the brain, which is aggravated by a tendency toward self-centeredness. If you want to avoid growing senile, spend a lot of time doing things to help other people, and do plenty of Ki breathing to keep the brain supplied with fresh oxygen.

There is no question but that modern medicine has greatly extended the average human life span. Not only has it conquered many diseases, but it has helped people to survive illnesses which once killed their victims. The primary weapons in the arsenal of modern medicine have been drugs and surgery. While these are often necessary in treating serious disease, people tend to forget that they both have negative side effects and rarely cure completely.

In Japan, a doctor can prescribe and then turn around and sell medicinal drugs for a profit. Tohei once met a Japanese doctor who let slip the comment that drugs were for selling and not for taking. He routinely prescribed larger than necessary doses, because he assumed that most patients forget to take their medicine regularly anyway. Worst of all, he refused to let his own family take some of the drugs which he sold to his patients, because he was aware of their harmful side effects. He further commented that doctors today would be better off going to engineering than to medical school, so that they could learn to replace faulty body parts with artificial ones that would not break down. An extreme case perhaps, but a good example of the danger of medical education which focuses on the body alone and ignores the person himself.

Surgery is sometimes necessary, but it should be a last resort. When you cut tissue, it never returns to normal. All tissue has a function, even if it is not well understood. They say that a Sumo wrestler is finished after he gets his appendix removed, even though doctors consider the appendix to be an organ which serves no useful purpose. Some doctors treat neuralgia of the face by cutting a facial nerve. This stops the pain for a while, but it tends to return along another nerve. If you keep cutting the facial nerves, you may kill the pain, but you also kill the facial expression. Kiatsu is a much safer way to treat such a problem. Exactly what is Kiatsu therapy and how does it work?

The Origin of Kiatsu Therapy

The word *Kiatsu* literally means "Ki pressure." It is not to be confused with *shiatsu*, or "finger pressure" therapy, from which it differs in a number of important respects. Shiatsu, also known as acupressure, is a form of massage therapy based on the theory and points of acupuncture and Chinese medicine. Kiatsu is a Ki-pressure therapy invented by Koichi Tohei and based on the Ki principles of mind and body unification. It is not a branch of Oriental medicine, nor a form of "faith" healing, but a practical method of helping release tension and revitalize the life-force. Kiatsu therapy is a method of directly or indirectly sending Ki to an injured or weakened part of the body, thereby rejuvenating the life-force and enabling the body to heal itself. Tohei came upon this unique method, like most everything else, from his own experience in applying Ki principles to solve real problems which he faced.

In the latter part of the war Tohei found himself far from home and without medicine or doctors. Maintaining health was a matter of survival and no one could afford to be choosy about what they ate or drank. One evening he suffered an extremely violent abdominal pain, apparently the result of food poisoning from some bad pork which he had eaten. Tohei remembered that some folk doctors practiced what they called *teate*, or "laying on of hands." Healing by touching goes back farther than that however, even appearing in the Bible. Tohei was familiar with all of these things, but himself harbored doubts as to whether it really worked. However, in severe pain, and without access to doctors or medicine, he decided to give it a try. Placing his hands on his stomach and pressing gently, he attempted to send Ki in an effort to ease the pain. He ended up going to the toilet seventeen times throughout the night, but each time felt a little better, so he continued this *teate* treatment. At last he was able to sleep for three hours and the pain went away completely. He skipped breakfast, but was able to eat lunch the next day without any problem.

Tohei had frequent recurrences of conjunctivitis in his youth, so he carried a lot of medicine for it when he went to China. But his medicine washed overboard on the way, so he had nothing to treat it with if it recurred. It severely affected his vision, which was a very serious problem, particularly if he needed to fight. When it eventually did recur, he washed his hands and applied the same kind of gentle pressure, not to the eyeball, but around the lid and socket. By the next day it was considerably improved, and it was completely healed in three days, this time with no recurrence. He found he could also use it successfully to treat various ailments among the soldiers in his charge. Later he treated all manner of injuries and illnesses among his students. Eventually he formalized his knowledge and techniques into a system which he called Kiatsu therapy.

The Interface between Eastern and Western Medicine

Propelled by science and technology, Western medicine has made remarkable advances in a short period of time. Once fatal diseases like tuberculosis, are no longer the source of panic that they once were; and vaccinations have nearly eradicated smallpox from the face of the earth. In addition, science has made possible the further extension of life through such things as heart and kidney transplants. New medicines are created everyday to treat a host of symptoms and illnesses.

One would assume that with this background, disease itself would be almost extinct. Yet nearly the opposite is true, disease is more prominent than ever. How can this be? Things in this world are relative. Whatever has a front has a back; good has a counterpart in evil. While medicines may be effective against certain symptoms, they also produce side effects. It is not surprising that the more proliferation we see in new drugs, the more the variety and complexity of the diseases that demand our attention. When several drugs are consumed simultaneously, they often worsen the patient's condition by producing a negative side effect that was not present before.

While Western medicine has followed the dictates of materialistic science, Eastern medicine has placed its faith in what might be called natural philosophy. Chinese medicine does not deny drugs, it simply prefers to use the medicines which can be extracted from herbs and barks. Its primary branches today are acupuncture-moxibustion, *amma* massage, and shiatsu therapy, each of which are based on the 3,000 year old Chinese concepts of *yin* and *yang* and of the Five Elements. Western medicine has begun to sense its own limitations in practice, and some doctors have begun to take a serious look at Oriental medicine to see if it offers any answers.

Dr. David Eisenberg of Harvard University began a joint research project under corporate sponsorship, with the Shanghai Oriental Medical College, in order to find the points of agreement between Eastern and Western medicine. In 1986, Dr. Eisenberg visited Tohei in Tokyo, through the introduction of Dr. Denji Suzuki of Jichi Medical College. Dr. Suzuki is the head of one of the Ki Society branch clubs at the Jichi Medical School, and one of his graduates had gone to Harvard and introduced Ki principles to Dr. Eisenberg. Learning that the Ki Society's approach was totally different from any that he had studied to date and that it was possible to actually physically test and experiment with Ki, he was interested enough to take the trouble to come to Japan and find out first hand.

Tohei told him that he thought it was a very worthwhile thing to do, but that there was one significant problem that would have to be resolved first, the problem of meridians. According to Oriental medicine, there are subtle pathways or circuits in the body for the flow of Ki, called meridians (*keiraku*). These pathways supposedly do for Ki energy what the circulatory system does for blood. They are also supposed to correspond to the movements of Ki in the universe at large, making the human organism a microcosm of the whole. Tohei asked Dr. Eisenberg if scientists have been able to find any evidence of the existence of these meridians. He said no, and that this was the very problem that was preventing them from finding the interface between Eastern and Western medicine.

Eastern and Western approaches to medicine both have advantages and, both have limitations. If we learn to recognize and set aside the errors of each, then we will end up with something far better. Dr. Eisenberg was apparently drawn to Chinese medicine because of its documented clinical effectiveness and long history, which is another study in itself. Western doctors have recently begun to shown interest in the fundamental unity of mind and body, although there is little agreement on what it means for medical therapy. In either case, it is much better to learn how to strengthen the life-force to prevent disease from occurring in the first place. Tohei has been teaching mind and body unification, and its practical applications in Kiatsu therapy, since the early 1950s. Doctors should not look for all of their answers in the field of Oriental medicine, for it is highly unscientific. It contains some good, much nonsense, and a great deal that is not testable.

The Fundamental Error of Eastern Medicine

In all fairness, it must be said that Eastern medicine is a mixed bag. Like Eastern philosophy, it can be very good or very bad. Like most folk medicine traditions, it is based on a combination of experience, observation, and superstition. Furthermore, there are many schools of thought within each branch. Not all acupuncturists think alike; nor do they all get the same results. However, its assumptions must be carefully examined, if we wish to get a better perspective on Ki.

The concept of meridians used in acupuncture is an idea that was created thousands of years ago, by people who had no accurate knowledge of anatomy or physiology. It is therefore not surprising that modern medicine is unable to find any evidence of meridians in the body. People assume that Ki is a mysterious force, and somehow look to archaic ideas in search of an explanation. However, inevitably there are problems in trying to force fit ancient ideas of Ki into a modern scientfic framework. Ki itself is neither mysterious nor ancient, but a natural and universal energy. Ki is the principle of the universe itself and therefore should not be outside of the terms of Western medicine and modern science.

Oriental medicine originated in China and has a 3,000 year long history. However, a long tradition by itself is no guarantee of validity. Many political, religious and even scientific traditions were followed for centuries until their limitations were made clear. Today even school children are taught concepts which were beyond the greatest minds of former eras. The only things which are valuable *because* they are old are antiques, and perhaps good wine. Theories do not necessarily improve with age. Universal principles do not change with time. We live in the same universe now as Christ or Buddha did then, and nature operates by the same principles now as it did before. The universe conceals nothing from those who are willing to see. Nature may be marvelous, but it is not mysterious or supernatural.

The absolute universe is all encompassing. It exists as a whole that nothing can stand outside of; that is to say, it contains everything. As the Japanese saying has it, the cloth of nature is seamless. But within this universal whole, we live in a world characterized by duality, the endless interplay of opposites. From our point of view, everything is relative. There is no front without a back, no top without a bottom. In the Orient this duality is known as *yin* and *yang*. In the West it is called plus and minus. As long as you are speaking in relative terms, nothing can be absolutely correct, for it all depends on your point of view.

The fundamental principle behind Oriental medicine is the theory of *yin* and *yang*, and its permutations, the Five Elements. According to this philosophy, the universe is composed of endless combinations of the opposites of *yin* and *yang*, which can be elaborated in great detail. The sun is *yang*, the moon is *yin*, man is *yang*, woman is *yin*, and so on and on run the expressions of duality. Furthermore, springing from these opposites are five material elements, represented by the qualities of wood, fire, earth, metal, and water. From these spring such things as plants, heat, soil, minerals, and fluids, which combine in endless permutations to create the world as we know it. According to Chinese medicine, our bodies are miniature models of this process, reflecting the movements of the stars and planets above. There are five organs in the body which correspond to these elements: the liver representing wood, the heart representing fire, the spleen representing earth, the lungs representing metal, and the kidneys representing water. Assisting these organs are the gallbladder to the liver, the small intestine to the heart, the stomach to the spleen, the large intestine to the lungs, and the bladder to the kidneys. To these are added invisible organs imagined to assist with subtle processes, such as the Heart Constrictor, and the Triple Heater. The ancient Chinese postulated that in order to help distribute energy to the organs that need it and drain it from the organs which have it in excess, a system of canals or passageways must be necessary, and this they called the meridians, each being named after an organ or its assistant. Chinese scholars compiled great encyclopedias categorizing many familiar objects, colors, creatures, and phenomena on this complex scheme. It is hard to imagine how they would go about making sense of the modern world, with all of its endless complexity.

This theory was developed by Chinese people living 3,000 years ago. They did not know that the earth was a roughly spherical body, spinning once a day through empty space in its annual revolution about the sun. To them the earth was as it appeared, a flat and unmoving foundation under the firmament of heaven. There was no means of travel sufficient to convince anyone that the earth did anything other than spread out indefinitely on every horizon, particularly on a continent as vast as China's. It seemed quite natural that the sun, the moon, and the stars should move as they appeared to move, that is rise from one edge of the world, travel across the sky, and set on the opposite side. This could only happen, they believed, if all of these heavenly bodies were connected by celestial meridians which the eye could not see. It seemed that in an orderly universe, the human body should be governed by similar phenomena.

A similar view dominated Western thought for centuries. Authorities taught and people believed, that the earth was stationary and flat, and that the heavenly bodies moved around it, embedded in a series of concentric spheres, each planet, star, and sphere being geometrically perfect. This ancient view was a combination of empirical observation, appearances, inference, and ignorance. It was accurate enough to navigate by, but awkward to work with, and completely wrong. In the West, people believed that there were only Four Elements, earth, water, air, and fire. In the human body, these elements were expressed by what medieval doctors called the four humours—blood, phlegm, choler, and black bile. These humours were related as much to the person's personality as to his physical make-up, and normal health was defined as a balance among the four humours. Doctors remedies ranged from the odd to the dangerous, and no doubt met with mixed success. Though many people long for the "good old days," few would want to return to the era of medieval medicine or dentistry. Why should their contemporaries in China be afforded any greater respect?

The ancient Chinese view of Ki traveling along meridians had some practical therapeutic value based on experience, but was extremely complicated and ultimately a doubtful description of the body. Western medicine has begun to face some of the limitations of its own method. An open-minded interest in alternative medicine may do a great deal of good for the medical establishment. However, ancient theories should be approached with caution, and with an awareness of the social and philosophical setting in which they were originally developed. Many of the ancient theories are not so much wrong, as they were vague. Like the theory of the planetary spheres, they may have served a useful purpose at the time, but were based on false assumptions of reality.

Ki is not an energy which runs through currents along prescribed lines in the body, rather it flows everywhere, as the body itself is ultimately made of Ki. It is more accurate to say that we are saturated with Ki than to say that it flows from here to there inside the body. Electricity can only be conducted along certain channels and through certain substances; but Ki can be conducted through anything, as it is the essence of things themselves. To say that Ki is "flowing" is really just another way of saying that everything in the universe is in motion, including the cells of our body, down to the subatomic particles of the most solid objects.

The field of Oriental medicine includes so many different therapies and interpretations, that it is very difficult to classify them under one name. Each must be examined under its own merits. Proponents of Oriental and alternative medicines point to the fact that they sometimes work. Acupuncture has drawn serious medical attention because of its effectiveness in treating certain illnesses and because it seems to offer a safe and effective alternative to anesthesia during surgery. It is licensed in many countries as a legitimate form of therapy. Every form of therapy has people who swear by it, or even claim miraculous cures. Many practitioners of alternative and folk medicine support themselves with their practice and get repeat patients. The advantage of the Oriental approach to healing is that it emphasizes natural methods and has few of the dangerous side effects of the more radical Western approach using drugs and surgery. The disadvantage of the Oriental approach is that it is based on questionable notions of how the body works, and may be too unscientific to be worth betting your life on.

There are many sincere and skilled practitioners in the business. But because alternative medicine is not legally recognized in most countries, it escapes the scrutiny of governmental and professional licensing organizations. Because it essentially operates "outside the law," there is far greater opportunity for abuse. The most common form of abuse is that the patient may be led to believe that he is getting more for his money than he really is. Anyone who is paying hard earned money for a treatment wants to believe that he is getting better. Most therapies do produce a real, if temporary form of relief. The problem is that the condition soon returns and another treatment is required. Most conditions require repeated treatments; but how frequently, and at what cost? A good therapist heals quickly, and with fewer treatments, earning income because he or she does the job, and gets referrals from satisfied patients. A poor therapist must rely on less ethical means to earn a living, which mislead or take advantage of a patient. Unfortunately there have always been quacks in the healing business, but that is another issue. The questions to ask of any alternative healing method are: Is it safe? Is it the best available? Is it in fact doing what it promises? Is it worth the time and money you must invest?

Even when healers are able to help a patient, they frequently acknowledge that they feel drained afterward. Particularly those who do a great deal of healing can themselves become physically weak or mentally unstable. Sick people are like sponges, soaking up any excess energy they can get from other people. As a result, most practitioners of these arts are forced to cut back or quit their practice by the time they reach forty, and spend most of their time teaching, while letting their younger students work on patients. This is a sure sign that they have weakened their Ki. It is dangerous to send Ki to others if you do not have mind and body unified, for you can quickly exhaust your own supply. One advantage of Kiatsu therapy is that it is based on mind and body coordination. Because practitioners learn how to replenish their Ki in daily life, it is safe to continue treating others well into old age. Furthermore Kiatsu does not use physical strength or force to apply pressure, so it can be done for many hours without fatigue.

Many practitioners of shiatsu, or finger pressure, use body weight or muscular force to press on the tissues, and may suffer from tendinitis as a result. You can break down stiff muscle tissue by force, but it grows only stiffer the next day, gradually developing a resistance to the massage, forming a kind of body armor which is very difficult to get rid of. With Kiatsu there is no forceful breaking down of the tissue, but rather a gradual restoration of its natural circulation and resilience. Some patients exclaim after a Kiatsu treatment that their shoulders feel so light that they seem to have disappeared.

Shiatsu makes use of pressure points, the same points used in acupuncture, which lie along the meridians. These points, often coinciding with large gatherings of nerves, are like traffic interchanges. The important thing is to improve traffic flow all over the body, working at the point of congestion, not at some remote spot. Oriental medicine frequently prescribes treatments on points at some remote place from the affected area, based on the theory that Ki is too congested or deficient, and needs to be "shifted" around the body. It is true that the human body has an endless number of circuits and connections, far beyond the human imagination, but the flow of energy takes care of itself if we do not interfere.

Ki flow does not occur along lines, but rather saturates the body, like water in a sponge. Tension squeezes it out. Relaxation allows Ki to flow freely throughout the body. This is a natural process, and not one which we are likely to be able to control mechanically. Everything in the universe moves. In a sense, sickness is really just sluggish movement of Ki. Kiatsu frees the movement of Ki in an area which has become restricted and the body naturally does what is necessary to maintain health. We cannot digest food any better by thinking about it, but we can provide conditions which make it easier to digest efficiently.

Many illnesses are a result of self-induced restrictions in the natural flow of energy in the body. If you can improve the circulation by removing those restrictions, many health problems take care of themselves. Kiatsu does not heal you directly, but rather like water which is poured into a well to prime the pump, it stimulates the life-force, which is ultimately what heals and protects the body. If you realize that your real body is made of Ki, rather than the bag of bones and ailments which plague you at the moment, then it is possible to renew and strengthen yourself. If your clothing is dirty, you wash it. If your body is weakened, you can strengthen it by cleaning it with fresh Ki. This is what is meant by mind over matter.

Chiropractors emphasize the importance of good posture to maintain health, saying that poor posture puts pressure on the organs and joints. While this is true, their treatment tends to be no more than a temporary adjustment. Even if the vertebrae are brought back into alignment, if habits of bad posture go uncorrected, the bones will soon need adjusting again. Without teaching a person how to coordinate mind and body, no amount of advice on good posture will stick. The same is true for health advice given by doctors and hospitals. A person may know that something is bad for his health, but be unable to stop doing it. This is partly what keeps doctors in business.

Some people criticize Tohei, saying he only teaches one point, whereas in Yoga they teach seven, or acupuncture they teach hundreds. People who have spent years studying these disciplines often possess very sophisticated intellectual knowledge about body energy, but may have little idea of how to experience or control it. Many have gained their knowledge from books, but find it very difficult to apply in daily life. By learning how to unify mind and body, and thereby how to use Ki in daily life, therapists may gain a new perspective on their own disciplines. The important thing to remember is that therapy is a means, not an end in itself. Medicine is a temporary measure, not part of a daily diet. The old quip applies: an ounce of prevention is worth a pound of cure.

A word should be said about remote healing, or healing without touching. In the early twentieth century, a Russian healer became famous for his ability to heal by touching. Using a technique known as *Kirlean Photography*, special photographs of wavelengths not visible to the naked eye revealed that the energy which came from his fingertips was particularly strong. Evidently some energy is transmitted, and this can have an effect on another person, even if that person is some distance away. The danger is that you may try to send out all of your Ki without first coordinating mind and body. This will exhaust you, and may even make you sick. Ki is a real force, but you cannot use it effectively unless you unify mind and body. More than one such healer has come to the Ki Society asking for help. They may have been able to help others, but they themselves were on the verge of nervous collapse. Remote healing can be done safely, but only if you first coordinate mind and body. The method is to first deeply unify mind and body, then visualize some unique features of the person you wish to help, perhaps the person's face, and send Ki strongly to that person. However, this should only be done when you are unable to give Kiatsu physically. Ki does not disappear over a distance, but its power and focus gradually dissipate. Considering the difference between a laser and a flashlight, it is better to touch the person directly, because focus and proximity have power. If you want to help a sleeping child, cup your palms on the child's forehead and back of the head, and while sending strong Ki direct a positive suggestion to the child for about thirty seconds. Even though the child is sleeping, he or she will react by smiling, sighing, or showing some sign of relaxing. The next morning the child will awake feeling bright and refreshed.

The Limitations of Western Medicine

Western Medicine has been carefully constructed by scientific inquiry, upon a foundation of facts and evidence. Unlike Oriental medicine, it does not try to fit observable data into a preconceived theory. Its progress is based on a step-by-step accumulation of objective data. This approach has led to astonishingly rapid progress and development in the medical field. Because the research of the past is used as a foundation for future inquiry, each generation has benefited from progressively more advanced medical knowledge.

Ironically, one side effect of scientific and technical advances has been the creation of new types of injuries, diseases, and dangers. While some diseases have been eradicated, the number of sick people and the variety of serious illnesses seems to have only increased. Moreover, the rapid proliferation of medical instruments, diagnostic devices, and chemical or mechanical interventions has so depersonalized the healing profession, that many doctors have lost the ability to detect oncoming illness by touch or by changes in face color. Only half in jest, some have begun to suspect that an engineering degree might be more useful to a doctor than medical study.

Perhaps now more than ever, we have come face to face with the limitations of our own strength in solving health problems. Though medicine has come this far, it is still far from being able to provide us with the degree of health that we need. Medicine has been at the leading edge of scientific research, having applied all of the methods and assumptions of strictly materialistic thinking, to the point where it has come to see the body as a complex machine. Each of its working parts has been so thoroughly examined, that we have an abundance of knowledge of the particulars, but we have forgotten how to see the body as a single living whole.

Taking a relative point of view may be unavoidable while living in a world characterized by opposites. But we must not forget that ultimately underlying this world is a universe which is perfectly interconnected. From the absolute point of view, the universe is seamless. Though we seem to have a separate mind and body, these too come from the universe. When mind and body are coordinated as one, we are close to our original nature. In overlooking the underlying unity of mind and body, medicine has fallen into a trap of its own making. Many medical professionals have become aware of this, and from these circles we have begun to see serious interest in a holistic approach to health.

As we have seen, to look for answers in the outmoded concepts of Oriental medicine is like trying to clean a window with a dirty cloth. Behind the dualism of *yin* and *yang* we must not forget that there is an absolute universe which is the origin of all. If modern medicine seeks to go beyond its present restrictions, it must seek answers in the concept of an undivided universe and in our essential unity with it.

The universe is a whole and any approach which is in accordance with this will be right. Any method which starts out attempting to consciously manipulate and balance opposites is doomed to fail. What works for one should work for all, any time, any place. The principles of the universe are not a mystery for the privileged few, nor are they partial to time and circumstance. We must seek to understand and share them without bias.

One of these principles is that the mind leads the body. In 1955, Tohei was invited to give a lecture on Ki and Aikido at an international medical convention being held in Honolulu, Hawaii. The speaker who introduced Tohei was familiar with his teaching that the mind controls the body, and asked the group of doctors if it was possible to change your pulse by your own will-power. All of the doctors present agreed that it was not possible, saying that the heart was an involuntary muscle. The speaker said that Tohei could do it, and if they did not believe it, they should test him. Tohei made the claim that he could vary his pulse rate at will, by thirty or more beats per minute. First he had the doctors measure his pulse in the left arm. When it registered at around ninety beats per minute, the doctors said it was far too high and that he should avoid heavy exercise. Then he asked them to measure the right arm. It registered about sixty beats per minute. At first they were confused at how the right and left arm could show a different pulse, but he explained that he had simply slowed it down. Each time of course, it was the same in both arms. Tohei explained to them that while it was true that autonomic nervous system itself is beyond the control of the conscious mind, it is possible to control one's emotions and therefore influence it indirectly. When you are angry, your pulse gets faster. When you are calm, it slows down.

Right away the doctors wanted to try it, but no one was successful. He explained that when they thought were angry, they were not really angry, and when they thought they were calm, they were not really calm. They were very eager to learn how to control the pulse with the mind, but Tohei told them that to learn the secret would cost them some money. Everyone was disappointed, until he smiled and said that the fee was $10, which was what it cost at the time to become a member of the Hawaii Ki Society.

Anyone who gets surprised or becomes angry exhibits a faster pulse. When the mind is calm the pulse rate naturally slows down. If you can control your mental state, you should be able to control your pulse as well. But this is easier said than done. Tohei repeated this demonstration across America, as a way of teaching that the mind controls the body. Before long he found that many scholars and medical professionals had taken an interest in the theme, and began to hear of research on how the mind affects the body. It was not long before the word Ki itself began to come into more common circulation in English.

An Overview of Kiatsu Treatment

We have seen how being alive is a state in which Ki in the body freely exchanges with Ki in the universe. If you extend Ki out then it is immediately replaced by fresh Ki, in a limitless supply. The free circulation of Ki is not only the most natural condition, but also the state in which the life energy is most active.

In order to increase the flow of Ki, it is first necessary to integrate the mind and body. Put the other way around, when the mind and body are unified, the exchange of Ki between the body and the universe is unrestricted, and the life-force operates at its maximum capacity. If we can maintain this condition in our daily lives, then we can enjoy a strong natural immunity to disease. In this sense, Ki is an elixir of life.

However, this is easier said than done. Even people who are aware of the need to coordinate mind and body in the midst of daily activities, usually consider it to be extremely difficult, if not impossible to achieve. The mind is intangible, but free to move about. The body is tangible, but restricted by its environment. How can two such unlike entities be unified, particularly when one is preoccupied with the demands of a busy schedule?

Even though you may be able to calm and concentrate your mind by sitting still in meditation, if you become distracted the moment that you move, it will not help you in your daily life. Many people in the past have sought to achieve peace of mind by undergoing austere training in meditation at mountain retreats, by sitting for long periods under a roaring waterfall, and numerous other strenuous methods of mental and physical training. Despite their numbers and efforts, very few were able to achieve this state in daily life. This is partly because of a basic error in their thinking. By assuming that the mind and body were two separate entities, they believed that constant vigilance and severe discipline were necessary to hold them together. Yet the strain of this misdirected effort was often great enough to prevent the very thing they sought to achieve.

As long as you think in relative terms, as if the universe were divided into parts and mind and body were separate, you will be unable to achieve mind and body unification. The word *universe* means, "all existing things regarded as a collective entity," coming from the Latin *universus*, meaning whole, entire, turned into one. The familiar world that we live in is a result of the endless combinations of opposites which have sprung from this universal womb. Because we live in a relative world, it is perhaps unavoidable that we think in relative terms. But we must not forget that underlying and supporting all opposites is a universe which is fundamentally indivisible.

Though we often use the word Ki in a relative sense, such as extending Ki, sending Ki, receiving Ki, strong Ki, weak Ki, and so on, in fact Ki is the energy and substance of the universe itself. It may be thought of as the connective tissue of the universe, a continuum of mind and body which includes ourselves, and much more. All things are essentially made of Ki, saturated and supported by it. In this sense, our mind and body are not only inseparable, but ultimately rooted in the universe itself. However, when we speak of mind and body in conventional terms, they exhibit certain properties which obey their own distinct laws. Our lives begin as a single cell, which contains within it the potential for brain, muscle, blood, hair, skin, and dozens of other types of cells, each of which operates in different ways from the original cell. Though the mind and body emerge from the same source, each operates according to its own distinct principles. To clarify this distinction, Tohei established the four basic principles for mind and body coordination, two for the mind (Keep One Point, Extend Ki), and two for the body (Relax Completely, Keep Weight Underside). By following these principles, anyone is able to experience Ki and learn how to apply it in daily life.

However, many people in the world remain unaware that this life energy exists and that it is freely available to them. Lacking sufficient access to this natural fountain of energy, they suffer needless degrees of illness and injury. Once the body is weakened by a disease or physical impairment, it becomes extremely difficult to recover by your own efforts alone. As a result, some people carry a physical problem with them for decades, resigning themselves to the thought that they must simply learn to live with it.

It is difficult to teach mind and body coordination to a person whose mind is preoccupied with pain, or who is suffering from a restriction which prevents them from living a normal life. Even if you try to teach such a person, they may lack the energy to put what they learn into practice. These people need a fresh supply of Ki delivered from the outside, like a jump cable start for a dead battery in a car.

When the water in a well loses pressure it will not produce water, no matter how hard you pump the handle. However, if you pour in a small amount of water at the top, it creates a seal, allowing the pump to build pressure, and then you can draw out as much water as you need. Similarly, if you apply Ki directly to the part of the body in which the life energy has become weak, this tends to call forth and renew the original flow of Ki to that area. When this flow becomes strong enough, it activates enough life energy to repair the damage and restore the healthy function of the part.

This is analogous to what happens when you press gently on a person's body and send Ki directly to the tissues through the fingertips. To give Kiatsu properly, you must first learn to coordinate mind and body according to the Ki principles. Then you must learn various techniques for extending Ki to the injured part. These techniques are difficult to learn from a book. For that you should seek instruction from a qualified Kiatsu instructor. Here we will examine the basic concepts and methodology of Kiatsu.

As we have seen, if you send Ki to another person without replenishing your own supply, there is a danger of draining and exhausting your own life energy. There are many sick people in the world. Even if you could help a few, what good does it do if it costs your own health in return?

How do you know if your own supply of Ki is low? The first sign is an inability to sleep deeply at night. Nervous irritation and tossing in your sleep prevent your body from achieving the state of total relaxation that is necessary to replenish your supply of Ki. If you allow your Ki to become depleted, you may experience weariness and feelings of lethargy, and become very easily fatigued. The danger of this is that it is very easy to contract a serious illness when the defenses of your immune system are down.

Faith healers and religious people who practice laying on of hands are often said to pick up the very sickness that they claim to heal. Some claim that to compensate for this sacrificial burden, they must also pick up a larger fee or donation. Actually what has happened is not that they have contracted the problem of the patient, but rather that they have allowed their own Ki to become depleted and this weakened state has brought on sickness.

If the air temperature in two adjacent rooms is different and the door between them is opened, soon the temperature will be the same in both rooms. Ki flows in a similar way, from the stronger person to the weaker one. Though it greatly benefits the sick person to absorb the Ki of the stronger one, this is hardly consolation for the one who may be weakened in the process.

To prevent this situation, Kiatsu therapists are first taught how to coordinate mind and body. A car can be run all night with the headlights on, because the battery is continually recharged as long as the engine is running. However if you leave the lights on with the engine off, the battery will run down in no time. As long as you send Ki to the other person while maintaining your own mind and body coordination, it is impossible to deplete your own supply of Ki. The more you send out, the more fresh Ki comes in, and the supply of Ki from the universe is limitless. A unique feature of Kiatsu therapy is that the more you practice it, the healthier both therapist and patient become. In many forms of therapy the reverse is true; if you treat too many people you can make yourself sick. This is true for both physical therapies and psychological counseling.

The person receiving Kiatsu treatment may feel a degree of discomfort at the point being pressed. However there is a fine line between what might be called "good pain," indicating that the sensation is returning, and the condition improving; and "bad pain," which results from the condition growing worse. In Kiatsu therapy one never presses with strength. The fingertips are simply applied to the area which is to be treated and Ki is extended to the tissues in a very natural way. As this Ki calls forth the patient's own life energy, gradually the area revives and begins to feel good. Though there may be some slight tenderness at first, it is usually experienced as "good pain" and is never painful after the pressure is released. There are no painful or dangerous side effects to Kiatsu therapy.

On the other hand, even if the patient experiences a temporary recovery, if he or she continues to live and act in the same way as before, the problem is likely to resurface sooner or later. To help eliminate the cause of the problem and prevent its recurrence, Kiatsu patients are also taught proper methods of health maintenance which they can practice on their own, particularly Ki breathing and Ki exercise. If you give a car proper attention and maintenance, you can double its useful life. Likewise we can increase the useful life of our bodies by giving them proper care and attention in daily life. Few forms of therapy give anywhere near the same emphasis on prevention of illness and maintenance of health.

Unlike shiatsu (finger pressure) massage which relies primarily on physical manipulation, weight, or pressure stimulation, Kiatsu therapy sends Ki directly to another person's body through the fingertips. But in order to be able to do this properly, you must first learn the correct method of extending Ki and how to direct it to another person. Merely imitating the outward appearance of the method without properly extending Ki will either be ineffective, or may actually endanger the therapist by causing a depletion of Ki. To ensure that Kiatsu is performed correctly, Tohei established five principles for Kiatsu therapy, which we will examine in some detail.

For Kiatsu Therapy:
1. **Extend Ki from the One Point in the lower abdomen.**
2. **Do not let tension accumulate in your body.**
3. **Press perpendicularly toward the center of the muscle without forcing.**
4. **Focus Ki continuously and precisely at the fingertips.**
5. **Concentrate on the lines, rather than the points.**

1. Extend Ki from the One Point in the lower abdomen.
Before you can effectively send Ki to another person's body, you yourself must be full of Ki and know how to send it out without depleting your own supply. The first principle of mind and body coordination is to keep One Point. When the mind is calm and focused at the One Point in the lower abdomen, the body is automatically filled with Ki. The more you extend Ki out, the more fresh Ki enters to replace it. This ongoing process helps maintain a healthy circulation of Ki. Just as water extends more forcefully from the nozzel of a hose, the extension of Ki is strongest at the fingertips.

We have already practiced the unbendable arm, in the section on the four basic principles. If you relax the arm completely and imagine that Ki is rushing out through the fingertips as though the arm were a firehose, your partner will have great difficulty in bending your arm. Extending Ki is not difficult. All you have to do is to correct your posture and simply tell yourself and believe that Ki is extending.

But even if you extend Ki from the arm, in order to do Kiatsu, you must first determine whether or not Ki is extending from the fingertips as well. Bend the fingers so that the middle three fingertips line up in a straight line, the palm held facing outward. Have your partner place the palm of his hand directly against your fingertips and try to push straight against your fingers. If you put tension in your arm or fingertips you will be easily pushed back. However, if you relax completely and concentrate on extending Ki at your fingertips, then your partner will have great difficulty even moving your hand. This will help you get the sensation of extending Ki from your fingertips.

The same thing happens when you extend Ki from the tip of the thumb. When water rushes out of a firehose, there is a great release of energy at the nozzle, where the water is confined to a narrow opening and suddenly extends out under pressure. The thumb is like the nozzle, in that you can feel a concentration of energy at the tip when Ki is extended.

Each of the four basic principles of mind and body coordination describe the same thing in different words. It is impossible to separate them. If you properly maintain one of the principles, you automatically have the other three. Similarly if you lose any one of them, you lose them all. However, it is impossible to think of more than one principle simultaneously. All that you need to do is to properly maintain any one of them. Although you may think that you are extending Ki, if you put tension in the thumb, then you violate the second principle, of relaxing completely. This tension actually stops the flow of Ki and you end up with mere finger pressure instead.

You can experiment in pressing with Ki by standing behind a partner who is sitting in a chair, and applying the thumbs to the large ridge of muscles on the shoulders, at the base of the neck. Your partner may also sit in the *seiza* posture, in which case you sit behind him, comfortably upright in a chair. If you press hard on the shoulders with strength, then all you do is to create a feeling of discomfort, pressure, or even pain in your partner's shoulders. On the other hand, if you do not apply any pressure at all, then your partner gets a vague feeling that you are not doing anything, and in fact the effectiveness is greatly reduced.

Before applying your hands to your partner's shoulders, first calm your mind at the One Point and relax your arms completely. Then lightly place your thumbs on the points where you will give Kiatsu. In this condition Ki is already extending strongly from your fingertips, and merely by touching the shoulders Ki automatically enters your partner's body at that point. In a few moments time, the muscles will begin to respond by relaxing and getting softer. At this point the thumb naturally follows by taking up the slack and gradually penetrates deeper and deeper. Your partner should be able to clearly tell the difference, as the feeling of Ki begins to penetrate the muscles. Though there might be slight pain if the tissues are particularly tense, it will be what we have described as "good pain" and is not uncomfortable. The feeling of receiving Kiatsu in this case is very satisfying, like scratching an itch.

If you put strength in the arms or fingers when you press, a third person should be able to easily pull your hand off of your partner's shoulder. This is proof of the fact that Ki is not extending. If you calm your mind at the One Point and lightly place your thumbs on the shoulders to give Kiatsu, because the weight is underside, the arm, the wrist, and even the thumb itself become firmly rooted to the shoulder and next to impossible to pull off. Because the weight is underside, naturally Ki is also extended.

2. Do not let tension accumulate in your body.
Many people have trouble at first distinguishing between concentrating Ki at the fingertips and putting strength into the fingertips. However as soon as you put tension in the body, you also reduce the flow of Ki. All you need to do is to think or imagine that Ki is flowing and concentrated at your fingertips. This is entirely sufficient. If you put tension into your hands, the flow of Ki stops and not only is the Kiatsu ineffective, but you risk getting tendinitis from holding your forearms tense for long periods, a frequent complaint of massage therapists.

If you remain calm and concentrated at the One Point and stay completely relaxed, tension should not accumulate in your body. However, if your posture is bad, or the position of the hands is wrong, you may gradually build up tension unconsciously. If your hands are higher than your elbows, so that you must raise your arms in order to press on the shoulders, even though you try to relax, you will gradually find your own arms and shoulders growing tense. You may find it easier to sit in a chair, and ask your partner to sit on the floor with the legs stretched out comfortably to the front. Because his shoulders are now lower than your arm, Ki easily flows out, like water running down a slope, and you can give Kiatsu without accumulating any tension in your own body. In principle, when you must raise the arms to give Kiatsu, Ki tends to stop. Therefore to stay relaxed, you should keep the elbows and hands down. This means adjusting your position according to the position of your partner. If your partner sits in a chair, you should stand.

By always seeking to maintain a comfortable posture with respect to your partner, one in which it is easy to extend Ki and remain relaxed, you can learn to give Kiatsu for long periods without getting tired. By adjusting your position, by working on various parts of the body and by occasionally using the three middle fingers instead of the thumb, you can be more effective and have better endurance. At first you may tire after a mere ten or twenty minutes, but with practice you can learn to give Kiatsu for more than an hour without fatigue.

3. Press perpendicularly toward the center of the muscle without forcing.
When you fill a tire with air, if the jack is properly plugged into the stem, the pressurized air naturally enters the tire until it is full and does not leak out at the sides. If the plug is not securely fastened, then most of the air leaks out without getting into the tire.

In Japanese *amma* massage, which involves deep kneading of the muscles, and in shiatsu massage, the fingers, heel of the hand, and elbows are used to squeeze and work the muscles until the tension is broken down. The treatment is often quite painful. Although this may give a feeling of temporary relief at the time, often the next day the muscles are as sore and tight as ever. If you then repeat the treatment, you get the same result, leading to a vicious cycle in which eventually the resistance of the muscles is so broken down that they cannot feel a thing without getting a truly rough treatment. The patient then demands more strength from the masseur. Many massage professionals have themselves broken down in fatigue for this very reason. In Japanese, such patients are said to have lethal shoulders, or shoulders which can kill a masseur.

If you leave a coiled rubber hose outside in the winter time it becomes very stiff. If you try to work the stiffness out by flexing and kneading the hose, you may damage it beyond repair. In the same way, if you try to massage or deeply rub muscles which are already weakened with tension, you will aggravate the problem. It then takes more energy to recover the original elasticity and circulation, but lacking this energy the muscles become stiffer and more insensitive than ever. In other words, most forms of massage simply fight fire with fire.

If you gently warm a frozen rubber hose it gradually recovers its elasticity without damage. In the same way if you gently apply Ki to stiff muscles through thefingertips, the circulation and life-force gradually recover and the muscles naturally become soft again. Far from making the problem worse, the shoulders become surprisingly light and flexible with Kiatsu.

Another traditional approach to fixing shoulder stiffness is the insertion of acupuncture needles. These needles are designed to stimulate the *tsubo*, or acupuncture points which are supposed to fall along the meridians (*keiraku*). However, repeatedly puncturing the skin with even a small needle inevitably causes the tissues to harden at that point. This is why doctors ask you to rub the spot after you get an injection, to help work out the stiffness the tissues produce in reaction to the needle. Repeatedly puncturing the skin at the same point causes stiffness which makes it even harder for the needle to penetrate with each puncture. Presumably a skilled acupuncturist should be aware of this problem and no doubt it is partly a matter of skill, but in any case a needle is a foreign body and will occasion some resistance in the skin. The stiffness resulting from the needling of an unskilled therapist may actually reduce circulation and put pressure on nerves, to the point that rather than easing the shoulder stiffness, it actually makes it worse. By carelessly combining other theories with Kiatsu treatments, you may actually be working against yourself and end up requiring much more time and effort to solve the problem.

How then can you learn to press perpendicularly to the center of the muscle, without damaging the tissue? Have your partner place one hand spread out palm down on the floor. First press with strength on the back of your partner's hand using the tip of the thumb, then ask your partner to try to slide the hand out from underneath. It should not be very difficult to do. Next try placing your hand on the back of your partner's hand in the same way, but this time pressing with the thumb, perpendicularly to the floor, thinking of your Ki as penetrating the hand and pinning it to the floor. Though this light amount of pressure, no more than needed to take up the slack, feels insufficient to hold the hand in place, in fact your partner will find it very difficult to move the hand at all. The same result can be achieved using the other fingers of the hand.

It is important to note that pressing perpendicularly does not mean standing the thumb vertically on end. All this does is to dig your fingernail into your partner's skin, cause your elbow to come up and out, and put tension in your arm, which cuts off the flow of Ki. This you can see immediately by having your partner try to pull up on your wrist while the thumb is held vertically.

The fingertip should be applied gently to the body, with the elbow naturally down. The first knuckle gently curves out, as when you grasp a large object. If you apply too much physical pressure, then the joint curves in, as it does when you extend your thumb in an exaggerated "hitch-hiking" gesture. When you press properly the weight is underside, the wrists and arms are virtually unliftable and Ki flows freely into your partner's body. It is Ki itself, not the finger, which enters perpendicularly into the center of the muscle. This you can experiment with, using the method of pressing on the shoulders described above.

When your partner feels nothing but pain and pressure, you have probably allowed too much tension into your arms. True Kiatsu creates no feeling of being physically pressed down upon, but rather gives a comfortable sensation of being gradually penetrated by Ki. It is helpful to ask your partner for verbal feedback when you practice, so that you can be sure that you are doing Kiatsu correctly.

4. Focus Ki continuously and precisely at the fingertips.

The effectiveness of Kiatsu therapy depends in large measure on the strength and consistency of the Ki of the therapist. If the therapist maintains a good degree of concentration, the therapy is many times more effective. The best way to maintain this concentration is by performing Kiatsu in a state of mind and body coordination. We have seen how the fingers and arm work in Kiatsu according to the principles of the body (Relax Completely and Keep Weight Underside). Now we will examine the state of mind in Kiatsu therapy according to the principles of the mind (Keep One Point and Extend Ki).

When Tohei traveled to major cities of America and Europe to teach Ki principles and Aikido, he often gathered as many as two or three hundred participants at each seminar. Frequently at the end of the training, a dozen or more students would come forward to request Kiatsu treatment. Because it was difficult in a short time to clearly demonstrate the results of treatment for such conditions as chronic stomach disorders or neuroses, Tohei choose people who had conditions such as migraine headache, shoulder stiffness, whip-lash injury, bursitis of the shoulder, sciatic pain, sprained ankle, and so on. Because of the number of people, he only worked on each person for only about five minutes. Audiences were often surprised to see how just a few minutes of Kiatsu on the neck and shoulders could restore freedom of movement to a person who was visibly stiff, or completely cure a headache. People who had been unable to raise their arms were able to extend them straight overhead after receiving Kiatsu. A few people with sprained ankles were actually able to set their crutches aside and walk almost normally.

Because of his strong Ki and years of experience, Tohei's Kiatsu is many times more accurate and effective than the average person. However, this ability is in no way exclusive. Anyone who learns and practices Kiatsu correctly can learn to give effective Kiatsu. The difference may simply be that rather than fixing the problem in five minutes, it may take you an hour or two; instead of fixing it in one session, it may take several, but the process is the same. For this reason it is important that the therapist develop enough Ki and concentration to be able to send Ki effectively to another person. With correct practice, what once took an hour to fix may be fixed in thirty, twenty, or even ten minutes. The restorative power of life's energy is impressive. Ki is freely available to anyone who is willing to practice its principles. Kiatsu works because it uses Ki to call forth the patient's own inherent life energy. It awakens the healing power that is already in the patient's body and helps it to perform its natural functions.

It is well known that there is power in belief and positive thinking. If you believe that Ki is extending, it follows accordingly. The stronger the conviction, the stronger the Ki. However, this is easier said than done. Ki has no describable shape or properties and it can not be palpably felt. How then can a beginner possibly believe in something that is so elusive? It is almost impossible at first to avoid wondering whether Ki is in fact extending, or how such a mild treatment could be effective. These doubts tend to arise in anyone at first. However, the moment that you entertain these feelings, you in fact cut off the flow of Ki. By vacillating between believing and doubting that you are extending Ki, you only reduce the effectiveness of the treatment, or increase the time required to fix the problem.

What should you do to ensure that your Ki is strongly and continuously flowing? The best possible way to guarantee that your Ki is not cut is to concentrate on the infinitely small movement of Ki at the fingertips. Imagine that the tip of the thumb is a small circle, which forms a unit of one. Picture this circle growing smaller each moment by half, without stopping. Very soon the circle becomes so small that you can no longer picture it, but you know that it cannot possibly be reduced to nothing. Let it go, just as you would watch water disappear down a drain. If you do this you will find that the resulting flow of Ki is so strong that the stiff tissues actually soften and yield, revealing new stiff surfaces below, which you can feel with your fingertips. When you concentrate on Ki growing infinitely smaller by half at the fingertips, the waves of your mind as well gradually calm down and you become capable of directing the life energy through your fingertips.

Modern science and technology have progressed to the point where we not only know much about the structure of the atom, but we have also discovered its awesome power.

A small object barely bigger than a matchbox has the power to blow away, or to supply energy for an entire city. The smaller the particle the greater the power. The mind has a similar capacity. When the mind is focused and reduced to fine particular elements, it has a tremendous power.

An old Oriental proverb says that when our mind is focused, it can penetrate a stone. Unfortunately, many people associate this idea with strange religious rites, in which priests burn cedar sticks, sparks fly; their eyes bulging and staring in an effort to focus the mind toward some magic purpose. True mental power has nothing to do with such primitive or occult practices. When the mind is calm and focused, it naturally is in harmony with the universe. Such a mind has great power of influence, which is why people with strong Ki also have strong will-power.

5. Concentrate on the lines, rather than the points.

The *tsubo,* or points used in acupuncture and shiatsu, are considered to be like way stations along the meridians (*keiraku*), at which Ki can be most easily stimulated or restricted. There is some evidence that these points correspond to points of greater electrical conductivity, or to concentrated gatherings of nerves. Precise location of these hundreds of points has never been considered easy, and the ancient Chinese meridian maps are imprecise at best. Acupuncture theory recognizes 360 major points and up to two or three thousand minor points, each of which have difficult names and functions. Students of acupuncture must go to school for two to three years just to learn the names and locations of all of these points. There is no question that the human body contains nerve concentrations that are sensitive to stimulation or injury from the outside. But these pressure points are by no means always located on the meridians, or even at the same place as the acupuncture *tsubo.* Particularly when you consider how easily skin and muscles stretch, the precise location of points seems a very formidable task indeed. Perhaps there is a simpler way to go about it.

Nerve impulses travel from the brain, through the central nervous system, and are communicated through peripheral nerves to every part of the body. Likewise, nerves from every part of the body send messages back to the brain. At no point in this complex system is there a gap or unrelated part. Our bodies are an integrated network of highly coordinated systems. There are places throughout the body where nerves are concentrated or dispersed according to different functions, like the interchanges on a superhighway system, which redirect traffic on and off of major pathways. These sensitive concentrations of nerve ganglia are often used as pressure points in the martial arts. They are more tender and responsive than other parts of the body. Nevertheless, the human body is an integrated whole. It is one continuous fabric from head to toe. If you pay attention to the overall flow of energy in the body, there is no need to be concerned about the individual points. Energy will naturally pass through every one, without any need for help from us.

Moxibustion is another form of therapy which uses *tsubo.* Small cones of an incenselike herb are placed on the skin above the point, lit and allowed to burn as close as possible to the surface of the skin. The momentary but sharp burning sensation acts to stimulate the point. One disadvantage of moxibustion is that it tends to leave burn marks on the skin. Because acupuncture and moxibustion both rely on stimulating points, they place great emphasis on these interchanges. You certainly cannot needle or burn the entire surface of the body. Kiatsu concentrates on the overall flow of energy in the body, and therefore allows you to treat the body as a whole. Even if you do manage to clear the intersections, if traffic is congested along the highway between the interchanges, it will eventually back up all the way. Only by improving the circulation of energy all along the way, can you keep the flow of energy vigorous and uncongested. This is what is meant by concentrating on the flow of energy rather than the points. *Tsubo* may be important, but is it really necessary to memorize the names of each interchange in the body? To travel from one city to another, you can travel straight along one highway, without needing to get off at each intersection along the way. If you have to make a stop at each one, you may never arrive at your destination. Furthermore, even though you make an ink mark for every *tsubo* on the body, it is very difficult to come back to exactly the same spot the next time. The position of these points changes considerably with each change in position or posture. Even if you can find a point once, there is no guarantee that you can find it again.

Kiatsu also makes use of lines, but these are not based on, or in any way derived from the meridians of acupuncture. There may be some similarity, due to the fact that both refer to the same human body. The lines of Kiatsu are simple guidelines to the anatomy of the body. Most of them follow major muscle groups or run along the edges of bones. Some of them simply divide the body into convenient geometrical segments. In any event, these are not described as lines of Ki flow, like meridians, but rather as reference lines to help people understand the body structure and to lend some order to the method of pressing. Students of Kiatsu therapy are taught how to find these lines in the body and they are described in Tohei's own book on Kiatsu therapy, but ultimately they are discovered through experience. It takes very little time to learn the major highways, or lines on the body used in Kiatsu therapy. Because all parts of the body are connected, by following the major lines, you can easily discover the parts that need attention which lie off of these lines. The purpose of Kiatsu therapy is to create a strong flow of life energy in every part of the body, from head to toe.

Getting to the Source of the Problem

The human brain sends messages to all parts of the body through the nerves, and the nerves in turn give the brain feedback on the condition of the body and environment. The body is literally laced with nerves. Furthermore, every single part of a healthy body is intimately interwoven, without a single break in the system. If the nerves are cut or damaged at any point, the result is loss of sensation, control, or movement, in other words partial or complete paralysis.

When there is a problem at some point in the body, the nerves report this to the brain in the form of pain or loss of sensation. The brain responds by motivating you to have the problem checked by a doctor, or by seeking some form of treatment, rest, or rehabilitative action. Without the problem being reported by the nerves, it would go unnoticed and could become irreversible with neglect.

One of the reasons that cancer is so feared is that it so easily goes undetected. By the time the symptoms become obvious or painful, the disease is already in an advanced state and may even be terminal. No one enjoys pain or loss of function, but perhaps by understanding that these are early warnings of potentially serious problems, we should be grateful for them when they come to our attention.

A common way in which modern medicine treats pain from such problems as neuralgia and soreness from whiplash injury is to give pain killing injections. These medicines merely remove the symptoms by temporarily deadening the nerves, and do nothing to fix that which is causing the pain. As soon as the medicine wears off the pain returns, in a vicious cycle. Our life energy can become weak at a certain place due to fatigue or injury. When this happens, it is often the case that the person's own life energy does not have sufficient momentum to overcome the problem without outside help, and the problem may persist for a long time. It is then when we can apply Ki to the injured area, like priming the pump of a well, and stimulate the patient's own life energy, which helps bring about a rapid recovery. Once the problem is fixed, there is no need for the nerves to report it to the brain any longer, so the pain naturally disappears and normal sensation returns to the area.

Oriental medicine is enjoying a surge of popularity today. However, its approach to pain is quite different from that of Kiatsu. In Oriental medicine, if you have a problem with your stomach, the area selected for treatment is more likely to be remote from the problem, using selected points on the bottom of the foot, or on the ear. While it is undeniably true that all parts of the body are connected, it is also true that the theory of Oriental medicine is based on an outmoded and questionable picture of the body. The notion of *tsubo* derives from this antiquated idea, so it hardly makes sense to base a method of therapy entirely upon it. Tohei often says in his Kiatsu classes, that if there is a traffic problem in downtown Tokyo, it makes no sense to try to clear the streets in a small town in southern Japan, even if it is true that all of the roads are connected.

To ignore the important message of pain or numbness coming from a distressed area, and try to treat it by stimulating a part of the body which is only remotely connected is not only a waste of valuable time, but potentially risky. Though some people claim to have been helped by such methods, we must remember that pain is often subject to suggestion or subjective interpretation. Actual cures by these methods are probably very few in number; which is not to say that they do not exist. Tohei tells his Kiatsu patients that they should rely on the diagnosis and advice of legitimate medical doctors, but do their best to combat the problem with Kiatsu before each medical test, and even before and after surgery if it is required. A number of people have thus avoided the need for surgery that was at first prescribed, the doctor's tests having indicated that it was no longer necessary. Others have been able to leave the hospital far sooner than the doctor predicted. In any case, it is a great tragedy to allow a disease to go unchecked and untreated, on the thin assurances of a healer.

Because the mind controls the body, it is possible that believing you have been cured can somewhat stimulate the life-force and make you feel a little better. However, if this was all that there was to it, then we would need no doctors, only faith healers. Yet despite the fantastic claims of many religious healers, there have been no scientifically documented cases of cures by these methods.

Ideally, it would be best to send Ki to the whole body by giving Kiatsu to every part. But as a practical matter, there simply is not time in anyone's schedule for that. Given the restrictions imposed by a normal schedule, we must make the most of the little time available, by concentrating our Kiatsu first on the part that needs it most. Whenever a part of the body has a problem, it is nearly always accompanied by some degree of pain and stiffness. If a person has stomach problems, you can give Kiatsu directly to the stomach, and to the nerves which help regulate its activity. By reviving the nerves and improving the circulation to the stomach, you can help awaken the inherent life energy which itself will heal the problem. Kiatsu merely sends reinforcements to the life energy, and helps it perform its natural function. With a little training, anyone can learn to find the stiff and tender areas in the body which need attention.

Depression

The incidence of neuroses and depression among people from youth to middle age has increased so rapidly that it has become a serious social problem. If measures are not now taken to deal with it, the problem could grow to serious and unmanageable proportions. It is a chilling prospect to speculate whether such people will be able to deal with the waves of change that the twenty-first century will bring, or whether they will be able to meet the national and international responsibilities that will face them. However, before we react to a problem, we must try to understand its causes.

First, particularly in countries which thrive on competition, parents push their children to get into the right schools. If the child's school marks are acceptable, the parents often consider their work done. But in all too many cases, important aspects of mental, emotional, and physical development have been seriously neglected for the sake of academic performance.

Secondly, many children who were born into affluent societies have grown up in pampered and easy circumstances. Never having experienced a day of hardship, they are accustomed to doing what they want, without regard to the needs of others. This has ill prepared them for facing up to responsibility or adversity.

Young people are often accused of lacking initiative, which in Japanese is called *yaru ki*. This word implies that Ki is something you give out, not receive. Ki should be extended out to people and things, not held within. As long as people are preoccupied with themselves and expect others to take care of them, it will be impossible to extend Ki. Stagnant water grows stale. Likewise, if Ki does not circulate, it goes bad. To be alive and healthy is to have the Ki of the universe circulate freely in the body. This is a result of always extending Ki out, so that fresh Ki may enter at any time. If mental and physical education are supported by a strong program of Ki training as well, there is no need whatsoever for people to suffer from neuroses or nervous disorders.

By always holding Ki inside, the mind and body grow so weak that the nerves become exhausted and break down in the face of even small difficulties. In the desperate period at the end of World War II, a majority of the Japanese people were not even certain of their next meal. Neurosis was a luxury that no one could afford. Anyone who allowed themselves to become preoccupied with their mental condition did not survive for long. Neurosis is often the luxury of those who face no serious problems, a by-product of weak nerves.

Medicine has typically thought of the body as a complex machine and tended to treat it in purely physical terms. But recent scientific research has demonstrated the powerful influence of the mind on the body. More and more physicians have come to recognize the essential unity of mind and body; and while they are a little late in making this discovery, it is a very healthy trend.

However, the mind operates by somewhat different principles than the body. Having reached an impasse in dealing with the body in purely physical terms, it is no solution to go to the other extreme and approach it from a purely mental point of view. Psychologists use hypnosis to dig deep into the patient's subconscious mind and uncover long forgotten troubles which may be contributing to the person's current ailments. There is no doubt that some problems in the past may contribute to disease in the present, but these are only a part of the problem, not the primary cause. More likely the problem resides in the person's incorrect use of mind and body. Nor is the environment the whole problem. An environment which causes one person to become ill may leave another unaffected.

Furthermore, even if one can discover the original cause of the disease, this is no guarantee of fixing the problem. For example, a person may realize that stress arising from unfair treatment by his boss has made him physically ill, but this awareness by itself will not easily rid him of that problem. Even a change in jobs is no real solution, because more conflicts may arise with people in the new work environment. The problem cannot be solved by trying to control the environment. Rather it is your self which you must learn to control. Learning to control and strengthen the self is the real basis for treating mind and body as a whole.

There are many things in the world which on the surface are quite similar, but in fact are totally different. For example, many people assume that they are relaxed, when in fact they are only slack and listless. Real relaxation is a state in which mind and body are unified, free of useless tension or anxiety, and strong enough to be able to let things take their course. True relaxation is based on the original unity of mind and body, as described in the four principles of mind and body coordination.

The condition that many consider to be relaxed is really no more than a weak and impotent state, in which the life-force is greatly depleted. If you pursue this counterfeit state of relaxation in the interests of health, you will end up with the opposite of what you seek. A person who wants to go north will not get any closer to the destination by going south, no matter how much effort he makes. Some people teach that you can recover health through limp relaxation. But far from regaining health, the more that you practice this wrong approach, the more you will aggravate your health problems.

Biofeedback instructors teach that when the mind is calm and relaxed, the brain produces alpha waves, which disappear the moment that the mind becomes agitated or upset. These waves can be measured by an electronic biofeedback device, which plays music when alpha waves are present, and shuts the music off when the alpha waves disappear. The purpose of the machine is to teach you how to always maintain the mental state which produces alpha waves.

However, there is one important complication. A great number of these devices seem unable to distinguish between the true relaxation of mind and body coordination, and the limp and listless state induced by the incorrect approach to relaxation. Both produce the same music. When asked how to account for this discrepancy, instructors replied that there are good alpha waves and there are bad alpha waves, and that one should strive to produce good alpha waves! If the patient could make this distinction, there would never have been a problem with neurosis in the first place. The real problem is that the instructors themselves cannot tell the difference.

As long as a person lives, the brain is engaged in constant activity. Every movement and thought is accompanied by brain waves. If you attempt to extinguish all thought, as some people attempt to do in Zen meditation, you will become neurotic, because it is impossible to totally silence the living brain. No matter how much you divide the number one by half, it will never be reduced to zero. Nothing comes from nothing, and as long as something is present, it can never be reduced to nothing.

What good is a state of mind which looks but does not see, and which hears but does not listen? It is not possible to reduce thought to nothing, but the waves of the mind can be made infinitely small and calm. This is what is actually meant by the Zen term, *munen musô*, or "free of thought, free of vain imaginings." The alpha waves which appear in this state must be what they call good alpha waves. However, as the biofeedback device fails to distinguish between these alpha waves and those which appear when the mind is vague and distracted, it cannot be of much help. If classical music played when the person coordinated mind and body and ugly discordant sounds came out when the person was absentminded, then the device would be somewhat useful. But at present there is no such device.

When it rains hard, you turn on the windshield wipers in your car. The movement of the wiper blades back and forth across the windshield does not interfere with your ability to see while driving, no matter how long you leave them on. If you were to become distracted and focus only on the wiper blades, you would be unable to see anything in the road ahead. Yet this is virtually what people do who suffer from neuroses.

The brain is constantly active, always engaged in thought. If you extend Ki out to the world around you, this activity of the brain goes largely unnoticed. However, if you become concerned about each and every movement of the mind, you will become unable to extend your Ki to the outside. A person who becomes wrapped up in himself in this way loses touch with the outside world, and even small and unimportant things become matters of grave concern and worry. The nerves respond to things way out of proportion. If the nerves accurately report a stimulus to the brain as it is, they remain healthy and normal. But if things are magnified a hundred, or even a thousand times out of proportion, the brain soon becomes overwhelmed. Such a person finds it difficult to go out of the house, or even get out of bed, and may only want to curl up in a closet and hide. Trapped in a whirlpool of his own making, the person may become incapable of helping himself. Even though an outsider may perceive an easy solution to his problems, taking this advice is no easy matter for the person who is suffering from the problem. The foundations of the world itself may seem to have been shaken loose, with no prospect of escape. How do you help a person in this depressed state?

You must approach such a patient from the angles of both mind and body and make efforts to help him change his entire attitude and approach to life. Begin with the mind, by showing him how he is essentially involved in a futile effort to look at the windshield wipers and forgetting to keep his eyes on the road ahead. If you can change the person's habits of speech, you can help him learn to extend Ki. Show him how to do the unbendable arm, and how strong the body becomes when Ki is extended forward. Help him to understand mind and body coordination as a direct physical experience. Then ask him whether or not he really wants to overcome his problems. Some people actually prefer being neurotic and refuse to make efforts to change. It is impossible to help such a person, as long as they insist on this attitude. If the person does want to get better, you should encourage him to practice extending Ki and show him how. It is important to arouse in the other person the will-power and desire to overcome the disease and return to a normal life.

Next, approach the problem from the physical side. People who suffer from a neurotic condition nearly always have a stiff neck, shoulders and back muscles, due to the constant strain of useless worry and stress. First help soften the stiff muscles and improve circulation to these areas with Kiatsu. Anxiety often reduces the appetite and excess nervous strain weakens the heart. Give Kiatsu to the organs to help free the person of the symptoms of stress. Improved circulation to the whole body helps deliver fresh blood to the brain, and helps the patient feel relaxed and clearheaded. This in itself may be enough to give the patient hope of his own recovery.

After that, what is important is daily practice of Ki breathing, which can only be practiced when mind and body are coordinated and which helps Ki circulates freely. If practiced daily, it ensures that you always have a fresh supply of strong Ki, which leaves no room for neuroses or depression to enter. This is the powerful method by which a person can get out of the vicious circle of self-pity, start each day with a clean slate, and quickly return to a normal and healthy life.

Stress

There are many people in the world who, while not yet neurotic, are quickly headed for that condition because they are continually under stress. After Tohei gave a lecture on how to overcome neuroses, one of the participants confided in him that he was somewhat neurotic and felt that Ki training might help him. At first glance, the man appeared perfectly normal, even healthy. But looking closely, his eyes did appear somewhat unsettled. Tohei realized that in a case like this you can see the problem very clearly if you mentally divide the face into upper and lower halves at the nose. Though the eyes may smile, the mouth appears to frown; though the person may wear a smile, the eyes seem close to tears. When there is an imbalance in the upper and lower parts of the face, this is a sign of trouble within.

The man went on to explain that he was a manager at the Bank of Japan and had graduated from one of the top Japanese universities. He was full of ambition when he first joined the bank, but gradually things had changed for him. If he had joined a small company, he would have stood out with such outstanding credentials, but nearly everyone at his bank had graduated from elite schools, and to make matters worse, each year's crop of newly hired employees all came from the top schools. Against this background, he merely faded into the wall. If he did not like something about his job, he was free to leave at any time, as there were any number of qualified people waiting to fill the position. He was literally surrounded by highly educated and extremely competitive co-workers. This predicament put him under considerable stress.

He could not consult the company physician, for fear of the rumors that might spread and damage his chances for promotion. He tried consulting with his wife about it, but she only scolded him more for slacking off when he had gotten such a good start in his career. In time, he found that he could not relax at work or at home. The effort to keep going had exhausted his nerves, and he finally came for consultation to the Ki Society.

After practicing Ki training for about a month, he became himself again. One day, before going home, he left a small booklet on Tohei's desk. It was written by the medical staff which worked with the Bank of Japan, and a copy had been distributed to all employees. The booklet covered various topics, but one of its main points was that neuroses were becoming more and more common among some of the very employees who were on their way to shouldering key responsibilities in the company. Among these were some of the most talented and most hopeful prospects for management. The medical staff's recommendation was that these people be given fewer responsibilities and allowed more free time to enjoy hobbies like golf and tennis, or even to just do nothing.

This is poor advice to a drowning man clutching at straws. For a person who is already worried about keeping up with the competition, to go on holiday or start taking it easy can only aggravate the nagging anxiety that one is going to be left behind. Far from preventing neurosis, this kind of approach can only plunge the person headlong into it. Any employee who is totally unconcerned about shouldering responsibility is hardly likely to make a contribution to the company. Lazy employees seldom become neurotic from overwork in the first place.

Although this may be an extreme case, there are countless people who overwork their nerves by fretting and worrying about things that need not concern them at all. By making an issue out of unimportant things, they accumulate dangerous levels of stress. In this condition, you are only a step away from a nervous breakdown.

When we coordinate mind and body the universe gives us the full use of our faculties, and allows us to develop our original potential. Human beings alone have the capacity to develop this ability freely, beyond that which we are born with. Tohei hopes that through Ki development, people in many countries can realize and use this ability to improve their lives. Once you coordinate mind and body and do your best, you may leave the rest to the universe. You can do no more. Anyone who does this will be free from the effects of stress and neurosis and able to live life to the fullest. A Japanese scientist named Shigeo Nozawa has done research on cultivating tomatoes under ideal conditions growing them in water, not soil. By this Hydroponica method, he was able to get one tomato plant to produce 13,800 tomatoes. Similarly, if we can remove the negative influences which hold us back, and renew ourselves constantly with Ki, then we will surely perform beyond our imagined limits.

People who try to learn Kiatsu from a book, or even just dabble in it without proper training may be disappointed to find that it does not do for them what it claims. Tohei teaches it in simple terms, as if all we need to do was to touch the patient and think that Ki is flowing in; but people forget that behind these words are many decades of hard training. Tohei was frequently asked by people in the bars and restaurants which he frequented to give Kiatsu treatments. On some occasions, people would actually line up from the kitchen, during their work and his dinner time, just for the privilege of experiencing Tohei's Kiatsu. He sometimes asked women working in the bars in Japan if their shoulders were stiff. They would ask in surprise, how he could have known. He replied that it was easy to guess, because nearly everyone had stiff shoulders.

Kiatsu feels best when it is needed most. Just as food tastes very good when you are hungry, Kiatsu feels very good when your Ki is weak. However when you are full of Ki, you may not particularly want or need Kiatsu, nor might you feel a major difference on getting it. In this case, you should be busy giving it to someone who does need it.

Kiatsu Therapy has several important points to recommend it.

1. It is comfortable and pleasant.
2. It has no negative side effects.
3. The emphasis is on achieving maximum results within a minimum number of treatments.
4. You learn the essential elements of mind and body unification.
5. You are taught how to prevent a recurrence of the problem through Ki breathing and Ki exercise.

These five advantages of Kiatsu therapy should be qualified however; for they only apply to Kiatsu which is performed correctly, according to the principles of mind and body unification. A person without formal training or skill in Kiatsu is not likely to get anywhere near the same results as one who is properly qualified as a Kiatsu therapist.

Tohei says that in some ways, you can learn Ki faster through Kiatsu than through Aikido, simply because you cannot fake the results in Kiatsu. A patient who is not healed may tell you he feels a little better out of politeness, but he will not come back. However, in Aikido, partners who become accustomed to each other often forget to really attack, and end up practicing as a form of mutual cooperation. In addition, the Aikido martial techniques cannot be applied in daily life, not because they do not work, but precisely because they are so effective. They must be used with maximum restraint, only when strictly necessary. Kiastu however, has no such restriction. No one will complain about gaining more health or vitality. Actually, mind and body coordination can be applied to anything in daily life. It is a great shame to limit it only to Aikido techniques.

Twenty Case Studies in Kiatsu Therapy

In April of 1982, Tohei opened the first course of a two-year Kiatsu Therapist School at the Ki Society Headquarters in Tokyo. In 1986 he opened a second branch of the school in Osaka, and in the same year a branch overseas in Amsterdam. Each year since he has sent graduates to many parts of Japan and overseas, to help people who suffer from physical or mental problems. Because the majority of Kiatsu therapists are still in Japan and because most of the documented clinical work has been done there, the following case studies are all about Japanese people. Still, they may serve as a useful reference for the kinds of things for which Kiatsu can be effective.

1. Eyes—Masayuki Shôda (eighty yeears old)
Diagnosed as having a mild case of cataracts. He was only able to see things in vague outline. This was compounded by severe back pain, and such bent posture that he could barely keep from falling forward. His cataracts cleared up completely after ten sessions of Kiatsu, and he now maintains himself in good health through Ki breathing and Ki exercises. Mr. Shôda continues to come for Kiatsu twice a month to keep fit.

2. Neck—Miyoko Murata (fifty-seven years old)
Employed as a hairdresser, she suffered from chronic stiffness in the neck and shoulders, and severe pain, particularly in the right elbow. Her job required that she work with her hands held up most of the time and she had reached the point where she had difficulty raising and lowering her arm. She came for Kiatsu treatment once a week, and by the third session was virtually cured of the problem. Now she comes for Kiatsu whenever she feels fatigue from overwork.

3. Throat—Noriko Kawano (fifty-eight years old)
Having lost her voice due to a cold, she came for Kiatsu in desperation, because she had to give a *Noh* theatrical performance only a week later. Her voice returned to normal after only a single Kiatsu treatment. Furthermore, for the previous six years she had suffered from chronic shingles rashes, and had extremely stiff shoulders and neck on the right side

of her body. She was extremely prone to catching colds, but after a period of Kiatsu treatment, each of these problems cleared up completely.

4. Spine—Sanae Shigeta (fifty-five years old)

Diagnosed as having spinal problems, she suffered from a number of other problems at the same time, including the onset of menopause, back and hip pain, chills and numbness in the legs. To stimulate her life-force, she received Kiatsu on her body and was taught how to do Ki breathing and Ki exercise on a daily basis. After three months her face color and attitude improved, and she was virtually free of most of the pains that had troubled her.

5. Chest—Shinji Nakajima (fifty-eight years old)

Though employed as a dance instructor, he had an irregular pulse, a weak gastrointestinal system, and suffered from chronic diarrhea. His face was an ashen gray color and he was concerned that he might have a terminal illness. He came for Kiatsu treatment and began doing Ki breathing and Ki exercise everyday. By the third treatment, his pulse had become regular and his diarrhea had stopped. Most dance instructors end up having to retire in their thirties, but though he is now near sixty, Mr. Nakajima continues to remain active in teaching and looks many years younger than he is.

6. Hip—Yuriko Tsukamoto (fifty-four years old)

Having injured her left hip joint, she became concerned about an increasing numbness in the area. She came for Kiatsu treatment just four days before she was to have a hip operation. She felt sharp pain even only slightly bending the hip. They began by giving Kiatsu very lightly, only sending Ki without pressing. Gradually they were able to apply pressure. After the first treatment the pain disappeared and she was able to walk home normally, surprising not only the patient, but everyone around her. She came in for Kiatsu everyday before the operation was scheduled, and on that day had the doctor check the hip again. She was told that there no longer seemed to be any need to give the operation right away, and that they should wait about three months, and have a second look. She still comes all the way to Tokyo from her hometown in Nagano once a month for Kiatsu, and twice a year for a medical checkup at the hospital. But every time that she goes, she is told that there is still no need to have an operation.

7. Abdomen—Masako Yoshino (thirty-four years old)

For ten years she had been on special medication for chronic constipation. Without this medicine, she was unable to have a bowel movement, even after a week's time. The side effects of the medication were such that she had stiff shoulders, menstrual irregularity, chills, and a face color that was so ashen that she almost forgotten how to laugh. She began daily practice of Ki breathing and Ki exercise, along with Kiatsu, in an effort to revive her own life energy. Although she had not been able to perspire for a long time, after three months of Kiatsu, she began perspiring again and her whole expression brightened. Although her illness was quite difficult, after six months she was able to entirely quit taking medicine and resumed normal bowel movements. This helped restore her overall health in other ways as well.

8. Hands—*Masayoshi Inoue (fifty-one years old)*

Mr. Inoue came to get Kiatsu for an elbow injury which he had sustained while playing golf. However, as president of a company, he was also under considerable stress, which had resulted in a stiff neck, shoulders, abdomen, and an extremely strained facial expression. The elbow pain disappeared after one treatment, but he continued to come in twice a month for Kiatsu to help with his overall tension. His face is much healthier now and he still comes for treatment whenever he is tired from overwork.

9. Knees—*Kimiko Gotô (seventy-eight years old)*

She was diagnosed as having a deformity in the knee. For twenty years she had endured pain in the knees, particularly in the right knee. This was accompanied by swelling around the kneecap and she was virtually unable to bend the one knee. Her legs were as stiff as wooden poles, and she had been unable to find anyone that could help her. After coming for Kiatsu for once a week for a period of time, the pain in her knees was no longer a problem. After a number of sessions, she was able to bend her knees about halfway. She still comes for treatment on a regular basis, but she no longer has pain or difficulty in daily life.

10. Legs—*Kumiko Tsuboi (thirty-seven years old)*

While working as a theatrical director, she injured her calf during an aerobics practice session. Though she experienced sharp pain at the time, she continued to walk on the leg for a week, until the pain and swelling were so great that she could no longer walk without crutches. The diagnosis revealed that she had torn the muscle in six places. She came in by taxi for Kiatsu everyday for a week. At first, the leg was so sensitive to pressure, that it was impossible to even touch the skin without causing severe pain. They gave Kiatsu at first without touching, by holding the hand near and sending Ki. After thirty minutes of this, they were able to place a hand on the injured area without causing pain, and from there began giving Kiatsu. After three treatments, the swelling disappeared. She was able to walk on the leg by the end of the first week. After that, she continued to come in for Kiatsu every other day for two weeks, by the end of which she was able to walk normally. She was so impressed with the effectiveness of the Kiatsu treatment, that she entered the Kiatsu school the next year.

11. Head—*Yasushi Hamaguchi (one year old)*

This infant was epileptic and suffered from rigid muscles and joints. He was born prematurely and began suffering from epileptic fits at the age of six months. The seizures were kept under control by medicine received at the hospital, but it left his body so limp and listless that he could not hold his head up by himself, and slept most of the time. A friend told his parents about Kiatsu therapy and they brought him in for treatment. After only a single treatment, the stiffness in the neck was gone and he was able to sit up without support by himself. By the second treatment, his face began to show expression, and his smile both delighted and surprised his mother and grandmother. After that they continued to bring him in once a week for Kiatsu, took him off of the tranquilizers, and no longer needed to go to the hospital. Other children in the hospital who had the same problem had shown no improvement and were still listless and bedridden. After six months Yasushi learned to walk while holding on to his mother's finger and continues to grow normally. His grandmother entered the Kiatsu school the following year.

12. Ears—Yoshi Izumi (eighty years old)

Mr. Izumi suffered from ringing in the ears and pain in both knees. Whatever hospital he had tried, he was always told the same thing: that it was an inevitable consequence of old age and that nothing could be done about it. His knee pain went away after only a single treatment. From the second session, the ringing in his ears began to fade and went away entirely by the fifth session. His family was very surprised that he was able to recover his health so easily.

13. Throat—Hiroki Nishijima (four years old)

Hiroki was diagnosed by the pediatrician as having asthma. His parents had started taking him to the hospital at the age of one, and he had been in and out of it three times by the age of three. The hospital's treatments appeared to have little effect. However, his symptoms eased every time he came for Kiatsu and the problem was entirely cured by the seventh treatment so easily.

14. Shoulders—Kazuichi Kodera (sixty-seven years old)

Many people in middle age suffer from chronically stiff shoulders. At first, Mr. Kodera thought that his shoulder stiffness would go away on its own, but the problem grew so severe, that he sought help from acupuncture, moxibustion, shiatsu, and even received injections at the hospital, which were designed to ease the pain. After retiring from his job, he had spent nearly five years at home, seeking help in various treatment methods, but nothing seemed to work. After the first Kiatsu treatment, he regained movement in his arm, which helped strengthen his grip. Chronic shoulder stiffness is not due so much to a specific injury, as to long-term accumulation of fatigue. It is brought on by maintaining the body in the same incorrect posture for long periods of time and is often accompanied by a dull pain and loss of flexibility. This pain was completely gone after only five treatments, and his shoulders were back to normal in three months of treatment once a week.

15. Heart—Takahiro Tokunaga (fourty-three years old)

He was diagnosed as having heart arrhythmia. The hospital had him taking over fifty pills a day and the side effects had given him severe stomach problems. His entire body was out of balance and the effect of the medicine so temporary, that he was continuously taking the pills. His irregular pulse returned to normal after only two treatments. His condition improved so much with regular Kiatsu treatments, that he gradually reduced his intake of the medicine and was off of it entirely in only three months. With Ki breathing and Ki exercise, he completely recovered from his problem. He is employed as the president of a company, which has him traveling all over the country, but he still comes in for an overhaul of Kiatsu once a month.

16. Gallstones—Setsuko Okajima (fifty-four years old)

After experiencing sharp abdominal pain, she was diagnosed as having gallstones. The pain had subsided somewhat, but she did not want to have an operation, so came to get Kiatsu therapy. This took the pain away entirely, and after just four treatments, she passed the gallstone in her urine, after which the problem was entirely cured.

17. Hips—Yoshiko Mori (fifty years old)

She suffered from both hip pain and chills in the legs. For the last three years, the hip pain had caused her difficulty in walking. Her legs were so numb, that she did not even feel pain when she accidentally cut herself with a knife and drew blood. However, she did feel pain on the back of her legs. In the first Kiatsu treatment they worked on her shoulders and abdomen, which became much softer. By the second treatment, she found that sensation was beginning to return to her legs. During the third treatment, she became able to stretch open her legs at a 120 degree angle, though before that 60 degrees was all that she could manage. With Kiatsu above the major artery in the groin, circulation to her legs so improved that they became warm to the touch. The pain in both the legs and hips had disappeared by this time. She maintained her health after that by daily practice of Ki breathing and Ki exercise.

18. Legs—Yoshio Inagaki (seventy-seven years old)
After a prostate operation, Mr. Inagaki experienced great difficulty in walking. His legs had become extremely weak and he suffered from severe constipation. He was also incontinent at night. The doctors told him that he was hydrocephalic, and that his condition would not improve. They began with Kiatsu to the head, abdomen, and legs, to stimulate his life-force overall. His legs began to warm up after the second session. At first, someone had to bring him by car, but in time walking became so easy that he came by himself, by train. He was greatly encouraged by his recovery and is spending much of his retirement traveling all over Japan.

19. Partial Paralysis—Mitsunari Fukuda (thirty-seven years old)
Having fallen out of a tree and injured his head as a child, Mr. Fukuda had since been partially paralyzed. He had virtually no sensation in his right arm and leg, and would not have felt pain even if they were burning. He was so helped by Kiatsu that he has been able to earn a living teaching Ikebana (flower arranging) and even joined the Kiatsu school. During his Kiatsu training, sensation gradually returned to his right arm and leg. Before graduation he regained full sensation on the right side of his body, and is now dedicating himself to helping others through Kiatsu.

20. Rheumatism—Kazue Shimizu (fifty-one years old)
Diagnosed as having rheumatism over her whole body, she was stiff and sore in her shoulders, arms and legs, and abdomen. She had virtually no strength in her grip, so that objects would literally slip out of her hands, and she could not even wash dishes. She came in for Kiatsu once a week, and after a month her shoulders were soft and pliant. Within six months her abdominal pain had gone and her grip was normal once again. After a year she had virtually returned to a normal life, and continues to practice Ki breathing and Ki exercise daily with enthusiasm. Three years later she felt that she had completely recovered.

Chapter 9: Daily Disciplines for Ki Development

Ki Training Methods for Daily Life

Even experienced students of Ki principles are often surprised to find how easily Tohei seems to be able to move them with his Ki tests. Most walk away with the impression that Tohei, or any of his advanced instructors, can move them anytime they want to, even though they seem to be using no more force in the test than would be required to brush aside a curtain. Tohei explains that by concentrating your mind at the One Point you become very stable, but that does not mean that a hole cannot be opened in your concentration. When he sends strong Ki, it always finds the hole, like wind blowing through thick foliage. Considering the difference in his years and intensity of training, it is not surprising that he can move a person at will. Ki training is without limit, a process of continual refinement, so you should never think you have arrived or graduated from it.

Though not strictly speaking a Ki test, Tohei often teaches his students how to suddenly throw a person to the ground, using no more physical force than a light hand on the shoulder or light tug on the sleeve. This is one of the more difficult things which he teaches, but he claims that it is the essence of Aikido. If you try to force the person down, you naturally meet resistance. Most beginners have trouble throwing their partner because they doubt that the technique would work, and try to use force in spite of themselves. Or they give up as soon as they feel they have collided with their partner's body. The secret is to maintain mind and body unification, and to drop the hand naturally without forcing. If you meet resistance, do not add to it, just keep going. When done correctly, even a small person can drop a much larger man to the ground, no matter how hard he resists, or how much he keeps One Point. If you move the mind, the body has no choice but to follow. It is impossible to gain the knack for this from a book, but knowing that it can be done may remind you of the depth possible in Ki training.

In anything that we learn, we like to measure our progress. Aikido has a clear system of ranks with specific testing criteria, as does Ki training. With Kiatsu, you know how well you are doing by whether or not your patient feels and gets better after treatment. For Ki in daily life there is always the measure of success and failure, and of whether or not you lead a positive life. But after you have learned the basic theory and techniques of Ki training, is there any way to increase the depth and power of mind and body unification? Can you be sure that it will serve you well in a crisis? And what can a person do to practice Ki training if he has limited or even no access to a dôjô or training center? These and other questions concerned Tohei deeply in his desire to make Ki training widely available to people around the world. If it were only for martial arts students, then it would be of little value to society. If it were not possible to practice Ki training in daily life, then it would only benefit those who were able to attend classes regularly. To make Ki training more relevant to daily life, and to enable a much broader spectrum of people to practice it, Tohei developed the third major branch of the Ki Society after Aikido and Kiatsu: the Jissenkai, or Group Study for the Practical Application of Ki. Anyone can start a Jissenkai, even with a single person, as long as you understand the purpose and methods of the special *gyô*, or training which he developed for it. These methods will be described in this chapter, along with the goals and benefits of practice.

The word *gyô* (practice) is an abbreviated way of saying the word *shu-gyô* (training), which is written with two characters that reveal a layer of meaning that does not come out in the English words "practice" or "training." The character for *shu* in Japanese is also pronounced *osameru*, which according to the dictionary means, (1) to make knowledge or skill one's own, and (2) to think and act correctly. The word *gyô* is also pronounced *okonau*, which is defined as to do or to put into practice, which is not the same thing as pretending or rehearsing. The word *shugyô* then, implies far more than simply training or practice, but rather the living performance or application of principles.

Sadly, our educational system neither rewards nor encourages such behavior. Because we are more often tested on theoretical knowledge than performance ability, when we learn something new we tend to stop as soon as we achieve a superficial intellectual grasp of it. This may be useful in helping you make a decision to commit yourself to something, but ultimately real knowledge consists of action. As Tohei is fond of saying, "I understand means I can do."

The *gyô* are special forms of Ki training, which Tohei developed from his own experience and training. Some of them derive from methods which were once considered secret. They were not taught publicly, because though very effective they could be dangerous if done incorrectly, that is without mind and body coordination. Tohei has modified some of the methods which he himself practiced as a young man, partly to make them safer, and partly to correct errors which he discovered in the traditions.

Most religions have sects or followers somewhere in their history who practiced asectic rites, or deliberate hardships designed to deny or abuse the body for the sake of spiritual elevation. Among these include fasting, celibacy, the wearing of hair shirts, and total disregard for physical or creature comforts. Even the Buddha practiced such things before his enlightenment, only eventually to deny them. Abusing the body for the sake of the spirit is already a sign of mind and body separation. You cannot achieve right results with wrong methods.

On the other hand, many people who have never experienced Ki training consider it to be just another form of ascetic punishment: getting up early, dousing the body with cold water, getting thrown to the mat, sitting for long periods in *seiza*, learning complicated Aikido arts, or training in cold weather. However the people actually doing these things have mind and body unified, so they are not bothered by them in the least. To the contrary, they enjoy their training, as is evident from their laughter and self-composed manner.

In what way does Ki training differ from ascetic austerities? For one, the purpose and the result of training is opposite. Ki training is designed to unify the mind and body, and help people to apply Ki in daily life. Practices which abuse the body in order to free the spirit attempt to separate the mind and body, and escape from daily life.

Hardship training was very common in the nineteenth and early twentieth centuries, but does not fit the mood of modern life. Today people seem instead to worship the body, and attempt to beautify and strengthen it by physical means. What people forget however, is that having a sound and healthy body is no guarantee of having a good character or fine spirit. Many cities have an abundance of sports facilities and sports enjoy great popularity, but this has not noticeably improved the attitudes or character of modern youth. Training the body and mind together is one thing, but physical training alone is no guarantee of health or good character, as evidenced by incidents of crime and drug abuse among professional sports players.

The purpose of *gyô* is to thoroughly unify the mind and body by changing the subconscious mind. This involves going beyond theory into action. Many people quote wise sayings or read books containing useful advice. But how many can put this knowledge into practice? Theory is useless without practice. To say you understand something implies that you are able to do it. Even advanced students sometimes tire of practice, because they think it is too basic, or they remember having seen or done it before. Ironically, many of the people who complain in this way are unable to perform the basics well enough to say that they already understand them. You will never be harmed by repeating something which is correct, no matter how basic. Ki principles cannot be exhausted. If you get bored with practice, it is a sign that you have stopped learning.

Others find it hard to practice Ki training because they assume that they cannot change themselves. If a person has a chronic illness or health problem that they have carried around with them for years, it is hard to convince them that they can overcome it. Tohei himself was very weak and frail as a child, but was able to completely change his body by changing his mental attitude and doing something to strengthen himself. He says that changing a weak body to a strong one is not so difficult. If you realize that everything is subject to constant renewal, then it is not unlike changing into a new set of clothes. People who wash the outside of their body often forget to wash the inside through Ki breathing. Still fewer people know the importance of renewing the mind. Although mind and body are essentially one, the mind is central. The mind controls the body, not the other way around. The body only controls the mind if you give up the initiative to your environment.

A person who has truly internalized Ki principles will act with grace, poise, and rhythm, even in simple daily motions. Many people have either lost, or never quite gained a sense for this, yet somehow long to have it. This explains the endless popularity of music, dance, theater, and even fashion; for these things provide a faint reflection of this state of grace. This does not mean that all artists and musicians understand Ki. Many of them are unable to sustain it in their own specialty, much less in daily life, because they try too hard to achieve what should come naturally. Some artists have a natural sense for Ki, but no idea of how to control it or teach it to others.

Tohei's Ability to Remain Calm in Extreme Danger

When Tohei's unit was under fire during the war, there were few places to hide. The foremost concern on anyone's mind was saving his own skin. When the danger passed, Tohei was always the first to come out of hiding. Few of his men noticed that he too had taken cover under fire. They assumed that he had stayed out in the open the whole time. Such was his reputation for courage in the face of danger.

Tohei started out in charge of a unit of fifty men. Later he received an additional thirty men from another unit which had been decimated and had lost its commanding officer. Tohei felt secure that as long as he maintained a calm mind and strong Ki, the universe would protect him. Though he had eighty men in his charge, he brought every last one of them safely back to Japan, something which was almost unheard of in an army which encouraged taking suicidal risks. Many considered him to be fearless. But rather than try to train himself to become strong against an unseen and unpredictable foe, he simply trained himself to become one with the universe by following its principles.

On one occasion, under heavy enemy fire he ducked suddenly, as if by reflex. When he looked up, he found a bullet buried deep in the tree behind his head. Another time a bullet actually penetrated the double shell of his helmet, spun around and out of the other side without grazing his head. A miracle, perhaps, but no one can count on or predict miracles. When he was in danger he always extended strong Ki, and somehow it saved his life. He took reasonable precautions, but walked without fear, for he trusted that the universe would take care of him. Often he was not fully aware of the danger that he was in until it had passed. Never did he consciously duck or try to deflect a bullet, which would have been impossible anyway. Call it luck, but on more than one occasion he made the right decision to take or not take a certain road, only to find that other units which went in later were ambushed or massacred to a man.

When they were pinned under enemy fire, he sometimes fell asleep in the foxhole. He reasoned that bullets traveled straight, and would not be able to find him by turning corners. As he kept One Point, even the sound of machine gun fire ceased to bother him. Somehow he was able to live on the edge of danger, without crossing it.

Before he left Japan for the front, Tohei was asked by his superior officers to prepare to die and not to expect to ever see Japan again. However, Tohei never agreed to say such a thing, insisting that he would return alive. His men had great confidence in him, saying, "Please take us back to Japan with you." Their faith in him was strong from the beginning. In the final days of the war it was not uncommon for whole units to be wiped out. Once Tohei's unit was completely surrounded. The only way out lay along the bottom of a ridge, practically under the noses of the enemy forces. The slightest noise would give them away and subject them to a hail of gunfire from above their heads. He told his men that if anyone was hit, they should die without making any noise, so as to avoid giving away the location of the rest of the group. With this, everyone became deadly serious and extremely quiet. Somehow they managed to get out of this apparently hopeless situation. Tohei taught them that they were much safer trying to protect each other than just looking after their own skins. He said that if you want to live, you never give up until you die; and that even if all escapes seem blocked, a calm mind will be able to find a way out.

Later he gave the same advice to people in financial, health, or personal crises. The solution to a crisis is often right under your nose, if you are positive and calm enough to look for it. Major scientific discoveries are usually the result of pursuing a problem to the utmost, and then getting a flash of inspiration when relaxed or half-asleep. Inspiration comes from the universe, which contains the potential solution to every problem. Ordinarily we use only a tiny fraction of our brain's potential. Those who are able to use more do so, because somehow they learn to unify their mind and body. The problem is how to get it back once you lose it. An artist or scientist who does not know how to unify mind and body is forced to rely on chance. If you experience writer's block, or find that you cannot sing in front of other people, this is a result of a subconscious assumption that you cannot do it. If you decide you can, you find that the block disappears.

In times of peace people become preoccupied with all kinds of superstitions, consulting astrologers about such things as which days are safe to travel, or when to engage in or refrain from business or love affairs. However, during a war or any other life-and-death emergency, no one can afford to think in such terms. The question of survival brings everything into clear perspective.

In the years after the war, Tohei frequently did things which appeared beyond the limits of normal human ability. Tohei once saw a group of priests trying to stare at the bright sun, but apparently having some difficulty. They believed that if they were pure they could look at the sun without blinking. Out of curiosity he joined them, and was able to look directly at the sun for a number of seconds, without blinking or looking away. They were all astonished and asked him how he did it. He said that the reason the sun appeared so bright to them was that they did not extend Ki when they looked at it. When he looked at the sun he first sent strong Ki. Therefore it did not appear much brighter than a light bulb. However, he cautioned them that they should not practice this, because without strong Ki they ran the risk of burning or damaging their eyes.

Tohei once took a twenty-hour train trip across the country. Because he sat upright and maintained mind and body unification, the trip was quite relaxing and comfortable. The person opposite him fidgeted the whole way, never being able to find a posture which was comfortable for more than a few minutes. Eventually the man was so tortured by the long trip that he had to get off of the train midway, even though he had purchased a ticket to the end of the line.

Tohei made many flights to Hawaii, and during one of them one of the airplane propellers failed. The plane was forced to circle the airport for an hour and a half to reduce the fuel and fire hazard in the probable case of a crash landing. The plane was not able to fly on an even keel, and most of the passengers were panicked at the thought that they might soon die if the plane crashed.

However, during this time of teary goodbyes and desperate final thoughts, Tohei took a nap. He woke up when the plane at last made its rough but safe landing. The person next to him asked him how he possibly could have slept under such conditions. What would he do if he were killed in a crash? He replied that if he were killed, there would be nothing he could do in any case, so why worry about it? He was convinced that if he was truly following the way of the universe, it would protect him and not snuff out his life prematurely without meaning. In this way he was able to remain calm.

One of the passengers, an older woman, had become so frightened that her eyeballs had become frozen in an extreme upturned position. Though wide open, all you could see were the whites of her eyes. Tohei knew that he could fix it with Kiatsu, but doubted that anyone would permit him to touch the woman without proper authority. He then flashed the honorary police captain's badge which he had received from the Hawaii Police Force, and started doing Kiatsu on the muscles around her eyes. They were back to normal in a few minutes.

Dealing with Conflict, Stress, and Danger

Many people get wrong ideas about danger by watching too many movies. Martial arts are portrayed in a particularly distorted way. Japanese sword fighting films usually picture the hero surrounded by multiple attackers, who are cut down one after another, until he emerges the sole victor, acting like it was nothing more than brushing away a few flies.

However, actual historical accounts of sword fights involving multiple attackers describe how after the first few men were cut down, the rest of them usually fled in fear. One story from Japanese history has it that a certain samurai demonstrated incredible courage by standing unmoved in the face of a number of foes. His dauntless attitude in the face of danger so upset his opponents that they ran away in fear. However, even after the danger had passed, the samurai remained frozen to the spot. His friends had to peel his fingers off of the sword handle, one white knuckle at a time. What appeared to an immovable mind, in fact was a mind which could not move. Evidently, there is a large gap between fact and fiction.

A similar story from recent times tells of a man who was able to sit calmly, while a burglar waved a Japanese sword in front of his face. The man's family was deeply impressed with his composure in the face of death, until he told them later that he had simply been too frightened to move a muscle.

As a youth, Tohei had read about swordsmen like the famed Musashi, and respected them very much for the way they trained their spirits to be courageous in the face of danger. But during the war he realized that an attitude which might work, dueling with a sword or spear against a single opponent, was almost useless against an unseen enemy with automatic weapons. Courage and self-confidence have their limits, and only serve to intimidate a weaker opponent. A truly immovable mind must be based on something much greater than your personal strength or skill; it must be grounded in the universe and its principles.

By keeping One Point in whatever you do, you can retain the initiative. Even if you must deal with a difficult person, you will not be upset by them. If you do not retain the initiative others will easily take it from you. It takes two to have an argument, so it is best to avoid letting yourself be caught up in one. If you are confronted with someone who is dangerous or criminally insane, such as a terrorist, the most important thing is to remain calm. This gives him nothing to react to, and helps him return to his senses. If you try to fight a desperate man you risk losing control of the situation. When dealing with an exceptionally strong, unreasonable, cunning or crazy opponent, the first thing to do is to recognize his existence: respect his Ki and do not test it. Then change yourself to a more positive state. No matter how scary looking an opponent may be, he has got two nostrils just like anybody else.

If someone stares at you on a subway, do not stare back or you will risk getting into a fight. Look calmly at the area around the person's nose and be sure that your whole body, and your eyes in particular, are totally relaxed. If you do this, you will not be particularly bothered by being stared at. The other person will feel no resistance and will soon lose interest. The same thing applies should you meet a bear or other dangerous wild animal in the woods. Do not panic or stare back, or you may well cause the animal to attack you. Just coordinate mind and body, show an attitude of unconcern, and calmly get to a place of safety. Tohei once tried an experiment with this, with various animals at the zoo. When he looked steadily at them, the monkeys nearly panicked. The cats stared back. Only the lion maintained the proper gaze, looking without staring; afitting form for the King of the jungle.

Men who ride the public transportation often try to steal a glance at an attractive woman standing nearby, while pretending that they are looking at something else. When the eyes and face look in sharply different directions you lose mind and body coordination, and look shifty-eyed and suspicious to people around you. When Tohei sees an attractive woman, he makes a habit of looking straight at her with relaxed eyes, which is more natural and less offensive than stealing glances. However, this does have one disadvantage. It once caused him to miss his train stop.

If you have a problem, it will only become more serious if you let it get to you by hanging your head or looking down. Make a habit of looking straight ahead when you walk, at a point just above the horizon. This will help you maintain a proper perspective on things.

196

The Real Secret of Self-defense

Lest people get the impression that Ki confers protective abilities only on certain people, or that Tohei is completely unique in this, it would be worth looking at a few stories of how his students have benefited from the same protective process. The body can suffer injury in many ways other than a physical attack. No knowledge of self-defense techniques will help you to survive an automobile accident, or a bout with cancer. To really put the process of self-defense into proper perspective, it will be useful to look at stories involving dangers other than that of being physically attacked by another person.

One of the most insidious attacks on the body is one which comes from the critical weakening or failure of a vital organ. Such attacks are often difficult to foresee, for they strike a person who is otherwise hardworking or athletic. Mr. Haruo Ema is a Ki Society member who works for a famous Japanese watch manufacturer in Tokyo. He was hardworking and successful, and so was given a promotion to middle management, and at the same time a transfer to the Osaka office. But with this promotion he had to manage men whom he not only did not know, but who were older and senior to him, and full of resentment at having to take orders from a younger man. Caught in the stressful middle level of management, his health began to suffer. He found himself tired most of the time. When he went in for a medical checkup, the doctor told him his liver condition was dangerously weak. When liver cells die they release their contents into the bloodstream, including a substance known as GTP. With the normal attrition rate for liver cells, GTP unit counts range from 20 to 47 for a person in good health. When many liver cells die, the number goes up. Mr. Ema's GPT count was 3,100. The doctor said that he was on the verge of collapse and made him check into the hospital on the spot, for intensive care.

The liver is one of the most difficult organs to treat. There is no effective medicine for it, yet if it fails, the chances of survival are zero. The doctor ordered strict rest, with no work or exercise. Mr. Ema had been a student of Tohei's and was familiar with Ki breathing, but had never really taken the time to practice it. Now was his last chance. Having nothing else to do all day, he practiced it in his hospital bed, from two to three hours per day. After one month of this, with no other particular treatment, the GTP number dropped to 800, a vast improvement, but still dangerously high.

Although the doctor gave strict orders to remain in the hospital, he felt that they were doing nothing for him that he could not do at home, so he left the hospital and continued his Ki breathing at home, two to three hours per day. After another month, the GTP number was down to a healthy 36, without having taken any medicine whatsoever. Now he is active once again in his company and holds a senior managerial position. He continues to practice Ki breathing daily.

Mr. Haruo Wada is a graduate of the Kiatsu Therapy School in Tokyo. Although his full time occupation involves international trade, he tries to find opportunities to help people with Kiatsu when he can. On one occasion, he met a person at a company party who was drinking powdered milk instead of alcohol. He asked the man if he had a health problem requiring some dietary restrictions. The man showed him how two of his fingers had turned bone white. The circulation was apparently so bad that his fingers had lost all color, and were extremely sensitive to touch. He felt sharp pain if his fingers even bumped lightly against a hard object. The doctors were strongly recommending amputation. The man was not sure that he wanted to take such an irreversible step, but did not know what else to do.

Mr. Wada taught the man how to do Ki breathing and told him that it might help his condition.

Ten months later, he met this person again. The man was overjoyed, saying that the problem had fixed itself. Desperate for some alternative which might save his fingers, he had practiced the breathing method for two hours everyday. Within six months all of the color and sensation had returned to normal. He could even drink alcohol again, and was extremely grateful for what Ki breathing had done for him.

Not all threats to the body come from disease. A serious accident can be just as dangerous and far more traumatic. Mr. Bunzaemon Kawakami is a Karate instructor who had just begun Ki-Aikido training in Osaka. One night after visiting his mother, he was driving his motorcycle home and had just pulled up to the intersection when suddenly he was hit by the car from behind, propelled over the top of the vehicle in front of him, then hit again and dragged some meters by a second car. He was taken immediately to the hospital, but so badly battered that no one expected him to survive. All of his ribs were broken, as was his right shoulder and arm. His right leg was bent the wrong way, perpendicularly at the knee. His whole body was bloody and bruised and he was unconscious. The doctors said that if he recovered, he would certainly be crippled and probably a human vegetable. The family had already begun arrangements for his funeral.

By morning he regained consciousness, but was unable to move a single muscle in his body. All he could do was to look at the ceiling and breathe. His whole body was racked with pain, but he was grateful at least to be alive. He remembered having been taught Ki breathing a few months before, and thought this was at least one thing he could do. He did it for many hours. By the next morning, the blood and mud encrusted on his face began to fall away, and he was able to move his finger a bit. This encouraged him greatly, so he continued to practice.

The accident occured in April, and by September of the same year, he was able to attend an Aikido training camp. No one present had any idea that he had been in such a serious accident just five months before. He was able to do all of the techniques as well as any beginner, and could even take falls fairly well, only slightly favoring his right side. Such is the protective and restorative power of Ki breathing. Mind and body unification would be of no value if it could only be used by special people under special circumstances, but these stories show that it can even save a life.

It can also help overcome chronic mental and physical weaknesses. Around 1960, Tohei met a Chinese-American in Hawaii named Wilson Lao, who had a serious problem with his vision. Tohei felt sorry for Mr. Lao, as he apparently had no control over the nerves which control the movement of both eyes. His eyes wandered aimlessly without stopping, so everything around him looked like it was in motion. He could not even keep his balance while standing still.

Lao had been trapped in the crossfire of allied and enemy troops in Italy in World War II, unable to advance or retreat. Most of his friends were killed. Somehow he survived, but with considerable shell shock, and total loss of control of his eye movement. He had seen many doctors, but all had given up any hope of a cure. The only son of a wealthy family, but virtually unable to lead a normal life, he was near suicide. He had come to Tohei's dôjô as his last hope.

Tohei talked to him, and confirmed that before going to Italy he had been able to see normally. Lao knew in fact that everything was not moving as randomly as it appeared.

Tohei said that in that case, it should be no problem to fix. He explained that just as people pay no attention to the movements of the windshield wipers when they drive, but look out at the road ahead; so he should send Ki ahead rather than focusing on the movements of his eyes. He taught him how to keep One Point and do the unbendable arm. Mr. Lao's whole expression brightened. Tohei taught him other Ki exercises, which he was able to do so well that he was unable to hold back his tears. Within a month he had changed completely. He could do everything by and for himself again, even drive a car. Later he became the owner of a large hotel bar and very successful.

If you were told that you must not blink for one hour, could you do it? It is almost impossible, especially if you try hard not to blink. Yet that is what Yasuo Sakamoto was told to do, when he was a young man working for the city ward office in Utsunomiya, Tochigi Prefecture in 1955. He was told he needed a major eye operation. The doctors warned him that if he blinked even once during the one to one-and-a-half hour operation, the operation would fail, and he might go blind. He had been near Hiroshima at the time the atomic bomb was dropped, and its delayed effects were causing him to lose his eyesight. At that time, this was considered a major operation. He had been doing Aikido for about one year and came to Tohei for advice.

He told Sakamoto that if he tried to avoid blinking, he would not be able to help doing so. Therefore he should simply concentrate on the One Point throughout the operation, even saying it quietly to himself. Then he could relax and take his mind off of his eyes. He had come looking discouraged, but this advice picked him up. The operation was a success, so it was followed by a second successful operation on the other eye two months later. The doctors said they had never seen anyone with such endurance. It is likely that he did blink during the operation, but that his eyelids were so relaxed that it in no way interfered.

What is a person's instinctive reaction if he suddenly meets an accident? He has a much greater chance of surviving it if he has trained himself to extend Ki. The same Mr. Sakamoto who had successfully endured the eye operation was riding in his friend's car, when suddenly the car plunged off a bridge into the Kinugawa River not far from Tohei's ancestral home, rolling six or seven times down the bank and then into the river. When the car lost control, he just rolled up his body, relaxed completely, and kept saying the words "One Point," over and over again. Both men were immediately taken to the hospital. Sakamoto was released the next day with no more than a few scratches. His friend behind the wheel was very seriously injured, a fate which Sakamoto apparently escaped by extending Ki. The average person may find it difficult to coordinate mind and body instantly in a crisis. Sakamoto was able to because he had been training on a regular basis, even though he was not yet even a black belt in Aikido.

Doctors know that the mind has an influence on health, but they are not sure exactly how, or what to do about it. Tohei once knew an old woman who had been diagnosed as having cancer. Shortly after that, her daughter was killed in an accident and she had to look after her only granddaughter, who was now an orphan. She became so preoccupied with taking care of the child, that she nearly forgot her own serious condition; only to find some months later that the cancer had receded, and she was declared free of it. Often the best way to protect yourself is to protect others.

Many accidents are preventable if handled well. Once an Aikido student was walking down a road, when a car swerved suddenly to avoid a dog and headed right at him. Instead of bracing for impact he jumped up; startling the driver who had not seen him until that moment, and causing him to apply the brakes in time. The Aikido student managed to land safely on the bumper of the car, but called out to the surprised driver, "You idiot! Watch where you're going!"

Pain is not always what we think. Not only children, but many adults dislike going to the dentist. A toothache is bad, but tolerable. The dentist puts you through more pain, so it is very easy to put off going, even when you know you should. Though the pain is no doubt exaggerated in the mind, still it is real enough. However, even real pain can be reduced by learning to change the way you see it. In Ogura, Kyûshû, there was a dentist named Hisaomi Matsumoto. He had practiced Aikido for years. He attended one of Tohei's lectures in Kyûshû, and became so wildly enthusiastic about Ki that he built a dôjô in his own house, and taught students between working hours. He had a good reputation among his patients, for he taught them to keep One Point during dental work; and found that there was not only less pain before and after pulling a tooth, but that his patients healed more quickly.

When doctors encounter pain everyday, they sometimes become hardened to it. The reason that some doctors give more painful injections than others is that they have stopped trying to find ways to reduce the pain of the injection. At one of Tohei's lectures a doctor confided that he had a bad reputation in this regard, and wondered what he was doing wrong? Tohei asked him how he gave injections. The doctor explained that he tried to get his patients to look the other way, thinking that if they watched the injection it would hurt all the more. He said many doctors did it that way, thinking this was the best way to reduce the pain.

Tohei explained that although that sounded right in theory, it did not work in practice. Human psychology is such that when told that you cannot look at something, it makes you want to look all the more. Even though the face looks away, the mind is left behind. Tohei advised him to have the patient look hard at the place of the injection for a count of one, two, and suddenly look away on three, when the doctor should give the injection. This way the entire mind and body become unified and it should hurt less. Using this method, the man later developed an excellent reputation as a doctor whose injections were painless.

Results You Can Expect from Ki Training

These stories show how various of Tohei's students have applied Ki in crisis situations. In most cases, their use of Ki was more of an unconscious reflex than a conscious application. Still it reflected a considerable dedication to Ki principles in daily life. In Japanese, the word crisis (*kiki*) is written with two characters, meaning "dangerous opportunity." In other words, a crisis is a situation which can turn out very well, or very badly, depending on how you respond to it. Many of the real dangers of life can often be avoided with a little wisdom and foresight. The problem is that we cannot always count on our personal knowledge, strength, experience, or talent to carry us through. We need something more. We need Ki.

If we practice Ki training in our daily life we form good subconscious habits, ways of thinking and acting which will help us live well and long. Some of the benefits you can expect from regular Ki training include the following.

Better Health: As you learn to extend Ki continuously in daily life, it will invigorate all of the cells of your body, improve blood circulation, and stimulate your life-force in general.

Better Performance on Tests: As you remain calm in daily life, you will find yourself unmoved by high pressure situations, such as examinations. With improved concentration under pressure, you will be able to remember and think better, and make full use of what you have studied.

Greater Success in Life: Whatever difficulty you may face, you will find that you are able to maintain a positive attitude. Not only will you be able to discover positive solutions to problems in daily and professional life, but you will also have the ability to act on them.

Personal Safety: As you can remain relaxed, you will find that you can stay calm and alert during long periods in traffic, and that your reflexes will be quick and appropriate to prevent accidents.

The Ability to Do Your Best in Sports: As you extend Ki well, even under competitive pressure, you will find that you can perform beyond your ordinary abilities. You will also be able to prevent sports-related injuries.

Strong Motivation: Without proper motivation nothing goes well. If you force yourself to do something without having your heart in it, you only suffer fatigue. When Ki is weak or insufficient, it is useless to try to force or even encourage others to work harder. Motivation to act is the same as extending Ki, and this is a more effective way to restore motivation.

Better Human Relations: Ki power is real power. If you have a bad first impression of another person or spend time finding faults with others, even if you do not say it out loud the other person can feel it. Gradually your relationship with that person turns sour. If you send minus Ki to another person, it returns to you in kind. If you dislike someone, they are certain to dislike you in return. If instead you seek out the good points of another and try to help encourage them, they will do the same for you. This is the way to lead a plus life.

Bridge the Generation Gap: If parents send Ki to their children, those children will grow and develop in healthy ways. If they do not send Ki to their children, they will not be able to expect it back from them either. The gap felt between parents and children is not due to insufficient time spent together. Even though separated by two continents, there are parents who maintain a firm Ki connection with their children and vice versa. The same is true between teachers and students. The real gap is not between generations, it is a gap of Ki.

Modesty with Self-respect: There are people who use negative words to describe themselves or their abilities, thinking that they are being modest. Negative words have a subtle power to gradually create a pessimistic self, and to attract unfavorable experiences. Nor do such words ever make other people feel good to hear them. It is much better to say that you are not yet fully mature. This means that someday you will be mature. The use of a single word can change the direction of your life.

Sending Ki to Other People: Recently a book on how to use your Ki in human relations became a best-seller in Japan, but the ideas in it are not quite right. If you are not careful, by sending your Ki out to others without mind and body unified you can exhaust your own supply. The real meaning of sending your Ki is to direct it fully to any person or object that you encounter. In this way, you can clearly understand what another person is thinking or wants. Then you naturally understand what must be done in any particular situation. By coordinating mind and body, you naturally send your Ki without danger or fatigue. And anyone can learn to do this.

Good Fortune/Luck: Some people complain that though they have not done anything bad in particular, nothing good ever happens to them. In many cases, neither have they done anything particularly good to deserve it. Furthermore, they spend a lot of time complaining. Such people should learn how to extend Ki and use it to do something good for other people. Then they will find that good things begin to happen to them as well.

Overcoming Fatigue: When you are truly healthy, whatever you do you do not experience fatigue. But when you are tired and force yourself to keep going, then fatigue can accumulate to a dangerous level. Such people should practice to replenish their Ki before it reaches a dangerously low level. By doing Ki breathing for thirty minutes, you can refresh and replenish your Ki. This will give you a second wind, just as others around you are beginning to fade. By calming the mind at the One Point just before going to sleep, you can get a full night's rest, even in a short time, and wake up with a fresh supply of Ki.

Training to Develop a Strong Will-power (*Chin Shin no Gyô*)

All successful people are possessed of a strong will-power, which enables them to see clearly, judge well, act appropriately, and overcome obstacles within and without. Tohei defines it as the ability to maintain mind and body unification in all circumstances. This is not a distant or unattainable ideal. By performing the *Chin Shin no Gyô* (Training to Calm the Mind), anyone can experience this state the first time that they try. Like anything else, the more you experience it, the easier it is to draw upon in other areas of your life.

All that is required is to assume a unified posture, and join your hands in a particular gesture called *Tôitsu-no-in*, or the "Seal of Unification." Tohei discovered that by folding the hands in this way, even a beginner could easily pass a rather difficult Ki test. Beginners tend to lose it the moment that they break the seal, while advanced students can maintain it for some time after. In either case, this gesture automatically unifies mind and body, whether or not you think of the Ki principles. It therefore offers a unique and convenient way for anyone to experience mind and body unification.

Here is how to make the Seal of Unification. It looks complicated at first, but not if you follow each step carefully. Be sure that you are sitting upright, either in a chair or in *seiza*, and have a unified posture.

1. Look at your left palm.
2. Place your right palm behind it, inserting the little finger, ring finger, and middle finger of the right hand between the same three fingers of the left, so that these fingers are parallel and the fingertips are touching. The left finger should be on the bottom.
3. Without letting these fingertips slip apart, touch the tips of both forefingers together. In doing so, the palms face each other and the first three fingers bend, making a comfortable but tight weave.
4. Keeping the forefingers relatively straight, fold the right thumb in, so that its tip touches the base of the right forefinger.
5. Complete the seal by folding the left thumb in the same way, so that it covers the right thumb, and its tip touches the base of the right forefinger.

Raise the forefingers to eye height, keeping the elbows comfortably bent. You may leave the arms in this position for as long as you can, though they may grow tired after a few minutes, or you may drop your hands as they are onto your lap. You need to do nothing more than make the seal and sit comfortably. There is no need to try to concentrate, for the seal itself automatically makes you unified. Whether your arms are extended out front or resting on your lap, you will find that you are suddenly many times more stable against any Ki test than you were without the seal. Your partner may try to push you very hard, or to distract you by testing in unexpected ways. You will find that you hardly notice, so secure is your unification of mind and body. When you can remain just as strong after breaking the seal, then you know you have made the first step toward transferring it into your daily life.

Once you understand how to make the seal, and appreciate what it does for you, there is no need to test it every time. The *gyô* are designed for practice. All you need is to make time and do it every day, anywhere from fifteen minutes to an hour. During this time you will find various thoughts come to mind. Anything is acceptable, as long as it is positive. You may choose to plan your day, practice positive visualization, or even memorize Ki principles. Because this posture has the power to focus and realize your thoughts, it is very important not to entertain dark or brooding thoughts. Eventually, your thoughts will calm down of themselves and you will experience deeper and deeper levels of unification. Moving water cannot be forced to calm down, but if you leave it alone it soon seeks its most tranquil state. The mind also calms down naturally if you leave it alone.

When the mind is calm it gains many powers normally considered hard to achieve: awareness, insight, intelligence, good judgment. These naturally translate into action, which is why we refer to as a will-power. Because it is based on Ki principles, there is no danger of this power being abused or used destructively.

What if you are in a situation, such as a business meeting, in which you do not want to draw undue attention to yourself? You can achieve almost as good a result by using a simpler variation on the seal, drawn from Zen meditation. Again, be sure that you begin in a unified posture. With palms facing away, lightly take hold of your right thumb with your left hand, and hold your hands palms up in your lap, so that the little fingertips touch in front of the One Point. The gesture should be comfortable and relaxed, and should not call any undue attention to itself. This can be extremely useful in helping you remain calm before a speech, in making a difficult decision, in controlling your temper, or in helping you understand what another person wants.

When Tohei first began teaching Ki meditation, he found that many people would only practice it in the dôjô when it was taught. Somehow it was too abstract to motivate students to practice at home. Even experienced students of Aikido seldom made time for Ki meditation in daily life. To give people a more specific, as well as infallible means of practicing Ki meditation, Tohei developed the Seal of Unification. It is extremely easy to do, and obviously a very effective means of unifying mind and body. It costs nothing except the time required to practice it. Considering the benefits of practice, one would assume that anyone who learned it would make a habit of using it. But people find it difficult to sit and do nothing. Therefore, to encourage busy people to practice, Tohei developed two tools for Ki Meditation, the Ki Stone, and music for Ki meditation.

The Ki Stone

Somehow, by folding the hands into a sealed gesture, it becomes much easier to experience mind and body unification. Ancient systems of meditation and prayer all contained such gestures, which were said to confer various powers upon the practitioner. At times they made use of implements for meditation, devices ranging from prayer beads to bells. Somehow these devices gave the mind a tangible point of focus. While many of these took on symbolic or religious significance, the original idea behind them was the same, to give form to that which was not obvious to our senses.

A related practice, with a long tradition in the Orient, is that of using *omamori*, a talisman issued by a shrine or temple, which was supposed to protect the holder or bring good luck, a practice which is still extremely common today, though people rarely think of it in terms of Ki. These come in various forms, ranging from small objects to envelopes containing various written messages. Their power is believed to derive from a blessing endowed by the priest, or from the cumulative prayers of people who have invested their hopes in it. One would assume that such relics have no place in Ki training, for it suggests reliance on something outside of oneself, and an object at that. The fact that these charms cost money makes them further suspect, as if the temples saw in them an easy source of revenue from unsuspecting believers. One is also reminded of how the church in former times sold dispensations into Heaven to wealthy contributors. But such abuses and superstitions notwithstanding, there is something about the *omamori* phenomenon which deserves our attention.

When Tohei was studying *misogi* breathing at the Ichikûkai before the war, there was an old woman at the dôjô named Kaneda. It was she who Tohei later realized was perhaps the only one with a correct grasp of Ki breathing, for she exhaled in long, steady, and quiet breaths. Mrs. Kaneda had taken a liking to Tohei, and out of concern for his safety during the war had given him an *omamori* before he left for China. This was not unusual, particularly in light of the fact that *misogi* has roots in the Shinto religious tradition of Japan. He had asked for another one for his friend who was being sent to New Guinea, a place where Japanese units had been experiencing major loses. His friend went to New Guinea, but soon became ill and was sent back to Japan, just a few days before his entire unit was wiped out. Coincidence perhaps, but he was the only one in his unit to survive.

After over fifty years of training, Tohei developed many methods by which anyone could easily experience mind and body unification. One of these was the Seal of Unification. He had long known that people giving Kiatsu almost automatically extended Ki. By focusing Ki at the fingertips it became very easy to unify mind and body. Somehow this gave him the hint that by holding an object, it might make it also make it easier to unify mind and body. The question was, did it matter what the object was? Like the *omamori*, could an object somehow become charged with Ki? Would such an object be useful to students of Ki meditation?

Any object which was to be used as a tool in meditation should be small enough to fit comfortably in the palm of the hand. It should durable and heavy enough to draw the mind to the lower abdomen, without being of a material or shape which could distract the mind from its original purpose. A round and flat polished stone seemed to be the best answer, one which was attractive to the eye and had a nice texture.

Certainly it is possible to charge an object with Ki. We do it all of the time. Handmade objects reflect the Ki of the craftsman. Original artworks are worth many times more than the best of forgeries. Two professional singers can sing the same standard number; one makes a hit, the other is hardly noticed. Food prepared with care is always better than anything mass-produced. Artists and craftsman can immediately tell the difference in holding a tool which has been used by a skilled hand, and one which has been abused by a careless worker. Even words contain Ki. Every handwritten letter contains its own non-verbal message and every spoken word says more in the tone of voice than the speaker realizes. Even the clothes that we wear take on our own shape. Everything that we touch or handle on a regular basis is charged with our Ki, weak or strong.

Metal conducts electricity, rubber does not. Batteries can hold an electric charge, paper cannot. Physical objects show varying degrees of electrical conductivity. However, all of these objects are ultimately made of molecules and atoms, which in turn are made of sub-atomic particles, which can be subdivided without limit into "particles" which we call Ki, as Ki is the essential substance of all things, as well as the energy which moves them. In this sense, any object can conduct Ki.

Tohei reasoned that if there were a Ki Stone, that is a small polished disk which could fit in the palm of the hand, helping the mind to focus, and with use becoming charged with Ki, it would be a very convenient thing to have. Like so many things in his life, once he decided it was worth doing, he did it. He had a large set of such stones made, in three sizes: large, medium, and small. The stones come in two colors, amber and aqua, and are made of semi-transparent, polished onyx. Each stone has the character for Ki carved on one face, and a fingertip-sized depression on the reverse side. Both the small and medium sized stones have a small hole drilled for a necklace cord, while the large one is solid.

To give the stones added value, he practiced a method he had learned in *misogi* training, in which he infused them with Ki doing Ki breathing in a cycle of 10,000 breaths. Considering that his breath cycle is longer than one minute, even with more than two hours per day, this takes nearly three months to complete. The process of infusing an object with Ki is nothing as crude as breathing on it. Rather, his Ki is mentally directed to the object during a state of deep mind and body unification, which is enhanced by Ki breathing.

Skeptics may doubt that such a thing is possible, but he has shown many times how, simply by holding the Ki Stone lightly in the palm of the hand, even a beginner can easily pass a difficult Ki test. When the stone is taken away, they can no longer pass the test. Advanced students however, can pass the test almost as well without the stone as with it, even though they claim to feel more stable with than without it. Tohei himself is equally strong with or without the stone. To those who question whether it might not encourage an unhealthy dependence on the stone, he says that it is simply a means of helping people to experience mind and body unification. Like the finger pointing to the moon, it is useful and necessary at first, to help you know where to look. After you have found the moon, you no longer need the finger, except perhaps to show others where the moon is.

Skeptics may also object to it, because it reminds them of healing crystals, sharpening razor blades with pyramids, and other New Age paraphernalia. However, here it is important to remember the ultimate goal of practice, which is to experience mind and body unification. In this sense the Ki Stone differs sharply from many of these paraphernalia. Objections should not be made on the grounds of superificial resemblance.

In Japan, moreover, it is not considered unusual that a person's Ki could somehow be contained in, or affect the quality of something. This is one reason why secondhand goods have never sold well in Japan. People prefer things which are brand new or fresh. When a new building is dedicated, the Shinto priests always performs a rite of cleansing the building and site of old Ki. Handmade crafts are valued very highly and food is considered best if prepared from scratch by hand, preferably using the freshest materials and in full view of the people who will consume it. Tohei is not a Shinto priest, but his Ki is exceptionally strong and he has charged the Ki Stones with it. Anyone can do the same, but you are not likely to achieve the same result.

For those who still have trouble accepting the idea of a charged object, it is possible to understand the effectiveness of the Ki Stone even without thinking of it in these terms. Its effectiveness does depend in part on a combination of belief and correct use. Once you have decided that something works, it is already 50 to 90 percent effective, because the mind leads the body. At the same time, you should remember that the purpose of the stone is to help you subconsciously remember to coordinate mind and body. What unifies and protects you, helps you to do your best, or brings good luck is not the material stone, but Ki itself. In order to use Ki, you must first unify mind and body. By holding the stone lightly in the palm of your hand, or even by wearing it around your neck, you give yourself a constant, non-verbal reminder to unify mind and body. Of course this is of no use if you make no effort to succeed, or have no understanding of Ki to begin with. The Ki Stone, like the Seal of Unification, definitely enhances the depth of your mind and body unification. This can be easily verified with a Ki test. You should remember that it is a means to an end. At the same time, if you do not make a regular practice of sitting in meditation with the stone, you cannot expect to subconsciously call upon it in daily life. It is a tool for practice; not a substitute.

The Ki Stone is a device for beginners. Tohei himself does not use it. But remember, even someone who possesses a high rank in Aikido may be a beginner in another field. Anyone can benefit from the Ki Stone in some area of their life. Even after Tohei overcame the fear of death on the battlefield, he was surprised to find himself anxious when his business went into debt. Never assume that any aspect of Ki training is too easy for you.

The Ki Stone is a non-verbal reminder to unify mind and body. The subconscious mind often responds better to non-verbal suggestions than verbal ones. The Ki Stone is empowered by Tohei, a Ki master, so it works better than another object which is not. It may be helpful as a supplement, but it is no substitute for Ki training. The Ki Stones are available from the Ki Society Headquarters. Their cost should be considered as a donation to the dôjô, not in terms of the material value of the stone. Ki itself, of course, cannot be packaged, bought, or sold. The real value of the Ki Stone depends on whether and how you use it.

How to use the Ki Stone
1. Stand with your feet slightly apart. The weight of your body should fall on a line between the ball of each foot. Relax your shoulders.
2. Sit down gently on a chair, without letting your weight sag or your lower back bend. Relax your shoulders once again.
3. Fold your hands in your lap, with your right hand underneath. Place the Ki Stone in your left palm, and hold it gently in place.
4. You may also sit in the *seiza* position in the same way, after standing on your knees and relaxing the shoulders as above.
5. After that, you practice in the same way as you would for Ki meditation, or for the Seal of Unification.

Music for Ki Meditation
Tohei was once asked by a student in Hawaii if it was acceptable to practice Ki meditation

while listening to music. At the time he said no, imagining the student trying to meditate to the sounds of the ukulele, a small four-stringed guitar popular in Hawaii, and a word originally meaning, "little jumping flea." Later he changed his mind, depending on the music.

Not surprisingly, the main precondition is to sit with mind and body unified. The second condition is to choose music which helps to calm and focus, rather than excite or upset the mind. Musical tastes are a matter of personal preference, and many types of music have been shown to produce brain waves associated with states of deep mental concentration. However, to assist students unsure of which music is best, Tohei had music specially commissioned for this purpose, from a famous Japanese composer of synthesized music by the name of Sôjirô. The resulting composition was *Ki no Sekai* (literally, "The World of Ki"), four pieces lasting just under twenty-five minutes in all. This music is richly textured enough to keep the mind interested after repeated hearings and contains subtle themes and undercurrents which help focus and calm the mind. It is uniquely designed to give you the light feeling of floating calmly in space, which is characteristic of Ki meditation. All you need to do is to unify mind and body, and simply listen to the music in a state of relaxed awareness. *Ki no Sekai* is available from the Ki Society Headquarters on both compact disc and cassette tape.

Training to Develop Strong Motivation (*Soku Shin no Gyô*)

We can do nothing in life without motivation. Whether it is a reason to live, a goal worth achieving, or even a simple stimulus and response, all of our behavior is motivated. Most of the time we are adequately motivated trying to earn a living, or seeking after things to make life better. But when things do not go well it is easy to become discouraged. Some people even become distraught in the face of adversity. However, when the mind becomes negative it loses all power to deal with problems, large and small. When this happens the breath always becomes weak and the mind preoccupied with negative words and thoughts. To fill the mind and body with positive Ki in short time, Tohei developed a method he calls *Soku Shin no Gyô* (Training the Mind through the Breath), based on the *misogi* methods he learned at the Ichikûkai. Using this method, it is possible for anyone to overcome neuroses, develop strong motivation, or gain inspiration.

The method that was taught at the Ichikûkai was extremely arduous and potentially dangerous. It involved loud chanting while swinging a bell for hours on end, driven by incessant pounding on the shoulders which was not unlike being lashed with a whip. There was little time for rest and little sympathy for stragglers. It was a method developed in the late nineteenth century by a demon of a swordsman, Tesshû Yamaoka, the purpose of which was to thoroughly banish fear and attain what he called, "the state of no-enemy." It was no place for the fainthearted.

Although it was through this training that Tohei gained his first insights into Ki, he found a number of things wrong with the method itself. First of all, the system of having someone pound on your back to "encourage" you to exhale more or chant more loudly, he considered more of a hindrance than a help. The timing of the blows was so difficult that if it was even a little off, it tended to cut short rather than extend the breath. Furthermore, in the intensity of the training, it was all too easy for the participants to degenerate into a rather frenzied form of sadistic or masochistic ritual. Since all genuine discipline is self-discipline, Tohei decided that striking the back was unnecessary at best and harmful in the end. Therefore he removed it altogether from his own adaptation, *Soku Shin no Gyô*.

Even without the striking of the back, repeated and forceful exhalations in a loud voice can put a major strain on the voice, and if done incorrectly can easily cause a person to pass out from hyperventilation. For this reason, the method was not taught to the general public. It was originally considered an advanced, if not secret method. But the truth is that *any* breathing method practiced without mind and body unified is potentially dangerous. The founders of various breathing methods are notorious for their tendency to die of natural causes, years short of the average life span. Those of their followers who do live longer tend to be the ones who did not practice the method very much. The reason for this is that whatever the intent of the original method, people tend to develop bad habits and start breathing in unnatural ways. The resulting tension accumulates as stress and they succumb to illnesses that leave the average person untouched. The best preventive for this is to practice with mind and body unified. However, lacking such a concept, or the means of testing it, this is usually not possible.

By even approximately following the Ki principles outlined in this book you will be able to unify mind and body well enough to prevent any danger of this sort. Nevertheless, it is highly recommended that you gain personal instruction by a qualified instructor, rather than try to learn it from a book. The method is briefly described here, not as a set of how-to instructions, but to give some idea of what is involved.

First students are taught how to sit in *seiza* with mind and body unified. The most important thing is that they learn how to relax completely without collapsing. Next they are taught the ordinary method of Ki breathing, particularly how to exhale without losing mind and body unification. Then students learn how to exhale in one forceful breath, almost like "barking" air, leaning forward slightly in a sudden and powerful movement. This sudden exhalation creates a vacuum of sorts, so that the next moment the lungs are full again, without having to consciously take a breath. If it is done correctly, it should be possible to repeatedly exhale completely in rapid staccato sequence, without becoming breathless or losing mind and body unification. All of this however, is still only preparation for the actual process of *Soku Shin no Gyô*.

The next step is to learn how to swing the bell, which is a sealed hollow canister on a metal stem, containing a number of small metal pellets. Although the bell is not particularly heavy, when you must raise it overhead and bring it down in a vigorous rhythmic motion for up to an hour's time without stopping, it can feel as heavy as a brick. The bell is held in the right hand, and swung in a way analogous to the cutting motion of a sword, from which the movement is originally derived. You must hold the stem lightly, that is totally relaxed. Still in the *seiza* position, you raise the bell high overhead. Here the important thing is that the stem face the ceiling at an angle, and not point toward the floor or toward the top of your head. If you tilt it back too far, you easily lose mind and body coordination. The bell is then brought down in a clean cutting motion, ending just over the right knee with the forearm extended, and facing the palm in at an upward angle. This causes the pellets to hit the bottom of the canister with a loud pealing sound. If done properly with Ki extended, the sound is clear and authoritative. If done in a tired or halfhearted way, it sounds more like Santa Claus in the mall ringing a bell for Christmas shoppers.

Having learned to exhale completely and knowing how to swing the bell properly, students are then ready to learn the chant. As described in Part I, it consists of the eight syllables *TO HO KA MI E MI TA ME*, which are then shorted to five sounds *TO HO KAMI EMI TAME*, then to two *TOHOKAMI EMITAME*, gradually blending into the sound, *TO-EI*. Again, this is not to be confused with the name To-hei, which only accidentally sounds similar. These syllables derive from an ancient Shinto chant and describe the sword, the mirror, and the jewel, each of which have profound symbolic meanings referring to different aspects of the mind. The meaning is no longer emphasized, but the sounds are retained, for they provide a proven means of focusing the breath through the voice.

The presiding instructor sits in front of the group on the right, facing his two assistants who sit opposite on the left. All members of the group face forward, and line up in rows and equal intervals. The bell must be swung in rhythm with the chant, the pace of which is set by the presiding instructor. At first, to ensure that the group is in harmony, the rhythm is slow, using a full swing of the bell on the stressed syllables and a light mid-level shake on the unstressed ones: *TO ho ka mi E mi ta me*. After a minute or so of this, the tempo picks up: *TO-ho kami E-mi tame*, gradually changes to *TO-hokami E-mitame*, gradually reaching a peak at *TO-EI! TO-EI! TO-EI! TO-EI! TO-EI!*, each syllable receiving a full swing. This goes on for about one hour, all in top voice and with full breath and Ki extension. Even in midwinter, it is only a matter of minutes before you are drenched in sweat.

If you are completely relaxed and maintain the proper rhythm, the bell seems to swing itself. Gradually you forget yourself and become extremely big, as if buoyed along by the waves of sound coming from the group. The Ki extension is so strong that you can easily imagine it driving away anything in its path. It is a kind of ecstasy without frenzy. At the end of the session, you feel tired but refreshed, as if the mountain winds had swept you through and through. Your arm may be sore, and your voice a little hoarse, but both return to normal after a short period of rest. Though your legs may be a bit stiff, somehow it was easier than just sitting still for an hour.

If you try to do all of this without first unifying mind and body, if you try to cheat by pretending to give it your all, or if you take a rest partway through; then you lose momentum and fall farther and farther behind. In this case, the result of an hour's training may be a sore arm which you cannot lift, a wispy or frog-like voice, and a sinking feeling that you let yourself down. Another interesting phenomenon occurs to those who lose the rhythm during the chant. The loud peal of as many as fifty to hundred bells, as well as so much Ki focused in loud and driving sounds, tends to wash together in an aural equivalent of an inkblot. It sounds like nothing in particular, therefore it can sound like anything at all. It opens up the subconscious mind, which may be filled with Ki, or may be a veritable Pandora's Box. The Ki energy is strong enough to sweep all the negative parts away if you put yourself into it fully. Otherwise you may find yourself becoming aware of negative or nasty voices in the sound mosaic. Some beginners have reported odd messages. One foreigner training in Japan said that he kept hearing voices saying, "Go back to Australia!" He did.

But for most people, particularly after the careful preparatory training, the whole experience is invigorating and surprisingly level-headed for all of the Mumbo Jumbo surrounding it.

Soku Shin no Gyô is not something which you can practice regularly or whenever you like. Your neighbors would probably drive you out of town if you did. Even in Tesshû's time they had to select the time and place for practice and many of them were harassed by the military authorities, who suspected them of belonging to a subversive group. At the Ki Society Headquarters in Japan the training is offered once a month. Some people engage in it only a few times a year, or whenever they feel they need a strong boost of Ki. Tohei says that it is concentrated and effective enough to cure most light cases of neuroses in a single session. For an otherwise normal person it is an invigorating and inspiring event.

The Ki Society Headquarters provides *misogi* bells to participants and sells them to anyone who wants his own. They are manufactured to specifications which Tohei determined as being ideal for weight, balance, and sound. Still, it is recommended that you only practice under the supervision of a qualified Ki Society instructor.

There is also a greatly simplified application of this form of breathing, which is unobtrusive enough to be used in front of other people, without anyone noticing. When you find yourself dominated by negative thoughts, or when you sense that you are in some danger, utter a quick, near silent, but decisive breath, almost like the sound of an arrow cutting the air, "*fut.*" This helps you extend Ki and cuts off the negative influence. A policeman in Hawaii tried this once when he sensed that he might be in danger. He miraculously managed to dodge three bullets fired from the shadows by an unknown assailant. Had he allowed himself to remain negative, he probably would not have lived to tell the story.

Training to Strengthen Your Life-force (*Shin Shin no Gyô*)

When the body is in a state of complete rest in deep sleep it can recharge itself, replenishing the Ki which was spent during the day. When we are healthy and full of vigor we have a full charge of Ki. When we are run down, we naturally get tired and feel a need to rest. You cannot charge yourself by trying to hold Ki inside. The best way to get a full charge of Ki is to relax completely. Just as opening all of the windows allows a room to become full of fresh air, totally relaxing the body allows it to become full of fresh Ki. The analogy of the charged battery refers to the result, not to the method. The method is to relax completely. Unfortunately, we cannot always go to sleep whenever we feel like it. On a busy schedule it is often difficult to get the amount of sleep that we need. Even if you could sleep whenever you wanted to, it would be all to easy to succumb to laziness.

Moreover, sleep is not the only way to recharge yourself. Any form of Ki training, particularly Ki breathing and Kiatsu therapy, produces the same result. Sometimes the problem is not so much a lack of energy, as a physical injury or weakness which makes it difficult to extend Ki fully. Ki breathing helps the healing process in a general way, but in such a case we need a more focused method for fixing the problem. A jammed finger, a sore muscle, a stiff neck, or a leg cramp may not respond that directly to Ki breathing. Unfortunately, you do not always have access to a trained Kiatsu therapist. In that case, a good alternative is to give Kiatsu to yourself. Using Kiatsu to heal yourself is a method which Tohei calls *Shin Shin no Gyô* (Training for Body and Mind), an approach which concentrates on fixing problems in the body.

The method is precisely the same as for regular Kiatsu, except that you do it on yourself. The advantage is that you can do it at your own convenience, and it costs nothing. The drawback is that it takes patience and persistence to be effective. Many people who try self-Kiatsu give up after a couple of minutes, saying that they do not feel any different. Not only does it take time to heal an injury, but you must be unified in mind and body in order to extend enough Ki to do the job. If you only give it a halfhearted attempt, or if you ignore the Ki and Kiatsu principles by trying to knead the muscle with force, then you cannot expect any clear results.

To learn Kiatsu therapy in order to treat others requires that you attend the two year school in Japan. Working on another person is a big responsibility, particularly when you accept money for your service. Even then you skirt the edges of the law if you promise to heal the person. Therefore, even though Kiatsu has been documented as being very effective for many serious conditions, it is still not legally recognized as a licensed form of therapy in many places. As such, you must advertise it in appropriate terms, saying that Kiatsu helps stimulate the life-force, which in turn promotes and protects health. However, as far as working on yourself goes, you are free of legal restraints.

Although some parts of the body are hard to reach, like the lower back, you have access to most places if you use a little ingenuity. Even though it is not a disease per se, one of the most common problems which plague people is stiff shoulders. Yet this is one of the easiest to fix using Kiatsu. Reach across your chest and place your three middle fingers on any obvious ridge of muscles between your neck and opposite shoulder. All you need to do is to send Ki through the fingertips to the center of the muscle, and try to be sensitive to changes in angle and stiffness. You can explore different angles by bending your head to the side, or by pressing in different places along the line. To help prevent yourself from pushing forcefully on the muscle, lightly rest your free hand on the forearm just above the elbow, where it crosses your chest. This prevents the elbow from coming up, a sure sign of pressing with strength. You may have someone test you, or test yourself, to be sure that your fingers are rooted to the muscle with Ki. If you use force, or if you fail to send Ki, the fingers can be easily lifted off of the muscle.

Other places which are easy to reach include the base of the skull. By pressing with your thumb, for at least fifteen seconds on each point along the rim of the skull, you can help remove the tenderness which you feel at first. This improves circulation in the neck, and can cure most headaches. Most big problems start out as little ones. By making a habit of giving your body daily maintenance and an occasional overhaul, you can prevent a number of problems from occuring in the first place.

You can also relieve a swollen or sore abdomen by lying down on your back, placing the hands palm down on the stomach, and pressing gently to send Ki with the fingertips. Be sure that the elbows remain lower than the fingers, and that the palms remain in contact with the stomach. If the pain persists you should probably have a doctor look at it. There are dozens of variations for self-Kiatsu, most of which are adaptations of regular Kiatsu therapy. Ultimately, you are better off receiving some instruction.

Training to Make Your Mind Positive (*Sen Shin no Gyô*)

We discussed before how you can change the subconscious by directing a strong suggestion to yourself in the mirror, right before going to sleep. But unless you reinforce this suggestion first thing on waking up, it is difficult to make it stick. Many people have trouble getting up in the morning. It may take several cups of coffee, and a few hours of activity before they are fully awake. Ignorant psychologists may describe this as a natural phenomenon, related to biorhythms or other such nonsense. In fact, to walk around in a half-dazed state is not only unnatural, it is very dangerous. The most natural way is to make a clear distinction between waking and sleeping. All too many people spend their waking hours in the twighlight zone of semi-consciousness and their sleeping hours in fitful or restless sleep. In this condition the body never really gets a chance to fully replenish its supply of Ki, making it more and more susceptible to diseases and stresses of all kinds.

Tohei developed a simple method which anyone can use to wake up fully, and begin the day with a strong and positive mind. Drawn from Shinto rituals of purification, *Sen Shin no Gyô* (Training to Cleanse the Mind) involves dousing the body with several buckets of cold water first thing on arising. This is done year round, even in the dead of winter. Surprisingly, once you get used to it, it actually tends to warm the body by stimulating better circulation. It also removes any trace of sleepiness or negativity. If you strongly exhale at the moment the water hits you, it helps to fill your body with Ki and fend off the cold. The sensation is brisk, but not unpleasant.

This is not a matter of endurance or abusing the body to harden the spirit. If you practice in that way you will only distort your character. A unified mind and body has a tremendous capacity to brush off stress of any kind, including that of a bucket of ice cold water on a winter's morning. Tohei recommends dousing the body with three to five buckets in a row, although when he was a young man he used to do twenty or more. An ice cold shower is not as good, for you miss the calming effect of the cold water hitting the body and running off in a moment's time.

Although this training is very stimulating and pleasant, it does take some getting used to. You may wish to begin it during warm weather and work up to it. *Sen Shin no Gyô* is always presented as an optional form of training. No one is forced to participate, and certainly no one is doused with cold water by another person. A women with long hair may prefer not to get her hair wet first thing in the morning, for it takes too long to dry. In that case, you may pour the water over your shoulder instead, with almost as good an effect.

Many people find that they cannot bring themselves to leap out of bed and rush to a cold water bath first thing in the morning. They should remember that the purpose is not self-punishment, but instant unification of mind and body, to begin the day filled with positive Ki. Even if you do not make it a daily habit, you may find it helpful when you face a difficult task.

At the Ki Society Headquarters every New Year's holiday, several days of events are held which ring in the new year with various forms of *misogi* training, especially breathing and cold water bathing. At 6:30 A.M. on January 3, at temperatures ranging down to 7 degrees centigrade below zero, well over a hundred Ki Society members spend several minutes bathing and splashing in the ice cold water of a pond made for that purpose. Sometimes they have to break the ice to enter the water, or brush the snow off of their bare skin. This is preceded and followed of course by some light jogging and exercise, after which students extend strong Ki with bell ringing and Ki breathing *(Soku Shin no Gyô)*. Even though the country air is biting cold and the whole training session lasts for several hours, no one seems to catch cold. Nor do they catch colds during the year. Even if they do, their recovery time is often very short. Somehow *misogi* Ki training greatly strengthens the body and its immune system.

Children as young as eight, and people as old as sixty are welcome to participate in this annual event. One year, a father enrolled his eight year old son, but he himself chose to watch from the sidelines, bundled in a warm overcoat. When his son emerged from the water shivering and obviously not very happy about it, his father told him, "Son, it's all in your mind. It's only cold because you think it's cold!" Young people have trouble believing adults who say one thing but do another. If you want to lead others, you must go there first yourself. It must be experienced to be understood.

Sen Shin no Gyô also clears the mind instantly of any negative thoughts or laziness, an experience which you can then draw upon at will, with or without the cold water. This in itself is the key to a healthy psychological outlook. Rather than carrying worries or resentments around with you all of the time, you can sweep them away simply by remembering the feeling of extending Ki when the cold water hits your body. Of course, the more often you have this experience, the easier it is to recall and draw upon in daily life.

Training to Move with Coordination (Oneness Rhythm Exercise)

Because much of the Ki curriculum has its origins in Tohei's early training, it tends to be associated with Aikido. Unfortunately, this causes the great majority of people to assume that Ki is only for Aikido students. Aikido is an important, but secondary branch of the Ki curriculum as far as Tohei is concerned. He is far more interested in promoting Ki development for daily life, than just for its limited application in one of the martial arts.

Many of the people who take Ki development also train in Aikido. Classes are often held back to back, with the same people practicing in the same uniforms, with the same instructor, making it difficult for a newcomer to tell where one starts and the other begins. To help overcome this misconception, Tohei developed a variation on the Ki exercises called the *Oneness Rhythm Exercise,* which is Japanese English for coordination of mind and body in rhythmic movement. Like the Ki development exercise for health, all movements are performed twice on each side. Some of the Aiki exercises were adapted and added to the routine, including dancelike movements of the whole body, and the entire thing was set to music.

The Oneness Rhythm Exercise was formalized and then recorded on a video cassette, copies of which are available from the Ki Society Headquarters. Because the models on the video are young Japanese women in leotards, many long time Aikido students assumed that the exercise was just for women and beginners, and had nothing to do with Aikido itself. However, Tohei pointed out that these same dance movements produce a state of mind and body coordination which can be applied very effectively in Aikido. People who have a habit of trying to force a technique to work, usually lose mind and body unification at the moment that they collide with the opponent. However, by taking the lighter and more fluid stance of the dance exercise, the student naturally relaxes and therefore extends Ki, making the Aikido technique all the more effective.

Even if a person was not interested in learning the dance form itself, many of the exercises within it contain subtle and ingenious variations on the original exercise, which make it almost impossible not to coordinate mind and body. Experienced Aikido students can usually coordinate mind and body in the midst of very complex and fast movements. However, beginners tend to lose it as soon as they move any part of their body, even in a simple gesture. Rather than require that everyone spend years learning how to do Aikido, Tohei developed this ingenious variation, designing it in such a way that even a beginner could experience mind and body coordination the first time, in spite of himself! Like the hand gesture for meditation and the Ki Stone, certain variations in the movements almost automatically unify mind and body. In this sense, the Oneness Rhythm Exercise is something which even experienced Aikido instructors can benefit from learning. It is filled with clever hints for teaching beginners.

The video is of course set to music, a composition that was commissioned specially for this purpose. Its rhythm is in common 4/4 time, like a slow blues dance number, and the beats are strong enough to be easy to follow as an exercise. Once you learn the exercise, it should be possible to do to other forms of music, as long as the rhythms are not too fast or complex. The purpose of the video is to give people of all ages an enjoyable exercise which can be easily performed at home, at work, or anyplace outside of the dôjô. It was intended to enhance, not to replace the Ki and Aikido exercises which came before it.

Training to Lead a Positive Life (Jissenkai)

It is easy to begin a new project full of enthusiasm, but difficult to sustain it long enough to produce tangible results. This is particularly true when working on something by yourself. Even when you begin with the best of intentions, as time goes by it is all to easy to fall back into old habits. Recognizing that people do better when they have a group to support and encourage them, Tohei developed a system of Ki study circles which he calls the *Ki no Genri Jissenkai*, an association for the practical application of Ki principles.

As powerful a training method as it is, Aikido actually has many drawbacks for the average person. It requires a teacher, time and a schedule which allow for regular practice, a facility for training with mats, a uniform, monthly fees, a certain degree of interest in the martial arts, some degree of youthful flexibility, and more often than not, an understanding spouse. This eliminates most people for one reason or another. Kiatsu too, as excellent a method as it is, has certain drawbacks. The average person may not have access to a trained Kiatsu therapist, or to Kiatsu training itself. They may assume that it is too specialized, too expensive, or too difficult for their particular needs. Yet Tohei's lifetime desire has been to spread Ki principles to all countries of the world, so that everyone may benefit from them in some way. Focusing only on the specialized applications of Aikido and Kiatsu would tend to limit this to too small a group of people. While both of these disciplines have their own internal standards and criteria of training, and specialists are certainly needed in large numbers, the average person may not have easy access to by either one.

To give the average person a serious format for Ki training, Tohei developed the Jissenkai. It is a volunteer study group, which meets on a regular basis, in an effort to understand and help each member of the group to apply Ki principles toward living a positive life. Members meet under the guidance of a leader, who has had at least the beginning level of Ki training, to read, discuss, and practice *gyô* with Ki principles for their daily life application. They also agree that during these sessions, they will only use positive words.

There are various ways to organize a Jissenkai, and no hard and fast rules, but it would be helpful to be sure that everyone present has a clear understanding of the purpose of the meeting, which is a plus life. For this reason, Tohei developed a set of principles, a kind of affirmation to be read aloud.

Five Principles for Applying Ki in Daily Life:
1. **From now on, I will think with a positive mind.**
2. **From now on, I will speak with a positive mind.**
3. **From now on, I will act with a positive mind.**
4. **From now on, I will treat others with a positive mind.**
5. **From now on, I will make a positive contribution to society.**

For those who prefer a more formal approach, there are materials available which can enhance the training: a scroll containing Tohei's calligraphy (*Shimpô Uchû Rei Kannô Soku Gen Jô*, meaning, "Believe in the universe and it will respond in kind."), wooden clappers to lead a group in Ki breathing, the Oneness Rythm Exercise Video, the Ki Meditation Music *Ki no Sekai*, and a small card contained in an envelope for writing down your goal or aspiration. Whether or not you use these materials, the important thing is that you gather with family and friends and actually practice the *gyô*.

On Lifestyle

Obviously, a major concern for any group concerned with Ki in daily life is the question of lifestyle. Cultural pluralism and the great rainbow of values which span modern society make it very difficult for anyone to say what lifestyle is right and what is wrong. Modern people do not take well to moralizing and there are often good arguments on both sides of any fence. Therefore, Tohei has wisely avoided specifying rules of behavior. What is right for one may be wrong for another, and few human beings are really qualified to judge. Ultimately we must make our own value judgments and let the universe settle all accounts in the end.

Still, there are certain value-neutral elements which can be considered fundamental to Ki training. Basically these are correct posture, positive words, and consideration for others. These elements are appropriate for Jissenkai study.

With poor posture you cannot extend Ki. Many children have grown weak due to poor posture, despite their young age. Adults do not emphasize posture in daily life as much as they once did and the results are detrimental. Physically, bad posture puts the organs under pressure, constricts the blood circulation, and weakens the life-force itself. Eventually such people lack the energy to solve their own problems, and then start to create problems for others.

Many of the problems with bullying and violence in the schools have to do with poor posture and attitude. In Japanese, the word *shisei* means both posture and attitude, which is a straightforward acknowledgment of the relationship between mind and body. By correcting your posture you also gain health, a strong character, and good judgment. However, correct posture should be defined in terms of mind and body unification, rather than outward form. It is quite possible for handicapped people to extend Ki, as long as they make efforts to correct their posture within their physical limits.

Words are a reflection of our thoughts and a predictor of our actions. Therefore we should take great care to only use positive words. If you think of your words as being requests for what you would like to have happen, then you will take more responsibility for what you say. If you cannot say anything pleasant about a situation, best say nothing at all, or find some way to offer constructive criticism. Empty complaining only guarantees that your mind will stay negative, and tends to draw to you the very circumstances which you seem to despise.

Some people find it strange that Tohei says so little about diet. Entire health systems are built around what you should or should not eat. The problem is that, like values and lifestyle, diet is a relative thing. So much depends on the individual, the culture, and how the person lives, that it is very difficult to set hard and fast rules. How many health food fanatics are in fact healthy? You can drive yourself into a nervous wreck by reading all of the labels and constantly worrying about whether you have been poisoned.

Furthermore, by maintaining good posture and doing Ki breathing on a daily basis, you can better digest and absorb nutrients, as well as eliminate poisons. Tohei's main advice about food is that you should eat with gratitude, and in moderation. He also says that people should eat more vegetables than meat, although he has never been a vegetarian himself. One significant difference between meat eating and vegetable eating animals is in how they release body heat. Animals like horses and cows, which live on a mainly vegetable diet, cool off by perspiring. Carnivores like dogs and cats do not perspire, but pant with the tongue to cool the body. Because people perspire rather than pant to cool off, perhaps they were meant to eat more vegetables. The proportion of molar teeth to canine teeth in the human mouth also suggests that we should eat more vegetables than meat.

Compared to before World War II in Japan, modern children are much larger in build and seem better nourished. On the other hand, they are also much weaker than children of Tohei's generation: easily subject to flu, often passing out while standing at the morning assembly lecture, easily breaking bones when they fall, and increasingly subject to adult diseases like hardening of the arteries, heart disease, and diabetes. One reason for this change is that parents who were worried over nutrition have forced their children to eat three large feasts a day, with lots of meat and sugar. High protein and high calories have ruined their health.

During Japan's medieval period of civil wars, soldiers would march for long periods, and fight carrying armor and weapons weighing over forty kilograms; eating only twice a day, and subsisting on little more than brown rice and a salted plum. This is obviously not sufficient by modern standards, but they managed to stay fairly healthy on it. Certainly any reasonable diet today should provide all that we need to stay healthy. It is not a subject worth losing sleep over.

Ten Characteristics of a Life with Ki

While Tohei has never been too specific in giving rules for behavior or lifestyle, he is quite precise when it comes to character. While every individual is unique, there are certain general characteristics which fit a noble character, without any need to sacrifice individual personality. These are described in the remainder of the chapter, not so much as things to practice, as ways of being. Consider them as descriptions of the character and attitude of a person who extends Ki in daily life. This should be a natural state, and not one imposed as a rigid moral code.

Develop a Universal Mind (*Uchû-Reisei*)

All things are born of the universe, and derive their life from it. By respecting the life of each individual thing, we show our ultimate respect to the universe. This should be the fundamental attitude of humanism and of democracy. However, as people today have forgotten this, democracy has become the champion of individual rights at the expense of other people: every man for himself.

All human beings are born with desires and appetites. Without desire, society and civilization would make no progress. But when it becomes too much, too selfish, then excessive craving tends to destroy society. On a larger scale this erupts into war, with the use of advanced technolgy by man against man.

Lao Tzu said, "When the Way (Tao) is lost, then human obligations appear. When human obligations are lost, then laws appear." Unfortunately, now even laws cannot stop the fighting. What real power does the United Nations hold over renegade nations? How long can international lawlessness persist before the world tears itself apart?

What can we do to prevent global disaster? Return to the Tao, or Great Way of the universe; return to the original nature from which we were born, return to ourselves. To be one with the universe is to be one with Ki, for they are ultimately one and the same. Ki is defined as the infinite gathering of infinitely small particles, in other words, the universe itself. We cannot really define this universe because it is infinite, without limits. Nor can it ever be reduced to zero. The universe not only contains all that is, but the potential for all that can be, whether we can see it or not. The universe has held more than one Japanese poet in awe:

> The mountain cherry blooms every year in the fields of Yoshino.
> Cut open the tree!
> Wherein can you find the flower?

The flower is not inside in any recognizable form, but it reappears every year nonetheless. Ultimately it comes from Ki, and returns to it. All parents were once children. Where in the child can you find the sperm and ovum? They appear later when the child matures. Therefore they existed in potential even in the infant. Many things in nature are hidden in this way in the potential of the universe, so small and undeveloped that we have no way of detecting them. All things which now exist have always existed in potential. In this sense, all things are born of Ki, all creatures are children of the universe.

The universe never stops moving and developing. We see its incessant motion in the seasons, in the forces of nature, in the circulation of our own blood, in the water cycle of rain and clouds and evaporation. What in the world is it that propels and sustains all of this motion?

Various of the world's religions say that it must be God, the Creator. Yet different religions claim different things about God. Religious fanatics are often willing to kill without compromise, just to protect their own self-generated beliefs. In the past, geographical boundaries represented real separations. People in different parts of the world could maintain separate and conflicting beliefs, without having much contact or interaction. However, the technology of communication and transportation have effectively made geography irrelevant. The world today has no boundaries, and we cannot afford to try to maintain them as we have in the past.

Furthermore, how could any god of man's limited imagination have created a vast universe that we can barely conceive of? The universe was not set in motion by a creator standing apart from it. As the word itself implies, the universe includes everything. It is a total living entity, which moves spontaneously. The word Tohei gives to this entity is *uchû-rei*, the universal spirit or mind. We ourselves participate in a small part of this whole, and the spark which we call life is our Ki. We are like branches on the universal tree. The more we recognize our natural condition and draw strength from it, the more we express our original form, and the more we are able to extend our full power. In the Shinto religion, they conceive of the body as being like clothing donned by a subtler spirit. The word for person (*hito*) originally meant "to hold the spirit."

> The body made subtle, we call the mind.
> The mind made visible, we call the body.

If we think of the spirit as central, and the body as an interchangeable garment, then we can easily change the body, renew and clean it as we do our clothing. If we think of the body as dominant, we over-attach to our egoistic self, and lose the capacity to renew ourselves. Once you recognize the source of yourself, then you can recognize your affinity with all things through the universal mind.

We can think of this mind as having five aspects.

Matter or Mineral Mind: The rock gardens of Japan are considered living expressions of the mind of the rock, the essence of nature in water, stone, and moss. We pay respect to the universe through its forms in nature as expressed in the garden. We ourselves are made of the same material. Our bodies function well by natural processes, with or without our conscious thought.

Vegetable or Organic Mind: Plant life grows and develops in myriad forms. It propagates, and covers the earth. One of Tohei Sensei's students, while studying at Fulton University in California, did an experiment with two plants. He gave each plant the same water, soil, and sunlight. One plant he praised constantly, and the other he subjected to considerable verbal abuse. After one month the first plant was thriving, and the second was in sorry condition. It was as if the plants had fed more on the student's words than water. Our organs carry out many vegetative processes. Almost everyone has experienced how certain sounds can make you feel good, or how unpleasant dinner conversation can spoil your appetite. While we need not be ruled by stimuli in our environment, we are certainly influenced by them. Much of this influence occurs in the organic mind.

Animal or Instinctive Mind: Without instinct, we would not be motivated to eat, be comfortable, or reproduce the species. Instinct is concerned foremost with survival and appetite, and it helps keep us alive. Animals live largely according to instinct and appetite, although many have highly developed social and behavioral patterns. Just as some animals are close to humans, some humans are not far from animals in their mental level. A baby tends to wake, sleep, and feed based on its bodily needs alone. As we grow we develop an awareness of the needs of other people, and lose some of the selfishness of childhood. When an adult acts only to satisy his appetites, people think of him as an animal. Delinquent youth are thought of as wild, because they act out of reckless instinct.

Reason or Social Mind: Civilization, culture, and society developed with the social or reasoning mind that says we cannot live on appetite or instinct alone, but must live and learn to work together for the common good. Animals possess a social mind to a certain extent. Bees and ants are models of industrious cooperation. Lions will not kill unless hungry or attacked. Even the jungle has its own rules. Only human beings, despite their more developed social mind, hunt for pleasure, wage war without thought of consequences, and ruin the environment without regard for the injury that it will cause others. The social mind developed after the animal mind, and is often not strong enough to control it. Instinct often dominates reason, usually with disastrous consequences, providing no end of material for detective stories and romance novels. Freud recognized this, but failed to see anything beyond it.

The first four aspects of mind develop sequentially, through biology, evolution, and history. They depend on the environment and other relative factors for development. They take time to develop. Reason appears at about age two or three, and must be cultivated with growth. As rare cases where children have been raised by wolves show, reason does not develop naturally, but must be cultivated. Education and family environment do make a difference. But reason is not strong enough to control all of the levels which appeared before it, some of which have powerful and ancient roots. The conflicts between reason and instinct make up much of the material of psychology, literature, and history. Knowing that tobacco is injurious to health has never been sufficient to make a person stop smoking, once he has developed the habit. Otherwise reasonable men in politics and business are often swept into self-destructive behavior that they never intended to begin with. It is always easy to find people who will encourage you to give in to instinct rather than try to fight it with conscience or reason. But where does this lead? If we are just in it for ourselves we will end up destroying whatever civilization has wrought. That way lies despair. Fortunately, there is a way out of this predicament other than retiring to a monastic existence.

Ki or Universal Mind: The universal mind is the mind which isfirmly unified in mind and body. It is stronger than all of the other aspects of mind because it underlies and encompasses them all. When waves on the surface of the water calm down, the water clearly reflects the moon above. This is often used as an analogy for what happens when the universal mind is made clear. This mind reflects the moon like still water, and its clarity overcomes the disturbing influence of the other aspects of the mind. The universal mind has always been considered an ideal of human development; but as we enter the twenty-first century it may become a necessity for human survival. The only difference between an angry man with a spear and an angry man with a missile is that the latter can do more damage.

The famous Heart Sutra of Buddhism states that form is void and void is form. In other words, no matter how much something is reduced it can never be reduced to zero. This means that everything is connected, even if the connection is not apparent to us. Even modern physics has discovered that the universe is a seamless web in a state of constant change. No one can say exactly what moves the universe, except that we can give it a name: the *universal mind*. We are all connected to it. Each of us participates in a small part of it. But only when we unify mind and body can we still the waves of our mind to the infinitely decreasing, imperceptible ripples which can clearly reflect things as they are. Tohei calls this *reisei shin*, the mind which sees the spirit of life in all things. When you think, speak, and act with *reisei shin*, the universe always responds to bring your intentions about. The mechanism for this may not be entirely clear, just as we may not see how form is void and void is form. Nevertheless, it works in practice. To use a crude analogy, *reisei shin* is like driving with a clean windshield. When you rely on reason or social rules alone, your windshield becomes so clouded that you cannot drive safely. The purpose of Ki training is to realize the state of *reisei shin* in mind and body, not just in theory, and thereby to refine and develop our character.

Love and Protect All You Meet (*Banyû-Aigo*)

The Buddha said that all things have Buddha nature. Everything is tied directly to the universe in spirit or origin. We are all parts of the universal body. A person who has developed this awareness to a high degree is one who has approached the pinnacle of spiritual development. No matter how clever a dog or monkey may be, it is incapable of knowing the universal mind. Although some animals can understand a limited amount of human conversation, no animal will understand you if you talk to it about the universal mind. Even a person who does not believe in God knows what is meant by the word. Whatever a person may think about it, everyone is in agreement that the universe exists.

To the degree that you identify with the universe itself, you must think and act in a manner befitting that stature. Recognizing that others have the same distinction, we must show love and protection for them. Brotherhood means not only respecting other people, but appreciating the value of everything that we use. We should not kill animals for sport, or waste food, for this shows a narrow and selfish attitude.

Buddha said that we must not take life. But in order to live we must take life. Everything that we eat was once a living creature. You only fool yourself if you think that being a vegetarian is avoiding the taking of life. Living beings are sacrificed that other life may continue. For this we must show gratitude and not waste food. The same attitude should apply to anything we use. Tohei is an ardently frugal in his daily work. He always uses both sides of a piece of paper, and is very strict when he finds office employees wasting time or resources. The best way to avoid wasting food is to make full use of what you eat by employing its energy to help you practice the way of the universe. Since we must sacrifice life to live ourselves, we should use it to do good rather than harm others or act for selfish gain.

After the Japan lost the war, despite severe food shortages few people died of malnutrition. Now with more food than ever, many people suffer nutritional deficiencies because they cannot make full use of what they eat. The best way to do this is to unify mind and body, as well as thought and action. All too many people preach love and brotherhood without practicing it. When the mind is calm, its relationship with other things and people becomes obvious. The desire to love and protect flow naturally from this awareness.

Show Gratitude for All You Have (*Kansha-Hôon*)

As long as we live we are protected by the universe. It is the source of everything that we need and want, and in that sense we are utterly indebted to it. The balance of nature operates constantly to our benefit. As long as we do not spoil it, we live in an environment ideally suited to our survival. Gravity holds us to the earth, while the centrifugal force of its rotation allows us to remain buoyant and move about. But like water to the fish or air to the mammal, Ki is everywhere so we tend to forget that it even exists.

Sex education is a lot more open today than in the past, but this has not helped to harmonize sexual relations or solve sexual problems. Indeed they seem to get worse. There seems to be more confusion than ever before and less concern for the lives of other people. The problem is that students are only taught the obvious physical facts of sexual reproduction. These are important, but do not tell the whole story. By teaching that human beings are merely the manufactured product of sexual intercourse, teachers inadvertently prepare students to treat life carelessly. Children should be taught that we are ultimately born of the universe through our parents.

Impertinent children sometimes claim that they never asked to be born, showing an ingratitude that must be very hard for parents to tolerate. No one came from nothing. Where were you before your parents met; or as they ask in Zen, what was your original face before you were born? The old tale of the baby being brought by the stork is metaphorically much closer to the truth than the scientific facts of sexual reproduction, because it implies that we existed in some form before we were born.

The traditional belief in Japan was that children are on loan to the parents from the universe. Far more valuable than silver or gold, they must be treated accordingly. We should be grateful that when we were born, the first face that we saw was the face of a human parent, and not that of a pig or lower creature. If children had this attitude, they would never carry out violence in their homes or schools. What they need is not sex education, but life education.

Everyone can find some reason to be grateful to everyone they meet, even if it be only for bringing them food, services, or for not doing them harm. Gratitude should be expressed in words, and it should be mutual, not a one-way street. In a dry desert of complaining and ingrateful people, grateful words are like an oasis to thirsty ears. If we had more of it, we could transform the world.

A child who says he did not ask to be born has truly lost the way, for he is ungrateful for all of the things people have done for him, no more than a selfish wretch. If a whole generation thinks only of taking and never of giving, then society itself is in danger.

Do Good in Secret without Expecting Reward (*Intoku-Kahô*)

During the period of China's medieval civil wars, people had the belief that if you saw a two-headed snake your death was imminent. A mother once found her son crying and asked him what was the matter. He told her that he had seen a two-headed snake and feared that he would soon die for it. She asked him what he did after he saw the snake and he told her that he killed and buried it, so that no one else would have to suffer his same fate. She was greatly relieved to hear this, telling him that because he had unselfishly done good in secret (*intoku*) without expecting any reward, then he would surely not die.

To do good in secret means to do good for its own sake, rather than for an ulterior motive. *Intoku* is the highest kind of morality. When you give money in exchange for goods or services, this is trade, not *intoku*. When you give money as thanks or reward for something done for you, or in order to have your name recognized, this is not *intoku*. Only when you do good for its own sake, without any hope of reward, can it be called *intoku*. This does not mean that meeting business or social obligations does not have its place; only that it should not be considered on the same level as unselfish giving.

A Zen story tells of a rich man who made a practice of donating money to the temple regularly. Because he never once received a word of thanks, he complained to the head priest, asking what he might expect in return. The priest scolded him, saying that he was the one who should have words of thanks, because he was the one ultimately to benefit for his charitable acts. While these might be considered ungrateful words coming from the beneficiary, at least they made it clear that the man's gifts apparently had some strings attached.

The literal meaning of *intoku* is "shadow-morality." This suggests doing the right thing because it is right, not only when someone is watching, or in exchange for another favor. Doing something without expectation of reward does not mean that you will not or should not accept a reward. The laws of nature and society alike ensure that good deeds are recognized and rewarded in time. Like water in a basin, the more you push it away the more it flows back to you, and the more you try to gather it to yourself the more it runs away. Learning to receive graciously is as important as learning how to give. However, we should let our good works produce their own rewards, without keeping accounts on what people owe us in return. Ki training is one of the best ways to accumulate *intoku*, for its cumulative effect always ends up helping other people. Think of your Ki training as a way of investing in the universe, knowing that it will pay you back with interest, in the form of improved health and a better life. No amount of money in a bank can buy these things.

Parents are naturally concerned about giving their children the best that they can within their means. However, even if you accumulate a fortune for your children, they will not necessarily protect it or spend it wisely. Even if you build a library of the finest books for your children, they will not necessarily read or understand any of them. The only thing that you can leave them that will certainly benefit them in untold ways is to accumulate *intoku* and leave them plenty of it. Parents are the universe's primary vehicle for transferring the accumulated *intoku* of the past to the next generation, particularly in the early years. But we should not try to live easily on the good we have inherited from the past. There is no guarantee of how long it will last, unless you yourself work to constantly build it up. Nor need we despair if we have received little of value from our parents, for many things can improve in a single generation.

People are sometimes surprised when a person whom they thought they knew well does something very good or very bad. However, nothing ever comes from nothing. Most things and people are simply too complicated to ever grasp in their entirety. Similarly, once begun nothing ever fully disappears, whether good or bad. If you sow good, you will naturally reap good. It is not possible or necessary to worry about exactly in what way the accounts will be balanced. Consider all of the people you can number among your ancestors for many generations back. Were they all good people? The good you enjoy is a result of the good they left you, though it is not perfect. Though it might be tainted by the misfortunes or wrong doings of certain people along the way, you should resolve to pass on only good to the next generation, whether or not you have children yourself. If you are not so fortunate, you can change your circumstances through your own efforts.

Even if you learn something valuable yourself, it will amount to nothing if you keep it inside and do not share it with others. Tohei says that selfish people have never understood and walked the way of the universe. If a country becomes prosperous due to the *intoku* of previous generations, and the younger generations squander it all on leisure and selfish pursuits, then that heritage, whether economic, environmental, or cultural, can be damaged or lost very quickly. People must always strive to work for a more positive world, for virtue is its own reward.

If we assume that our actions will go unrewarded we will act in shortsighted ways, as if there will be no accounting later. But both history and the daily news show that this approach does not pay in the end. The universe has perfect reckoning, though on a scale too vast and complex for the human mind to follow in detail. This means that we can act positively with the assurance that good will come of it, without needing to demand immediate results.

Have Soft Eyes and a Composed Manner (*Jigan-Onyô*)

When Tohei was a young man he studied Zen meditation. To build his powers of concentration, he was told to stare at the mat in front of him, and try to burn a hole in it with his spiritual energy. He was never able to do so, nor was anyone else. Instead, he found all that this staring did was to give him a headache.

Tohei briefly participated in various forms of group religious training in his youth, in his search for a method that would work. One of the more bizarre of these groups had the participants sit still for an hour without moving. Tohei was the only one in the group who was able to do this, because he knew how to calm his mind to an imperceptible and infinitely rapid movement. This made it look like his body was not moving at all. But when later they were told that all of those who moved did so because they had done something bad in a previous lifetime, Tohei quit the group. Not only did they give the wrong reason why people moved, but they were unable to teach anyone how not to move. Therefore he decided not to waste any more of his time.

Everyone knows that you must concentrate the mind to be effective, but most people are unable to tell the difference between a mind which is concentrated and one which is simply mesmerized. When you fix your gaze and tighten your face you are not concentrating, only limiting your vision. You are also inviting a host of other problems by putting tension into your body. Tohei's Zen teacher gave instructions that the students were to put strength in the stomach and never let their attention flag. Rather than clearing his mind, Tohei found that this approach gave him headaches, dizziness, and hemorrhoids. After sitting this way for hours, he would eventually fall asleep from exhaustion, while still in the sitting position. When he awoke he found his mind clear and refreshed. In time he realized that it was not the sleep but the relaxation which produced this rejuvenating state of awareness. At the same time he realized what a mistake it was to put strength in the eyes, because tension soon spread to the whole body.

When you relax completely your eyes naturally become soft and humane. This gives you a composed manner and the stability of a rock. Whatever thoughts you hold in your mind immediately appear in your body. It is not just the eyes which are a window to the soul, your whole manner gives you away. Over time your thoughts can completely change your face and character, for better or for worse. If we do not take responsibility for what we think and say now, we shall have to live with the consequences as we get older.

Beauticians may not belong to the world's oldest profession, but they have been around since the beginnings of civilization. Cosmetics is a thriving industry today, and plastic surgeons do a steady business with patients wanting to improve their looks. Unfortunately, cosmetic measures are superficial and temporary at best. The best way to improve your face is to have soft eyes. When you wash your face in the morning, do not forget to check your eyes. Do not begin your day until you have checked to see whether your eyes are relaxed and calm. If you make this a daily habit you will not only look your best, but you will gradually develop your character as well.

The Asakusa Temple in Tokyo has a gate guarded by two large muscular statues, with glaring eyes and bulging muscles. A samurai once said of Zen meditation that beginners should sit like these temple guardian statues. He claimed that only after much practice could one develop the soft eyes of the Buddha figure within; for if one began too easily, there was a risk of giving up before achieving enlightenment. He separated the end from the means. In fact, if you practice with hard eyes you will end up wearing a scowl on your face. Tohei himself practiced this way at first, putting strength into the lower abdomen and the eyes, trying to burn a hole in the mat in front of him. But he found this approach to be totally useless when his life was in danger. Many martial artists make this mistake and develop hard eyes. The figure of Kannon inside the temple is the Buddhist goddess of compassion and mercy, with soft eyes and a composed manner. The guardian statues outside are nothing but gatekeepers. Being dedicated to the way does not mean to be a fanatic with fiery eyes, but rather to be totally composed, with a spirit like that of a mild spring breeze.

Be Large-hearted and Forgiving (*Kanyû-Taito*)

When you assume the correct posture and calm your mind at the One Point, then your heart feels open and free of trivial concerns. When you lose mind and body unification, then even small things get under your skin. In the Chinese *Saikontan,* the first book of philosophy which Tohei read as a young student, it says the mind should be clear like a mirror:

> The superior man takes things as they come.
> When things pass, his mind is once again clear.

This is no easy thing to do, for we tend to stick to things in the past and worry needlessly. No matter how smart a person may seem, if he has a habit of complaining, he inadvertently shows how small his emotional capacity is. The smaller the mind, the greater the tendency to gather up negative things about others and complain. It is easy to find fault with others, for there is not a single human being who is free of faults. The more you focus on the shortcomings of others, the more they will find fault with you. In time you will not be able to find a single good person left.

On the other hand, if you look for and focus on the good points of others, and overlook their faults, then they will do their best to never let you see their bad points. In time you will be surrounded by good people.

Every child is a mixture of good and bad. Usually, if there are eight good parts and two bad parts, you think of him as a good child. If the child has five good points, but five bad ones to match them, the child is thought of as not so good. But if there are two good parts and eight bad ones, the child will be thought of as very bad. However, if you spend all of your time focusing on the bad parts, soon the good ones will vanish from sight and the child will take vengeance by proving you right. Real education must cultivate the good, and let the bad perish from neglect.

Parents and teachers tend to favor a child who sits quietly, studies as he is supposed to, and never makes trouble. But this type often turns out to be the worst troublemakers when they get older. Children are full of Ki energy and this must not be suppressed by a parent's limited judgment of what is right and wrong behavior, or a teacher's desire for orderly behavior. We must learn to see what is really good. To do this, parents and teachers must first calm their own minds and learn to see clearly. Then you can recognize and reinforce the good accordingly. There is no better way to give your child a good education.

A fighting mind seeks an outlet in everything from a petty argument to the horrors of war. Fundamentally it is a result of being overly critical of the faults of others and not sufficiently aware of one's own shortcomings. The more you learn to observe and correct yourself, the more forgiving you can become of others. Many people assume that to be the first to apologize is to lose the argument. Actually the opposite is true. By being the first to forgive, you show that you have a superior capacity, like the great ocean which accepts and absorbs all of the rivers, come what may.

Once you pick up a negative attitude and start to complain, you can find fault with nearly everything you see. Critics and skeptics often pride themselves on their intelligence, but they rarely see how much they limit their capacity for wisdom as a result. There is much talk today about equality of the sexes. While there are undeniably wrongs which must be righted, equality is not a matter of everyone doing the same things, and having the same roles. Nature endows each sex with different characteristics. Equality does not mean that both sexes should be the same. The sexes are equal in the sense that one is not better or worse than the other, they are simply different. One leads and the other follows, depending on the task. Problems develop when both insist on leading at the same time.

When a person seriously loses mind and body coordination, it is sometimes difficult to tell at first glance if it is a man or woman. A person who is vague about his own sexual identity does not project it very clearly to others either. Men should be masculine, women feminine. Masculinity is not the same as macho behavior, which is often no more than excessive tension. Nor is femininity equated with passivity, which is often a result of weak Ki. A tense woman can be macho, just as a weak man can be effeminate. Moreover, a man can be gentle without being effeminate, just as a woman can be strong without needing to act like a man. If you unify mind and body then you will be both strong and gentle, whether you are a man or a woman. The mountain does not criticize the river for being lowly, and the river does not criticize the mountain for being solid. All things and all people are unique, each has special qualities, and we should learn to accept these and bring out the best in them.

The One Point gives us the capacity to accept positively all things and circumstances that come to us. However many bad habits another may have, you can always find something good to praise and cultivate. If you make a habit of this, in time the good will outshine the bad. Every light casts a shadow. It is up to you to decide whether to look at the thing itself or at its dark shadow.

Think Deeply and See Clearly (*Shinryô-Meisatsu*)

In the past, when people were geographically isolated, local errors had local consequences. In the global community, now the mistakes of even a single person can have consequences for us all. We can no longer afford to be careless about the way that we live. Chicken Little worried constantly about the sky falling. The fact is that he was in greater danger still from the anxiety which wore him down as a result.

It is an unalterable fact that someday every one of us must die. But it is also true that as long as we are alive, we are not yet dead. Therefore, instead of wasting your life worrying about when it will end, the best way is to live it fully, with all of your power, until you die. Only those who live halfheartedly are panicked at the thought of dying, for if you do not do your best now, you may seriously regret it later. To worry about results without making efforts to improve anything is a foolish waste of life.

A chess master will carefully consider the possiblities ten or fifteen moves ahead before making a play. In our lives too, we must carefully think things through, then make our moves without regret. In a board game you have but one opponent; but in life the universe is your challenger and it is no easy thing to anticipate its next moves. A business executive may do his best to make the proper decision; however if he misjudges, the negative consequences will affect not only him, but all of his employees and their families. Great generals also have to make critical decisions, sometimes with little to guide them but intuition. Consulting an oracle is no answer, for as the proverb says, "Sometimes it's right, sometimes it's not." When the mind is clear and calm it can draw on the universe itself for an answer, the correct answer. This does not come as a voice from heaven or as a mystical dream, but rather as a sudden and sharp sense of certitude, one which brings with it the confidence and energy for action.

Courage is necessary in the face of difficulty or disaster, but courage without good judgment can be dangerous. Decisions are difficult enough for adults, who have a wealth of life experience. How can young people cope, who increasingly have to make adult decisions in a fast changing and unpredictable world? As long as we live, our brains are in a state of constant activity. This activity produces measurable brain waves. The calmer the waves, the more relaxed the body and clear the mind. Calm waves allow us to reflect things clearly, and therefore to make good judgments. We cannot stop these waves, but we can reduce them to a state of crystal clarity. Each of us are given the capacity by the universe to reflect like a mirror and to know what is right. Confucius said that it was not until the age of seventy that he learned how to let his mind do what it will, without risk of error in judgment. Perhaps with Ki training, we need not wait that long.

Maintain a Spirit of Unshakeable Composure (*Taizen-Fudô*)

During the Meiji Restoration (1868–1912) many samurai went overseas to learn the ways of the West. They also taught some of the ways of the East, such as *Jû-jutsu*, to the FBI. One large bearded martial artist, greatly respected in Japan, went to the United States and was challenged by a professional American boxer. The boxer circled him many times, but the Japanese remained unmoved. Finally the boxer laid him flat with a single punch. This martial artist bluffed that he was brave, but when he needed to move he could not. He was all show. Like the coward who talks big, he had no real power. Tohei knew a number of braggart soldiers during the war who argued with people all of the time. But when the bullets started to fly, these strong men were usually the first to run and hide. One got a bad fever after shivering all night under attack. Despite the image which Hollywood purveys in its movies, big muscles and a big mouth mean absolutely nothing in a real crisis.

It is not hard to find people who act big in daily life. Most of them would fall apart in a crisis. Any challenge with no guarantee of success is a real test of mettle. Genuine courage comes from daily efforts at self-control and self-improvement. Put all stress into the One Point, and you can develop the spirit embodied in the poem:

> Though the eight winds blow,
> The moon in Heaven remains unmoved.

There was a family in Tohei's home town which was robbed by a thief wielding a real sword. The old man sat unmoved throughout the entire experience, and earned the admiration of all of the family for his courage, until later they found out that he was just too petrified to move. Bravado and fear are identical twins.

There is a world of difference between saying "I will not move," and saying, "I cannot move." A common misunderstanding of the idea of the immovable mind (*fudôshin*) is assuming that you should never react or show emotion, even if your parents die; that you should pretend that you are warm, even if it is bitter cold outside. Tohei insists that he gets surprised just like anyone else, only that he does not stay surprised. He feels and expresses emotion with his whole body, only without losing One Point. It is natural to react, but it is not natural to overreact. Saying that it is cold is stating a fact. Complaining about the cold is overreacting. Your complaints will not affect the cold, but they will affect your mind. Real *fudôshin* means acting like a lightning rod, taking in things fully as they occur, but not holding on to them after they are gone.

Be Vigorous and Full of Energy (*Seiki-Hatsuratsu*)

Great people in the past have always had the energy or Ki to overcome difficulties and accomplish important tasks. As long as we live, we exchange Ki with the universe. When this exchange is vigorous, we have plenty of life energy. Too many people today identify themselves only with the small and visible parts which they can see, ignoring or forgetting the vast potential that they could draw on. This leads to a crisis in which they have less and less confidence and energy, and become more and more isolated, weak, lonely. In short, they have a deficiency of Ki.

You can tell at a glance the difference between a person with or without Ki. A person who lacks Ki looks listless, has poor facial color and unhealthy skin, is negative in speech and thought. A person who is full of Ki is energetic and healthy, calm and bright. As the proverb says, "Laugh today and laugh for life. Cry today and cry for life." It is easy to be happy when things are going well. But all of us are subject to ups-and-downs, advances and reversals. It is during the downs and reversals that we must remember to extend Ki and remain positive.

When your mind is positive you enjoy whatever you do. Food has a wonderful taste. The reverse is true when the mind is dark, for you lose the essential joy of living. Do not limit yourself to what you can see. Expand your mind to your greater self and you will have abundant energy to share with others.

We have a choice in this world to be plus or minus at any moment. But whichever we choose, that choice implies a certain degree of inertia, or tendency to keep going in that direction. In order to truly take responsibility for our lives, we must choose only plus, and constantly strive to find it. An alert person dare not choose minus, because he can see where it leads, and therefore refuses to entertain useless and negative thoughts. This attitude gives you a tremendous amount of vitality, because with it you are fully unified with no need to fight against yourself, or anyone else.

Persevere as Long as You Live (*Shishi-Futô*)

Dripping water has the power over time to drill a hole through rock. Wind is nothing but air, but when it is concentrated it can transform a landscape. Nature is filled with examples of the power of persistence.

Nothing can succeed without persistence. A Japanese proverb practically equates the two in saying, persistence brings power. Unsuccessful people have one thing in common: they easily change their minds. Many have a bad habit of shopping around for just the parts of something that they like or believe in, based on their limited and narrow experience. They try to build a philosophy of living from bits and scraps of truth and error, and ultimately come out more confused than ever. What can you create from the head of a lion and the legs of a giraffe?

You must learn to persevere if you wish to accomplish anything great. This is no easy task in learning something new, for soon after you make a little progress, you always encounter a wall. If you give up whenever you meet resistance, then soon your whole life will follow that pattern. But just as the "endless" rain of the rainy season someday lifts, nothing in the universe continues as it is indefinitely. If you persist and wait, there will sometime be a change. All survivors know this instinctively. Once you experience this, you have access to a tremendous power.

However, if you want to persevere, it makes sense to pursue what is right. What good can possibly come of practicing the wrong approach for a long time? The problem is, how do you know what is right? It is almost impossible to make this judgment based on your own limited knowledge and experience. This is one reason why people are often surprised when jobs, marriages, and friendships turn out to be other than what people expected in the beginning.

The best way to develop good judgment is to learn to calm the mind and see clearly through Ki meditation. Then when the way is clear, resolve to pursue it to the end. By realizing and practicing the principles of the universe, doing your best and letting everything else take its course, you can learn to see and do what is right. When you set out on a path, you cannot reach your destination unless you pursue it to the end. Since the universe has no end, we must persevere indefinitely, as long as we live. This is a matter of being natural, not of showing superhuman effort and endurance. To persevere without stopping means to be one with the universe, to participate in its growth and development. Eventually we can actually transform our subconscious mind, so that perseverance is effortless, and the mind is free to do what it will.

Teaching Ki Principles in Japan and Abroad

Fig. 11. Tohei at the age of thirty-six, teaching police officers in Hawaii (1956).

Fig. 12. Group photograph with the Maui Police Department.

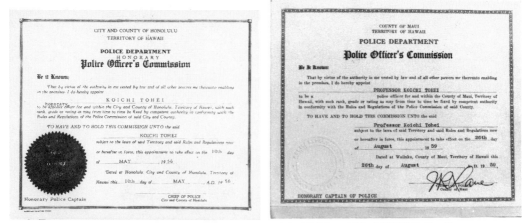

Fig. 13. Police officer commissions granted from the Honolulu (1956) and Maui (1959) Police Departments.

Fig. 14. Police captain's badge received from the County of Maui.

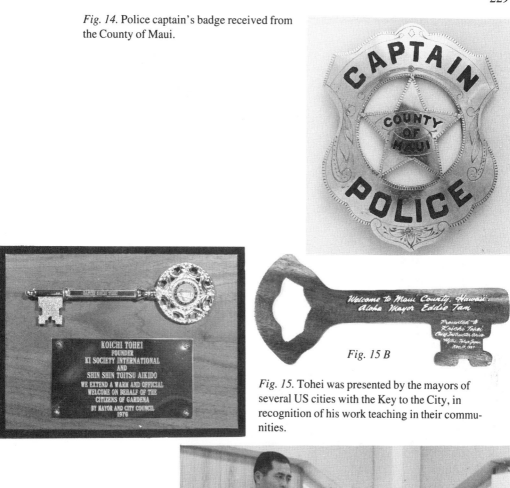

Fig. 15 B

Fig. 15. Tohei was presented by the mayors of several US cities with the Key to the City, in recognition of his work teaching in their communities.

Fig. 16. Tohei at the age of fifty-eight, teaching Sadaharu Oh, the "King" of baseball (1976).

Fig. 17. Tohei with two baseball champions to whom he taught Ki principles. Shigeo Nagashima (left) and Sadaharu Oh (right).

Fig. 18. Tohei with pitcher Suguru Egawa, when he achieved fame for his performance in the nationally televised high school baseball competition.

Fig. 19. Hiromitsu Ishige (left) of the Seibu Lions baseball team with the author (center), participating in New Year's River *misogi*.

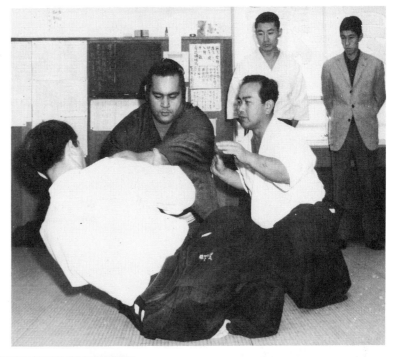

Fig. 20. Tohei at the age of fifty-two, teaching Ki principles to Takamiyama, the popular Sumo Champion of Hawaiian birth (1972).

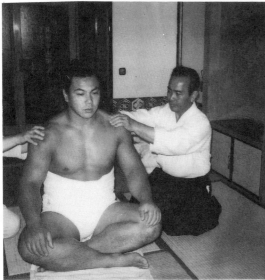

Fig. 21. Tohei giving Kiatsu to Chiyonofuji, the famous Sumo Champion, after he had dislocated a shoulder during a Sumo competition.

Fig. 22. Tohei with the singer Don Ho in Hawaii, one of several performing artists to whom he taught Ki principles.

Performing Aikido Arts

Fig. 23. Tohei doing a Ki-Aikido lecture and demonstration before a group of 3,500 people, at Lewis and Clark University (around 1974).

Fig. 24. Tohei holding the *jô*, or wooden staff used in Aikido.

Fig. 25. By keeping One Point, Tohei could make his body unliftable and even sit unmoved in a chair while being pushed by a number of people. In New Zealand, he demonstrated how he could absorb the pressure of six large lumberjacks pressing on his extended little finger (1975).

233

Fig. 26. A series of photographs taken of a *randori* (free style), in which Tohei successfully throws multiple attackers

A

Fig. 27. Demonstration of an Aikido throw called *kokyû nage.*

B

C

D

PART III

Putting the Universe in Perspective
with Ki

All are but parts of one stupendous whole,
Whose body nature is, and God the soul.
—Alexander Pope

Chapter *10:* Retracing the Way

Important Influences on Tohei's Thinking

Truth needs no authority; it speaks for itself. If something is right, it is because it is true, not because someone says it is right. Authority has given itself a bad name over the years, recalling images of communism, fascism, and tyranny. Even the respected authorities of science and the church often turn out to be wrong, or at least to have had a limited view of truth. Anyone who claims to be right anymore is almost automatically suspect. This has given rise to a tendency to emphasize each individual's right to his own opinion, as if truth were anything that you wanted it to be; a kind of tyranny of the subjective self.

Yet by always focusing on our differences, we tend to forget how much we actually do have in common. There are wartime stories of people fighting on opposite sides, who meeting a common crisis such as thirst or disease, sometimes forget that they are enemies. We may have real political differences, but they amount to little when we realize that we all breathe the same air.

Tohei's lifelong effort has been to distill out that which is true for everyone, that which works anywhere and anytime, that which can be called universal. No one man, not even all of humanity can claim to know everything about the universe. But one man, every one of us, can come to know some aspects of the universe which qualify as true. Calling the sky blue does not say everything that can be said about the sky, but it correctly describes one aspect of it. Tohei learned from many teachers, but mostly he learned by trial and error, not only his own, but those of everyone around him.

Today he rarely talks about the books he has read, or the various disciplines he once pursued. One of his favorite expressions is something which roughly translates, "The proof is in the pudding." He says that nothing should be considered true just because it has a thousand or more years of tradition behind it. Right is right. Wrong is wrong, even if the majority of people and the top authorities all believe it.

When asked if anyone might not arrive at the same place he did by studying the same things he did as a young man, he replied that they would, but only if they did so with the same intensity and thoroughness. Remember, he found many that of the things which he was thought did not work in real life. Reading Chinese philosophy made him feel like a wise man, but when he put the book down he was his own miserable self again. The martial arts of Judo, Karate, and Kendo promised to make him strong, but he found the larger man always won anyway. *Misogi* training made him stronger, but was too abusive of the body and too extreme to have broad appeal. Zen Buddhism provided a philosophy and a method of calming the mind, but when he practiced Zen meditation exactly as he was taught, it gave him a headache; furthermore, it seemed better suited to life in the temple than to life in the outside world. Aikido techniques seemed very effective in Japan, but over half of the ones his teacher had taught him were ineffective against the people he encountered in Hawaii, who played by different rules. Furthermore, Aikido was so specialized that it only appealed to a narrow range of people already interested in the martial arts. Yoga postures, and its methods of breathing and meditation were impractical for daily life, and often based on archaic ideas about the body. So much did he modify and change what he himself had been taught, that he even came to regard his own earlier writings as not worth reading, to the extent that they reflected these early influences.

Many of the errors he found in these teachings were not errors of theory, but errors of method. The traditional teachings were often vague and subject to free interpretation, or they were based on ideas about the earth and the body which were clearly false. One reason for the persistence of these methods was that the people who pursued them spent more time talking or writing about them than actually practicing them. Anyone can practice a wrong method for a few hours a week, but Tohei wanted something which he could apply in daily life, twenty-four hours a day. This desire was simply incompatible with most of the methods he was taught. When he did stumble on the right approach, as judged by his ability to do a task, or achieve a desired result, he found that he was always centered, relaxed, calm, and positive. From this experience he developed the four basic principles of mind and body unification, and the entire Ki curriculum which is based upon them.

Tohei was never sure if the vague aphorisms of Zen or Chinese philosophy were meant in the same sense as he understood them, for they were vague enough to mean different things to different people. When Chuang Tzu wrote that the body should be like dry bone and the mind like dead ashes, what exactly was he trying to say?

Tohei developed a unique ability to interpret traditional proverbs in a sense different from what most people took them to mean. For example, the proverb, "Compassion is not for other people (*Nasake wa hito no tame narazu*)," is taken by many Japanese young people to mean that compassion should not be wasted on others. Tohei says that its real meaning is that compassion ultimately benefits you as well as others. He found clever ways to make his teaching points clear, such as distinguishing between living calmness and dead calmness, between relaxation and losing power, between concentration and attachment. He even invented words to make distinctions in meaning when he could not find an appropriate expression in ordinary usage, such as "jump down," which means to drop the body down as a unit from the One Point, without lifting the shoulders first to wind up; or "cutting Ki," which means to give up mentally before you are finished. These expressions came to be known as "Tohei" English, although apparently they are just as original in Japanese.

Nevertheless, many students of Ki development are curious about the teachings which Tohei was exposed to as a young man. To even begin to explore the roots of these teachings, or the lives of the more significant men who taught and influenced Tohei, would require a separate book altogether. But it is worth looking as some segments of these influences, particularly those which echo the teaching he ultimately developed.

Chinese Philosophy

The first significant book in Tohei's life was the *Saikontan*. This Chinese classic of philosophy was introduced into Japan during the Edo period (1603–1868). The Japanese translation is so close to the Chinese that it requires a modern interpretation even for Japanese to follow it. The book reflects a combination of Taoist, Confucian, and Buddhist influences, and is still read today by business executives with an interest in Chinese thought. English translations do exist, but make for somewhat uninspiring reading, for the original places a great deal of emphasis on moderation and the avoidance of extremes, and goes on at length about the value of adversity for spiritual development. Readers will find only faint echoes of Tohei in it. It is of interest however, that it was this book which he practically memorized, parts of which he often recorded from memory in his military diary, to the astonishment of his superior officers. A small collection of relevant quotations follow, some in abbreviated form.

People who are faithful in their pursuit of truth suffer temporary isolation. Those who prefer to be flattered with power gain temporary benefit, but ultimately suffer permanent isolation. The master of living is not caught by the fleeting values of the world, but sets his sight toward eternal truths. Even though you suffer temporary setbacks, you must not choose the way of permanent isolation. (verse 1)

If your ears always ring with painful self-reflection, this becomes the whet stone on which you polish the blade of your spirit. If your ears are always filled with sweet words and flattery, you gradually poison yourself to death. (verse 5)

Mercy is not for others. This does not mean that you should be hard on others, it means that compassion ultimately comes back to and helps ourselves. (verse 17)

If a family can maintain the way of Buddha, they express the truth in their daily life. They show sincerity and get along well with one another. With smiling faces and peaceful conversation, parents, children and siblings live as one and fully understand one another. This has ten thousand times the value of any difficult meditation or spiritual practice. (verse 21)

Rather than our usual custom of being hard on others and easy on ourselves, we should learn to be hard on ourselves and easy on others. This is the key to smooth human relations. (verse 53)

Before reading words of wisdom from the past, we should first purify our own minds. Otherwise, if we seek to use them for selfish gain, it will only do us harm. This is like giving a weapon to the enemy, or giving a thief the key to your home. (verse 54)

The fish swims freely about in the water without being aware of the water. The bird flys freely on the wind, yet does not know that wind exists. If we understand this principle, we can move freely in the Way. (verse 68)

The calmness which you find at rest is not true calmness. Only the calmness which you find in action is genuine. Similarly, the peace of mind which you find in retirement is not true peace of mind. Only the peace of mind you find in the midst of struggle is true peace of mind. (verse 88)

When we are in difficulty, everything around us has the potential of being our ally, only we fail to notice it. When things are going well, everything around us has the potential of being our enemy, only we fail to see it. (verse 99)

Do not be careless because you assume a task is unimportant. Do not cheat just because no one is watching. Do not be negligent in times of misfortune. This is the secret of developing a fine character. (verse 114)

If left alone, waves on the water naturally calm down. The mirror reflects clearly if there is no smoke. Similarly, there is no need to try to make our mind clear. All we need to do is to remove the things which cloud it and make it dark. Then it is naturally pure. There is no need to try to force pleasure. If we remove the cause of suffering, we naturally experience joy. (verse 151)

We are like people who, though possessing a limitless inheritance, act like beggars knocking at our neighbor's gate. You who, though having newly acquired wealth remain poor in character! What are you boasting about? If you look about you, smoke rises from every chimney. (verse 159)

If you believe in other people, they will not necessarily all be worthy. But at least you yourself will be worthy. If you doubt other people, they will not necessarily all be wrong. But you yourself will be suspect. (verse 162)

The mouth is the gate to the mind. If you are not careful, it will spill all your secrets. Intention is the feet of the mind. If not controlled, it will carry you forthwith down the wrong path. (verse 220)

Zen Buddhism

Zen is a sect of Buddhism which thrived and developed in China and Japan. Along with Confucianism, Zen had a tremendous formative influence on the thought, behavior, art, and lifestyle of the medieval Japanese samurai. Tohei does not speak well of it, partly because he has a distaste for the vague paradoxes that so characterize Zen teachings, and because of the errors he found in the way it was taught. But he is careful to remind people that he never said that Zen was wrong, only that wrong Zen was wrong. Some important Zen priests lived in the past and no doubt there are some worthy Zen masters living today. Tohei was even asked by a Zen priest to form a new sect of Zen, but he declined, saying that it was not a good idea to build on a shaky foundation. All the same, through the martial arts and simply by having been born Japanese, Tohei was greatly influenced by Zen in many ways. It is these aspects of Zen which concern us here, not a comprehensive view of the subject. Many volumes on the subject of Zen have been written in English, for those who wish to pursue the subject further.

The most favorable remark which Tohei ever made about Zen was to say that it could get you into the metropolitan area, but that it dumped you there without an address or phone number to call. The original teachings of the Zen masters were not so much wrong as vague. However, the interpretations of Zen which their students and later generations wrote are filled with errors and absurdities, particularly those which have become popular in the latter half of the twentieth century.

Nevertheless, there are a few pillars of the Zen tradition which Tohei admits as being close to what he teaches, at least in principle. Tohei studied Zen from the head abbot of

Daitokuji, one of the most famous temples in Japan. The founder of the Rinzai sect of Zen was Daitô Kokushi (1281–1337). Like many Zen priests, he wrote poetry.

If your ears see,
and eyes hear,
Not a doubt you'll cherish—
How naturally the rain drips
From the eaves.

Considered by the Emperor in his time as the "teacher of the nation," he was therefore given the title *Kokushi*. His teaching was characterized by references to the importance of the Original Face, likened to the master of a house, or the mind over the body. The purpose of all of the *kôan*, or problems for meditation, was to free the mind from distractions and bring forth the Original Face.

One of the most famous priests of this sect was Takuan Sôhô (1573–1645), who was appointed abbot of Daitokuji, in Kyoto, at the young age of thirty-five, and was both friend and teacher to the famous masterless samurai, Miyamoto Musashi. He was also a consultant to the third Tokugawa Shogun, and taught Zen to Yagyû Munenori (1571–1646), head of the Yagyû Shinkage school of swordsmanship. In his famous letter to Yagyû, he refers to *mushin*, the unconscious from which a tremendous power can be released, seeming to come from nowhere but possessing the whole field of consciousness. He tells him not to stop the mind; not to let it abide, for this is ignorance. He taught him not to let his mind be caught by his opponent's sword or movements. Fudô Myôô is a Buddhist god known as the Immovable, representing immovability in mind and body, but not the same as stopping. It contains the potential for all movements. Another symbol is Senju Kannon, represented with a thousand arms, each holding a different instrument, which is symbolic of the mind not stopping at any one particular place. Takuan produced the analogy well-known among students of the sword, of seeing all of the leaves of the tree, without getting stuck on a single one.

Takuan also refers to the small interval between the flint as it strikes steel, which gives rise to a spark, and repeatedly says that a swordsman must leave no more than a hair-breadth interval. Another analogy he frequently makes is that of a man calling out in response to hearing his name, immediately and without deliberation on what the other person might want. He talks of the need for *kufû*, or skillful means, to gain real knowledge of the One Mind. *Kufû* means to strive, wrestle, and find the way out of a problem with one's whole being, not just intellect. Just as we cannot satisfy our hunger with a book on cooking, we must seek to know the truth in action.

As to the important question of where to locate the mind when you hold the sword, Takuan says that it should not be on the sword or the opponent, or even on yourself, but in the lower part of the abdomen below the navel, which will enable one to adjust in accordance with the shifting demands of the moment. Even then it should not stop there or be localized anywhere, but rather fill the whole body. He taught that one should let the mind move freely and unhindered, so that it can be expressed in action without hindrance.

Takuan described the right, or true mind, as equally distributed over the body, and the partial or one-sided mind as divided and stuck. The right mind behaves like water, whereas the confused mind is congealed, like ice. The Zen mind is compared to a gourd, which when pushed under water, bounces back, floats, and will not stay in place.

How can one have both immovability and fluidity at the same time? Put another way, how can one remain relaxed and alert at the same time? *Munen musô* is defined as the state of no-mind or no-thought, in which you have perfect fluidity and fill every space, like the flowing stream. In swordsmanship, hampered movements are said to produce dangerous openings, or *suki*, through which your opponent can strike you down. A Yagyû poem reads,

> Behind the technique, know that there is the spirit.
> It is already present.
> Open the screen,
> And lo, moonlight fills the room!

Only fully qualified disciples were eligible to receive the secret teaching, called "The Moon in the Water." This was evidently a reference to the state of mind which is calm enough to reflect clearly. The crests and sword guards of the Yagyû clan were filled with such symbolism, though it is unclear exactly in what way and to what extent they understood it.

Tohei studied Zen largely through meditation. As his teacher was a member of the Rinzai sect, they made extensive use of *kôan*, the ambiguous paradoxes given to Zen students to ponder and solve through meditation. Tohei passed the entire series of *kôan* problems, no easy task in itself, because the Zen master judged your attitude as much as your answer. Tohei found out later however, that it was fairly easy to face death in the abstract, sitting on a meditation cushion; not so on the battlefield when unseen enemies are trying to kill you.

What exactly is a *kôan*, and how does it work? A *kôan* is a concise principle of the universe, even though its meaning may not be obvious at first. It only becomes obvious after thorough investigation through meditation. Just as science isolates certain phenomena for study under controlled conditions, the *kôan* isolates a particular dilemma of life and presents it in an concentrated way, free from the distractions of daily existence. Many of the *kôan* are nothing more than short stories or statements about the enlightenment experience of various Zen masters in the past, often after as many as thirty years of effort. A great number seem impossible to solve intellectually, yet treating them like riddles by explaining them in philosophical terms does not qualify you to pass. The real answer must be a living demonstration, not just a parroted response.

Many of the Japanese arts which have been influenced by Zen take the attitude that real understanding means being able to show your knowledge in action. Tohei himself frequently reminds students who think that they know because they have already heard a certain explanation, that in fact they have only just heard about it. Understanding means being able to do and show. The higher ranks of black belt examinations in Judo include an interview. Students are asked various questions, such as to give the definition of *shizentai*, the basic natural stance used in Judo. A student might answer, "*Shizentai* means to stand upright and relaxed, with the feet about twelve inches apart, and the center of gravity midway between the feet." This is the correct answer, but for the student to pass, he must be in that posture as he says the words, or even when the question is asked. No excuses or corrections are allowed.

The answer to a *kôan* cannot be faked to one who knows it through experience. Even in business, no matter how sophisticated the words, the voice of inexperience sounds fake.

One Zen master described the voice of the immature student as sounding like a little girl talking about the joys of marriage, or a boy scout talking about the hell of war. Beginners often repeat what they have heard or read and it may be perfectly correct, but the fact is they do not know what they are talking about. Knowledge must be expressed in action, not just in words. The answer to the *kôan* does have some structure, as it is supposed to be expressed in terms of the theme of the original problem, either through verse or action. Theoretically all *kôan* lead to the same answer, but each must be expressed uniquely in order to pass and qualify for the next *kôan*.

This method is used especially in Rinzai and to some extent in Sôtô Zen, although the emphasis and approach is different. A *kôan* may be used simply to focus the mind, or even dropped if not solved after five years of study. In the Kamakura period (1185–1333), *kôan* were often associated with problems about which students had some direct concern, including military and other arts. The student was expected to pass some 200 of them, though there are 1,700 listed, under seventeen major themes. Some well-known examples include short stories of Buddhist origin, ending in questions such as: What is the sound of one hand clapping? Does a dog have Buddha nature? What was your original face before your parents were born? Many of them are like children's riddles: If you brought up a bird in a jar and it grew too big to get out of the jar, how can you free it without killing the bird or breaking the bottle? The *kôan* often asks for impossible feats of action or judgment. It may require you to stop a ship on a distant ocean, which may have to be answered in verse, but must be convincing and not merely clever.

Kôan are often compared to good chess problems, in that the answer exists, but is not at all obvious, and only comes to you after extended consideration of the problem from all angles. Zen training is severe, with austere food, little sleep, and several visits to the master a day. Many of the Japanese arts were heavily influenced by Zen, which often converted the chores of daily life into an art form. Wooden floors were polished by hand without wax, until they became like mirrors. Calligraphy students practiced painting the same characters over and over again, until they were able to recreate the spirit as well as the form of the master copy.

Given such a long and well-established tradition, why did Tohei have problems finally accepting the Zen method? After all, he did manage to pass all of the *kôan* tests, he sat far more intensively than the average monk today, and was even a favorite of his well-respected teacher. Much of Tohei's poetry reflects a Zen influence:

> The rock stands unmoved under the pounding wave.
> It stands alone in the wind driven snow.

All of us would like to develop an attitude in which we can stand up to anything and not be swayed by the pressures of our daily lives. The problem is how to realize this state of *fudôshin* and use it in a practical way. While he was practicing *zazen* intensively, Tohei felt that he had this noble state of mind. One day he found himself standing on the train tracks, thinking that the oncoming train was nothing to be afraid of. Fortunately, he snapped out of this dazed state without needing to put it to the test. It was then that he realized what it meant to be sick with Zen. He had seen many examples of people who could maintain a noble bearing in the temple, but easily became upset or even lost their temper when they were out in society. While he respected some of the teachings of Zen, it seemed to have serious limitations.

Tohei also had problems accepting the posture specified in the classic Sung Dynasty Chinese text, the *Zazengi*, which specified that the ears should be held over the shoulders and the nose held over the navel. Instead he found he was much more stable by putting the forehead over the One Point. The same book said to stare at the mat with fiery eyes, as if to burn a hole in it with the power of the mind. Instead he found that soft eyes were the way to relax and unify mind and body. He once tested a Zen priest sitting in the meditation posture, with just a little pressure on the shoulder. The priest remained with legs folded in the lotus posture, but rolled over on his back like an inanimate object. Because his legs were still folded, he claimed that his mind did not move. Tohei has little patience for people who just want to make believe that they are strong. When he saw how the hippie movement used Zen as an excuse for doing nothing, he determined to find a more reliable way of conveying the idea of *fudôshin*.

Shinto: *Misogi* and Aikido

Shinto, a word meaning "Way of the gods," is less a formal religion than a collection of beliefs and practices. One of these practices is *misogi*, or ritual purification, which has been practiced for centuries in Japan. Through both his association with the Ichikûkai and his study of Aikido, Tohei was probably more heavily influenced by Shinto than either Chinese philosophy or Zen Buddhism. Although he is not formally associated with Shinto in any way, there are many parallels in Tohei's teaching and Shinto practices. This should not be taken to imply that Ki development is a branch of Shinto, only that it has been influenced by it. Like everything else he studied, Tohei transformed and left his own mark upon it.

Shinto is characterized by festivals, ritual cleanliness, and the belief that all things are alive or contain spirit. It has had a major influence on Japanese architecture, customs, calendar, and even other religions in Japan. Because it is associated with reverence for the Emperor of Japan, it has been subject to the abuses of Imperial power, as well as associated with many of the fringe and fanatical religious groups of Japan. Yet its aesthetics and basic beliefs are very much on the side of life, and have had a beneficial influence on Japanese customs for centuries. Shinto has no founder or scriptures, although the word originated in China and can be found in both Confucian and Taoist texts, referring to anything from the mystical rules of nature, to the path to the grave, or to the realm of the gods. Chinese characters are poetic, but imprecise. Shinto does have a number of myths associated with it, mostly describing the "unbroken" Imperial line descended from the gods and the creation of the Japanese islands.

Shinto can also be read as the "Way of the *kami*," or the way of the noble and sacred spirit, which all beings are thought to possess, even natural objects and phenomena, and are therefore considered deserving of respect or admiration. The *kami* are considered to have protective powers, which they grant if properly addressed and given attention in the form of offerings. There is no supreme *kami* in Shinto, so many Westerners consider it a form of animism or paganism.

Shrines are considered divine dwellings and contain many sacred symbols like the guardian lions and the red *torii* gate named after the bird's perch, the long and serene *sandô* or path of approach to the shrine, the giant sacred ropes and white zig-zag strips of paper representing clouds and lightning, the purification wand for the sweeping away of harmful influences (*harai*), the ceremonial dress and dances, and offerings, and the mirror, sword, and jewel which metaphorically lie hidden in the inner recesses of the shrine. Even words are considered to have spirit. Master Ueshiba made frequent reference to *kotodama*, which are words and sounds considered to have inherent spiritual power. The syllables TO HO KA MI E MI TA ME used in the bell ringing chant were once considered to be *kotodama*.

Commercial activities and anything involving the intervention of fate and fortune is considered closely tied to the *kami* and to the shrine. Many come for blessings and talismans, on occasions such as consecration of a new building, for protection of a new automobile, to give strength to a loved one in the hospital, or even to ask for the blessings of the neighborhood. Even foreign businesses, such as Kentucky Fried Chicken, participate in Shinto rituals, ostensibly to appease the spirits of the dead chickens, but no doubt also to maintain harmony with suppliers and neighbors.

Nature is practically worshiped in Shinto and many natural features are treated with respect bordering on reverence, especially mountains, trees, stones, and rivers. Death is considered an evil, though dead people are considered to live on as spirits, who need constant attention and respect.

Shinto works hand in hand with Buddhism and Confucianism. Japanese see no conflict in belonging to more than one at a time, although few take their religion as seriously as do people in the West. Each way of belief is thought to fulfill different functions for human life. Therefore, it is not unusual for a Japanese to have a Christian wedding, a Shinto blessing, and a Buddhist funeral, while holding a degree in engineering and working in the tough world of international business negotiation. This contributes to great religious tolerance in Japan. New religions are welcomed simply as expressions for different *kami*.

The character for *misogi* is composed of two radicals, one meaning a religious altar, and the other meaning pure, righteous, manly, and decisive (*isagiyoi*). *Misogi* is purification by bathing in cold water. It is only part of the thorough and ritualized cleansing that includes the entire grounds of the shrine. From *misogi* come the practices of cold water bathing, deep breathing, strictness about cleanliness and order, as well as the idea of using Ki to sweep away harmful influences (*kibarai*). Parts of the Ki Society General Headquarters (Ki no Sato) are faintly reminiscent of these Shinto practices, although without the pious or exclusive atmosphere characteristic of many shrines. These Shinto influences were greatly modified through Tohei's experiments and experience.

He must have also been influenced by his teacher Morihei Ueshiba's close association with Shinto. Ueshiba's later years at the dôjô in Iwama were rather secluded from worldly affairs. Ueshiba rose every morning at 4:00 A.M., doused his body with cold water, and then went outside to greet the morning sun, meditating before the Aiki Shrine for an hour and a half, feeling the communion of being in harmony with the universe. Tohei's teacher became a follower of the Omoto-kyô religion, after having a mystical experience in which he felt himself to be a vessel for the divine energy of the universe. He would practice *chinkon-kishin*, a Shinto meditation technique for centering the mind and body, with gestures and invocations performed at sacred spots and shrines. He also practiced *misogi*, the ritual washing away of impurities with cold water, in streams and waterfalls. Although it was quite different from the method Tohei developed for Ki breathing, Ueshiba also practiced deep rhythmic breathing to purify the blood and regenerate the mind and body. As evidenced by his writings, Ueshiba's approach was deeply mystical, and openly religious. It certainly did not fit Tohei's temperament or style. Ueshiba would tell students that the reason he held his opponents so lightly was that he was old and the *kami* had entered his body on a purple cloud. Tohei held his opponents the same way, but explained that it was because he had too much to drink the night before. Tohei did not explain further out of respect for his teacher; but as soon as the master passed away, Tohei began openly teaching in terms of the four basic principles, saying that anyone was stronger when they were relaxed.

Ueshiba did not like people imitating his practices of *chinkon-kishin* and *misogi*, urging them instead to purify mind and body and bring peace to the world through the discipline of Aikido. The other practices he considered too difficult for those of little faith, or perhaps he believed that no one else could follow them. Indeed his explanations were so obscure, that none of his students could possibly understand or interpret them to outsiders. Tohei learned to ignore what Ueshiba said and instead watch what he did, which were sometimes different things.

Many of his students welcomed the religious meditations and breathing, more because it gave a respite from the rigorous physical training than out of any religious devotion. The Omoto-kyô was a religious movement founded by a man named Onisaburô Deguchi in 1913, a movement which gained a membership of several million people. Deguchi was a healer, psychic, and interpreter of Shinto practices. Omoto-kyô also taught that agriculture and natural farming methods were the basis of the new world order, and Ueshiba thus developed a love for farming. Certain members of the Omoto-kyô religion started rumors that Deguchi would usurp the Emperor and become the new spirtual leader of Japan. The order was then raided by government agents, and Deguchi was arrested in 1921, after which the movement was subject to constant harassment from the government. During World War II the religion was almost crushed. Many members were arrested, some lost their jobs. Their leaders were tortured and the Omoto-kyô facilities were destroyed.

Ueshiba taught Aikido to Japanese and Chinese officials who had been appointed to serve in the Japanese puppet government of Manchukuo from 1932. But he was always opposed to the use of martial arts for killing, instead trying to emphasize its need for peace. He never believed that Japan could win a war against a large and wealthy country like the United States. From 1935 to 1942 he began aquiring land in Iwama for a dôjô, with a farm and an Aiki Shrine. Ueshiba died on April 26, 1969 at the age of eighty-six. He was an outstanding martial artist, many large and highly trained men could not lay a hand on him, without first being thrown hard to the ground, never knowing what happened to them. He was known for incredible strength, almost supernatural awareness, and powerful technique. But his life is so surrounded by myth and unverifiable stories, including teleportation and other doubtful feats, as well as writings which are obscure and mystical, that we cannot really know in detail what actually happened.

Ueshiba learned Aiki from Sokaku Takeda, the founder of the Aikido style of Daitô Ryû, which was said to have been passed down in essence to the Takeda clan, from the famous Minamoto clan around A. D. 1100. The martial art went through a number of names, from Daitô Ryû Aikijutsu to Ueshiba Ryû Jûjutsu, and others, until 1942, when it was simply called Aikido. The organization which Ueshiba founded survives as an international organization today under the name of Aikikai, under the charge of Ueshiba's son Kisshomaru. Some old films remain and are available on video, but the master's writings were rather unspecific: half-poetry, half-religion, with a dash of common sense, and a strong emphasis on peace and love. Although the famous Buddhist scholar Daisetsu T. Suzuki called Aikido a form of "moving Zen," in fact Ueshiba never studied Zen. His background had much more to do with Shinto.

Though they never met in person, Tohei was also indirectly influenced to a large degree by the teachings of Tesshû Yamaoka; indeed he studied *misogi* from Yamaoka's top student, Tetsuju Ogura. Born in 1836, Yamaoka studied Confucianism and martial arts in order to gain *fudôshin*. He was greatly attracted to Zen as well as the martial arts, and in 1853, was adopted into the Yamaoka family, as a student of their School of Spear fighting. The training was intensive, often lasting all night long, including cold water baths in the dead of winter, and up to as many as 30,000 thrusts with 7 foot long bamboo poles, or 1,000 thrusts with a 20 pound spear. Yamaoka was a wild man outside of training as well, responding to eating and drinking challenges such as eating a hundred boiled eggs, or drinking nine bottles of *sake* at one sitting.

There was at the time a zealous political movement which ran under the slogan of "Revere the Emperor and Expel the Barbarians." The movement was set in motion by xenophobic Japanese, following the challenge and military threat of Admiral Perry's Black Ships in 1853. But by 1867 he had switched affiliations and worked in the personal guard of the Shogun Yoshinobu Tokugawa. He braved enemy foreign lines and went in alone to negotiate with Takamori Saigô, one of the leaders of the Meiji Revolution. When Saigô asked him how he managed to penetrate the lines and get as far as he did, he said he just walked down the main road. Yamaoka returned safely with a letter of passage from Saigô.

Yamaoka studied the Ittô Ryû (One-Sword School) and eventually developed the Mutô Ryû, or School of No Sword. Yamaoka and his students would train like wild men from morning to night. When asked the source of his boundless energy, he simply replied that there was no secret, just to keep the mind empty so that it reflects the shadows and distortions of the opponent's mind. In swordsmanship this shows you where to strike, in daily life it lets you see into another's heart. He faced and won thousands of challenges and constantly preached that to a fearless man, nothing is impossible. He later became a personal teacher and confidant of the Meiji Emperor.

Yamaoka was also appointed the fifty-first Headmaster of the Jubokudô School of Calligraphy, passed on from the famous Buddhist priest Kûkai (774–835) who was known both as a great healer and master of the brush. Kûkai had lived for a time in China, studying the calligraphy of the greatest of Chinese calligraphy masters, who lived in the fourth century, Wang Hsi-chih (O-gishi, in Japanese). One story tells of how an ignorant servant, not recognizing it as the master's brushwork, tried to sand the markings off of a piece of wood. No matter how he scraped and cut, the ink had penetrated so deeply that it was indelible. *Jubokudô* means the Way of Penetrating Wood, and is known for its emphasis on putting strong Ki energy into the brush strokes.

Tohei's primary contact with Yamaoka's teachings was through the Ichikûkai. We have seen how he benefited from it and what he changed in his approaches to breathing, chanting, and bell ringing. Yamaoka may have been an outstanding martial artist, or even a powerful example of the spirit of *misogi*, but he was hardly a model which most modern people could follow, or even find inspiring. Indeed, he would probably today have been regarded as a dangerous fanatic. Aside from his political zeal, he was a heavy drinker and womanizer, and worked his students like slaves. One story suggests the extreme quality of his character: after one of his students vomited from too much drink, Yamaoka lapped it up, saying that it was not right to waste so much food.

Classical Budô: The Tradition of the Samurai

Any modern student of the martial arts is curious about the roots of his study. What is the history behind the martial arts in Japan, a tradition marked by extremes of violence and peace, of crude behavior and elegant refinement, of barbarism and classical wisdom? It would require a separate volume even to scratch the surface of this fascinating subject, and much has already been written about it. However, there are certain things which may be relevant to our story, for many of the misconceptions surrounding the martial arts naturally affect people's perception of Aikido, and therefore of Ki.

A distinction should be made between *bujutsu*, or martial techniques for self-protection, and *budô*, which is the martial way of self-perfection and development. Two forms of Confucianism were prevalent in Tokugawa Japan: the Neo-Confucianism of the Sung Dynasty philosopher Chu Shi (1130–1200), known as Shu-shi in Japanese, which focused on human relationships and suited the policies of the military government. Rivaling it was the Wang Yang-ming (1472–1529) system, known as O-yômei in Japanese, which was completely personal and intuitive, emphasizing systematic physical effort and actions to control the mind, very similar to Zen.

The classical *budô* were developed for the dual purposes of killing in war (self-protection), as well as to provide a physical means for character development, self-control, and the study of Zen concepts. *Bushi-dô* has been compared to Western chivalry. Just as few people today would see fit to return to the forms that were developed by and for people in the feudal societies of the middle ages, *bushi-dô* is probably no more than an anachronism today. How many modern students of the martial arts would really want to go all the way and practice loyalty, honor, reverence for the lord and master, service, patience and obedience, and be ready to throw their lives away at a moment's notice to defend these virtues? How many of these classical values still have a place in a modern democratic society? How many might wish to commit *hara-kiri* for the sake of honor, or relegate women to a third-rate status? Various feudal lords had family constitutions with rules and precepts for behavior, many stemming from Confucian thought. Most of the rules were a common sense means for maintaining order and discipline in an uncertain society: being alert and well-behaved, never being cowardly, always remembering your parents, being moderate and patient in all things, never asking your lord for money, land, or rice, always making efforts and telling the truth, guarding against spies, studying Zen, taking care of one's horse, being fair, avoiding gambling. No wonder that the martial arts have had to change to survive.

One of the classical schools of the sword which had an indirect influence on Tohei, both through Yamaoka and Ueshiba, was the Yagyû Shinkage Ryû. Its history is long and involved, and closely tied to significant political events in Japan's history. During the period of the Civil Wars, around the fifteenth century, there were three major schools of the sword: Shintô Ryû (religious), Ittô Ryû (swift single stroke), and Kage Ryû (secretive). The reputation of the Kage style greatly improved with famous and true tales of how its members could cut an enemy down with a single stroke, which seemed to emerge from nowhere. Musashi had also learned from this style and remained undefeated.

The Yagyû village was located in the Kinki region, between Nara and Kyoto Prefectures. Around them the Kamakura Shogunate fell and was replaced by the Ashikaga, which lasted for two hundred years. The Yagyû samurai became an extension of the government, tending the land and teaching sword techniques to government officials. They had an excellent reputation.

In the mid-1500s revolt broke out and was repressed. As the Yagyû had assisted the losing side, they were soon attacked by government. They held them off for three days, but then were forced to surrender and recognize the government. It was around this time that they began to refine the inner and secret aspects of the art.

In April of 1565, the founder presented Yagyû Muneyoshi (the first headmaster) with a certificate in the Yagyû Shinkage Ryû. The single guiding principle was to never stop the mind.

Up to then, no one had successfully been able to take title of Shogunate, until Tokugawa Ieyasu defeated his rival Ishida Mitsunari, a story which was portrayed in the well-known novel and film, *Shogun*. Iishida's castle at Osaka was too well fortified, so Tokugawa wanted to draw him out into the plains. He enlisted the help of Yagyû Muneyoshi. His oldest son Yoshikatsu had been wounded and crippled, so could not take over the school. Munenori (born in 1571, the youngest of eleven children of Muneyoshi) was very determined in practice, would often train in the snow, cutting at balls suspended from tree branches. He specialized in *kumi-uchi*, a set of techniques for taking away weapons, which evolved into modern *Jû-jutsu* and Mutô Ryû, and had a major influence on Aikido.

Yagyû Muneyoshi impressed Tokugawa by taking away his wooden sword in one stroke. He then installed Munenori as Tokugawa's personal instructor, thereby assuring the future of the school. Munenori persuaded his father to help Tokugawa against Ishida at Sekigahara (Japan's Gettysburg) on September 15, 1600. Munenori took up a real sword to help protect Tokugawa's claim to the Shogunate from his rivals at Osaka Castle. He won acclaim by dealing with multiple attackers in scenes that would later become part of Japanese martial arts films. Later descendents refined the no-sword techniques, and other methods for disarming an attacker.

Takuan, the Zen priest, was born in 1573, the son of a samurai. He became a Buddhist priest at the age of nine, and the head of Kyoto's Daitokuji at thirty-five, which indicated that his remarkable abilities were recognized by people in power. In his travels he met Munenori, and taught him the Zen of no-mind. It was during that time that he wrote his famous letters to him on not stopping the mind.

Stories abound of how people outside of the martial arts had also mastered the technique of standing without fear or flaw, although it was considered a secret method. A Noh actor was once praised by the Shogun and his Yagyû teacher, for a performance which allowed not a single opportunity to strike. One samurai came to the Yagyû dôjô, saying he knew nothing of the sword, but was able to face Munenori without fear of death, and so was given a certificate on the spot.

Within a few generations, the school had split into two or more major branches, which still survive today under the instruction of Yagyû descendents. Many expert swordsmen emerged from both and some became sword smiths as well. In 1867 the Meiji Emperor disbanded the Tokugawa government and abolished feudalism. There was rivalry along the way between the major Yagyû branches, and during the Meiji Restoration some fought on opposite sides. Most of them were killed in the civil war, a fulfillment of the old prophesy: those who live by the sword, die by the sword.

Mind and Body Unification

Tohei learned from many teachers, but perhaps the most well-known (at least in Japan) and remarkable of them all was Tempû Nakamura, the man who first used the term mind and body unification, and helped Tohei realize that the mind leads the body.

Born in 1877 of a noble family, Nakamura became a military detective, and was known in the Russo-Japanese War as a fearless and awe inspiring figure. He traveled to America and then to India in an effort to cure his tuberculosis condition, which was in his day a potentially fatal illness. Nakamura graduated with a medical degree from Columbia University and became the first man to introduce Yoga to Japan. He served as the chief director of a major bank in Tokyo (Tokyo Jitsugyô Chozô Ginkô), as well as serving on the Board of a Milling Company (Dai Nihon Seifun). He led a very eventful life, and in his later years became well-known as a teacher of the Philosophy of Success. Among those who considered Tempû Nakamura as a major influence in their lives were: Kônosuke Matsushita (chairman of Matsushita/National-Panasonic), Fukujirô Motono (consulting advisor to TDK Corporation), Kazuo Inamori (chairman of Kyocera), John D. Rockefeller III, Shuzei Kurata (former president of Hitachi Manufacturing), Seizô Iida (former president of Nomura Securities), Jin Sano (former president of Kawasaki Heavy Industries), Prime Minister Kei Hara, General Gensui Tôgô of WWII, Gonroku Matsuda (a Living National Treasure), Jirô Osaragi (a well-known author), and Tatsurô Hirooka (baseball critic, former manager of the Seibu Lions, the man who helped introduce Tohei into the baseball world).

It was from Tempû Nakamura that Tohei got the idea for mind and body unification, through the words that the "mind leads the body." This Nakamura taught through exercises, examples, and stories which reinforced the importance of developing a fine and strong character as the basis for health and happiness. He taught the importance of establishing one's humanity as the basis for success. He emphasized that we need to do more than just exist, that we should make the most of our potential. He stressed the need for the mind to be strong, positive, right, and to follow the natural principles of mind and body.

Nakamura taught that the mind must always be focused in what it is doing and that the body must be trained to be strong in order to operate at its best as a matter of habit. He said that it is better to practice than to learn, for this is the way to change the subconscious mind. He taught that mind and body unification was the fundamental principle for both health and good fortune.

From his own experience he realized that no matter how wealthy you are, you cannot buy health. The world's richest man cannot buy his way out of a terminal illness. No medicine or famous doctor can help, only the life-force, which he defined in specific terms of physical vitality, courage, judgment, self-discipline, sexual vitality, and ability. Rather than worry about what happens if you die or if there is an earthquake, he said that you should devote yourself to living your life fully. Nakamura said that you should have sexual vitality at any age, quoting an old Zen enlightenment poem, addressed to Daruma, the patriarch of Zen.

Daruma-san, look this way.
The world is moonlight, snow, and flowers.
Wine and women.

He became ill with a respiratory disease during the Russo-Japanese War, even though he had had quite a reputation for fearlessness and physical vigor. Gradually he became more and more concerned about his health and forgot the condition of his mind. Then he remembered what Thomas Edison had said, about how though people assumed his many discoveries came from deep academic learning, in fact they came from the observation of the most mundane and commonplace events. Nakamura resolved like Edison to find truth close at hand, in everyday life. Then he realized that he had forgotten about the importance of his mental state and desired ever more to know what that state was. He searched many of the best thinkers and philosophers in Japan, but they could not help him. Then he found an untranslated English copy of *How to Get What You Want*, by Lauren Swede Mardin, and was so inspired by it that he determined to go to America and learn the secrets from the author himself. But the author was totally unhelpful, saying that he never asked him to come anyway, and that he should just try to memorize his book. Even if he died before he could do so, Nakamura felt that it was better to be one step closer to the truth. This was bitter medicine to a man who had illegally smuggled himself out of the country to meet the author whom he so admired.

Then he set out to study a health method called *Motion Motive*, which did not help him at all. Following that he inquired after a philosopher called Carrington, who had apparently helped treat Edison for a illness he had developed from an electric shock. Carrington praised him for being interested in developing his mind at such a young age, rather than just pursuing material things.

Nakamura went to London and met H. Addington Bruce, who taught him that the best way to strengthen the body and train the mind was to forget useless or worrisome things; not to try to go to sleep, but to forget about sleep and fall asleep naturally. He sought out many others, and eventually went to Columbia University, ultimately to graduate as a medical doctor. Still he felt unfulfilled, and on his return journey in 1911, at a hotel in Cairo, he met an Indian guru named Carippa, and decided to follow him to the mountains of India to study Yoga. During his two years and some months of training there, his Yoga teacher told him that he relied too much on the teachings of others and that he should find this power within himself. He told him that the reason for his search for the truth was his illness; but that having no guarantees, and not knowing the day of his death, why not live his life with more fortitude? The teacher was ruthless in demanding that Nakamura live for himself, and Carippa resorted to means that would be considered cruel today.

Nakamura realized that negative thoughts and attitudes unbalance the nervous system and prevent it from supplying the extra life energy we need for health and success. He determined to go back to Japan and die on Japanese soil, and eventually did so on December 1, 1968; but not until he had influenced a whole generation of men, including Koichi Tohei. Nakamura was well into his eighties when he died.

His Yoga teacher taught that the body was a reflection of what was in the mind, that the internal organs' conditions reflected mental states, but that mental states could also exert a positive influence on the organs. He said that even though the body becomes ill, there is no need for the mind to be sick as well. Even though you suffer a setback in life, there is no need for the mind to be set back as well. His teacher asked him in the Himalayan mountains, if he had ever considered what it was that human beings were born on earth to do. After much thought he decided that it was to participate in the plan of universal development and improvement, that human beings were in this sense lords of creation. There he developed the ideas of suggestibility and the subconscious, as well as the mirror method of suggestion. One of his favorite poems read,

It is the mind which confuses itself.
Let the mind take hold of itself.

Nakamura's teachings still have a major following, and there is a group in Tokyo called the Tempûkai which publishes and teaches about them. His methods of giving positive suggestions to the subconscious mind are contained in essence in the methods which Tohei developed from them, including the use of the mirror to give the subconscious a strong suggestion before going to sleep, as well as the emphasis on completely positive thought and action. His other teachings consist of good psychological common sense, showing gratitude, avoiding fear and anger, dealing with people in a cheerful manner, and living in the present.

What Nakamura lacked was the idea of how to test mind and body unification, which is what Tohei supplied and developed to a high degree. Tohei did not agree with all that Nakamura taught, particularly about meditation and breathing, perhaps because he had discovered better methods elsewhere. What he particularly rejected was the Kumbahaka method that Nakamura had learned in India. This was a method to help you in an emergency or crisis, or when emotions or sensations threaten to overcome you. The Kumbahaka method was to first tighten the anus, while at the same time relaxing the shoulders and filling the lower abdomen with strength. The breathing method was little more than deep abdominal breathing.

Nakamura offered suggestions and principles for recitation, a practice which Tohei adopted, although he used his own Ki principles instead. To offer an example of the difference in tone of Nakamura's principles, this is a translation of the oath he wrote for daily recitation:

Today all day
I will not anger, fear, or feel sad.
Honest, kind, and congenial,
With strength, courage, and faith,
I will take responsibility for my own life,
Never losing the spirit of peace and love,
And realizing my potential as a human being.
This I solemnly vow.

While Tohei differed from Nakamura in several important ways, he was probably closer to him in spirit than any of his other teachers. This is important, because many people only know of Tohei's Aikido associations with Ueshiba, and some view him as nothing more than a renegade has-been of the Aikikai organization. Some members of that organization have gone to great lengths to eliminate Tohei's image from their own history, by such means as airbrushing him out of old photographs and films. This must have been very difficult, as he was at Ueshiba's side in a great many of them, and while Ueshiba had many important students of Aikido spanning four generations of men, Tohei was too important a part of Aikido history to ignore. Tohei's own view is that he would prefer to be remembered first as the founder of the Ki Society, and only incidentally as a teacher of Aikido.

Undeniable Aspects of the Universe

We live in a complex and fast changing world. It is no wonder that so many people lose sight of themselves and do not know what to believe in. Religions new and old are enjoying unprecedented growth, a reflection of the insecurity of the age, and the frantic search for something to believe in. Belief is so powerful that it exempts itself from the ordinary criteria of human judgment. Belief does not need proof, it goes unquestioned. Those who believe live in bliss, because their belief frees them from the anxiety of the age.

The problem is that one person's belief is often the cause of another person's unhappiness. Most religions define themselves to a certain extent in terms of their denial of other sects or religions. Next to sex and politics, religion is the one subject best avoided if you want to maintain a harmonious relationship with another person you have just met. Yet there is below the surface a raging current of doubt. When everyone claims to be right and no one has any definitive proof, how can anyone know the truth? A shocking percentage of the world's population is willing to kill for their beliefs; or at least is willing to tell the rest of the world to go to hell, or even take them there personally. At the same time, many people have turned their backs on any religion which is too remote to be tangible, or which demands blind faith. When you see how some religious leaders and members live, it makes you wonder all the more, who and what is right?

When we all live in the same universe, why is it so difficult to agree on the nature of that universe? The voice of tolerance might say that all religions represent different paths to the same summit. Yet to the extent that a religion defines itself in terms of local customs and cultures, it can hardly be said to represent a universal view. And that is where the trouble begins. One person may accept something just because his religious authority said it was so, while another one says something else, pointing to a different authority. If the only basis for their discussion is their own belief, the more they talk the more intransigent they become. At best they may write the other person off. More likely they will try to convert them. In the worst case they will cut his throat, without a trace of remorse, for the other person represents the devil incarnate. What should be our standard for accepting something as right?

The universe is obviously beyond the power of our senses and intellect to fully grasp. We can only stand in awe of its vastness. Infinitude is the great silencer. Like the owl in the Mother Goose nursery rhyme,

> The more he sees the less he speaks.
> The less he speaks the more he sees.
> Why can't we be like that wise old bird?

We cannot be like the birds and the beasts because human beings have the ability to think. We have the capacity for both belief and doubt, and neither will leave us alone, as long as we live. If we attempt to extinguish one in favor of the other, we risk either rigidity or despair. The dilemma of belief is that the moment you believe, you cast seeds of doubt. And when you doubt, you are insecure. In what then, should we believe?

Just because Buddha or Christ said something does not make it right. First of all, we cannot be absolutely certain that they said it in that way, because neither of them left any writings whatsoever. All sayings attributed to them were recorded by their disciples and were very likely colored by their own interpretations. And always there is the danger that something was lost in the translation. After all, neither one spoke English. Out of deep respect for the Buddha, people in the past devised stories telling how he was born out of the armpit of God. For Christ, there is the Immaculate Conception. Few people today take such statements literally.

An old Chinese story tells of man by the side of the road who had painted a very life-like picture of a snake. Passersby complimented him on how good it was. He then said that he could make it even better and added legs to the creature. But then the people left, saying that since it now had legs, it was no longer a snake. This is not unlike what has happened with many of the world's religions and philosophies. The founder gained some universal insight into the nature of the universe and our place in it. The founder was of such noble character, that he could heal, lead, and inspire people by his presence alone. In time, the remarkable truth became so decorated by the fantastic myths surrounding him, that no one could really be sure what was truth and what was fiction. The easy way out is to claim that religious writings are beyond any human being to question, because they are the word of God. Unfortunately, there are other groups with different ideas making the same claim.

Is it not odd that in both East and West, religious priests cannot explain the universe without reference to ancient scriptures? We live now in the same universe that people did then. The fundamental things still apply. Basic universal truths are plainly available to anyone who has eyes to see, without needing to rely on ancient authorities. The universe exists, with or without us, and it is beyond our ability to fully measure or define. The world that we know and live in however, is a world marked by relativity, a constant interplay of opposites, a world of light and shadow, right and wrong, me and you. While it may be true in some respects that the universe is benevolent, a case can also be made that it is random and chaotic, depending on your point of view.

But underlying all of the opposites is the universe itself, which joins them as figure and ground. As they say, we are all in it together. Universal brotherhood is not true *because* Buddha or Christ said it, rather when they spoke of it they simply spoke the truth. Anything which is in accord with universal principles must be right, and anything which opposes them must be wrong. Despite our differences, there is a common ground on which we all stand. If we can find this common ground of agreement, the petty squabbles of politics, religion, and cultural differences can be easily set aside.

But what if, in trying to define universal principles we run into the same problem of reconciling differences of opinion. The problem comes in trying to describe the entire universe in words. It cannot be done, no more than you could paint a picture of everything in the world. The Chinese Taoist sage, Lao Tzu, put it very plainly when he said that the true Tao is not the Tao which we can talk about. All of nature and our very existence is supported by universal principles, whether we believe in them or not. We may not believe in a particular set of beliefs, but we all believe in the universe. We recognize that it exists and that we live in it. To live well we should try to understand and follow its principles. But how?

One way to start is by establishing the most fundamental statements that we can make about the universe, ones on which anyone anywhere can agree. We can acknowledge that these statements do not tell it all, but at least are true. As to the aspects of the universe on which there is disagreement or uncertainty, of which there must be many, we can admit that we are not sure and leave them for later. The first priority is to establish that on which we can all agree and live according to it.

The universe is greater than the sky or the galaxy, it includes everything. In order to grasp the nature of this cosmos, we must begin by trying to describe its contours. Of course infinity itself is beyond intellectual comprehension, but at least we can arrive at some basic statements about the universe on which everyone can agree. By creating an acceptable definition of the universe in which we live, we can begin to understand how to live in harmony with it. Tohei proposes three statements about the universe, which fit this criteria. At least no one can deny them with certainty.

1. The universe is like a sphere with a limitless radius, and a limitless circumference.
The idea that the universe extends infinitely in all directions would surely have been ridiculed by anyone who lived as little as 400 years ago, when the earth was generally believed to be flat and motionless. The idea that the earth was a huge ball hurling through space has been known in theory since then, but it was not until photographs were actually taken of it that people had a real feeling for it. The term *Spaceship Earth* is still more of a poetic reference than an actual feeling. In our daily conversation we still refer to up and down, and say that the sun rises and sets, even if we know better.

Though it may not look or feel like it, each of us stands at a point from which the universe extends equally and infinitely out in every direction, above, below, and to every side. It does not stop at the ground. Therefore it can be said that each of us is standing at the center of the universe, though that center is not fixed. Moving one step to the right or left does not get you any closer to the edge of the universe. That fact remains unchanged no matter where you go. Though difficult to express in words, this is another way of saying that the universe has no outer limits.

Problems arise when you think that you are the only one standing at the center of the universe. All things are equally at the center in a sphere whose circumference is nowhere and whose center is everywhere. Buddha said, "Heaven above and Earth below. I alone am the Honored One," suggesting that the Buddha nature was at the heart of the universe. His disciples in later generations misunderstood what he meant, insisting that Buddha existed at the physical center and all other beings were more or less away from that center, toward the edge. They never stopped to think what could be outside of that edge. The universe is a limitless sphere with a limitless radius. It has no center or edge as we know it. It is inconceivably large, an infinite macrocosm.

2. The universe is an infinite gathering of infinitely divisible particles.
If the number one is divided in half, that half can still be considered a unit of one itself. It may be further subdivided an infinite number of times in half, and will never reach zero. Nothing comes from nothing. As long as there is a unit, it is always further divisible. Anything which exists may be divided into parts, however small. The word *atom* comes from the ancient Greek word, *atomos*, which means indivisible. Atoms were supposed to be the smallest and most basic building block of matter, which itself was considered to be a hard and definite substance. Now we know that even the tiny atom is composed of numerous and complex subatomic particles, and that even the densest metals are made of atoms which are almost completely empty space at the subatomic level. It is almost as if each atom were a tiny solar system, so that you could shoot a large object right through it and

never have it touch anything on the way through. Even our bodies are made of countless tiny cells, each of which is a universe in itself, all the way down to the atomic level as far as we can see. Scientists can say with confidence only that a certain subatomic particle is the smallest one *yet* to have been discovered. And even these cannot be measured or described with certainty. We simply cannot pin the universe down. It is always larger than we thought and smaller than we can imagine. Even the laws of physics seem to operate differently on both the macrocosmic and microcosmic scales.

An infinite gathering of infinitely divisible particles is immeasurable and therefore difficult to comprehend. To give it a name, we may simply call it the absolute universe. Another name for it is Ki. Our sun is now an actively burning star. What was it before? It had to have come from something, for it did not just appear out of the blue. We must assume that the sun, and whatever processes created it, emerged from the infinite creative potential of the universe, in other words, from the Ki of the universe. We ourselves are no different. Though our bodies may be traced to the union of the cells of our parents, where did they come from? No matter how far back you pursue the question, the conclusion is the same. Our bodies and our life energy is born of the universe itself. All things are born of Ki. When we begin to grasp the implications of this, we understand that love and brotherhood are not just for our fellow human beings, but for all creation.

3. The universe is constantly changing and never stops moving.
Everything in the universe is in total and constant motion. From the rotation of the earth, to the passage of time, and the cycle of the four seasons, nothing ever stops moving, even for an instant. If all of the blood vessels and capillaries in your body were to be measured in their total length, they would form a line 96,000 kilometers long, enough to go around the world two and a half times. Yet for the blood to leave the heart and travel this incredible distance once around the body takes only twenty-two seconds. A small scratch on the skin scrapes off tens of millions of dead cells, while tens of millions of new cells are born to replace them. The process of metabolism is one of constant change and renewal. The law of the universe is change. To some this means chaos, to some growth and development. It is not, as some scientists claim, all downhill.

There is plenty of scientific evidence to support these three assertions about the universe, aside from the fact that the same conclusion can be reached through sensory observation or intuitive reasoning. Yet the idea of Ki as being a universe which is both infinitely large and infinitely small, and undergoing constant renewal and change, is fundamentally different from the many of the traditional assumptions about Ki found in Oriental medicine and the martial arts.

The Archaic Approach to Ki

The word Ki itself derives from the Chinese character, which originally represented the fundamental energy of the universe. The original character portrays what looks like an eight-directional compass, suggesting that energy is extending in all directions. This portion of the character can also mean rice, a source of food energy. The character was simplified by the Japanese Ministry of Education after World War II, into an X-like cross, a symbol meaning to close off or seal inside. This may make the character easier to write, but it totally distorts the original meaning.

Nevertheless, people in the past had their own limited view of Ki, based on ignorance and superficial perceptions. The ancient Chinese, and the Japanese who learned from them, believed that Ki was a force which existed in nature, and was constantly circulating about like the wind. Three or four thousand years ago people had no possible means of imagining that the earth was round, or that it revolved around the sun. The sky above appeared limitless, as did the horizon. Heaven appeared infinite, but not so the earth. The ground was solid and immovable. People naturally looked to the earth as a source of stability, and this was reflected in both posture and attitude alike. It can still be seen today in the low fighting stances commonly used in the martial arts.

The universe was thought of as a vessel filled with Ki which moved about from place to place. When Ki gathered and accumulated in one place, this was known as *seiki*, a sign of good fortune and Heaven's favor. When Ki went someplace else, it was known as *suiki*, declining or failing Ki. At such times it was best to stay home and do nothing, until Ki returned and was with you. As a result, the ancient Chinese did everything they could to store and accumulate Ki within their bodies, and not let any of it escape. The ideal condition was considered one in which Ki was drawn in from the top of the skull at a point called "Heaven's Passage" (*tsû-ten*), circulated around the meridians (*keiraku*) and accumulated at an area in the center of the abdomen near the navel called "field for the Ocean of Ki" (*seika tan-den no ki kai*). When a large measure of Ki was stored in the abdomen, it was thought to swell out in such a way that the navel pointed up toward Heaven. Statues and drawings of the Saints made by the ancients often depicted the anatomy and the belly in this fashion.

While the old ideas of Ki make a fascinating study from the point of art history or cultural anthropology, they hardly make for a framework reliable enough to chart our course by. To train according to ancient concepts and outdated traditions which long ago filtered into Japan from India and China is to repeat their errors. It does not matter what ancient tradition says. What matters is what is right.

Fortunately, Tohei has developed a method of Ki testing which allows us to verify for ourselves whether a training method is right or wrong. The problem of training without Ki testing is that it is very easy to believe that you are indeed developing Ki, getting stronger, or healing yourself, when in fact you may only be fooling yourself. Many of the ancient methods do produce a feeling of energy or strength, but it is only a feeling, like getting dizzy from hyperventilation. One Karate teacher's comment is worth keeping in mind: everyone he had ever met who practiced the ancient Chinese Ki methods said that they felt as strong as tigers, but they always lost in martial arts competitions. Talk is cheap, feelings are subjective; only action speaks for itself.

The Energy of Life

Benjamin Franklin was partly right when he said that while God heals, the doctor collects the bill. Our health is sustained by the life-force, which is actually a function of Ki itself. This life-force heals sickness, repairs injury, and maintains our immunity against disease. No matter how skilled the doctor, no matter how potent the medicine, there can be no healing or recovery once the spark of life is gone. Heart and kidney transplants, and other miracles of modern medicine are only possible because the life-force is still active in the patient. An organ transplant is obviously useless once the patient is dead.

One of the reasons that modern medicine has reached an impasse despite its technical progress, is that it has not given serious enough attention to how to strengthen this life-force and prevent disease from occurring in the first place. What good does it do if a drug fixes the headache, but its side effects cause stomach problems? No drug is entirely free of side effects. While stimulating the life-force in one place, it interferes with it in another. When a patient is simultaneously under several, or even several dozen types of medications, the combined side effects are dangerous and unpredictable, and almost certain to weaken the very life-force which is the mainstay of health.

Doctors must recognize that their role in healing includes early discovery of the symptoms of disease: as well as finding ways to work with and strengthen the life-force. What actually heals the patient however, is his own inherent life energy.

We are aware of the food that we eat until it passes our throats. The processes of digestion in the stomach, chemical breakdown in the liver, and absorption in the intestines is largely beyond our conscious control or awareness. Furthermore, the nutrients of our food are not incorporated as they are into our flesh and blood, but are rather synthesized into usable elements, according to our bodily needs and structure. Only then is this food transformed into useful life energy. Our bodies are like extremely sophisticated, custom-made chemical factories for transforming food into energy.

The process of metabolism which sustains life, goes on without stopping until the day that we die. It operates without any conscious effort on our part, whether we wake or sleep. What makes life work is still a mystery, even to medical science. For lack of a better word, we may simply call this mysterious force *life energy*.

Our individual lives are inextricably tied to the life, energy of the universe itself. The universe is a whole and we are a part of it. Our life energy cannot be sustained for an instant without it. When we maintain a good circulation of Ki with the universe, the life energy operates at maximum efficiency and gives us a natural immunity against disease. As a result, the autonomic nervous system is kept in balance, the blood circulation to all parts of the body is good, and each organ plays its appropriate role in maintaining health.

There are dozens of health methods to choose from, ranging from dietary regimens to exercise programs. However, many of these are based on limited insights, or narrow points of view. People tend to rely on what they believe is the answer, without realizing that some of these systems actually run counter to natural principles. Far from increasing health, many of them actually can damage it. It is not surprising that many of the founders of these systems, from jogging to extreme dietary methods, actually die at an earlier age than the average person who pursues none of these methods. Anything which violates natural principles is bound to fail. The correct method for maintaining health is to coordinate mind and body, and follow the principles of the universe.

The Rhythm of Life

The famous early Jazz pianist and vocalist, Thomas "Fats" Waller, was once asked by a lady what rhythm was. He replied, "Lady, if you got to ask, you ain't got it." Rhythm, and indeed music itself is something which must be perceived with more than just the ears. Claude Debussy went so far as to say that the music was between the notes. This is a helpful analogy in understanding Ki, as a real but intangible force.

The Taoist philosopher Chuang Tzu said that Ki (*Chi*) was what was between all things, connecting them throughout the universe. The separation between things is only apparent, an optical illusion. Many familiar daily phenomena are actually quite different than they appear. The water on the ocean seems to travel across the surface in waves, while in fact it moves in place, up and down in a circular motion as the wave of energy passes through it. This is why a tidal wave will pass unnoticed under a ship at sea and only reveal its true size when it climbs up on the beach. Scientists and artists may become aware of some of the subtle forces which our senses miss, but they often tend to overlook Ki, because like the air, Ki is everywhere.

The one aspect of Ki which is obvious is change, and the law of change is rhythm. Life is constant change. How well we live and how much we enjoy our lives, depends on whether we can be in harmony with the rhythms of life. Those who ignore or oppose rhythm risk imbalance and suffering. This does not mean that we must be slaves to the rhythms of the sun and seasons, for human beings are not just passive recipients, but active participants in this rhythm. Sailing is a frequently used analogy for living. Our bodies are like vessels: prisons if poorly used or abused, yet tremendously useful and adaptable if properly understood.

Change is constant, certain, and increasing all of the time, throwing many of our values and assumptions into question. Yet if we want to live well, we must welcome change, and not be swept away by it. Tohei frequently quotes a poem about the moon which remains in the heavens, though it is swept by the eight winds. The last part of the poem reinforces this with an image of a lone rock standing firm in the wind blown snow.

There is something sad about a life without synchronicity, a lack of harmony in human relationships, poor coordination in movement or bodily functions, a spoiled environment. Is there a way to live in balance in the midst of chaos? Can we find the eye of the hurricane? Human beings from all cultures have striven to find the answer to this question through religion, philosophy, art, science, and the many pursuits of civilization. Ki development can help provide the answers, for it gives us a sense of mind and body harmony from within. If we only have this, then the products of our civilization will reflect it, as they have in all the great renaissances of the past.

The Instinct to Survive

When the life-force is strong, it gives all life forms a strong survival instinct. When Ki becomes weak, so does the instinct to survive. One of Tohei's senior students, Mr. Koretoshi Maruyama, once found a praying mantis trying to cross a road which had fairly heavy traffic. Usually green, these insects turn brown before dying, and this one had already begun to change color. He picked up the praying mantis and turned it back toward the grass, thinking that it would be safer there. The insect turned around and headed again for the road. He turned it around again, and again it came back several times, each time growing angry at the interference. Finally he gave up and let it go where it wanted. The praying mantis was run over by the next car that passed. Apparently in nature there is an instinct to die as well as live.

Before beginning his study of Aikido in 1962, Maruyama Sensei had worked in his family's business. On one occasion he was sitting in his usual place at his desk, thinking that it was earlier than he usually went to lunch, but deciding to make an exception that day. Moments after he left his seat a runaway truck come crashing through the window, completely crushing the desk and chair where he had been. He himself escaped with a few glass cuts on his hand. The driver had fallen asleep at the wheel and there had been no warning of the accident except an unconscious urge to move, which saved his life.

This instinct to move to safety does not operate equally for us all. When the life-force is weak, its protective instinct sometimes works in reverse. Maruyama Sensei once had to meet with the section chief of a client company. He remembered thinking that the man cut a rather small and sad figure from behind as the man was leaving his office, and wondered if he would be alright going home. The next day he read on the front page of the newspaper that the man had been stabbed to death later that night, while trying to stop an argument between two young punks. The accident occurred in a part of Tokyo which was known to be quite dangerous late at night. When Ki is weak, people tend to take unnecessary risks, and even flirt with danger.

Scientists often view the universe in terms of entropy, that is in view of its tendency toward chaos or disorder, as if everything were gradually running down and running out. But living things demonstrate countless examples of life's incredible energy against entropy. Evolution itself is the story of indomitable Ki. Salmon swim upstream to lay their eggs, animals in the wild struggle and survive against incredible odds, people adapt to extreme changes in the environment, or even challenge new and hostile environments.

There are also many examples of self-destructive behavior, particularly among human beings. Life consists of opposites, light and dark, plus and minus, health and sickness. Both are real, but we do have the capacity to choose plus, life, health, and survival over their opposites. One student of Chinese philosophy challenged Tohei on this point, saying that just as *yin* and *yang* both existed in the universe, we should balance the good in ourselves with bad. This student was under the illusion that he could personally manage the accounts of nature, and his life was shackled by endless rules of what he should eat, wear, and do, all in an effort to balance *yin* and *yang*. The only difference between him and an ordinary neurotic was that he was philosophical about it.

It is true that we live in a world in which death, disease, war, and poverty are daily realities. However, we need not forget that every situation contains the seeds of its opposite, and that we can always turn minus into plus. The force of life is plus, extending out, known in Japanese as *yô-ki* (or *yang* Ki), a word also meaning cheerful, bright, and positive. Its opposite is *in-ki* (or *yin* Ki), which means gloomy, depressed, and pessimistic. Extending Ki is plus. By extending Ki we invite favorable circumstances. By pulling Ki within we only ask for the worst. It is nothing so simplistic as trying to maintain a moderate balance of good and bad. All we need do is to recognize that we have a choice. We may not be able to control all that happens to us, but we can see to it that we are always in a positive state, ready to receive and to create good. Freedom from bondage to the duality of good and evil really means that we have the freedom to choose plus. The life instinct gives us the energy and resolve to choose. Without it, we find ourselves unhappy slaves of circumstance.

The Web of Cause and Effect

Negative people are attracted by philosophies which teach determinism. All cultures have them, or manage to give a deterministic interpretation to an existing philosophy. Buddhism teaches that life is a web of cause and effect. A crude interpretation of this is that whatever we do comes back to us in the form of *karma*, that we cannot escape the consequences of our actions. Even if you manage to escape the hand of the law, they say you will be punished for wrongdoings by the universal law, in this lifetime or the next. When the laws of man are ineffective in maintaining order, the idea of universal justice does have a certain intuitive appeal. Anyone who has been wronged would like to believe that the wrongdoer will get his just desserts someday.

The problem is that this belief can serve as an excuse for inaction. One French student, who considered himself a Buddhist, claimed that parents could really do nothing to help their children, since the child's character and destiny were already largely determined by what he had done in his past life. The man had no children of his own and was completely enamored of his own philosophy. He was basically a fatalist and had his own peculiar view of Buddhist thought.

The more you analyze something, the more it becomes apparent how intricately connected it is with everything else. The question of reincarnation aside, we are all a result of a complex mix of influences: hereditary, historical, and cultural. It is easy to see that the whole influences the part, but we tend to forget that the part can also influence the whole through the same mechanism. One of the fundamental principles of Buddhism is right effort. If you make right effort, you get right results. If you make wrong effort, you get wrong results. But if you do not know what is right, how can you make right effort?

Many people complain that although they have not done anything wrong, they are still unhappy; though they work very hard, they are still poor. At the same time, others seem to be born into wealth or good fortune that they do not deserve. By all appearances, the distribution of good luck is far from fair. But this is deceptive, because people only look at what is at hand and fail to take the long-term or wholistic view. In fact, the universe is extremely fair and consistent in its law of cause and effect.

If you throw a stone in a pond, it makes visible waves, which soon vanish from sight, but are they really gone? Actually they never really disappear. The same is true of our words, thoughts, and actions. Once issued, they never truly disappear. Each becomes a cause in itself, plus calling forth plus, minus attracting minus.

How do you explain the unequal distribution of wealth, intelligence, and good circumstances at birth, without relying on the theory of reincarnation or assuming that it is a Godless universe? Consider your parents, and your parents' parents, going back as far as thirty-three generations. Your ancestors in the last 1,000 years total a number rivaling the current population of the earth. Through means which are neither mysterious nor occult, all of these ancestors have contributed to make your life possible today. Of all of these people, how many lived good lives? Even of the good people among them, there must have been good and bad days, or right and wrong deeds. We are subject to all of this influence, and through them the indirect influence of everyone else's ancestors. Not surprisingly, this results in individuals whose situations are totally unique, and circumstances which range from the best to the worst.

Those born into good circumstances benefit from the right actions and good fortunes of their ancestors, and vice versa. But if you were not born into good circumstances there is no need to be disappointed. The universe is constantly changing and we are not totally passive recipients of fate. Our present state may reflect our past, but it need not foreshadow our future. Starting where we are, we can change it for the better by choosing to lead a plus life.

Regardless of your personality tendencies or physical inheritance, everything can be changed by what happens in-between your birth and death. A talented youngster can be ruined by manipulative adults, just as a spoiled child can be made great by caring adults. Nurture can do much to offset nature. *In-ga* is the Japanese word for cause and effect. There is also a word for what can happen in-between, the intermediary influence of *en*, a word meaning "edge," or "relation." The endless permutations of *in-en-ga*, cause turning into effect and effect turning into cause, with constant interference from the edges, make for the dynamic and constant changes of the world. What is important for us in Ki development is to remember that our efforts, attitudes, and actions are also *en,* and that through them we have the power to change our circumstances.

It is as possible to squander a hard earned fortune in one generation as it is to earn one. It happens all of the time. If you just ride on your luck, without sowing positive seeds yourself, someday you or your children will feel the effects. We should feel grateful to those who went before us and gave us an opportunity to learn the way of the universe. If a person is shown the way, and does nothing about it, you can assume that they had not enough *en* to recognize the value of what they were shown.

Rather than moan and complain about your situation, you should take advantage of your free time and think and act positively to change it. Gratitude is possible for some aspect of any situation, no matter how bleak. If you are poor, you can be grateful that you are healthy. If you are sick, at least you are still alive and may recover. Look at those better off as an inspiration to make effort, and look at those worse off as a grateful reminder of how well off you are. This process applies not only to your circumstances in general, but to every word you speak and every action you take. Think of yourself as standing at the center of two radiating cones, one accepting the influences of the past, one extending influences into the future. Take responsibility to stop the bad influences of the past in your lifetime and only pass on the best ones to future generations. If everyone took this attitude, the earth would soon be transformed into a paradise. This may seem like a utopian dream, but it is not impossible. You can at least determine to start with yourself.

Flaws of the Self-centered World View

Much of our thinking is still heavily influenced by our ancestors' belief in an earth-centered universe. Note the pervasive influence of Newtonian and Euclidean thinking on science and daily life today, even though it is well established that neither of these fully describes the real world that we live in. Like the optical illusion that the sun is rising and setting, these views may be useful, and may roughly apply in some situations, but they are not accurate descriptions of the way things actually are.

The mechanistic view of the world spawned philosophies in the nineteenth century like Social Darwinism, which said that in society as in nature, only the fittest are entitled to survive. This was a polite way of saying that you should take what you can get. Its counterpart was Imperialism, which continues to haunt us today. You do not have to scratch the surface of today's trouble spots very far to find feelings still festering from events which occurred during the last few hundred years.

If we want to live at peace in one world, we must learn to see the world as it is. This does not mean joining a utopian society, following a mystical seer, or becoming indoctrinated into a new political cause. We have already seen how none of these things work, and how badly they can deform people when carried to extremes. The more we try to insist that other people live or act in a certain way, the more resistance we are likely to get. People follow others much more faithfully if led than if forced. In order to lead others, you must first learn to integrate and control yourself. This is only possible by learning to unify mind and body.

Family, church, and school have created moral injunctions, shoulds and should-nots, rather than teaching people to behave in an intelligent manner out of enlightened self-interest. There is ample evidence for the interdependence and interconnectedness of all phenomena. This applies in our environment and society, where it has an immediate and personal relevance. Yet we continue to think, speak, and act as though it were not so. We may know that it is better to give than to receive, but we do not act that way, partly because we do not understand why it is better. If we saw ourselves not as isolated individuals, but in relation to other people, then we could directly perceive that giving is one of the best ways of receiving. What we send out comes back to us; or if you like, what goes around comes around. If you try to keep everything for yourself you tend to lose or spoil it. This is illustrated in the story of King Midas, who in his avarice was granted the golden touch, only to find he could touch nothing and no one without turning it into an inanimate gold object. Zen has a similar parable, about a nun who tried to make all of the incense smoke go to her Buddha statue alone, only to find that it blackened the statue's nose. Japanese villagers used to say that if you try to keep all of the water in your rice paddy, it not only runs off, but you wind up the outcast of the village. In Taoism, water is used as a metaphor for the Way. If you push it away from you, it comes back; if you try to gather it to yourself, it runs away. Like Ki, it stays fresher when it circulates freely.

Believing in the Power of the Mind

While it is obvious that changes in the mind produce changes in the body and vice versa, the question to ask is, which one is more central, closer to the roots of the self? The spiritualists and materialists have been arguing this point for hundreds of years, and neither school seems to have arrived at a workable approach for improving the self. Even though the mind and body are one, they operate by different principles, in different dimensions of the same reality, so to speak. It is not possible to be effective if you ignore one in favor of the other. Some religions teach that disease is all in the mind and that if you hold images of health in your mind, the disease will go away. However the results of such approaches are often tragic, particularly if no physical attempts are made to treat the problem at all. People assume that sports helps to build fine character and some sportsmen do have a fine character; but many do not, and the relation between the two increasingly seems incidental. Just as an axle needs two wheels to be useful, we need to develop both mind and body if we are to stay in balance.

On the other hand, the power of suggestion or belief is well established. Psychologists have researched the process thoroughly. Hypnotists use it and get results. When a suggestion forms part of a set of beliefs about the self, it becomes our self-image. The effect of the self-image on our abilities and behavior is well documented, including the fact that this image can be changed.

While the body may be subject to various illnesses and limitations, the mind need not be controlled by the body. If the mind remains free and strong, then it can rejuvenate the body and bring it out of trouble, but only if it does not try to escape into a separate reality. More accurately, even if the body or mind fall ill or out of balance, Ki itself need not grow weak.

266

By training to unify our mind and body and learning to extend Ki anytime, we can avoid most of the problems which plague the average person, and become stronger in both mind and body. Ultimately, we can train ourselves to have a strong character which cannot only overcome personal problems, but become a valuable and positive influence to other people as well. In this way we will leave the world a better place than we found it. The word *karma* means work or action, as well as consequence, and in this sense it is the same as *en*. Tohei calls it mind over matter.

To apply this with confidence, we must confirm for ourselves that the mind leads the body. We often tend to act as though the opposite were true. If we are easily swayed by our appetites and circumstances we have no freedom, because everything is determined by forces beyond our control. It is the mind which tastes food, through the organ of the tongue. It is we ourselves who take a walk, not our legs. A person whose body parts move at random or without control is in trouble, because mind and body are not unified. This does not mean that handicapped people cannot be helped. Whatever the cause of their disability, as long as they have an ability to communicate and a desire to improve, Ki training can be of tremendous benefit. Tohei has taught at the Friends of the Handicapped Organization (Shin-shô Tomo no Kai) in Japan, concentrating on Kiatsu, Ki breathing, and the four basic principles of mind and body unification. Even for people who had been handicapped for years, the results were so impressive, that in 1977 he received official recognition from the Imperial Prince Akihito of Japan, who is now the Emperor.

A Chinese saying has it that if the mind is not in the tongue, there is no taste; if the mind is not in the eyes, there is no sight; and if the mind is not in the ears, there is no hearing. We know this because we all have experienced varying degrees of presence and absence of mind, particularly while reading or engaging in any task requiring concentration.

How can you believe in Ki when you cannot see it? We must and do believe in many things for which there is no tangible evidence or guarantee whatsoever. Without this we could not live and society could not function. How can you be certain that your parents are really your parents and that you were not adopted? How do you know that the food you have ordered in a restaurant is not poisoned? Why do you trust any product that you ever use? How do you know that you will not die in your sleep? Ultimately we must believe in the universe and that it will protect us, otherwise we would end up insane and unable to function. Compared to these things which we normally believe in and take for granted, it must be relatively easy to believe in Ki.

Freedom of Choice

The philosophical problem of freedom and determinism is an old one and has been argued at length by intellectuals for centuries. What many of them misunderstand however, is that this is not an intellectual problem, but an experimental one. It is possible to muster quite convincing arguments both pro and con, because it is a relative issue and opposites are always partly right. However, relative conclusions are dead ends, because they never present the whole picture.

With the experience of mind and body coordination we are given a new option, the possibility to explore and experiment with the range of our potential, knowing that it has no limits beyond those that we ourselves impose. We have a choice of either unifying mind and body and controlling our fate, or allowing ourselves to drift apart in the sea of change.

Given the choice, would not anyone prefer a bright happy life to a dark gloomy one? Who would not prefer to be healthy than sick, prosperous than poor, loved than hated? Oddly, the answer is that a great many people find this a difficult choice. Why is the decision difficult? What is the source of their dilemma?

It can only be assumed to be ignorance, wrong ideas, false perceptions, ways that do not work. Where do these things come from? Eastern religions have it that delusion come from the illusions of the relative world. We are deceived because we believe that things are as they appear on the surface. But there is another, more obvious answer. They come from our past. History tells the story of man's follies and errors more eloquently than any philosophical or religious theory. We have inherited our past, and man has made a mess of the world. Yet we also have the hope that through our actions in the present, we can transform ourselves and our world, even in our lifetime. Once this is clear and the impact of its responsibility and privilege is felt, then there is no longer any dilemma, indeed no longer any question of what to do, only how.

Old World Thinking in the New Age Dogma

A Chinese parable tells of a man who was aboard ship, when he accidentally dropped his sword overboard. He carefully marked the side of the boat at the spot where he had lost his sword, so that he could look for it when they arrived on shore. The allegory suggests that many of our frames of reference are irrelevant, because things keep changing. As old as this story is, it is still relevant today and pinpoints the reason why we should not stick to the teachings of the past.

Many of the disciplines of the past which are enjoying a great revival in the present are the remains of teachings which, while they may have had value in the beginning, over time have degenerated into irrational or irrelevant practices. For reasons ranging from political oppression to sheer ignorance, some of these disciplines evolved in an atmosphere of extremely ascetic or monastic conditions. They were practiced in a master-disciple relationship, which required relinquishing of the world for the demanding pursuit of exclusive occult traditions. Many of the approaches taken in the past are either archaic or counterproductive for modern people.

Today, relative freedom of expression removes much of the need for secrecy. Moreover, the urgency of environmental and other problems with global impact requires an approach which works quickly and efficiently, without wasted effort. The pace of life will not allow people today the luxuries of time taken by people in the past.

Old world thinking can be defined as any idea which ignores or denies the fundamental principles which we have established about the universe, particularly the essential unity of mind and body, and the universe as a macrocosmic, microcosmic totality in constant change. Extreme examples of old world thinking include: the flat earth theory, Ptolemaic cosmology, the ghost in the machine concept of spirit in body, the theory of humours and meridians, racism, nationalism, war, crime, a list as old as history.

The New Age movement refers to a collection of diverse schools of thought and practice, each of which is seeking an alternative to the institutions and beliefs of the past. The Age in reference is the Aquarian Age of astrology, in which there is supposed to be a higher spiritual consciousness and a more enlightened society. While much good has come of this movement in raising general consciousness about important issues and assumptions, the movement has also generated much mischief and confusion. In its worst aspects, it can be associated with people who have gone totally off the deep end. It is ironic that much of the so-called New Age movement is based on thoroughly old world concepts. The term *old world* does not necessarily refer to any time or sequence in history, rather to things which have been shown to be false, out-of-date, or inappropriate to the present. Antiquity is not a criteria for truth. Tohei is fond of saying that the only things which are valuable *because* they are old are antiques. What is true is true, regardless of who said it, or how long ago.

Many sincere people are involved in the New Age movement. It is not our purpose to deny or reject wholesale the New Age approaches, but only to offer a word of caution, that they do not all necessarily lead in the same direction as Ki development, and that a few can be actually dangerous. The best advice is to look before you leap, make an intelligent choice, and do not try to mix the contradictory elements of different approaches.

Some New Age disciplines make use of machines to monitor or alter consciousness. One of Tohei's students brought him a machine which could supposedly measure alpha waves, the brain waves associated with relaxation and mental concentration. Indeed, one of the senior teachers present could generate alpha waves without any effort. But when one of the junior trainees tried it, he was unable to generate any alpha waves. Everyone assumed that it was a matter of lack of training. But suddenly, when he heard the cries of the sweet potato vendor outside, the machine responded by showing a stream of alpha waves.

Researchers have tried using the same machine with men who were established masters of concentration, a Zen priest, an Kyûdô archer, and a professional Japanese chess player. None were able to produce alpha waves. The explanation was that the professionals were probably too nervous about the results to concentrate. What surprised one researcher was that a gum chewing boy of fifteen was able to produce a steady stream of alpha waves. His explanations was that there were good alpha waves and bad alpha waves, and that the machine was not sophisticated enough to tell the difference. Tohei remarked that if it could not distinguish between concentration and daydreaming, such a machine was not reliable enough to be of any use. Besides, what use was it in daily life if you had to be hooked up to an expensive device in order to know if you were relaxed?

Some New Age techniques are designed to enhance whole-brain thinking or create super-intelligence. Much of this is common sense under new names, or approaches using music or drawing which create a relaxed state. Relaxation is the *real* reason behind the improved performance when it occurs; the method itself is incidental. However, whether for brain or body, any overemphasis on strengthening a part of the human being can lead to a neglect of the other parts. If pursued by an unbalanced character out of greed or selfishness, the technique may work, but the end results may not produce anything very pretty.

Also common in the New Age movement is the analysis, re-creation, and exploration of dreams as alternate realities. It is true that the so-called *hard reality* of social norms can damage mental health. The world of the artist's imagination deserves our enthusiastic support. However, in work with dreams there is a danger of people taking their own subjective experiences as true and reliable reference points, gradually losing the ability to empathize with others or be objective about themselves. It is easy to dream about your progress, but you cannot eat the food in a picture. And you cannot develop Ki without mind and body unification.

New Age therapies come in all varieties, from acupuncture and massage, to counseling and occult sessions. The failure of conventional approaches, as well as the need to restore balance is obvious. But people too easily assume that the alternatives must be better simply because they are different, or because someone is enthusiastic about them. Many alternative therapies represent poorly digested and incomplete interpretations of the original. We need to apply the same critical thinking to them that we do to any professional legal, financial, or health services we might enlist. There have always been a lot of charlatans in the healing field. Sick people are suckers for them. So-called *psychic surgeons* from the Philippines carry out "operations" with their bare hands, removing what they claim is a cancerous tumor. Many accept a large fee for this service, more than enough to pay for the chicken livers, blood bags, and cotton swabs which they use to create the ruse.

Many New Age groups use the word Ki, but the important thing to remember is that they do not all mean the same thing by it. If you press them, you will find that many do not really know what they mean by it, except that it is an ancient word for energy. The problem is that ancient ideas of Ki were heavily influenced by wrong ideas about the earth and the universe. The approaches taken by these disciplines were often designed around astrological superstitions, or otherwise self-centered thinking. Despite all of the health methods man has ever devised, the best one seems to be the simplest: avoid extremes and do not worry about small things. To put it positively, learn how to relax and enjoy life. One thing is clear, that which heals is not the medicine or the knife, or even the positive thinking, but rather the wondrous workings of the human life-force, of Ki itself. Anything we can do to increase that life-force, or our free exchange of it with the universe, will increase our health, extend our lives, and protect us from illness and accident. Rather than pursue the endless remedies and complicated rituals which *might* make us better, why not begin with the simplest, most practical approach for daily life, Ki development?

Another characteristic of New Age methods is the seeking of instant enlightenment using variations on ancient disciplines. The appeal of the instant approach is obvious in modern society. The use of various machines to measure consciousness and devices to alter it must appeal to people who use machines to accomplish almost anything else that they do. For all its utility, the automobile has caused people to stop walking as much as they used to, with an attendant decline in health. You need to be careful about anything which takes you someplace too fast.

Another danger of using machines is that they mask the other side of convenience: easy come, easy go. In any real crisis you go in alone, therefore it is not a good idea to become too dependent on external devices to strengthen yourself. People often enter a spiritual discipline in search of what they think they want, peace of mind, higher awareness, or freedom from fear, without really having any idea of what these things mean, or of what it takes to achieve them. It is very easy to be satisfied with a substitute experience. A counterfeit experience is often much easier to obtain than the real thing. Indeed, there are those who package these things very slickly, and would be more than happy to take your money and time for them.

As to occult psychology and practices, there are many documented examples of charlatans using dime store magic tricks and posing as Ki masters or supernatural shamans. It takes a sophisticated eye to catch a trained person at sleight of hand, and there are plenty of gullible people who will fall for it. One "Ki" master, who calls himself Mr. Maric (a contraction of the words Magic-Trick), demonstrated on Japanese television how he could burn a ¥10,000 note in front of everyone and then "restore" it as if brand new, using Ki alone. His proof was that the serial numbers were the same, both notes ending in the number 14. It is true that no two notes are issued with the same number, but close examination of the video reveals that he had penciled over the last digit, turning an 11 into a 14. The distance between the last two digits was much smaller on the "Ki" note, than on the original. He was lucky that he was not arrested for burning legal tender.

Another of Mr. Maric's "Ki" demonstrations involved making a cigarette roll freely on the table, using energy which he projected from his hands. When an American magician, James Randi, challenged him to do it again after sprinkling tiny shreds of tissue paper around the cigarette, Maric refused. He knew that the paper would fly when he blew on the cigarette at right angles, causing it to roll. He could blow a stream of air without being noticed, but so can ventriloquists, who can do even better by projecting their voice to a puppet! All you need to do is to pick up a good book on how to do magic tricks, and you too can be a "Ki" master, as long as you do not tell anyone your secret. For a thorough unmasking of these kinds of charlatans and their methods, readers are referred to two excellent books, *The Faith Healers* (Buffalo, N. Y.: Prometheus Books, 1987), and *Flim Flam!* (Buffalo, N. Y.: Prometheus Books, 1982) both by James Randi.

Another reflection of our times is seen in some of the New Age methods which recommend chemical and other artificial approaches to altering consciousness. The use of drugs, electrical stimuli, even nutrients to change consciousness or performance is obviously possible, usually illegal (as in the Olympics), almost completely untested for long-term side effects, and has extremely dangerous potential for abuse. All of these approaches are also subject to one fundamental flaw: they assume and act as though the body leads the mind. As with any chemical dependency, the more the crutch is used, the lazier the body becomes, and the more it loses its capacity to sustain itself. Using drugs to achieve higher consciousness is the Russian Roulette of the New Age.

Lastly, we should remember that the way of the universe is simple. Anything which is too complicated, too hard to grasp or put into practice, should be looked at very carefully. A truly universal principle should be universally true (it works everywhere), repeatable (anyone can do it, more than once, without needing special conditions), and observable (not based on someone's word or subjective experience).

If we keep our approach simple we can walk the way of the universe: the road that anyone can walk. Truth is not something written in a book, nor is it based on one person's limited opinion or experience. It is clearly before our eyes, and it is everywhere we look. We cannot grasp it all, but we can learn to work with it, not to fight it; and to respect those of its principles which we do understand. Fortunately, we need take nothing on blind faith. The intellect may not be able to control mind and body on its own, but it can understand and appreciate what is happening. If we work with Ki, it will work for us.

Chapter *12:* Ki Perspectives for a Society in Balance

What It Means to Live a Plus Life

If you consider the incredible odds against the particular union of cells which made your life possible, you realize how lucky you are to have been born at all. For this we should be grateful and work to live our lives to the fullest. Awareness of the unique opportunity of birth is the source of insight into what we each are meant to do, as well as of the energy to do it. We either embrace life or we wait for death.

The universe itself is beyond opposites; but the world we live in is a relative world of opposing forces, plus and minus, *yin* and *yang*. Every light casts a shadow. Reality is a mixture of good and bad elements. It is a matter of personal choice whether we choose to view our lot as a cup half-full, or a cup half-empty. It is still the same cup. As Shakespeare noted, there is nothing either good or bad, but thinking makes it so. If we would live a good life, we must strive to eliminate all negative thinking from the subconscious mind and fill it with only positive thoughts. Tohei uses the analogy of a cup of tea, which can be changed to pure water, one drop at a time, or in a flood. All that is required is the steady effort to think, speak, act, treat others, and contribute to society in a positive manner.

There are those who object that positive thinking is too idealistic for the real world. The traditional approach is to assume that since you cannot really eliminate evil or darkness, you must learn to live with it, or seek peace of mind in retreat from the world. Unfortunately, there are also plenty of people who take the attitude that breaking the law is only wrong if you get caught. A positive life is one lived in accordance with the principles of the universe, a negative life ignores or goes against them. We have a choice, although many people choose minus out of ignorance, which is a lack of understanding of the way things are. A plus life is all to our benefit, but no one is forced to choose it.

We get lots of bad news through the media. Whatever good news there is gets quickly drowned out by the next crisis, natural disaster, outbreak of war, revolution, assassination, senseless crime, the list is endless. How is it possible to maintain a positive mind in the face of such misery? Hiding one's head in the sand will not make the problems go away. The important thing to remember is that having strong Ki does not mean being naively optimistic, and smiling no matter what happens. It is perfectly possible to express anger, surprise, or sadness, or any other human emotion without cutting Ki. Bad news may occasion a variety of emotions, but it need never cause you to slacken your Ki. Instead, one should look for lessons in it, and try to find ways to help, no matter how remote. When the bad news is close at hand, you must act rather than react, and this requires mind and body unification.

We have examined in detail the methods which Tohei developed for individual mind and body unification, but what of society at large? What are the consequences of Ki development for politics, economics, the family? These areas are as value-loaded as individual lifestyle, so Tohei has deliberately avoided giving overly specific prescriptions for what is right. But these issues concern us all and Tohei's comments on Ki development and society are worth serious consideration. People directly involved with these issues may be in a position to do something about them. If so, Ki development will help them find the strength and the means to do so.

Political Renewal

In Japan, political activity was originally referred to as *matsuri-goto*, or festival celebrations. All over Japan throughout the year, people celebrate festivals for all kinds of reasons. Typically they are celebrated to show gratitude to plants, animals, fish, even needles and other objects which are sacrificed so that human beings may have a better life. Of course there is also plenty of food, drinking and dancing, but that is not the original purpose of the festival.

In any society, it is impossible to achieve total fairness or satisfaction for all groups and individuals. Peoples' needs are just too complex. The purpose of politics is to remind everyone of their mutual interdependence, and to regenerate the desire to work together as best as possible with a spirit of gratitude. However when people forget this, they focus on what they themselves or their group can get, without any regard for the whole. Democracy is widely considered the most workable political system in the world; but real democracy focuses on mutual satisfaction, not just individual rights. We should try to remember the original spirit of the *matsuri,* and direct our efforts toward creating good without seeking direct reward in return. The words of John F. Kennedy are immortal: "Ask not what your country can do for you, ask what you can do for your country."

Politicians should think in long-range terms for the good of society, rather than simply reacting to the pressure groups of the moment, out of their own desire for reelection. They should make decisions and take actions which are respectable in the eyes of the universe, not just to please their constituents. In feudalistic societies it was enough for the lord of the region to look after his local affairs. Now politicians must look after the interests of entire nations, and increasingly, even these boundaries are becoming less and less meaningful. We live together on a single planet. What you thought was over there may soon be over here.

To be narrowly concerned about national interests and ignore the massive sufferings of people in other countries is against the way of the universe. When so many are starving, it is vicious and shortsighted to restrict food production for economic reasons. Many countries do provide foreign aid or money, but what they give is really a pittance compared to the magnitude of the problem. Even in disaster areas when thousands of people are dying everyday, relief is often delayed for bureaucratic reasons; delivered too little and too late. Foreign aid is not usually a national priority. If you superimpose geographical and political maps, you see clearly how arbitrary our national boundaries are in the scheme of nature. Nature recognizes no passport, for we are all citizens of the same earth. A responsible politician knows that his neighbor's problems are his, or will be soon. Confucius said that if a man takes no thought about what is distant, he will find sorrow near at hand.

One of the most serious responsibilities of a nation's leadership is to prevent the outbreak of war, while at the same time maintaining a degree of order and respect for international law. The reason for law is to uphold the idea that right makes might. However, the dictators and renegades of the world operate from the opposite assumption, that might makes right. History has shown that one gives in to such people only at a great cost, for they stop at nothing to achieve their own selfish ends. Still, no moral nation feels right about going to war in order to prevent war. What then should be done?

Regardless of the errors or intransigence of the other side, it always takes two to make a fight. If the leaders on one side can negotiate with the calmness of *fudôshin*, the immovable mind, rather than the tension of self-righteousness, then there will be an opportunity for peaceful resolution without compromise. But this can only happen when there is a meeting of the minds, which means that the opposing leaders must meet face to face and talk, preferably on neutral territory. There is always someone whose self-interest will be sufficient to make them willing to act as intermediary in such a negotiation. Things are never as black-and-white as they appear on the eve of war.

Winning a war never solves a problem without creating other problems in its wake. Every war in history can be explained in terms of the conflicts which have preceded it. This means that the original wounds were never healed. You cannot heal a wound by wounding it further. Perhaps through Ki principles, politicians could gain some insight into the practical applications of non-dissension. No ruler rules alone. If cooler heads prevail around a president, he himself will keep a level head. If the people thirst for blood, how can they expect anything else from their chosen leaders?

Economic Improvement

Along with democracy, capitalism has shown itself to be among the most successful of economic systems, even though it is far from perfect. The basic goal of capitalism is to create wealth by gaining the greatest return on the smallest investment. This works in theory, but with the world's economies so completely intertwined, with the intense turnover of new products and markets constantly in flux, this is no easy task.

Of course effort is important for success, but effort alone is not enough. A single unforeseen event, an oil crisis, or a war on the other side of the globe, can undo years of well meaning effort by corporations and governments. To succeed in any business, you need a combination of good fortune (chance), sincerity (plodding along), and patience (stamina), known in Japanese as *un-don-kon*. Though effort and persistence are important, in the end it is often good fortune which spells the difference.

There was a wealthy merchant of lumber and other goods, who lived in Japan during the early Edo period (1600s), named Kinokuniya Bunzaemon. He was hired by the military government to carry out many important civil engineering projects. He made a fortune by braving extremely rough seas and delivering a load of mandarin oranges to the markets of Edo. People assumed that this success was just a matter of luck. But at that time, faced with the decision of whether or not to attempt the hazardous voyage, he meditated silently and gained a strong resolve that he could make it. Of course a variety of factors must have played a part, but without a calm mind he would not have been likely to succeed. Even so, fortune proved fickle. He later earned the enmity of both the people and the government through his greed and ostentatiousness, and his great fortune was lost in a single generation. The universe does not play favorites.

The same thing can happen to people who are successful in business today. Indeed, a large fortune can be lost in less than a decade. By making use of insights gained from the universe, a person can become very successful in business. But greed, laziness, or indifference toward employees and customers can cause that success to come undone just as quickly. The old maxim about money still applies: easy come, easy go.

John D. Rockefeller Jr. said that the *only* question with wealth is what you do with it. Executives and economists should take thought for how to repay their employees and reinvest their profits into the society which helped them, not just how to get rich. A critical way in which corporations can contribute to society is by acting in environmentally responsible ways. The environment includes the social and aesthetic, as well as the natural environment, for the quality of life includes all of these factors. Money is not the only measure of wealth, though it is an important one. Creative effort is the best way to increase wealth, and sharing the wealth is actually the best way to keep it.

On the other hand, no philanthropist or taxpayer wants to see his money wasted on people who expect handouts as their birthright, and make no effort to take care of themselves. Even if a great fortune were distributed equally to everyone in the country, it would amount to a little bit of nothing for everybody. Unless money is focused and put to creative use it has not power to help anyone. The private foundations and government agencies which are responsible for the use of this money are expected to have the public welfare in mind. The best way to know what is right for the public welfare is to maintain the perspective of a universal mind.

Science and Technology

Science grows by building on its own foundation. The discoveries and experiments of scientists in the past produce a cumulative body of knowledge which is passed on to future generations. Elementary school children today are taught things that the leading minds of past generations could not even have conceived of. Isaac Newton claimed that he could see farther than others only because he stood on the shoulders of giants. It is ironic that standing on Newton's shoulders, so few people today can see beyond their five senses. We enjoy the products of science, but seldom maintain the spirit of scientific inquiry in our daily lives. Things are not the way they appear. When someone told Einstein that his theories did not fit the facts, Einstein jokingly said that the facts were wrong. The history of science is the history of the rediscovery of the world.

The influence of science is everywhere, and it is here to stay. But this does not mean that science has conquered nature; not by any means. The man who believes that he has conquered Mt. Everest simply by climbing it is just satisfying his own ego. Nature is not mastered by man's use or abuse. The universe contains limitless power and potential, and its wisdom can be ours if we just learn how to draw on it. Nature holds no secrets from the person who seeks truth. Only when we delude ourselves by closing our eyes to truth do we fall prey to illusions about life.

Scientific progress does not depend on effort and accumulation of data alone. The greatest leaps of science have been made through inspiration. These flashes of insight come from the universe to the scientist who is receptive, by being unified in mind and body. Inspiration comes from the universal mind, so we must seek to apply this knowledge from the same perspective if we want to use it properly. If we use it for selfish or short-term gain, we may expose ourselves to terrible risks. Too many scientists in the past and present have cooperated with governments which make immoral uses of their knowledge. No scientist can claim immunity in the name of pure research. There is no such thing as pure research, for every action has a consequence.

Scientists must take some of the blame for the environmental problems which technology has created. But it is too late to turn back now, and it may be science itself which can provide the answers we desperately need. It is possible to bury nuclear wastes for a period of time, but no container lasts forever. Rather than trying to bury or simply contain dangerous contaminants, scientists should apply themselves to find a way to make use of it, to turn minus into plus. Just as every benefit contains negative side effects or possibilities, the reverse is also true. By unifying mind and body we learn how to find the positive side of any situation. This gives us access to universal wisdom, which is the real source of cultural development.

Ki training is highly compatible with science, for both are products of a mind eager to know the truth through experimentation. Both look beyond the surface, and assume that all problems have a solution. With Ki development as with science, progress halts the moment you assume that you have arrived, or think that you know all of the answers. Many people mistakenly believe that Ki is mystical, and therefore beyond science. They assume that somehow in the pre-technological era, mankind enjoyed an idyllic harmony with nature. However, both history and archaeology provide evidence that all of the evils of man against man existed long before science and technology held sway. The only difference now is that technology amplifies the consequences of our wrong doings. There is no reason why it cannot also increase the power of our good deeds. There is nothing inherently evil about technology. Instead, we should be more concerned about the man behind the wheel.

Education and Human Development

Education means developing through teaching. As human beings, we were born with a capacity to understand the universe. No monkey or dog has this ability. A person may not believe in God, but he understands what is meant by the word. As human beings alone have this capacity, they are in a sense spiritual lords of creation. Man has the potential to reach the pinnacle of development of the universal mind. Each of us was given special talents and advantages by the universe. When the mind is unsettled, it cannot reflect clearly enough to discover what these gifts are. The purpose of education is to help us find our talents and put them to best use.

Farmers trample wheat several times, but because the roots are secure it always grows back, and in time yields a plentiful crop. If it is not trampled, its yield is very poor. Cultivated vegetables always produce better than those in the wild. Somehow pruning them back makes them more productive. Many parents today think that all they need to do is to provide for their children's physical needs or whims. Yet money cannot buy what they really need. Unless children are given the care and resistance implied by education, they will not be able to weather the pressures of living in the world. Parents should do their best to trim the weak points, and cultivate the strong traits in their children while they are still at home. No child is a perfect angel, but neither is any one a total devil. True education takes place in the home.

In the past, children were educated in most of the details of daily living at home. Now parents expect the schools to do it and schools expect the parents to do it. Delinquency and bad behavior among youth reflects the lack of training at home. If you expect someone else to do it for you, you may find someday that it is too late to start. All babies have the potential to turn out good or bad. There is no such thing as an delinquent infant.

Nevertheless, the age of juvenile delinquency continues to get younger, and the behavior wilder. Strict laws are notoriously ineffective in correcting this situation, while permissiveness only seems to let the problem grow out of hand. Parents and teachers must first reflect on their own responsibility for this state of affairs and how to correct themselves. This is the fastest and most effective way to help young people.

While it may be necessary to reform the educational system, we should not stop there. What good does it do to reform the curriculum and textbooks, if we do not first reform the educators themselves? One student refused to remove his hat in the classroom, saying that teachers were laborers working for pay (because they went on strike for higher wages) and that students were customers in the business. He explained that the customer was King, so there was no need to take off his hat. You cannot force students to respect their teachers. As long as teachers teach for pay rather than for love of teaching, they cannot expect students to respect them. Teachers should reflect on themselves first, on their real motives for going into education. Then they will earn the right to ask for higher pay, as well as student and parental respect.

Charles Darwin was asked by a mother with a three year old child, when she should begin the boy's education. He told her that she was alreay three years too late. In Japan, it is commonly believed that education begins in the womb. Many mothers take this very seriously, and try to provide an environment of music and cleanliness to welcome the coming child. But later they go wrong by overemphasizing education as a means to get ahead in life. Educators should devote themselves to finding the unique potential and value of the individual, and helping students to realize it in their lives.

Educators devote enormous amounts of time and energy to preparing students to pass examinations in which they have little interest, and which have little relevance to their daily lives. Most experienced teachers would agree that students are more concerned with their peers than with their studies, and in any event are extremely inefficient learners. Some teachers think that education is too good a thing to waste on children. A child whose mind is clouded with fear, anxiety or social concerns is not prepared to learn well, in either physical or academic education. If Ki development could be added to even a small part of the school curriculum, it would pay enormous dividends in rapid learning both on the sports field and in the classroom. Ki training is extremely relevant to the student's own immediate concerns, how to be stronger, look better, perform with confidence. With the school's support, the student could find school to be a fascinating laboratory for applying Ki in various areas. Teachers with strong Ki would be respected as people students wanted to follow and spend time with, and many disciplinary problems would disappear of themselves.

Family and Social Life

Experience and environment tend to give everyone a different opinion of marriage. Some believe that marriages are made in Heaven. Others see it as a cage in which, as Montaigne wrote, those outside are desperate to get in, and those inside are desperate to get out. Most would agree that if you are to be married, it is best to be happily so.

People have enough trouble keeping themselves together, much less maintaining a lasting relationship with another person. Couples grow and develop as separate individuals, at different rates and in different directions. This is why initial compatibility is no guarantee of lasting happiness. On the other hand, individual differences may be a better reason for staying together than for coming apart, for one partner may compliment what the other lacks. Yet no matter how compatible two people are in background or personality, unless they enjoy a healthy bond of Ki, their relationship must experience some degree of strain.

When each is convinced that the other is wrong, it is very difficult for either party to be the first to apologize. Actually there can be no winners in an argument between people who depend on each other. The secret is to view the conflict as one in which you must win out over yourself. The way to do this is to unify mind and body and forget your differences. Human psychology is such that it is hard to remain angry with someone who agrees with, or is willing to listen to your opinion. You can say yes, in the sense of "Yes, go on . . .," without meaning "Yes, you're right." It is perfectly possible to hear another person out without compromising yourself, but only if you maintain mind and body unification. By changing yourself, you automatically change the other person. By remaining calm yourself, you become like a mirror and reflect everything back to the other person. It is very difficult to stay angry all by yourself. If your partner is upset, you should remain calm and the storm will pass. Then you can face the problem as reasonable adults, rather than as bitter and biased enemies.

Sexual roles are continually being redefined. This is a complex issue when argued in the abstract, but not so difficult when viewed in the context of the people involved. Is militant feminism really any better than male chauvinism? Both are creeds for the battle of the sexes, not for equality. Even equality can become a source of conflict if people try to impose it artificially. It is impossible to divide all of the household chores, family income and assets equally. As long as your foremost concern is getting your share or being treated fairly, you will never be satisfied. It may be 80/20 today and 40/60 tomorrow, but it can never be 50/50 all of the time. If the bond of Ki is strong, such contractual issues never even come up.

Marriage is often thought of as a relationship between two people, but in fact it includes the extended family as well. The old expression is literally true, that you marry into a family. There is no doubt that the extended family is weakening as an institution. If current trends continue, then even the nuclear family is in danger of drifting apart. Children spend more time away from home, and old people are often relegated to institutions rather than living with their families. People who assume that parents have an obligation to rear their children, sometimes act as if children have no similar obligation to take care of their parents in old age.

Because people live longer today, the average age of the population keeps increasing, and with it the tax burden on working people to help suppport the elderly. The Japanese government is trying to encourage old people to retire overseas to help alleviate this problem, but all this does is to shift the problem somewhere else. In the past, people would sometimes abandon elderly parents on the mountainside when they could no longer take care of them. Now they try to get someone else to take care of them. But this is no guarantee of good care; for no one really cares as much as a relative. Rather than encouraging the breakup of the family, governments should find ways to help older people contribute and remain productive.

The communication gap between generations is not so much based on different lifestyles, as on a lack of Ki exchange. What will bridge the gap between generations is Ki, not money, education, or health care facilities. In the past in Japan, when a family member would travel or have to be away from home, the ones who stayed behind would go through elaborate rituals to sustain the Ki contact, even talking to them aloud and praying for their safety during their absence. When Japanese children leave the house, they are taught to say *itte kimasu*, which means, "I am going and coming back." This is an important custom, for it not only lets the parents know that the children are going, but it establishes a bond of Ki which helps protect them when they go out into the world. Ki knows no boundary of time or distance, which is why parents and children can remain close despite physical separation.

If parents always send Ki to their children and protect and love them when they are young, then the children will show the same love and protection for their parents when they grow up. Within a family there should always be a feeling of mutual awareness, respect and protection, which is based on the free exchange of Ki among them. Parents may not all be able to practice Ki training with their children in a dôjô, but if Ki can become a natural reference point in daily life, it can do a lot to further mutual understanding and support.

Health and Medicine

Water exists originally in a pure form. Even if it becomes polluted, the contaminants can be removed and the water is pure once again. It is the same with the Ki in our bodies. If we remove the causes of sickness and maintain a healthy exchange of fresh Ki, then we can age gracefully, without breaking down and getting sick.

If you want a bright, happy, and healthy life, you should choose it and act upon your choice. On the other hand, no one will stop you if you want to choose a dark, gloomy and sick existence. In fact, you will find that misery loves to have plenty of company. Even if an illness is not of your own making, you will never overcome it by moaning and complaining. Some New Age thought blames all illness on the person's wrong attitude or behavior, if not in memory, then in a past lifetime. This causes a tremendous amount of guilt and does nothing to fix the problem. While it is true that some illnesses are mentally induced, or at least aggravated by a poor attitude, one can hardly blame a small child or disaster victim for his wrong way of living. Some illnesses and injuries have purely physical causes. Your illness may not be your fault, but it is certainly your responsibility to try to get better. Who else really cares as much about your recovery?

The first thing to do is to start by making your mind positive. A negative mind is filled with hatred, fear, envy, and selfish thoughts. A positive mind is generous, joyful, and shows concern for others. The world has many negative influences, so it requires great effort to remain plus and not be influenced by a negative environment.

If we know that we are part of the universe and that our bodies contain Ki like a sponge, then we can refresh ourselves any time by extending Ki out so that fresh Ki can come in. While we are awake and active, we gradually consume Ki and become tired. It is very important that we daily replenish our Ki through relaxation, deep sleep and Ki breathing. This has an effect like clearing stale air from a room by opening the windows. Daily renewal of Ki builds the foundation for a healthy life.

The nature of water is pure. Only when something is added to it does it become polluted. If the foreign elements can be removed, you once again have pure water. It is impossible to pollute water permanently, for it can always recover its original state. In the same way, Ki is originally pure. Human beings are born of the Ki of the universe. Although a person becomes injured or sick, by sending them a fresh supply of Ki through Kiatsu therapy, the person's own life-force has a tremendous capacity to regenerate and restore the tissues to their original state. The purpose of Kiatsu therapy is to help remove the things which have accumulated in the body and interfere with its health.

However, even if a person receives Kiatsu, if he or she continues to maintain the same mistaken postures, behavior, and lifestyle which originally caused the problem, the problem is likely to recur. Until the person is willing to make a change in these areas, it will be impossible to truly maintain good health.

What does it mean to lead a healthy lifestyle? For the mind, it means always extending Ki, thinking positively in all circumstances. A positive mind calls forth positive people and gains positive results. A person with a positive mind naturally improves his own life circumstances and naturally enjoys good health. The more you extend Ki, the more you receive a fresh supply of universal Ki. As the circulation of Ki improves the life-force is fully activated, and naturally maintains the body in a state of good health.

We must put aside the notion that it is natural for the body to be weak, sickly, or to begin to break down in middle age. Rather, these things should be considered a consequence of negative thinking. It is important to remember that the mind leads the body. To create a strong and healthy body, you must think of the body as being naturally healthy. Even if the body does experience illness, there is no reason for the mind to succumb as well. Bodily illness is a superficial thing, like getting dirty. Mental illness is serious, more like getting stained. If the mind is strong it has the capacity to shake off physical illness.

We must also consider health from a physical standpoint, including correct posture, eating habits, and breathing. Correct posture is any posture in which the mind is calm and focused at the One Point, and body is completely relaxed and free of excess tension. This posture is not only the most comfortable, it is the strongest and most stable. Furthermore, it is only when mind and body are coordinated in such a posture that the life-force is fully activated. However, if the wrong approach is taken to relaxation, the body becomes limp and slack. This will eventually lead to a breakdown of health and immunity, even if it is done in the pursuit of a so-called "health method."

Correct breathing is also extremely important. Ki breathing is a practical means for restoring health. We have already examined the method and benefits of Ki breathing; but it is worth taking a second look, in the context of how to live a healthy lifestyle. We take food into our bodies and metabolize it to create energy for life. We absorb oxygen from the air, which is necessary to the process of metabolism. We breathe air into our lungs, and from it absorb oxygen into the bloodstream, which is carried to every part of the body, where the oxygen helps metabolize nutrients for the cells. The by-products of this process include carbon dioxide and various waste products, which are carried out again via the bloodstream. Carbon dioxide is then expelled from the lungs to complete the cycle of respiration. Correct breathing is breathing in which the exchange of oxygen and carbon dioxide is complete. In other words, the best condition is one in which the major arteries are rich in oxygen and the major veins are rich in carbon dioxide.

The human lung capacity ranges between 3,000 to 4,000 cubic centimeters of air. However, the average person only exchanges about 600 to 700 cubic centimeters of this air with each breath. This means that ordinarily we only exchange about 1/5 to 1/6 of our capacity. Consequently, the blood that travels through our arteries only holds a fraction of the oxygen that it could.

A great number of people suffer under such nervous strain that their muscles are chronically stiff and circulation extremely poor. The tiny capillaries which lace the body tend to close off under this tension, causing an insufficient delivery of oxygen to many areas of the body. Excess carbon dioxide and unmetabolized wastes tend to accumulate. This reduces the body's immunity by increasing the burden on the life-force, and invites all kinds of physical problems.

If a gas stove burns inefficiently it produces dirty smoke. If you clean the oven however, abundant oxygen reaches the flames and the stove burns cleanly, without smoke. Similarly, when you relax completely, the small capillaries open up and help improve the overall circulation in the body. This results in a cleaner, more complete metabolism of nutrients, as well as a more efficient disposal of waste products. Metabolism turns the food into energy, which activates the life-force. In other words, proper breathing is a process which activates Ki and invigorates the whole body.

After standing for a only a short period of time, an anemic person can physically collapse. This is increasingly becoming a problem among young people in their teens and twenties. Doctors have found that after collapsing, the victim's lungs tend to be full of oxygen, with hardly a trace of carbon dioxide. Japanese doctors named this condition *Excessive Breathing Syndrome*, following the lead of a French physician, assuming that these people had breathed too much oxygen. The suggested remedy was to have the victim breathe into a sealed plastic bag, forcing him to breathe his own carbon dioxide.

It is hard to believe that despite the advances made by medical science, doctors could still make such mistaken judgments about such a fundamental biological process. At one time when pneumonia was still a major problem, rehabilitation centers were built in mountainous and well-forested areas. The presence of many trees provided an oxygen-rich environment, which was considered beneficial to people suffering from lung problems. This is also behind the thinking today that says that people need fresh air baths as much as they need sunbaths. According to the thinking behind the excessive breathing syndrome theory, a well-forested area would be the worst place for a person to go who had fainted from pernicious anemia. Their method of treatment is rather like sticking the victim in the dark, smoky corner of a nightclub, where the air is as bad as possible.

One of the problems with the current trend of modern medical thinking is that it regards the body as a complex machine. It tends to consider only the part which has broken down and how to repair or replace it, without any regard for the living organism as a whole. Naturally if you consider only the lungs, it might appear that there is an excess of oxygen and a deficiency of carbon dioxide. But if you look at the whole body instead, you would find that although oxygen has accumulated in the lungs, it has not been well absorbed into the blood, which itself is overcharged with carbon dioxide. Far from having an oxygen excess, the entire body is suffering from an oxygen deficiency.

The only way to treat this problem is to restore the correct and complete exchange of oxygen and carbon dioxide through Ki breathing. People tend to think that an anemic fainting spell is caused by a low blood count, but in fact it is caused by an insufficient supply of oxygen to the brain. A low blood count may contribute to the problem, but if the blood is oxygen rich, the person will not faint; and even if the blood count is high, without sufficient oxygen the person will collapse.

Although Japan now boasts one of the highest longevity rates in the world, at the same time senility has increased so fast as to become a major social problem. Reduced mobility due to old age is one thing, but when large numbers of elderly people become both bedridden and senile, this poses a major burden on the younger generations who must look after them. Many young people have found that caring for senile parents and relatives has significantly interfered with their jobs or careers.

Although we must look after those to whom this has already happened, those soon to enter old age themselves can learn a lesson from it and resolve not to be a burden on the generations to follow. It is never too early to start preparing for a healthy and mentally alert retirement.

Premature senility is brought on by a chronic oxygen deficiency to the brain. Fully one-third of the oxygen in the blood is consumed by the brain. When working at the peak of your career, the brain requires and usually receives a full supply of oxygen. When it is used up, the brain demands fresh oxygen, which is supplied according to need. During this time, the brain is well fed and has no opportunity to grow senile. However, when a person retires from these responsibilities and begins to lead a sedentary existence, the brain no longer demands, or gets the full supply of oxygen that it needs, and it is not long before signs of senility set in.

To prevent this from happening, older people should busy themselves finding opportunities to be of use to others, or to make a contribution to society. Even if a retired person is financially secure or cannot find paid employment, there are endless opportunities to volunteer if you only look about. One has to respect the occasional elderly person who devotes free time to cleaning up trash in the park, or removing dangerous broken glass from childrens' playgrounds. Older people who occupy themselves in trying to help others need not worry about senility.

Having purpose or meaning in life implies that society or other people benefit from your actions or existence. If on top of this, you ensure that your brain always has a fresh supply of oxygen through Ki breathing, your mind will remain clear and alert well into your eighties or nineties and you will be able to fully enjoy your last years.

Modern medicine has achieved a major success in developing the ability to detect cancer early, a disease which was once both dreaded and obscure. The fear which cancer induces is partly related to the fact that its symptoms are nearly silent until it is almost too late. It takes hold and grows quietly, without drawing attention to itself. By the time it becomes obvious or starts to hurt, it is often too late to save the patient. If a person with cancer is lucky enough to have it detected early, the chances of recovery are excellent. But since the symptoms are so subtle, it often goes undetected.

On the other hand, some people are so anxious about the possibility of getting cancer, that they find every possible excuse to run to the doctor to have it checked. One man began to suspect that he had a tumor in his throat when he noticed a hard lump. It turned out to be his Adam's apple. He had never paid much attention to it until he started looking for tumors.

Apparently, all of us have cancer prone cells in our bodies. These cells are kept under control when the immune system is strong, but tend to multiply when defenses are down and the protective life-force weakens. It is possible that a person can actually trigger a cancerous growth by exhausting the nervous system through chronic neurotic concern about the possibility of getting cancer.

Medical research has found that cancer cells often do not survive in an oxygen-rich environment, but that in an oxygen-poor environment even radiation therapy cannot stop them from coming back. This suggests that when the breathing process is correct and continually supplies fresh oxygen to all parts of the body, the immune system operates at peak efficiency in preventing cancer. It also reminds us of the importance of regular practice of Ki breathing.

An article in an American newspaper reported that cancer researchers were trying to

282

find a way to create an oxygen-rich environment for victims of cancer. However, even if the patient sat in an oxygen-rich room for several hours, although the lungs became full of oxygen, it did not reach the cancerous cells where it was needed. Oxygen cannot be injected or taken orally in pill form. Therefore the research was considered inconclusive.

It is relatively easy to get oxygen into the lungs. The problem is how to get it from the lungs to the bloodstream and to all parts of the body, especially those which contain cancer prone cells. When the mind is upset and the body stiff, the blood may become oxygen-deficient and many important cells may fail to receive a proper delivery of oxygen.

The only way to ensure this proper delivery of oxygen is to relax completely, allowing the capillaries to open, then breathe deeply and correctly. Unless the capillaries open to allow full delivery of oxygen to the tissues where it is needed, no amount of oxygen in the lungs will suppress the growth of the cancer cells. The proper way to achieve this is through Ki breathing.

Of course, if a person does get cancer, it is urgently important to follow the doctor's advice and deal with the problem through surgery or other recommended means. This is especially important for younger people, where the growth of cancer cells can be very rapid. After receiving medical treatment, practice Ki breathing daily and the steady supply of oxygen will help keep the problem under control. The operation removes the most dangerous of the cancer cells. Supported by a rich supply of fresh oxygen, after that the immune system should be able to prevent a recurrence of the disease.

We have looked at the implications of Ki development for politics, economics, technology, education, family, and health. But there is an undercurrent running through all of these: that of the environment, which may be thought of as our common body. The environment is our commonwealth, as well as the foundation of our common health. Politicians must learn to put a higher priority on environmental protection before it is too late. The environment must not be sacrificed to shortsighted or self-serving economics. The best time to convey these concepts is early, in the schools and in the home. What is the reason why we should all be environmentalists? Need it be asked? Aside from the issue of man's stewardship of the earth, of respect for the beauty and power of nature, of the fragility of ecosystems and species which were a millennium in the making, of the fact that time is running out, there is a more basic and selfish reason: our health and happiness depends upon it. It was true in ancient times and it is true today, the foundation for success in all things is a sound mind and a sound body. This is only possible if we live in harmony with nature, if our lives are based on a feeling of unity with the universe. That which can help us achieve it is Ki.

Chapter *13:* In the Words of the Master

Up to this point, the contents of this book have been about the life and teachings of Koichi Tohei and how he developed a practical system of Ki development for modern people. This information was based on the author's years of study with Tohei Sensei since 1972, on interpretations of previously untranslated writings by Tohei and on many hours of interviews and note taking. A translation of his books would not have been appropriate, because the structure of Japanese language and reasoning differs from English. Too much goes implied and unstated, and the presentation of ideas in Japanese is not as tight as is required in English.

However, it would not be right to complete a book about Koichi Tohei and his teachings without letting the Master speak for himself, through a translation of some of his original writings: worthy sayings based on remarks he made during training, and poetry which he has written to express different aspects of the Way.

These will give the reader a better feeling for the personality of the man, and for his deep insights into Ki and human life. Most of these sayings were recorded by his closest students over the years, or have appeared in Tohei's own writings. Here is a sampling.

Selected Quotes

• Even your own training can be considered as *intoku* (good done in secret), because someday it will bear fruit in the ability to help others develop.

• Some people are quick to find reasons and excuses why they cannot do things. This cuts their Ki and in time stifles their motivation altogether.

• Motivation is extending Ki, not receiving it. People today are more concerned with what they can get, than what they can give or do for others. That is why they cannot extend Ki.

• Until you can clearly make up your mind, you are better off not doing something. Make a habit of being decisive in your daily affairs.

• When you teach people, it is useless to try to change their character. Correct their bad habits first, then their true character can come out.

• Public school teachers must have a positive mind. If their attitude is negative, it infects their students. Students cannot learn from bad examples until they develop their own powers of judgment.

• However good the teaching sounds, look at the person teaching. Whenever you teach, you yourself are the best representation of what you are really saying.

• Begin with form, then transcend it. When the correct form truly becomes a part of you, then alone can your individuality come out. A twisted form can never express a person's uniqueness. There is a world of difference between individuality and idiosyncrasy.

• Young people today overuse the words "my pace" or "my style." In essence, all that they have done is to abandon their pursuit of excellence.

• The word mirror in Japanese (*kagami*) originally meant "to observe the temporary or superficial self (*kari no ga o miru*)." People should use the mirror occasionally for self-reflection, not just to fix their faces.

• There are people who say, "Oh, I've heard that story before," when they listen to a Ki lecture. In doing this, they miss the chance to discover something new in it. The fact that it sounds the same to them is just proof that their mind is too small to contain it.

• Some people can be heard to say, "What'll I do if I get killed?!" If you die, there is nothing that you can do. Whatever you have to do, do it now, while you are still living.

Ki Sayings from Master Tohei

The following sayings were recorded by several of Tohei's top students, during their years of intensive training in all aspects of daily living, and published in a book of his sayings. They are presented here for the first time in translation.

1) We gain wisdom from the universe when the waves of the mind are made calm by half, half, half, until it reflects all things clearly like a mirror. In the movies you sometimes see a figure struck by the voice of God as loud as thunder, but this is fiction. The universal mind only becomes clear when the mind is calm.

2) You must practice to be able to return to essential principles at any moment.

3) We are able to sit calmly on the ground because we are held in a perfect balance between centrifugal and centripetal force. If centrifugal force were too strong, we would be cast off into space. If centripetal force were too strong, we would be held fast to the ground. Just thinking about this fact alone makes you realize the degree to which we are utterly dependent upon the universe for our life. Unless we start with a spirit of gratitude we will be wrong from the beginning.

4) What does it mean to be right? You cannot say that something is right just because Buddha or Christ said it. Things are not right because anyone says so, they are right if they are in accord with universal principles. There are many such principles, but to be considered universal it must be possible for everyone to achieve complete agreement on them. If even one person says no, then it is not universal.

The four basic principles meet this criteria. For example, consider number three, "Keep Weight Underside." Is this right or wrong? No one would claim that the weight is underside in Japan, but upperside in America. If everyone can agree upon it, it must still be right even a thousand years later. Such a principle may be called universal and therefore right.

5) The Chinese philosopher Lao Tzu said that if the Great Way is lost, then humanity and justice appear. When humanity and justice are lost then criminal laws come into being.

We must return from criminal law to the Great Way. Criminal law is only capable of apprehending petty thieves. Truly evil men slip through its fingers.

6) The Ki of the universe is absolute. There is no such thing as strong Ki versus weak Ki. Correctly speaking, Ki is strong only because it is strongly extended, weak only when it is not extended strongly. There is no limit to how strong your Ki can become if you train yourself to extend it strongly.

7) "Sensei what exactly do you mean when you say become one with the universe?"

"That means to have a universal spirit."

"Then what does it mean to have a universal spirit?"

"That means to go beyond the concern of life and death."

8) The Ki of the universe has never for a moment stopped moving. We call this continuous growth and development. Do you not think it strange that human beings seem to be the only ones trying to stop the movement of Ki?

9) As long as you live, the universe has a use for you. When you die, you might say that this is no longer true. Leaving the question of living and dying up to the universe, this is what I call true relaxation.

10) The famous swordsman Miyamoto Musashi said that God was to be respected, but not relied upon. In his later years he sought but was unable to find the truth and he died a miserablr man.

I rely entirely upon the universe, leave everything up to it. That brings great peace of mind. But this is not a state of dependency. I first establish my center and leave the rest up to the universe. There is a fundamental difference in the attitude of being dependent and that of letting things take care of themselves.

11) You should not carelessly utter high sounding philosophical quips about being beyond life and death. If you really understood such a statement, you would not talk about it, but instead be able to remain truly undisturbed.

12) Smaller than molecules and atomic particles, there are mind particles yet undiscovered by science. You will see in thirty to fifty years people will be quoting me on this.

13) The space we live in is permeated with wind. As proof of this, anytime you wave your hand, you feel a breeze. The same can be said of sound. Whenever you clap your hands you get a sound.

14) Be vigorous and full of energy, and make ceaseless efforts. As instructors you must always be full of positive Ki. This means that little things do not discourage you and that you approach all things boldly with an attitude of determination.

15) Time has its own flow. It is very important, particularly for politicians, to have an accurate grasp of the flow of events. In order to achieve this, you must have a sense of the rhythm of the universe. This is something you know with your body, not your intellect.

16) When you coordinate your mind and body, you have unlimited access to the wisdom of the universe.

17) No matter how well you hide your actions from other people, you cannot conceal them from the universe. It is very important that you always act in such a way that you need feel no shame before the universe. As the saying goes, "Know Heaven, know earth, know others, know yourself."

18) The Buddha explained things in plain terms to the common people around him. How could they have been expected to understand a text so difficult that even a university professor needs a dictionary to read it? The principles of the universe are very simple. Only mankind has made them mysterious and difficult to understand. I think anyone can follow the four basic principles which I teach, don't you?

19) Before awakening, your mind is always ill at ease. After awakening, you realize that things are just as they are. If the universe had a limit, you might wish to go to see it. But when you realize that it is limitless, there is no need to try to go. When you understand that it is limitless, you can remain where you are and be at ease.

20) Some people believe that they have achieved the highest understanding, or reached enlightenment. This is a very foolish notion. Only because they have not yet realized that the universe is limitless can they say such a ridiculous thing.

21) "Do nothing" does not mean "Don't do anything." *Mu*, or "nothing" is not merely the lack of something. It refers to the state in which the mind has grown imperceptibly calm, and then allowed things to take their natural course.

22) Anyone can walk the Great Way. That which only certain people can walk is called the small way.

23) Ishida Mitsunari (1560–1600) was offered a persimmon just moments before his appointed time of execution. He refused it, saying that it might upset his stomach. Many of the spectators laughed at the spectacle of a man about to die, still thinking of how to care for his body. But Kuroda Saburô removed his own military halfcoat and put it about Ishida's shoulders, then offering him a bow of deep respect.

In any circumstances, we should always give our best. This is what is meant by a man who has achieved full maturity.

> The lady divers wear their straw raincoats
> all the way to the beach
> In the drizzling rain.

24) If you can leave things entirely up to the universe and not put up the slightest resistance, then you can pass the *Okuden* (highest level) Ki test.

25)
> Don't get stuck on any particular way,
> Think of your body as a ship sailing
> before the winds of time.
> Go with the current.

The meaning of this poem is that you should be a balanced person, coordinated in mind and body, so that the winds of change do not disturb you. If you know how, you can use the winds to take you wherever you wish to go.

26) Whenever you enter the dôjô you must be in a positive frame of mind. Your students come to the dôjô in order to change their minds from minus to plus. If the instructor is minus, there is no need to come.

27) In the United States when a person says "Hello" by telephone, the other party answers "Hello" without delay. There is no gap between the sounds. Wherever you go in the world, Ki is communicated instantaneously.

28) A wise man is simply someone who has manifested the universal mind.

29) If a child usually listens to what a parent has to say, then the parent will overlook an occasional misbehavior. Similarly, if you continually live by the principles of the universe, it will extend sympathy and pull you out of trouble when you go wrong.

30) Things appear very complex, but underneath they are quite simple. People complicate things by superimposing their own viewpoints and advantages. If you remove all that is superfluous, most problems have very simple solutions.

31) To let the universe take its course, this is the most natural condition. Human beings have an infinite capacity for development. They change and grow every day.

32) After realizing a principle, unless you learn it with your body you cannot expect to get true understanding. Scholars in particular tend to learn in theory only.

33) "Sensei, you always say that we should feel gratitude to the universe. What exactly does that mean?"

"It simply means realizing that your life comes from the universe."

34) You must never become bored with life. If you take the initiative to find work yourself, there is no limit to the number of things to be done. If you really run out of things to do, do not just sit there blankly, but go right to sleep. When you sleep you can replenish your supply of Ki from the universe and wake up eager to go back to work.

35) "Sensei, when do you train yourself?"

"I practice twenty-four hours a day."

36) "Sensei, what you teach us turns out to be so plain and obvious, why is it that we don't notice these things for ourselves? Why is it that you can see it for yourself and we can only see it after it is pointed out?"

"That is because I am always totally committed to finding the Way. When you search, the universe shows you what you need, when you need it. The difference with you is that you only search when you think you need it."

37)   Casting off the world,
          As if I were already dead and gone,
          The snow fallen day is crystal cold.

The state of enlightenment is merely a condition in which you perceive beautiful things just as they are.

38) The truth of things in any era always spreads plainly before our eyes. Why chew over the same tired materials from the past? We should direct our efforts to learning from what we see, in the world that we now inhabit.

39) There are people who attribute their unhappiness to their parents' neglect, or try to blame society for their problems. But waiting for your parents or the politicians to change is like waiting for the river to clean itself. It may take a hundred years.

If you change yourself, then you can live well wherever you go. If all you have to do is to change yourself, then you can start anytime.

40) What do we mean when we talk about a full life? We mean that our life is full of the Ki of the universe.

41) If might is right, then the world will tear itself apart. We must strive to create a world in which right is might.

42) It is as true for individuals as it is for the world itself: everything comes in waves. Small changes every ten years, large changes every hundred years. There are even changes every day.

If you ride the waves of change, you succeed. If you ignore them, you fail. When the wave is down, most people resist it by trying to go up. When the wave goes up, you should go up with it. When it comes down, you go down.

43) When you go with the rhythm of the universe then you are able to grasp the overall situation. Then you are able to influence the flow of events.

44) The universe is limitless. If you trust the universe, then you have access to limitless strength.

45) You must lead other peoples' minds. But before you can do this, you must learn to control your own mind. That which goes against principle is called forcing. You cannot force other people. That which goes with universal principles is called correct.

46) If you trust the universe completely, then you are able to free yourself from worldly cares. When I go to sleep, I always extend Ki and ask the universe to take care of things.

This was how I was able to sleep peacefully, even on the battlefield.

Whenever we encountered danger, I always woke up in time. The universe wakes you up when it is necessary. It is the same now as then.

47) I believe that as long as I am living, the universe will protect me. This means that as long as I have work yet to do, there is no possibility of dying prematurely. There is no need to think about how to defend your body. All you need to do is to try your best to practice the correct way.

48) You should not waste even a single sheet of paper. Nor should you cut a flower without good reason. All things have life.

49) I am glad that I was not born a cow or pig. Otherwise I might have ended up as someone's steak dinner. We were born of the Ki of the universe, but through our parents, so it is natural that we feel gratitude toward them.

Parents are pleased about almost anything that their children do for them. Anyone who is incapable of pleasing his own parents must also be incapable of doing any important task.

50) Human beings cannot grow without feeling gratitude. Gratitude toward things is an attitude which fosters growth.

51) An old proverb says that the man of virtue does not talk of supernatural powers. Even if you could knock a man down by staring at him, or hold your breath for a year, what good would it do?

Recently there have been television programs which claim to show such kind of supernatural demonstrations. They say that the world is more advanced now, but apparently many people are still taken in by this sort of thing. You must develop the ability to distinguish between the real thing and the fake.

52) Earthworms eat sludge. Even human feces can be used for fertilizer. Nuclear wastes are still a product of the universe, and hence must have some positive application. To look only at the negative side of things is to have warped vision.

People take the irresponsible way out by dumping wastes in the middle of the ocean. But if they were to look seriously into the matter, there is always a possibility of finding a practical use for it.

53) Bring to life the small self, and live in the larger self. During World War II, it was common to say "Sacrifice yourself for the good of the nation." But sacrificing yourself is a negative suggestion.

When I went off to war, I refused to say like the others, "I will never again walk in my homeland," or "I shall die to serve my nation." All I said was, "I'll be back." I always said that I would go, but that I would also return.

54) There was an old woman who practiced some religion and was always heard saying, "Thank you Lord, I'm so grateful." But after her son got married, all she did was complain about her daughter-in-law.

It does not do any good to express gratitude if it is only superficial. It must be genuine if it is to have any meaning.

55) Once in the New York subway I got up to offer my seat to the elderly man standing in front of me. He snapped back, "I don't need your seat! You think I'm too old to stand up?!"

He had lost his ability to perceive human kindness. People should not be close-minded. We should see things as they are.

56) I do not like killing living things. That is why I do not fish or hunt. If I were invited

to go along on a hunting trip, as soon as I saw a wild pig, I would fire a warning shot in the air to help him escape. If I went fishing, I would stir up the water with my pole to scare off the fish. Saying such things I never got invited to either!

It is alright to kill for the food you need to live. But you should never kill for sport.

57) If you showed the unbendable arm saying that God's power resided in your body, then people would probably believe you.

But the truth of the matter is that the mind leads the body. I do not use God's name so carelessly. That is because I have seen a number of religions from both inside and out.

58) Even if a hundred ton boulder should fall, I would be safe! When I say this, everyone laughs and wonders how. No need to try to stop it, just move out of the way. You do not have a problem if you do not try to take it on yourself. Most people in the world suffer because they try to take upon themselves things which they do not need to.

59) As long as you are alive, you must do your best. After you die, you must still do your best. I do not know whether I will go to Heaven or Hell after I die, but even if I end up in Hell, I will gather the devil spirits and conduct Ki classes.

60) Sometimes at night, instead of going out drinking, you should spend time gazing at the stars. They move. Through this you can grasp the movement of the Ki of the universe.

61) Because the four basic principles are ultimately the same, if you get one, you naturally have the other three. However, in practice it is not that easy. When you teach from one direction, you tend to go too far, and when you approach from the other direction, you tend to do likewise. So you must swing back and forth like a pendulum, gradually approaching the center. It seems after all, that you do need four different approaches.

62) What good does it do you if you can only coordinate mind and body in a quiet place? Even the Buddha did more than just sit in one place. If you cannot be unified in the midst of your daily work, what good does it do you?

63) If you want to experience true calmness, you must find ways to calm the waves of your mind in daily life.

64) If you truly adapt to things as they arise, you have no need to put on a show of bravery. If you have mind and body coordination, you just accept things as they are. The saying goes, "It is easy to lose your temper, but difficult to accept things as they are."

65) You must use your mind in a unified manner. Some people are unable to study or read a book without at the same time listening to the radio. You surely cannot call this coordination of mind and body.

66) It is not possible for beginners, but if you really have a deep state of mind and body unification, it is possible to maintain it in any posture. A great actor is capable of playing the part of a fool or drunk, without losing form for a moment.

67) Someone asked a well-known actor how to improve one's acting ability. He answered that you must become the part completely. When playing the role of Kudô Suke-tsune, due to poor stage construction a piece of bamboo came loose and fell right in front of him. Without missing a beat, he exclaimed, "How poorly made, these rented rooms." This produced a great reaction from the audience. Such an improvised response could not have come from one who lacked mind and body unification.

68) When giving a lecture on mind and body coordination, you must keep in mind the following principles:

1. Clarify the importance of mind and body coordination.
2. Explain why it is not as difficult as is ordinarily assumed.

3. Show that mind and body are essentially one.

4. Teach the principles of the mind and of the body.

5. Ask whether mind is central or body is central.

69) By trying to get rid of distracting thoughts, that very effort only further disturbs the mind. Just as you cannot calm waves on the water's surface by trying to smooth them out with your hand, the mind cannot calm itself.

However, the mind can grow calm by infinitely pursuing the One Point, half… half… half…, until it appears empty and clear.

70) If you assume the Zen meditation posture described in the *Zazengi*, in which the nose is placed directly over the navel, you are unable to move or deal with any kind of frontal attack. The correct way to sit is to put the forehead over the One Point. In this posture your mind remains calm and clear, and you are able to perceive and respond to your opponent's Ki.

71) Gautama said, "Above and below, I alone am the Honored One." Jesus said that He was Son of God. But this did not apply to them only as individuals. All of us are originally Buddhas, each of us children of God. Each person contains the center of the universe in the One Point in the lower abdomen. The universe condensed becomes ourselves and this further condensed becomes the One Point.

72) The One Point in the lower abdomen is like a magic pot. It contains whatever you put into it. No matter how big the thing, it vanishes in the One Point. By containing the universe in the One Point, that which is infinitely small becomes infinitely big.

73) You should not endure or supress things. Instead, put them into the One Point and let them pass. Tokugawa Ieyasu said that, "Our life is like a long journey, carrying a heavy load." But if we put the excess baggage into the One Point, we hardly feel the load and we are able to walk lightly. This is how we should live. Calm the mind in the lower abdomen, and the load is lifted off of your chest. You can walk through life without hesitation.

74) Thinking with the abdomen (getting a gut feeling) is a matter of unifying mind and body, and thinking with a calm mind. It does not mean that your brain is in your belly.

75) As a young man, I engaged in intensive Zen training and passed the *kôan* tests (Zen riddles for meditation). In so doing, I assumed that I understood. However, during the war, I found that when bullets started to fly I easily lost my composure. It is relatively easy to face death sitting on a *tatami* mat, it is another thing to face it in fact. You can imagine you are swimming while sitting on dry land, but that is not the same thing as actually swimming in deep waters. It was through this difference that I came to understand the One Point.

76) You cannot very well train yourself by rushing off to war, or experiencing near fatal illness. Instead you can develop yourself with Ki testing.

77) There is a difference between unification and attachment. If you are so absorbed in a book that you cannot hear someone calling your name, it simply means that your mind is caught in the book. If you are so caught up in a movie that you do not notice someone picking your pocket, then your mind is simply attached. Whether you read a book or watch a movie, you must do so in a unified state.

78) Putting strength into the lower abdomen is a form of attachment.

79) Watching famous gymnasts on television, their arm and leg movements clearly originate from the One Point. Somehow they have achieved it naturally. But how many of

these same people can teach others how to do it? Teaching Ki principles is a very difficult thing.

80) I can tell by watching Mr. Oh (Yomiuri Giants baseball hitter) at the plate on television whether he is standing with living calmness or dead calmness. When his mind is stopped, it does not matter how hard he tries, he cannot hit a home run.

81) If you try too hard to extend Ki, you become tense and it does not work. If you try too hard to calm the mind at the One Point, you become too tense to do it. Rather than think that you must extend Ki or keep One Point, just think that Ki is already extending, or that your mind is already calm at the One Point, and let it alone.

82) One person fell over easily when lightly pushed at the shoulder as he did Zen meditation. He claimed that though his body moved, his mind did not. It does not work that way. When the body moves, it is proof that the mind also moved. It was to make this clear that I developed Ki testing.

83) Ki power is real power. If you send it out, it goes out. In this way it is possible to protect someone at a distance.

84) When you believe and act as if Ki power is real, then it becomes effective.

85) In most cases, people look only at the results of other's successes and forget the roots. The root is mind and body unification. I have met many successful people over the years, and in all cases, unconsciously they have absorbed the essence of mind and body unification. If you teach them the four basic principles, they can do it immediately.

If such people could be taught how to teach the four principles to young people, the world would derive great benefits. Young people are never motivated simply by hearing about the success stories of others.

86) "Love and Protect All Creation." If you always seek out and focus on the faults of others, you develop very hard eyes. Though the temple guardians have been standing and staring for years, they are still nothing but gate keepers. Real mind and body unification is shown by Kannon, the Buddha inside the temple.

87) It is not right to try to keep customers here when they come, and to ask them back when they leave. Whether they come or go, the god of fortune smiles. He smiles today, and he smiles tomorrow.

88) All you have done until today is to train, train, train. Your body is so overtrained that your forehead is always wrinkled. You do not even smile at your own child. You have got to develop a softer manner. I will give you this calligraphy (have soft eyes and a gentle manner). Look at it everyday and hurry up and get rid of the wrinkles on your forehead.

89) The body has limits, the mind does not. It is fine to train your body, but you should not stop there. While you are still young, you must train your mind. The body ages, but the mind does not.

90) They say that a lion puts his all, even in catching a rabbit. You should make a habit of putting your all into every little thing that you do.

91) A poorly made sword does not warrant any particular care, but a fine sword must be kept polished and sheathed. In the same way, when a person develops a better cutting edge and the eyes to see through other people, he must learn to keep this ability well-wrapped and sheathed.

92) "Sensei, what should I do about this?"

"Calm your mind at the One Point, sleep on it, and make your decision in the morning."

93) You should not be disappointed if you are clumsy or slow at learning. A quick

learner can do it the first time, while a clumsy person may have to repeat it ten times. This repetition is actually the only way to put it deeply into the subconscious. It will stand you in good stead later on.

94) It is a mistake to be too concerned about a person's intelligence while they are still young. Far more important is whether they are capable of self-control.

95) The story goes that when someone mentioned to a famous general how hot a day it was, he replied, "That's all in your mind, how you look at it." If he were truly a great man, he would never have said such a thing. To say that it is all in your mind is proof of how his mind is caught by the heat. If someone says that it is a hot day, the proper reply is, "Yes it is, isn't it?" What is not good is to be bothered about it. When water is cold, it is cold. What is wrong with calling something hot, hot?

96) If you are faced with an important crisis in business, you should calm your mind at the One Point. Then the right answer will come to you.

97) Individuality is a good thing, but it must be genuine. If your individuality is based on a false idea, then it is nothing more than a bad habit, a matter of self-importance.

98) If you are trying to write, you should just write down whatever comes to mind, and edit it later. If you try to edit before you set words on paper, you never get anything written.

99) All things in the world, whether good or bad, can teach you a lesson.

100) When you are teaching others the Way, they view that Way in terms of your actions and personality. Do not act in a manner which belittles what you teach.

101) Who put this book on the shelf upside-down?! There is not anything which is alright to do without presence of mind. Not noticing this kind of thing is where slackness begins. Put things back properly!

102) Look at my appointment book. When I have something to do, I write it down. When it is finished, I cross it out. When it is for a future date, I fill it in the appropriate place. In that way, I never forget what I have to do, and I am able to organize my work.

But it will not do you much good to try this if you forget to look at your date book!

103) You have got to learn to be neat and organized in whatever you do. Take a look at the bills in my wallet. They are all lined up in the same direction. This kind of care is important.

104) When you are involved in some task, you lose sight of everything else going on around you. You never make progress with that attitude. You have always got to remain aware of the whole. Never lose sight of the big picture.

105) Thinking you must not move, must not lose, must not get upset, this is all relativistic thinking.

106) Being unaware of the area around your feet is proof that you are not calm. When your mind is calm, you can always see clearly what is around you.

107) Even if you are able to remain calm on the field of battle, if you shrink from the debt collector, you cannot be said to have *hara* (mature strength coming from the lower abdomen).

108) Just because you were able to do it before, do not assume that you can do it as well the second time. Each time you do something, you must return to your beginner's mind, and give it your best.

109) When the famous tea master, Sen Rikyû, instructed the carpenter to drive a nail in a pillar of a tea house, he was so particular about where it should go that the carpenter be-

came irritated. Thinking to show the master a thing or two, he made a small mark which only he could see on the place where he had been instructed, and then deliberately dropped the nail.

Again the tea master led him through a series of trials and errors, only to arrive at precisely the same point. The carpenter was greatly humbled by this. Rikyû, after all, must have had great mind and body unification.

110) You yourself do not heal the other person with Kiatsu. By filling your own body with the Ki of the universe, you are able to then put it into the other person's body, stimulating that person's life-force, which is what does the healing. In order to do this, the person giving Kiatsu must first unify mind and body.

111) In order to bring forth the universal mind, you must practice Ki meditation.

112) The purpose of all religions is to bring forth the universal mind. I was asked by a minister in Portland, Oregon whether or not Jesus, Moses, or the Buddha would have passed the Ki tests. I said, "Of course!" He asked me why, and what proof I had of this.

Until the end, Christ smiled and prayed for other people. Buddha taught the Way even upon his deathbed. Without fully bringing forth the universal mind, such things could never have been possible. Without unifying mind and body, it is not possible to realize the universal mind. Therefore, it is obvious that they would have passed the Ki tests. The minister was very pleased to hear this.

113) The earth is moving around the sun at an incredible speed, yet we do not even feel it. It is so fast, that it feels like no motion at all. Extreme states of motion have a tendency to become very calm.

114) One of the founders of *misogi* cold water training said that in the winter, we hold fast to the pillar. Superficially, people might think that there is little work to do in the cold, so we stay at home, but what he meant was something entirely different. The pillar refers to the center of the universe, in other words to the One Point in the lower abdomen.

115) If you throw a stone into a lake, it makes waves on the surface. Eventually the waves disappear, but just because you can no longer see them does not mean that they are really gone. They have just become too small for us to see. In the same way, we calm the mind by half, half, half...and the waves of the mind become infinitely calm. They never actually stop.

116) There is a difference between calm stopping and dead stopping. We can distinguish between living calmness and dead calmness. While you are alive, please practice living calmness. After you die, you will have plenty of time to practice dead calmness.

117) In Japanese aesthetics, many references are made to *seijaku*, or a state of quietude which implies solitude. This is not merely a matter of being lonely or alone. As the Haiku poem says,

> The stillness is so loud
> When the shrill cry of the locusts
> Penetrate so deeply into the rock.

Although the sound of the locusts fades from our ears, it does not truly disappear. It is only made infinitely small, giving the poet the impression that it penetrated deeply into the rock.

118) In Japanese Buddhism, the term *munen musô* is often misunderstood. In English it

may be rendered as, "Think nothing. Do nothing." But this is not to say, "Don't think or do anything." The same mistake is made when we fail to distinguish between living calmness and dead calmness.

119) There is a difference between the state of true open-mindedness and that of being empty-headed. The word *mushin*, or "no-mind," refers to the pursuit of the mind toward the infinitely small.

120) Have you ever heard the poem? (There is here a humorous play on words which is not translatable.)

> What a world of difference between the clear and the clouded.
> People swallow tea, snakes swallow people.
> What a world of difference between the clouded and the clear.
> The brush has hair, the bald man does not.

121) I understand that Zen meditation enjoys great popularity in America, but if you practice it the wrong way, you run the risk of becoming weak and flaccid. Some people practice forms of meditation in which the mind is allowed to travel freely, say to London or Paris. But eventually it must come back to the body and face reality. If meditation is used as a mere escape, it will not help you to solve your problems. You must not separate the mind and body.

122) Freedom to move is very important. Coming and going, the mind and body must be relaxed, otherwise such freedom is impossible. That is what is missing in today's politicians. If they would learn to coordinate mind and body, they would be able to make good politics.

123) Actually, even death is not dead calmness. It is merely a change in form, not a true end. If the waves truly stopped, they would never be able to come back again.

124) All things come into being from a state of infinite reduction. The Zen priest Dôgen said, "Even if you cut me, it is as though the lightning cuts the spring wind." He was referring to this state of infinite potential.

125) When they say to throw away the small self and live in the large Self, it is easily misunderstood. Just as the universe is both infinitely small and infinitely large, the mind can be likewise. As there is no need to be caught in your physical condition, there is also no need to throw it away.

126) When forced to do something, you might as well see it in perspective, calm the mind by half, half, half... and just walk along.

127) In its original form, all water is pure water. If you remove the impurities, any water is clean water. Human beings are the same. If you remove the impurities of evil thoughts and evil actions, all people are essentially good people.

128)
> The saints appear as foolish men.
> The wise appear plain.

We should just be natural. In order to do this, we must first unify mind and body.

129) When the mind is calm, your face always appears at its best.

130) They say that when you apply your will-power to something, it will always be realized. But this power is only possible if you unify mind and body.

131) Once you learn to use your will-power, you must never apply it to harm another.

Remember that when you curse another, it always comes back to you.

132) An old Japanese saying has it that a hundred preachings can be blown away by a single fart. Just as you cannot know sugar without tasting it, how can you know truth without putting it into practice?

133) Even though you come to the dôjô to learn the correct method of sitting in *seiza*, why do you not continue to practice it in your daily life? Mind and body coordination can be practiced twenty-four hours a day. If you can maintain it while working, playing, or sleeping, then you have the real thing.

134) When I went to San Francisco, I saw a hippy sitting in a state of blank meditation. I tried to take his picture, but he demanded a fifty cent modeling fee!

How could he possibly have been sitting in a state of *munen musô* (no-mind: no-thought)? If you misunderstand this idea even a little, you run the risk of becoming lazy and unmotivated, to the point where it is even too much trouble to walk.

135) Once a hippy came to practice at the San Francisco dôjô, but his body was so filthy and bad-smelling that no one wanted to practice with him. I asked him if he never took a bath. He replied that since it was natural to sweat, it was unnatural to wash it off.

What a joke! Even a dog has enough sense to jump in the river when his body gets itchy. After I cautioned everyone to wash their training clothes, the next day everybody returned with clean uniforms.

This is an example of what can happen when you misunderstand the meaning of "Be natural."

136) The reason that you should not make noise while you are eating is that you should maintain a spirit of calm in whatever you do.

137) Do not accept anything simply because another has said it. Always check things out for yourself. It is best to maintain enough composure to be able to think things out in this way.

138) How can you ever manage to carry out such a big responsibility if you do not first pull yourself together? Take a bigger view of the whole. If you cannot calm yourself, then whatever you do will come out half done. Practice Ki meditation to collect yourself.

139) Kusunoki Masashige, who fought Takeda Shingen, was often taken advantage of by petty merchants. In his daily life he himself was honest and straightforward, and never resorted to petty tricks. That is why he was able to act as such a great general. If you resort to small tricks in your training, you will never achieve the real thing.

140) I heard that there are many seminars teaching meditation in America which charge large amounts of money for a few days of instruction. Many of the people who attend are wealthy and do not want to feel that they wasted their money, so they try very hard, and have nothing bad to say about the seminars.

In the same way, betters at the race tracks never talk about their losses, but only about the money that they made. The organizers of these events have found a clever way to take advantage of human psychology.

141) "Sensei, what should I do if I find every path blocked?"

"You must be joking! If every path is blocked, the best thing is to do nothing. Rather than exhaust yourself with useless activity, sit in Ki meditation. In time the flow of events will change, and you will discover a way out."

142) Since you have got to keep breathing as long as you live, you might as well practice Ki breathing.

143) From the moment a newborn baby utters its first cry it starts breathing. Soon the

small child is talking. By the time the child is an adult, it has done an incredible amount of talking, but this is no guarantee that the same person can talk in front of a large group of people.

Everything from breathing, to walking, to public speaking has its own principles.

144) The blowing of the wind and the flowing of clouds are expressions of the rhythms of the universe. Each individual leaf that falls off of a tree falls with its own rhythm. The same is true of Ki breathing. There is a proper rhythm to exhaling and inhaling.

145) When I was young and practicing breathing methods at the Ichikûkai, there was an old woman next to me named Kaneda (the mother of the current vice president of the Gakushûin University), who breathed so quietly that it seemed as though she were sleeping. I assumed that at the age of eighty, that was all the physical strength that she could muster.

Later when I went off to fight in the war and practiced Ki breathing 200 times per day, I realized for the first time that her breathing was actually the correct way.

146) With whole body breathing, the entire body becomes filled with fresh oxygen and the mind becomes very clear. This must be a very good thing for the child of a mother who is pregnant. It will ensure the child's good health.

147) The Chinese sages were said to breathe through their heels. When standing with the mind focused on the One Point, the weight of the entire body falls on the bottom of the feet, perhaps creating the impression of breathing through the feet. This does not mean that the feet suck in air as does the nose and mouth! However, the heels are the wrong place for this feeling. When you stand correctly, the weight always falls on the balls of the feet, not on the heels.

148) People think that Aikido with Mind and Body Coordination is strange or mystical, but it is the easiest to explain in terms of physical principles. That is because all of its arts are based on principles. There are forms of Aikido which ignore principles, and I feel sorry for the people who pay money to learn them.

149) There is a difference between compromise and harmony. When I agree to fall for you if you fall for me, that is called compromise. There is a way to help your opponent to do his best, and in spite of this to lead him without conflict. This is the way of harmony.

150) If you practice Aikido for ten years, and can still do nothing but techniques, then you are greatly handicapped. All you have done is to reinforce your own bad habits. If you truly learn essential Ki principles, then you can lead and demonstrate to them in how you live your life.

151) In Zen they refer to the tile which knocks on the gate, and the finger which points to the moon. The techniques and exercises are like this, they merely point the way. Through them you must grasp the Way itself.

152) Does the rim along the edge of this *tatami* mat appear to you as a straight line? It looks curved to me. Is it not true that if you extend this line out indefinitely, it will circle the earth and come back to itself? Then it must be curved.

Aikido techniques are said to consist of circles, but these circles are not small ones. They must be thought of as circles on a universal scale, if you want the arts to work properly.

153) One of my students found himself called overseas on a work assignment, after he had completed a mere three months of Aikido training. He was disappointed that now he might forget all that he had learned. I told him that if he reviewed the techniques which he

had learned once a day in his mind, that they would penetrate ever more deeply into his subconscious, and that he would be even better off.

154) People who are fast learners tend to pick things up so quickly that they lose out on the opportunity for repetitious learning. Even if you learn something quickly with your conscious mind, you will easily forget it after you stop practicing. That which is learned with the subconscious mind is not easily forgotten. Therefore, to learn something with the subconscious mind, requires months and years of training.

155) In the game of Go, there are patterns of master play called *jôseki*. Until you absorb these basic patterns, your play never goes well. The same is true in learning other things. If you devote yourself conscientiously to learning the basic master patterns, then in time you will achieve a great result.

156) In Go *jôseki*, not a single wasted move is permitted. The same is true with the movements of your body.

157) When you run into a wall in your practice, it is proof that you have progressed to that point.

158) They say that you must sit upon a rock for three years. If you persist at something for that period of time, you will generally achieve a tangible result. When you meet an obstacle in your training, you should just quietly persevere. You will then always be able to overcome the obstacle, though later you will meet another. This process is repeated indefinitely. But the reason that you can go on is that you know that the wall will eventually disappear. Is that not the same as having no wall to begin with?

159) When learning something new, you must never be critical at the beginning. Always do your thinking after trial and error. Most people make up their minds one way or another before they even get started. The most important step is to remove your colored glasses and get a clear view.

160) I tried everything. If you approach things with the view that you do not want to be deceived, you never learn anything from anyone. What is right and wrong will be clearly apparent. If you shut it out from the start, you will never really know. Take in the good and bad together and make your choices later.

161) After you learn the correct principles, seek out their applications for yourself. If you forget the basic principles, then the applications which you find will be aberrations.

162) There is a difference between being open-minded and having blind faith. If your mind is calm, it will clearly reflect what is right and what is wrong in another person. If does not mean that you should blindly accept whatever comes along.

163) The word *sunao* means straight from the source. It refers to an open mind which reflects all things clearly, and so is free of error. Everyone is too much on guard. If they would just take a good look, they could see things clearly. If you do not know, just say so.

164) You must not think of what you learned as belonging to you. Your learning was only possible because of the people who taught you. If you forget this, before you know it you fall under the illusion that you are the only one who can do it, or the only one who understands. This is called being full of yourself.

165) If you go charging on ahead and insist that others try to keep up with you, they soon lose motivation. When learning something for the first time, if the student feels a great gap in ability from the teacher, the instructor should take care and try to maintain a humble attitude, one of learning together. Just as you should not criticize the faults of others, so you should not boast about your own strengths.

166) There is a difference between being calm and being slow. Even a bow has its proper rhythm. If your bow is too slow in an effort to be overly polite, you disturb the natural rhythm.

167) It is wrong to think, "I am strong," because this strength is nothing but weakness turned inside out.

168) You must think of how to act with universal principles.

169) When a watch is broken you take it apart to analyze what is wrong with it. When a technique does not work, if you analyze it carefully you can always find out what is wrong.

170) When teaching, always compare the correct way with the incorrect way, side by side. Then the reasons for the correct way become obvious. You must know both.

171) When your techniques are rough it means that you are forcing against the principles; proof that you are still immature. You will not be able to stand up to a stronger opponent. You must try to follow the principles.

172) The secret to successful sales is aftercare. In the same way, the secret to successful teaching is looking after your students.

173) Your character comes out in your techniques. So do the habits of your mind. By correcting the techniques, you can correct the bad habits of your mind.

174) If you constantly collide with others in your practice, your mind will develop a habit of clashing with other people.

175) Practice is not a matter of years and months. It is a matter of concentration.

176) Aikido with Ki becomes effective the older you get, because you become less attached to your physical strength and so can relax completely. Aikido without Ki becomes weaker and weaker with age.

177) People are willing to pay extremely high tuitions to learn tea ceremony or flower arranging, because these things have useful applications in daily life. However, with the martial arts, the stronger you get, the less permissible it is to use them in daily life. No one wants to spend a lot of money on something that they cannot use. Even in America, the martial arts boom has passed.

So what should be the objective of our teaching? Correct thinking, correct action, and a correct attitude toward life. How do we determine what is correct? That which is in accord with universal principles, I call correct.

178) How can you ever improve your character by forcing against your opponent and causing pain? That which is in accordance with universal principles is harmonious, that which is against them is in conflict. This is called the principle of harmony and conflict.

179) Though I am not physically large, whenever I taught large men overseas, they always said that I looked big. This was because I looked directly at them and made sure that their whole body was in my field of vision.

After practice, when we took a group picture, everyone was always surprised to find out how short I really am (162 centimeters, less than 5 feet 4 inches).

180) Nature appears to us in four seasons. The spring is bright and warm, the summer lazy and hot. The fall is decked in color with a trace of sadness, and the winter frosted and severe. Similarly, the movements of Shin Shin Tôitsu Aikido are rich and varied. There is both severity and kindness, speed and calmness. It is designed to express the many moods and characteristics of men and women, old and young.

But if it for one moment varies from the principles of the universe, it is no longer Aikido with Ki.

181) By refining the rhythm of your bodily movements and learning to move in accor-

dance with the rhythm of the universe, you can learn to make use of the universal rhythm. Other places teach about philosophy. Here we practice it.

182) The real work of a musician is to reveal the way of the universe through music. The calligrapher and artist do the same using a brush. Is not Ki-Aikido an art designed to reveal the way of the universe through movement?

183) If you become confused by apparent contradictions among things said by your seniors, then go back to the four basic principles and find out for yourself.

184) If you practice Aikido with Mind and Body Coordinated, then you will clearly understand the intimate relationship between martial arts and dance.

185) The purpose of Ki-Aikido is not self-defence; that is a mere by-product. It is far more important to learn to control mind and body.

186) It is too late to try to calm the mind after you take up the sword. First you must calm the mind and then extend the sword.

187) When you raise the sword overhead, do not cut your Ki. Continue to calm the mind by half, half, half. . . and create a living calmness in that infinite reduction.

188) When practicing cutting with the sword, you will find infinitely more value in cutting just five or ten times with Ki fully extended, than you would in cutting a thousand times with mere physical strength.

189) I spent no more than a week or so learning sword from Master Ueshiba. Most of what I learned came from solitary practice, aiming my sword at a tree behind my house, keeping the tip calm. I did this everyday, for thirty minutes to an hour, and eventually learned the meaning of the immovable sword. You can practice sword movements for ten years and never understand the immovable sword.

190) Most people today who practice sports or martial arts train to achieve faster or more powerful movements. I teach how *not* to move. No matter how fast you run around a 100 meter track, you will never be faster than the person who starts at the finish line. The most important thing is to develop an immovable mind and body.

191) Can you cut your own image in the mirror using a wooden sword, before it cuts you? The image moves at exactly the same speed that you do, so it seems like double suicide. However, it is possible to do.

Before you cut with the sword, cut with Ki.

192) When your mind is calm you can understand *ma-ai* (the distance at which your opponent must take a step forward to attack you).

193) Ki-Aikido is a way of perfecting the principle of non-dissension. However, it is only human nature to want to compare, to evaluate which is superior to the other. If you are going to compare, it is best to compare the right things, with the correct criteria. This is why I designed the *taigi* and organized the Taigi Competition, in which we compare and compete on the criteria of how deep is the state of mind and body coordination.

It turned out to be a good idea. I had no idea that people would progress so quickly because of it. This is the third year we have done it, and it promises to get even better. Someday we will hold an international Aikido exhibition and people will clearly be able to see the difference in our style.

194) Ever since we started holding the Taigi Competition, people have shown great improvement in their techniques. If you do not perform with mind and body unified, you cannot place in the competition, so everyone puts their best into it and maintains mental calmness.

I am particularly impressed with how much the university clubs and other students have improved. They seem to realize the importance of mind and body unification. With this approach, now I feel assured that Ki-Aikido can continue to develop properly, even without my direct supervision.

195) If you are under stress, you cannot sleep properly. When you are sleeping, you are completely relaxed. In the same way we should remain relaxed during our waking hours. This way we will not experience fatigue.

196) It is not enough just to relax when you are sleeping. Some people cannot even relax then! I remain relaxed regardless of whether I am awake or asleep.

197) Relax both shoulders. That is the real meaning of having an open and expansive chest, of holding no secrets.

198) If the mind is free, so should be the body.

199) Stand light and tall, like a crane alighting on the ground. This is the correct posture. I understand that an elephant easily breaks its bones, even if it jumps from a short height. If you stand like that, with so much weight on your feet, you will not be much better off.

200) Standing with your feet dug into the ground, or sitting with your upper body held tight is no way to calm your mind. It is completely wrong. If you press down on the ground, you collide and the earth pushes back. The correct posture is one in which you are floating and centered.

201) Most hospitals put up a sign on the walls of their corridors saying, "Please walk quietly." Only when you put excess tension into your legs do you make noise when walking. If you relax completely, you can walk silently.

202) When you relax completely, the capillaries all over your body open up and your circulation improves. This is very good for health.

203) If you go into a high-class restaurant with only a little small change in your pocket, you cannot relax or enjoy yourself. But if you had plenty of money it would not be any problem.

If you want to learn to relax, you must learn to give your best to whatever you do. If your mind and body are unified, then you can relax under any circumstances.

204) The purpose of a Ki test is to know the state of the mind. Whether or not you move is nothing more than the finger pointing to the moon.

205) In order to lead with confidence, you must first have Ki extended.

206) As the saying goes, "Think of the first 99 miles as half-way to 100." The moment that you think you are almost done, you tend to cut your Ki. You tend to get tired just before you reach your goal. If you think that your goal is still far, far ahead, then you will not cut your Ki.

207) You should not mumble like some young people do. You cannot speak clearly unless you extend Ki.

208) Whenever you undertake a task, before you begin you should tell yourself that you can and will do it. If you make a habit of this, you will find that you can accomplish most anything that you try.

209) If you find yourself forced to go into a dangerous place, it is all the more important to extend very strong plus Ki.

210) If you pour fresh water into a cup which is already full, all it does is overflow. First you should empty the cup and then pour in the fresh water. When you set out to learn something new, first you should remove your preconceptions. Otherwise you will never understand what you are being taught.

211) If something is genuine, it has Ki. If it is fake, it does not. You can tell the difference by looking for the Ki.

212) Before constructing a building, the architect makes a design and plan. In the same way, if you want a positive life, you must design and plan for it.

213) Instructors must always be positive. Even if someone fails at something, you must have the energy to help them turn it into a success.

214) When you fold your hands in a gesture of salutation or prayer, then you join the Ki of both hands and make it stronger. You may not be able to light a match for your cigarette on a windy day, but if you put two matches together you can usually light it. In fact it is stronger by many times than two matches lit separately.

But if a person folds their hands without extending Ki, then it produces no power at all.

215) If you let yourself take things easy after you have finished a major task, then your Ki slackens and you will be unprepared for the next job. As a teacher of Ki, how can you expect to get anything done this way? If you do not slacken your Ki, then you will not be caught unprepared.

Why do you think we practice the eight-way exercise for sending your Ki equally in all directions?

216) When teaching children, the most important thing is to find the child's bad habits and correct them from the beginning. Figuring out ways of correcting them is one of the teacher's most important challenges. Doing this, both teacher and student make rapid progress.

You cannot expect to accomplish very much if all you do is just practice.

217) When correcting someone in teaching, even though you find ten things to correct, you should focus on no more than two or three. It is impossible to correct everything at once. It is important to be kind, and correct the student gradually over time.

218) When teaching your juniors, you should not always be nice and easy. At times you should be very demanding. It will not help your students grow if you always go out of your way to be easy on them.

219) Education is not a matter of oppression.

220) If you put a rock on top of a weed, it will seek a way to grow out from under the sides. Similarly, if you constantly reproach and repress a person, they will find a way around you and go off in untold directions.

221) When a child does something bad, you should scold them sharply. However, you must never hit them on the head. If you must spank a child, spank his bottom. Hitting a child on the head stunts his growth. Spanking him on the bottom gives him the message to grow up.

222) If you do not send Ki to your children, no amount of dialogue between parent and child will close the gap.

223) As you learn, always consider how you can teach what you have learned. Do not just let it stop there. What you learned today you can teach tomorrow.

224) Teachers complain about violence in the schools, but today's teachers are too lax. If you really set your mind to it, you can lead young people. But it is not easy to set your mind. It is not even taught anymore in school.

225) Education in the home is hardly what it should be. People misunderstand the meaning of taking good care of their children. Raising children is a little bit like cultivating a garden. You must weed out their weak points and encourage their strong ones. Then they will amount to something.

It is almost too late to do this if you start when they are already fifteen or sixteen. By the age of ten you should have weeded out their bad points. Then they will develop into fine adults, even if you let them go their own way.

226) You should not run away from difficulties. Even if you escape to a far away mountain, they will follow you there. If you have a problem, think of it as part of your training and face it head on. Have not I taught you how to control your mind?

227) You must never write a letter when you are angry or confused. When you must write a letter, wait one day, sleep on the problem, and write it after your mind has calmed down.

Make a habit of responding immediately with a positive letter and of waiting a day before answering a letter when you are upset.

228) Up to now, at the Ichikûkai you have trained yourself for a long time into a hard shell, to the point where you cannot see anything else around you. I will break that shell for you, but I think it will take about three years of *uchi-deshi* training to do it.

229) Your voice carries well when I hear you sing in the same room. But with the door closed from the next room, there are places where the sound is lost, where you cut your Ki. Try to find out how not to cut your Ki.

230) Your eyes should face forward, or even slightly up. If you look down, your Ki collides with the ground. When a person cries, he looks down, not up. Young people should train themselves to look ahead, even when sad or in trouble.

231) I have been going to the same barber for thirty years. And I would continue to go, even if it were out of my way. This is because I value the connections I have with people.

232) Even if you fail at something, you should immediately reflect on the reasons why and correct yourself. Do not waste time regretting and blaming yourself. If you continually correct yourself, you will not be the same person today as you were yesterday. Therefore there is no need for regret.

233) Because I scold you in order to help you, there is no need to become negative when you are scolded.

234) You should never drink to forget your troubles or to complain about things. When you come out of it, you will only find your troubles increased. When you drink, you should always do so with a positive mind.

235) No matter how much I drink, I have never been late to early morning practice. If you cannot get up in the morning, do not drink! It does not matter how much you drink, as long as you can fulfill all of your responsibilities properly.

236) You should not drink heavily before an important event. It will cloud your mind. Instead get a good night's rest and fill yourself with the Ki of the universe.

237) Many people have the bad habit of criticizing others when they drink. You should not do this. Before you know it, you have said too much.

When you drink, you should drink to enjoy yourself, not to put others down. What a waste of good alcohol! Because I enjoy drinking, my students love to go drinking with me. Unfortunately, in this way, we end up drinking too much.

238) Sometimes I catch one of my students sleeping in, and being late for practice. It may have been the first time that they did it, and were just unlucky that I happened to catch them, but it still reflects the wrong attitude. You should train yourself without slackening your Ki.

239) What do you mean, you do not think you can start a new branch dôjô?! How do

you ever expect to accomplish anything with such weak Ki? If you assume that you cannot do it, you are doomed from the start. All you need to say is "Yes! I'll do it!"

240) It has been three years since you started that dôjô, and you have finally gotten the spirit of training. It seems after all that unless you give a person responsibility, they do not take things seriously.

241) I have no interest in teaching people who only wish to train themselves. The proper attitude is one of wanting to learn and help others learn. I taught you; what you learn one day you can teach another.

242) If a person is stuck in a swamp, you will never get them out by refusing to lend a hand and simply calling to them to come out. You have got to go in yourself and lead them out.

You cannot teach others by simply telling them they should follow. Only when you put yourself in their place can you lead them to a higher level.

243) A kindness done to another is always well remembered, in any time and in any culture.

244) People used to say it in the past, but if you have a basin of water and try to scoop the water toward yourself with your hands, it all runs away from you to the other side. However, when you try to push the water away from you, it all comes back.

In the same way, if you think of nothing but your own profit and gain, it will all slip away from you. But if you think only of what you can do to help others, it will all come back to you in time.

245) Many people think only of what they can do to benefit themselves. You should become a person who lives to bring joy to others. This does not mean acting as a volunteer from time to time, but rather being able to please others as a matter of course.

246) A person who is born with confidence and courage is not much use in a real crisis. Far more important is the person who though weak, becomes aware of his weakness and trained to thoroughly overcome it. Such a person is careful in little things, and so can be courageous in big things. Such a person is of real use in a crisis.

247) By taking care to approach the tasks of daily life with mind and body unified, no matter how small and troublesome they may be, they all take on a tremendous interest. In this way you will become able to direct your Ki even more to the things which you really like and really enjoy your life.

248) In writing a letter, even though you must report something unpleasant, always do so first and end with a positive conclusion. Say that although this is the situation now, you are doing this or that to correct it. Do not focus on the negative parts of the situation; rather focus on what you can do to make them positive.

249) Do not be a bad correspondent. No matter how busy I am, you notice that I always make time to answer and write letters. When I receive a letter from someone, the first thing that I do is to address the envelope of my return letter. That way I do not forget and usually find that I can get the letter off in a few moment's time.

250) In a lecture, people usually laugh at the most commonplace things, because it reflects what they themselves are doing in their daily lives.

251) It is more important to make efforts to avoid making one enemy, than to try to gather a million allies.

252) When you must spend time in a hospital, it is extremely important that you continue your Ki training. People in a hospital tend to be negative, and it is very easy to get

drawn into that atmosphere. When you leave the hospital, your Ki should be stronger than ever.

253) Psychologists refer to the so-called *Law of Reversed Effort*, by which you achieve the opposite of the desired effect by trying too hard. But that is not what actually happens. Wrong effort produces wrong results. Right effort produces right results. It is that simple.

254) You should never think that you have reached the limits of your strength. Nor should you assume that you can extend Ki without making efforts. This is called conceit.

255) You should make it a habit to look into the mirror and smile broadly once a day. This is the secret to leading a plus life. Real beauty comes from inside; it cannot be purchased or produced by decorating the outside.

256) You should not think only of how you can be loved. If you love other people, then you will naturally be loved in return.

257) People will not gather around a negative place. When teaching others, the instructor must be very positive. Whatever you have to say, say it in a positive way. No one will follow you if you speak in negative terms.

258) Make a habit of using positive words in daily life. Children should be taught to speak only plus from the very beginning. This creates the foundation for a plus life.

259) There is a plus way of laughing as well as a minus way of laughing. Laughter which is full, pleasant, overflowing, this is plus. Laughter which is cruel, cold, or spiteful, this is minus. It is not good to laugh with the mouth while scorning with the eyes. The only natural way to laugh is with both the mouth and the eyes together.

People who have lost the ability to laugh naturally tend to have very tight face muscles. They should look in the mirror first thing in the morning and smile.

Unless you can laugh when you are in trouble, then you are in real trouble.

260) When your Ki is extending, then your appearance from behind is quite different. You cannot fake this because you cannot see it.

261) Until you change the subconscious mind, you cannot say that you have learned something. If something is worth learning, you should stick with it until you have changed the subconscious mind.

262) If you want something to go smoothly, send your Ki to it fully. Being lazy only makes it harder. Ultimately, you give up. Sending your Ki to something is the easiest way to proceed.

263) If you hold a wooden staff with a tight grip and try to raise it overhead, it feels quite heavy. If you hold it lightly, it feels light.

In the same way, you should not approach things with too serious of an attitude. Take a lighter point of view. In other words, think positively.

264) In the Ki Society, we give our staff and *uchi-deshi* (live-in students) big responsibilities from the start. This is not because they are capable, but rather because by doing so, you quickly discover their abilities and bad habits. Because the *uchi-deshi* are only here for three to five years, we want them to gain as much as possible from their short time of training here.

265) If you watch people waiting at the bus stop, you find that few of them seem to have a happy face. There seems to be little expression of the joy of living.

But when they meet someone they know, they suddenly put on a forced smile or exaggerated face. Why can't they learn to have a more natural smile?

266) Do not be late. When you keep someone waiting, you waste that person's time. Be careful about that.

267) When you are late for something, you are late in life. If you do not want to be left behind in life, make a habit of respecting time commitments.

268) Training has a lot in common with mountain climbing. Do not look down, do not stop, do not give up partway, or you may fall. When you push a car uphill, if you stop or cut your Ki it will roll back. Ki training is just the same.

269) Some people have a bad habit of being indefinite about whatever they say. If you are indefinite in your speech habits, you will be indefinite in your life. You will not extend enough Ki to do the job.

270) People who are bothered about things are always in trouble. It is too hot or it is too cold. The yen is valued too high or too low. They even start complaining when they greet you. These people spend their whole lives in trouble.

271) When I call a person's name, I never talk down to them. I always say Mr. with their name. This is because I think of them as being equally at the center of the universe.

272) What do you mean by saying that you are sorry?! Do you think you can excuse yourself in being late for practice, keeping people waiting? In a case like this, you should apologize like you mean it.

273) People sometimes excuse their foul mouth, saying that inside they have a good heart, but this is not true. Only what is in the heart can come out of the mouth.

It might be a different story, however, if they really expelled all the bad stuff inside when they spoke, but there is usually quite a bit left.

274) Be careful about the expression in your eyes. If a person has a bad expression in his eyes, his life will turn bad.

275) What do you think my tie pin is made of? People ask me if it is a saphire jewel, but it is only imitation glass. I bought it for ¥500. The appearance of an object changes according to what is inside the person wearing it. On the other hand, there are people who look small in the face of a real diamond.

276) I once mentioned in a Ki lecture on health, that I always had three bowel movements a day. One woman present exclaimed, "That's dirty!" But I asked her: which is the more unclean, passing it out, or carrying it around with you all of the time? People who suffer from constipation should receive Kiatsu therapy and improve their digestive tracts. This is very important for health.

277) Of course I expect you to read my books. But when you are young you should read a great variety of books. Otherwise, how can you expect to develop into a well-rounded person?

278) It is very important to form good relationships with others. Understand their position, what they want, and help them to get it. Even when you seem to have no relation to another, probably you are just unaware of it. As Buddha pointed out, all living things are connected.

279) You should not raise children telling them, "Don't do this. Keep your hands off that." If a child grows up like the three famous monkey carvings at Nikkô, "See no evil, hear no evil, speak no evil," then they go into retirement before they get a chance to grow up. Such a child has a dark future. Children should be brought up knowing how to control themselves.

It's alright to look and listen,
Go ahead and speak your mind,
Lest you a monkey become.

Poetic Writings

Song for Training with the Wooden Staff

Training with the wooden staff consists of several forms, both with and without a partner.
The ones which are performed without a partner are usually counted aloud, to help maintain the proper rhythm. In the early days of his Aikido training, Tohei used to teach his
students to swing the stick while they sang the following words which he composed, set to
the music of a traditional folk song. The song had ten verses, and was performed at a
somewhat slower speed, to clearly articulate each movement of the form. The song reflects
something of the hard discipline and military spirit of the early days of Aikido, as well as
the embryonic stage of some of the Ki principles before the Ki Society was formed.

1) This is the first! How few know the Way of Aikido,
    the secret to unifying mind and body!
        How wondrous is this Ki! How wondrous is this Ki!

2) This is the second! Let the wind and rain blow,
    it is nothing to one who has trained!
        How wondrous is this Ki! How wondrous is this Ki!

3) This is the third! Through to the last, through Aikido,
    the Ki of the universe, deep in the abdomen!
        How wondrous is this Ki! How wondrous is this Ki!

4) This is the fourth! Riding the crest of the waves of the world,
    hold high the emblem of your training!
        How wondrous is this Ki! How wondrous is this Ki!

5) This is the fifth! Training under any sky,
    in time bears its fruits!
        How wondrous is this Ki! How wondrous is this Ki!

6) This is the sixth! Don't think anything beyond you,
    laugh and lead the way you please!
        How wondrous is this Ki! How wondrous is this Ki!

7) This is the seventh! Do not say you have little strength,
    polish your spirit while you can!
        How wondrous is this Ki! How wondrous is this Ki!

8) This is the eighth! Though the mountain is smashed apart,
    the abdomen is undisturbed!
        How wondrous is this Ki! How wondrous is this Ki!

9) This is the ninth! If you don't surpass yourself,
    you'll never weather the storm!
        How wondrous is this Ki! How wondrous is this Ki!

10) This is the tenth! Let's join hands together
      and rejuvenate the world!
        How wondrous is this Ki! How wondrous is this Ki!

Poetry Written in the Traditional Chinese Style

Tohei has always had a strong poetic leaning, although it is little known among his foreign students because most of them cannot read Japanese. Even today he studies Japanese ink painting, which has long held a close association with the poetic tradition. Many of the Chinese classics which he studied as a youth were written in poetic classical Japanese. Not only were many philosophical teachings conveyed in poetry, but it was considered the mark of an educated man to be able to compose and recite verse. The following poems were written by Tohei during the war, while he was in China. He even had the opportunity to study with one of the best poets in the traditional Chinese style of his day. This teacher remarked that anyone who had the spiritual maturity to write poetry in the face of death would surely survive the war.

AT CHÛTONSHI

A lone mountain in the wind blown snow, the bridge slants sharply.
Snow blown, like petals from a thousand trees.
My mind goes back to the festival red hues
in the aftermath of a party long ago.
Filling my glass alone at home.

BEFORE THE BATTLE

The moon sinks in the shadows of the mountain, spreading the evening cool.
The wind whips up the lights of a thousand fireflies.
I sleep lightly in the moments before we fight, dreaming of home.
When I awake, I see the road ahead stretches long.

THOUGHTS UNDER THE MOON

Beyond the long and desolate field,
the moon is clear and bright.
Here have risen and fallen countless generations.
It is cold the whole night through.

Now is the time for a great undertaking.
In the past this land enjoyed the protection of many gods,
Now it seems only the dream of a frail flower.
High winds have thrashed and ravaged this field.

The blessings of Heaven were not ours to receive.
Just when we were in our prime,
Having courageously braved the storm,
What good now does our courage do?

308

The world has always come and gone in waves.
Are these the same fighting men who were full of fight,
Now sighing and weeping below the moon?
The air is filled with the songs of army men.

SONG OF RETURN

The whipping winds of war are now still.
Walking across the same fields on which we fought,
We find that we have been spared.
But the tragedy of our homeland wrenches us deeply.

Even the shadows are cold under the starry sky.
Opening the letter which bring news from home.
The wails of my countrymen
Move my heart and make a grown man cry.

No flowers bloom in Konan,
What of the flowers in my homeland?
Don't cry country, don't cry home town.
Someday we will again see the days that we once knew.
Wait for us, for we shall soon return.
Having dedicated this body to my country,
Now I think only of return.

Poems in the Traditional Japanese Style

Much of Tohei's writing contains poetry, freely mixed with prose in the traditional style. These poems are written in archaic Japanese, more like poetic prose than formal classical poetry. It is safe to assume that some of these are references or quotations from the Chinese classics, of which Tohei was an avid student. Until recently in Japan, it was common to quote poetry from the classics without footnotes. Probably, much of it was done from memory and was so well-known that its original author was long forgotten. It is interesting to note that even past the age of seventy, he frequently quotes this kind of poetry in his Ki lectures. Much of it takes on added dimensions of meaning when seen in the context of Ki development.

When the mind is empty of thought,
the sounds of the world come alive.
Is not the dripping of water from the eaves
the sound of my very self?

The mountain does not laugh at the river because it is lowly.
The river does not speak ill of the mountain because it cannot move.

Though cast adrift in the storm, I harbor no tension in my heart.
It is only clouds, sweeping across the great sky.
After *satori*, you think to be free of your body.

But when the snow is falling, how cold it really is!

Though it is only cold,
people complain that it is too cold.
The mouth is harder to shut than the doors on a summer evening.

The more you think about it
the sadder life becomes,
when the mind has no sway over the body.

To the mind which is bright, there is a clear sky even in a dark room.
To the mind which is dark, a bright day bears gloom.

Don't tarry on the way.
If you travel far enough, there are many new worlds to see.
Even though you walk with the oxen.

A beautiful flower bears no substantial fruit.
Be a person of substance,
not a flower of form.

The changing seasons bring many views of the moon.
But if you look closely,
you see they are all the same.

Everyone has their own point of view,
But how crystal clear the autumn moon appears
from high atop the mountain.

Flowers of the spring, the nightingale in summer.
The moon of an autumn sky.
How cool the crystalline snow of winter.

How sad the form of man,
who through the ages speaks to pass on what he knows,
but is remembered not.

The bow is drawn,
but before releasing the arrow,
the mind is already deep in the target.

Strong Ki can penetrate even solid gold.

Come what may, my mind is serene.
When I awake, the eastern window is already filled with the sun.
When you look at things calmly, everything follows its own way.
Throughout the seasons and whatever occurs,
We are much the same.

The Buddha mind is fluid and free.
For better or for worse, the devil mind resists.
Calm the mind in the lower abdomen,
and the mind flows freely as a river.

Though the eight winds blow,
The moon remains in the sky.

The rock is not moved by the waves.
It stands alone in the blowing snow.

How small the mind that complains.

Favorite Japanese Proverbs

A proverb is a short sentence based on long experience.
—Miguel de Cervantes (1547–1616)

The following proverbs and expressions are ones that frequently come up in Tohei's lectures and conversation. They are all listed in Japanese dictionaries of common expressions, but when collected and organized as follows, they offer some insights into the things which Tohei considers important. Some conventional wisdom he actually opposes, which is indicated below in parentheses.

On Truth:
• *Sei sei ruten shite, shunji mo todomaranai.*
Everything in the universe is constantly moving and developing.
• *Fueki ryûkô.*
Fashions come and go, but essentials never change.
• *Yanagi no shita ni wa dojô wa inai.*
You will not always find the fish under the willow tree.

On the Real versus the Fake:
• *Dasoku.*
Legs on a snake.
• *Heta no kangae yasumu ni nitari.*
Poor thinking is like no thinking at all.
• *Yaochô.*
A fake, frame-up, counterfeit, put on, sham, pretending.
• *Ataru mo hakke, ataranu mo hakke.*
Fortune-tellers! Sometimes they are right and sometimes they are not.
• *Rikô na hito wa baka na mane wa dekiru ga, baka wa rikô na hito no mane wa dekinai.*
A clever man can play the part of a fool, but a fool cannot play the part of a clever man.
• *Nite hi naru mono.*
Some things which appear the same are fundamentally different.

• *Warawareteiru no mo shirazu, baka chikara.*
Not even knowing that people laugh behind his back, the tough guy.

On Mind and Body:
• *Kokoro koko ni arazareba miredomo miezu.*
If your mind is not present, you look without seeing.
• *Zukan soku netsu.*
Cool head, warm feet.
• *Kenzen naru seishin wa, kenzen naru shintai ni yadoru.*
A sound spirit resides in a sound body. (Opposes, saying that a healthy body alone is no guarantee of a sound mind.)

On Learning and Teaching:
• *Ichi o kiite, jû o shiru.*
Hear one, but understand ten.
• *Ikkyoshu, ittôsoku.*
The movement of every hand and foot is important.
• *Kata yori irite, kata yori izu.*
Enter through form, but transcend it.
• *Saru mono wa owazu.*
Do not chase after those who chose to go. (Opposes, saying that you must actively recruit students, rather than waiting for them to come to you.)
• *Meijin ni nidai nashi.*
Genius cannot be taught. (Opposes, saying that Ki, the essense of genius, can be taught.)
• *Suki koso mono no jôzu nare.*
When you enjoy something you naturally improve at it.
• *Nakute nanakuse.*
Even if you think you have no bad habits, you have got at least seven.
• *Hito o mite hô o toke.*
Change your teaching according to the person.
• *Hito no furimite waga furi naose.*
Observe others and correct yourself.
• Easy come, easy go.
(No Japanese equivalent, but one of Tohei's favorite expressions.)
• *Uma o kawa ni tsurete iku no wa hitori demo dekiru ga, uma ni mizu o nomaseru koto wa jû nin mo dekinu.*
One person can lead a horse down to the river, but ten people cannot make it drink.

On Attitude:
• *Sumeba miyako.*
If you learn to live where you find yourself, anyplace can be paradise.
• *Dai wa shô o kaneru.*
The large overcomes the small.
• *Me wa kokoro no kagami.*
The eyes are the mirror of the mind.
• *Yanagi ni kaze.*
The willow bends freely in the wind.

• *Yuiga dokuson.*
I stand at the center of the universe. (Buddha)
• *Waga mi o tsunette hito no itasa o shire.*
Pinch yourself and you know how another person feels.
• *Waratte kurasu mo isshô, naite kurasu mo isshô.*
The happy are happy for life, the unhappy are always unhappy.
• Ask not what your country can do for you; ask what you can do for your country. (John F. Kennedy)
• *Chikara wa seigi nari.*
Might is right. (Opposes, saying that, "Right is might.")
• *Kuchi wa kitanai kedo hara wa kirei.*
He talks bad, but he has a good heart. (Opposes, saying that our words reflect our state of mind clearly.)

On Action:

• *Ichinen no kei wa gantan ni ari. Ichinichi no kei wa asa ni ari.*
Plans for the year begin on the first day. Plans for the day, in the morning.
• *Ichi nen koru tokoro, iwa o mo tôsu.*
When focused, the will-power can penetrate a stone.
• *E ni kaita mochi.*
Painted rice cakes (will not feed you).
• *Ron yori shôko.*
Do not talk about it, do it. Show, do not just tell.
• *Awateru kojiki wa morai ga sukunai.*
The poor man who cannot sit still remains poor.
• *Sugitaru wa nao oyobazaru ga gotoshi.*
Doing too much is no better than not doing enough.
• *Nito o ou mono wa itto omo ezu.*
Chase two rabbits at once and you lose them both.
• *Ni no ashi o fumu.*
Taking double steps. (The implication is that rather than hesitate, it is better to get it right the first time.)
• *Hone ori zon no kutabire môke.*
You try so hard that all you do is to break your bones and get exhausted.
• *Nai kane wa tsukawanai.*
Do not spend money you do not have. (Do not force the situation or try the impossible.)
• *Muri ga tôreba dôri hikkomu.*
If people force then the right way is lost. (Opposes, saying that ultimately, the right way always prevails.)
• *Happô fusagari.*
All directions blocked. (Opposes, saying that nothing blocks Ki.)

On Human Relations:

• *Issun no mushi ni mo, gobu no tamashii.*
Even an inch worm has half an inch of spirit.
• *Nasake wa hito no tame narazu.*
Showing mercy is not for other peoples' benefit (it is for your own).

Chapter *14:* Putting It All in Perspective

A Lifetime of Ki

The first twenty years of the Ki Society, under the leadership of Tohei Sensei, bespeak a long list of achievements at an astonishing rate of growth, culminating in the establishment of a major world headquarters training campus, located on the very property where he grew up. People who knew Tohei at various stages of his life were amazed to see years later just how much this one man had done. Many Ki Society members doubted or questioned projects proposed along the way, but Tohei never failed to carry them out. Working against enormous odds, he consistently and effectively worked to build the organization, being careful to develop its people and leave a trail of tangible achievements which someday would be recognized by society at large. As many of these achievements have to do with the organization and development of a system for teaching Ki principles, their story is better told in light of Ki training and philosophy itself, which is covered in detail in the earlier parts of this book. However, to put Tohei's life work in perspective, it would be helpful to view its highlights as a whole. Then we can truly see the measure of the man, his idealism and commitment, and his inexhaustible capacity for action, in a word his Ki.

A Profile of Tohei's Life Achievements

1920: January 20: Born in Tokyo's Shitaya.
1923: Moved with parents back to Tochigi. Was sickly as a child and eventually encouraged by his father to train in Judo.
1935: He received black belt in Judo at the age of fifteen.
1937: Entered the Preparatory School for Keio Gijuku University. Due to overtraining in Judo, suffered an injury which developed into pleurisy, forcing him to miss school for one year. This sickness inspired him to strengthen himself through Zen, *misogi,* and waterfall training. He studied Zen from Jôsei Ohta, the chief director of Daitokuji in Kyoto. He studied *misogi* from Tesshû Yamaoka's top student, Tetsuju Ogura and his follower Tessô Hino.
1939: Enrolled in the study of Aikido with Morihei Ueshiba.
1944: Sent to China during World War II, as an officer responsible for eighty men. Through his wartime experience, he realized the difference between martial arts as a sport and true life and death fighting. Through this he realized the principle of calming the mind at the One Point, in a situation where the slightest flagging of attention could mean death. Also, through his experience of getting sick on the battlefield without access to doctors or medicine, he developed Kiatsu therapy. On his return after the war, he began again training in Zen, *misogi*, and Aikido. He also studied Mind and Body Unification taught by Tempû Nakamura, at Gokokuji in Otowa, Tokyo.
1953: Traveled to America as the first Japanese to teach Aikido and Ki principles. Between 1953 and 1982, he went to America, Europe, and even the South Pacific, a total of twenty-eight times to teach seminars.
1969: Was awarded the tenth degree of black belt in Aikido, the highest rank available, from his teacher Morihei Ueshiba.

1971: September 16: Established the Ki Society International with just six members, based on the four basic principles which Tohei formulated for mind and body unification. At first, Ki classes were held just three times per week at the Olympic Memorial Youth Center in Yoyogi.

1972: Jaunuary 15: Established a temporary office for the Ki Society in Ikebukuro, Tokyo. June 7: Officially appointed instructors and established a formal system for ranking and promotion. June 18: First formal public Ki lecture (held three times per year thereafter) by Tohei, as founder and president of the Ki Society. July 16: First International Friendship Lecture in Hawaii. November 3: On the first anniversary of the Ki Society, established a new office in Haramachi, Shinjuku, in Tokyo.

1973: January 1: Year-end Breathing training, and first issue of *Mind and Body Unification* newsletter, 1,000 copies. January 3: First public-participation cold river training sponsored by the Ki Society. January 29: First week-long, Mid-Winter Intensive Ki Breathing Training (held annually thereafter). May 21: First Ki lecture delivered to a group of nine universities. August 20: First Aikido training camp (held twice per year thereafter).

1974 : March 29: Tohei traveled to America to help recruit members for the Ki Society. May 1: Established the Principles of Aikido with Mind and Body Coordination and held a founding party at the Imperial Hotel in Tokyo.

1975: May 1: Established an *uchi-deshi*, or residential student system to train professional Aikido instructors. Established a dormitory for training them in all aspects of daily life.

1976: January 2: Established Osaka HQ and dôjô. May 1: Established *uchi-deshi* system and dormitory in Osaka, Japan. October 3: Fifth year anniversary party held at the Palace Hotel in Tokyo.

1977: March 3: Created a system of thirty Taigi, or sets of related Aikido arts performed in sequence, to help teach the applications of basic arts and to prevent the distortion of the teaching in future generations. October 19: Received government accreditation for the Ki Society from the Ministry of Health, for spreading Ki principles to preserve and protect health. This is a much coveted and extremely difficult status to achieve and reflected much background work to establish credibility. November 20: Party to celebrate accreditation, held at Palace Hotel.

1979: March 3: First All-Japan Taigi Contest, held at the National Olympic Youth Center (held annually thereafter). Traditionally, there are no competitions held in Aikido, to reflect the spirit of non-dissension. The Taigi Contest is not a competition between partners, but rather between pairs of partners, to see which ones best demonstrate the qualities of mind and body coordination, rhythm and timing. As in the Olympics, outstanding performances are recognized by Gold, Silver, and Bronze medals, and Gold medal winners receive a promotion of one level of black belt. June 11: Went to Europe to teach Ki principles and Aikido as well as help establish a European branch of the Ki Society, visiting Belgium, Italy, France, and England.

1980: February 24: First Public Ki Lecture-Demonstration, held at the Shinjuku Cultural Center. April 10: Established a two-year school to train Kiatsu therapists, to help stem the increase of sick and weak people in modern society. October 5: Fifth anniversary party for the Osaka regional headquarters.

1981: January 20: Established the Ki no Genri Jissenkai, or organization to spread Ki principles and practice, to help people practice Ki training in their homes, especially Ki breathing, Ki meditation, and Kiatsu. June 1: Established a system for training Jissenkai instructors.

1982: March 21: First graduating class from the Kiatsu Therapists School. August 7: First post-graduate training for Kiatsu (held monthly thereafter).

1983: April 10: Established a two-year school to train Aikido instructors, with an intensive and comprehensive format, to increase the number of qualified instructors throughout the world.

1984: March 8: First public Aikido demonstration, held at the Asahi Seimei Hall. March 17: First graduating class from the Aikido Instructors School.

1986: January 6: Began formal preparations to build the World Headquarters in Tochigi Prefecture, to be completed four years hence. April 10: Established a second Kiatsu school in Osaka, Japan.

1987: October 8: First public demonstration by university student clubs, held at the Japan Youth Building. November 7: Party held at the Palace Hotel, to celebrate the tenth anniversary of the Ki Society.

1988: July 6: First public Ki lecture by chief instructor Koretoshi Maruyama, held at the Asahi Life Insurance Building (held three times per year thereafter).

1989: February 5: First Jissenkai Public Lecture, held at the Japan Youth Building.

1990: October 28: Opening ceremony to celebrate the completion of the New Ki Society World Headquarters Campus, on the twentieth anniversary of the Ki Society. This massive training center is called *Ki no Sato*, or the "Homeland of Ki," based on the fact that it is located on the property where Tohei spent his youth. Ki no Sato includes a number of training halls, each one specially designed for a particular type of Ki training, as well as a Ki Museum. The entire campus covers 30,000 square meters of land. A detailed explanation follows.

A Detailed Description of Ki no Sato Facilities

Ki Meditation Hall (Tenshin Gosho)

A place for reflecting on your true self, and experiencing the calm essence of Ki. A training hall rich with the cool fragrance of cypress wood, and 250 square meters of space.

Ki no Sato. The Ki Society World Headquarters (October 28, 1990)

Fig. 28. Bird's eye view of Ki no Sato (artist's drawing).

Here you can experience and study Ki meditation and Mind and Body Unification, the tranquil side of Ki development. Music specially commissioned from a famous contemporary Japanese composer (Sôjirô) for Ki meditation literally envelops you, reverberating from a high-quality sound system. Effective use is made of soft interior lighting to refresh and clarify the mind during Ki meditation. Tenshin Gosho is an excellent place to overcome the stresses of business and private life.

Fig. 29. Tenshin Gosho (inside). Meditation Hall, training for unification of mind and body.

Fig. 30. Tenshin Gosho (outside). Meditation Hall.

Misogi Bathing Hall (Senshin Tei)

A place to train your mind to become firm and resolute, by filling a bucket of water from a fresh well; and dousing your entire body against the strength of a penetrating *Kiai*, or focused projection of the voice. Performed in the open air before sunrise, this training method can change a negative mind to plus in an instant, and help you begin the day full of Ki. At the Senshin Tei, you can renew yourself by fully refreshing your mind and body.

Fig. 31. Sen Shin Tei Misogi Well.

Kiatsu Therapy and Training Hall

A place to stimulate your life-force through Kiatsu therapy. By learning to use Ki, an energy we all possess, we can prevent or overcome illness. Kiatsu therapy is very effective and has no harmful side effects. Tohei Sensei hopes someday that no family will be without access to a Kiatsu therapist, so that people anywhere in the world can enjoy the opportunity to lead a healthy and joyful life. Here too, it is possible to gain professional training as a Kiatsu therapist.

Main Dôjô and Training Hall (Tenshin Kan)

A place where you can fully express and develop yourself, by exploring the active side of Ki. A large training hall with 2,000 square meters of space. Here you can learn to maintain mind and body coordination in the midst of any movement. With 520 *tatami* mats and a ceiling 14 meters high, Tenshin Kan is the largest such training hall in Japan. When Ki is

Fig. 32. Tenshin Kan (inside). Shin Shin Tôitsu Aikido Dôjô, training for coordination of mind and body.

Fig. 33. Tenshin Kan (outside). Aikido Dôjô.

applied to Aikido, it becomes the art of Shin Shin Tôitsu Aikido, or Aikido with Mind and Body Coordination. Here too, it is possible to gain training which leads to professional credentials as an Aikido instructor.

Group and Dormitory Facilities

With an emphasis on cleanliness and a pleasant living environment, these facilities include a large and comfortable lounge, a multipurpose hall, a relaxing dining room, and comfortable bathroom facilities. The dormitory facilities are kept clean and

Fig. 34. Dormitory Facilities

Fig. 35. Interior Facilities

fresh, so that everyone may train in the most agreeable environment possible. There are also private rooms available for people who wish to stay for long periods of time.

The Grounds and Tohei Ancestral Residence

The Tohei ancestral home was a Chief Magistrate's Residence during the Edo period (1603–1868). Including the footpaths, which are lined with trees hundreds of years old, the entire Ki no Sato campus expands across approximately 30,000 square meters of land. This is a place unique in the world, the first of its kind. It was established so that people could gather from all over the world to learn how to develop Ki in ways which can enrich their daily lives.

Fig. 36. Entrance to the old Magistrate's House.

Fig. 37. Gate to the 300 year old Magistrate's House.

Fig. 38. 1,000 year old zelkova tree on the grounds.

The Museum of Ki Science

There is so much popular interest now in Ki, that the media has actually referred to it as a Ki "boom." However, in its popular use, the word Ki includes so many interpretations and such a diversity of disciplines, that it is difficult to group them together. One organization may present Ki in religious terms, while another uses the word to refer to supernatural powers.

The Museum of Ki Science was established in order to clarify the basic questions that people have about Ki, and to search for a scientific rather than a mystical explanation of Ki. This museum was built by the Ki Society International, and while taking an eclectic approach to the subject, leads the visitor to a basic introduction of the teachings of its founder, Koichi Tohei. The Director of the Museum of Ki Science is Tatsurô Hirooka, the well-known baseball manager and critic.

Fig. 39. Ki Museum (artist's drawing)

Visitors to this museum will not only come away with a clear idea of what Ki is, but also a recognition of the fact that it is something we all possess, and which we can easily extend and use in our daily lives. The museum provides an explanation of Ki from a variety of technical and cultural viewpoints, and even offers an opportunity for visitors to experience Ki first hand.

Foundation Purpose of the Museum of Ki Science

In an age of rapid growth and high technology, we find ourselves increasingly driven by things and systems. Gradually we are beset by stresses which we cannot even clearly identify. Our lifestyles allow for increasingly less of the basic human communication and communion with nature which we need. The damage and social problems which this complexity has brought on are widely acknowledged.

Considering the scale of the problem and the importance of what is at stake, there is a pressing need for a space in which to acknowledge and communicate on this vital subject. Ki is the underlying theme for this museum space, through which people can gain a glimpse of their essential nature. Visitors to the Museum of Ki Science will hopefully come away with a fresh viewpoint on their lives, putting material things and technology into proper perspective. The Museum of Ki Science was established to offer an opportunity for more and more people to recognize the importance of our original nature, and its role in helping us to reestablish person-to-person communication.

Ki is not something in which people have only recently gained interest. It was experienced by ancient man, and finds expressions in the cultures of China, Greece, India, and many countries of the world. This itself suggests that Ki is something real and universal. This series of exhibits begins by looking at the historical expressions of Ki, and ultimately considers Ki to be the basic essence of the universe itself. We ourselves, animals, plants, even minerals consist of Ki. What is presented here are knowledge and materials which show that Ki is indeed universal. In addition to the exhibits, there are opportunities to actually experience Ki for yourself.

General Information and Explanation of the Exhibits

Entrance
The gateway to the world of Ki. Panels explain the exhibits in the Museum of Ki Science. Major panels are translated into English. Most of the exhibits are highly visual, so they can be enjoyed without needing a full translation of all of the panels and tapes. However, in time a full English pamphlet will be available for visitors from overseas.

Fig. 40. Entrance   *Fig. 41.* Ki in Nature

The Ki Society International
Explanation of how the Ki Society developed from its beginnings into a large, international organization.

Ki in Cultures throughout the World

Early Ideas of Ki
Early man made use of Ki in a natural form. Explanation of the world of primitive man through a dramatic representation.

Fig. 42. Ki for Primitive Man

The Chinese View of Ki
Explaining the ancient Chinese view of Ki and the universe, through the teachings of Lao Tzu, Confucius, and Mencius.

Fig. 43. The Chinese View of Ki

Fig. 44. The Japanese View of Ki

Fig. 45. Ki in the Western World

The Japanese View of Ki
Explanation of how Ki has been expressed in Japanese culture, through the Noh drama and other art forms.

The Western View of Ki
Concepts of Ki existed in the Western world, as well. Explanation of how the ancient Greeks and people of India viewed Ki and the universe.

Ki in Science, Art, and Nature

The Tip of the Iceberg
Numerous specific examples of how human beings ordinarily use only a small fraction of their subconscious potential.

Ki in the Arts
Evidence of how great philosophers and artists in various cultures had an understanding of Ki, as illustrated by their words and works.

Ki, Man, and Nature
Using images which illustrate the ecological system and natural environment, explanation of the importance of Ki, and the connection between Ki, man, and nature.

How to Experience and Measure Ki

Fig. 46. Ki and the Environment

The Experience of Calmness
A space for experiencing the calmness of Ki, letting go of preconceptions and experiencing Ki with an open mind.

Fig. 47. Pyramid and Mirror Room for Experiencing Calmness

Fig. 48. Devices Which Measure Ki

How to Experience Ki

Various instruments and devices which measure the flow of Ki, as well as an introduction to Ki testing. Here is an opportunity to verify the existence of Ki for yourself, by seeing the immediate effect that mind and body unification has on your brain waves and other physiological states.

The Tohei Approach to Ki

An explanation on video tape of how anyone can learn to extend and use the Ki that they possess.

Ki Library

Numerous references, books, and information on the subject of Ki.

Fig. 49. Corner for Experiencing Ki

Fig. 50: Ki Library

Museum Shop

A variety of Ki-related paraphernalia and souvenirs are available for sale at the Museum Shop, including Ki meditation music, videotapes, books, clothing and accessories with Ki no Sato emblems and design; as well as many of the implements used in Ki and Aikido training, including high-quality wooden swords and staffs, *misogi* bells, Ki Stones, and so on.

Fig. 51. Ki Museum Shop

For Visitors to the Ki Museum

The Museum of Ki Science is located approximately 15 kilometers east of Utsunomiya-shi, in the Haga Township, Ichikai City of Tochigi Prefecture just north of Tokyo, Japan. The museum grounds cover about 10,000 square meters of land, while the museum itself has 943 square meters of floor space, in two stories.

- *Admission Fee:*   Adults/¥600
  Elementary and secondary school students/¥300
- *Museum Hours:*   9:00 A.M.–5:00 P.M.
- *Museum Holiday:*   Monday. When national holidays fall on a Monday, the museum will be closed the following day as well.

- *Transportation:*
  - From the Tôhoku Highway:
    — From the Kanuma Interchange (IC), follow the Kanuma Road and the National Highway 123 toward Mito and follow the signs.
    — From Utsunomiya IC, take the National Highway 119 to National Highway 123 toward Mito and follow the signs.
  - From the Jôban Highway:
    — Get off at Mito IC onto National Highway 123 toward Utsunomiya and follow the signs.
  - From the Japan Railways Utsunomiya Station:
    — Take the JR Bus Mizuhashi Route bound to Ubagai and get off at Kami-Akabane. It takes about 40 minutes by bus, or about 30 minutes by taxi.

- *Inquires can be directed c/o:*

  The Museum of Ki Science
  378–1 O-aza Akabane
  Ichikai-machi, Haga-gun
  Tochigi-ken, Japan
  Tel: 0285–68–4012

Appendix A: A Summary of Ki Principles

The following is a list of Ki principles written by Master Tohei originally in Japanese. The translations are not always literal, but stay very close to the intended meaning of the original. For example, the third principle for Keeping One Point in the original reads: *Musoku no Shisei*, which translated literally comes out, "a posture of no breathing." I have translated it simply as: "Your breathing is calm and subtle," for it certainly does not mean that you should hold your breath! Each of these principles have been covered in detail in various sections of the book, but are presented here again for easy reference.

These criteria are given to ensure that you gain a proper understanding of each principle and discipline. Each set contains five criteria, each of which describes the same attitude, posture and bearing from different points of view. At times, one criterion will seem easier to understand or practice than another, but you should always remember that they ultimately describe different aspects of mind and body unification. You may find it useful to write them down and refer to them often, perhaps choosing a new set for study each week, until you are thoroughly familiar with them. One suggested use for these principles is to insert copies of them into your appointment book or other place of easy reference and use them as suggestions for daily life. Knowing them implies more than just reading about them. You must be able to put them into practice to solve real problems.

Four Basic Principles for Mind and Body Unification

1. Calm and focus the mind at the One Point in the lower abdomen.
2. Completely release all stress from the body.
3. Let the weight of every part of the body settle at its lowest point.
4. Extend Ki.

Abbreviated version:
1. Keep One Point.
2. Relax Completely.
3. Keep Weight Underside.
4. Extend Ki.

Principles for Mind and Body Unification

For Keeping One Point:
1. Center on the point in the lower abdomen where you cannot put tension.
2. Let your body weight fall on your One Point, not your legs or feet.
3. Your breathing is calm and subtle.
4. You can accept whatever happens without losing your composure.
5. Therefore you can do your best at any time.

For Relaxing Completely:
1. Each part of your body settles in its most natural positon.
2. You relax positively, without collapsing or losing power.
3. Your sense of presense makes you look bigger than you actually are.
4. You are strong enough to be relaxed.
5. Therefore you have an attitude of non-dissension.

For Keeping Weight Underside:
1. You maintain the most comfortable posture.
2. Your body feels light and does not sag.
3. Your Ki is fully extended.
4. You are flexible and can adapt to changing circumstances.
5. Therefore you perceive everything clearly.

For Extending Ki:
1. You are not overly conscious of your body.
2. You make full use of centrifugal force in your movements.
3. You have soft eyes and a poised manner.
4. You show composure in your posture.
5. Therefore you are bright and easygoing.

Principles for Ki Development

For Ki Testing:
1. Not a test of strength but a test of whether or not the mind moves.
2. Give instruction appropriate to the level of the student.
3. Test in order to teach, not in order to contest.
4. Learn by testing others.
5. The test merely points the way and is not an end in itself.

For Ki Exercise:
1. Movements center on and begin from the One Point in the lower abdomen.
2. Ki is fully extended in each movement.
3. Move freely and easily.
4. Do not feel any tension in the muscles.
5. Show and feel a clear sense of rhythm in your movements.

For Ki Breathing:
1. Exhale gradually, with purpose and control.
2. Exhale with a distinct, but barely audible sound.
3. At the end of the breath, Ki continues infinitely like a fading note.
4. Inhale from the tip of the nose until the body is saturated with breath.
5. After inhaling, calm the mind infinitely at the One Point.

For Ki Meditation:
1. You maintain a posture of mastery.
2. You have a sense of freedom.
3. You create an atmosphere of harmony.
4. You are vividly aware of the spirit of life in all things.
5. Therefore you can feel the movement of Ki in the universe.

Principles for Aikido with Ki

For Ki-Aikido:
1. Ki is extending.
2. Know your opponent's mind.
3. Respect your opponent's Ki.
4. Put yourself in your opponent's place.
5. Lead with confidence.

For Training with the Wooden Sword:
1. Hold the sword lightly.
2. The tip of the sword must be calm and steady.
3. Make use of the weight of the sword.
4. Do not slacken your Ki.
5. Cut first with the mind.

For Training with the Wooden Staff:
1. Hold the stick lightly.
2. Control the stick with the rear hand.
3. Manipulate the stick freely.
4. When changing the position of the stick, one hand must always have hold.
5. The line traced by the stick is never broken.

Principles for Kiatsu Therapy and Health

For Kiatsu Therapy:
1. Extend Ki from the One Point in the lower abdomen.
2. Do not let tension accumulate in your body.
3. Press perpendicularly toward the center of the muscle without forcing.
4. Focus Ki continuously and precisely at the fingertips.
5. Concentrate on the lines, rather than the points.

For Sleeping Deeply:
1. Always unify mind and body before you go to sleep.
2. Believe that the mind controls the body.
3. Calm and collect your thoughts before you go to bed.
4. Maintain a cool head and warm feet.
5. Use your mind to direct the blood to your feet.

Principles for Learning and Teaching

For Learning Ki:
1. Be flexible and open-minded.
2. Never tire of training or repeating fundamentals.
3. Be resourceful in applying Ki in your daily life.
4. Change your subconscious mind.
5. Learn it well enough to teach others.

For Teaching Ki:
1. Trust and have confidence in universal principles.
2. Share what you learn with others.
3. Practice and apply what you teach.
4. Teach according to the person.
5. Maintain the attitude of learning and growing together.

For Raising Children:
1. Be resourceful in letting them play and enjoy what they learn.
2. Never allow them to injure themselves or make serious mistakes.
3. Always relate each exercise to their growth and use positive words.
4. Make it perfectly clear what behavior is good and what is bad.
5. When they misbehave, scold them firmly but with a positive attitude.

Principles for Ki in Business

For Office Work:
1. Take initiative to find work without waiting to be told.
2. Make a habit of taking notes to organize and improve your work.
3. Do not postpone something that you can do now.
4. Before going to sleep, plan the next day's work.
5. Make a habit of reviewing your notes first thing in the morning.

For Sales:
1. Know the value of what you are trying to sell.
2. Approach your customer or client with positive Ki.
3. Focus on customer benefits, not whether or not they buy.
4. Always provide responsible after-sale service.
5. Even when you do not make a sale, always leave a positive impression.

For Management:
1. First become a positive person yourself.
2. Do not work for selfish gain, but see how your work benefits others.
3. Be calm enough to be aware of larger trends in society and the world.
4. Always make efforts to help your employees grow and develop.
5. Return your profits and benefits to society in some way.

For Public Speaking:
1. Begin with a strong and clear introduction.
2. Write down the key points of your talk and keep them in mind.
3. Extend Ki from your whole body when you speak.
4. Speak slowly and punctuate your remarks.
5. Always conclude with a positive story.

Principles for Jissenkai and Daily Living

For a Plus Life:
1. Always think with a positive mind.
2. Always speak with a positive mind.
3. Always act with a positive mind.
4. Always treat others with a positive mind.
5. Always make a positive contribution to society.

For Character Development:

These are not so much things that you practice, but rather characteristics of a person who has mastered the art of mind and body unification. These qualities are universally admired in all cultures, and serve as reminders of the ultimate purpose of Ki training: the development and growth of ourselves as human beings.

- Develop a Universal Mind
- Love and Protect All You Meet
- Show Gratitude for All You Have
- Do Good in Secret without Expecting Reward
- Have Soft Eyes and a Composed Manner
- Be Large-hearted and Forgiving
- Think Deeply and See Clearly
- Maintain a Spirit of Unshakeable Composure
- Be Vigorous and Full of Energy
- Persevere as Long as You Live

With the opening of Ki no Sato in October of 1990, the Ki Society celebrated its twentieth anniversary. Already it had a substantial worldwide membership, which it hopes to increase through the effective use of this training center in introducing Ki principles and their application to daily and professional life, to visiting groups and individuals from around the world. In addition to Ki no Sato, which is the Ki Society's official world headquarters, there are offices and training centers located in Tokyo and Osaka, Japan. There are high school, university and corporate clubs active in twenty-two Prefectures throughout Japan.

Ki Society regional branches, some of which have been active since the 1950s, can be found in fourteen major cities throughout the United States, as well as in Canada, England, Australia, and throughout Europe. All in all, Ki Society branches can be found in a total of seventeen different countries. As of the October 28, 1990 Headquarters opening, the Ki Society had 25,170 members in Japan and approximately 100,000 members overseas. A partial list of regional headquarters follows. Space prevents a full listing and new ones may have been formed since this book was published, so please contact the one nearest to you to find out about local clubs. Please note that the addresses given are contact points for information and not necessarily the address of the dôjô itself. You can check local phone directories for phone numbers, or write to inquire about branches and clubs which might be located near you.

JAPAN

Ki Society World Headquarters/Ki no Sato
Ki no Kenkyûkai So-Honbu
3515 O-aza Akabane
Ichikai-machi, Haga-gun
Tochigi-ken
Tel: 0285–68–4000

Ki Society Tokyo HQ
Ki no Kenkyûkai Tokyo Chiku Honbu
101 Ushigome Heim
2–30 Haramachi, Shinjuku-ku
Tokyo 162
Tel: 03–3353–3461
Fax: 03–3353–1897

USA

HAWAII
Honolulu Ki Society
2003 Nuuanu Ave.
Honolulu, HI 96817
Tel: 808–521–3513
Attn: Harry Eto
      Clayton Naruai
or
1511 Ipukula St.
Honolulu, HI
808–373–1864
Attn: Seiichi Tabata

Big Island Aikido-Ki Club
P.O. Box 438
Papakou, HI 96781
Tel: 808–964–1480
Attn: Takashi Nonaka
      Hajime Ueki
      Richard Okano

Maui Aikido Ki Society
P.O. Box 724
Wailuku, Maui, HI 96793
Attn: Shinichi Suzuki
     Isamu Takaki
     Lawrence Shishido

Kauai Ki Society
3325 Alohi St. Lihue
Kauai, HI 96766
Attn: Tetsuji Masumura

WESTERN USA
Northern California Ki Society Federation
2531 Titan Way
Castro Valley, CA 94546
Tel: 415–481–1734
Attn: Hideki Shiohira

Southern California Ki Society
P.O. Box 3752
Gardena, CA 90247
Attn: Ed Grover
     Masao Shoji
     Clarence Chinn

Northwest Ki Federation
P.O. Box 2143
Lake Oswego, OR 97035
Tel: 503–684–0185
Attn: Brenda Tam
     Calvin Tabata
     Louis Sloss

Seattle Ki Society
6106 Roosevelt Way, NE
Seattle, WA 98115
Tel: 206–527–2151
Attn: Dick Hanshaw

Arizona Ki Society
P.O. Box 13285
Scottsdale, AZ 85267
Attn: Kirk Fowler
Dôjô:
7845 E. Evans Rd.
Suite F, Scottsdale, AZ
85267
Tel: 602–991–6467

MIDWESTERN USA
Chicago Ki Society
7721 S. Luella
Chicago, IL 60649
Tel: 312–478–4464
Attn: Jonathan Ely

St. Louis Ki Society
6006 Pershing Ave.
St. Louis, MO 63112
Tel: 314–726–5070
Attn: Mark Rubbert

EASTERN USA
Virginia Ki Society
5631 Cornish Way
Alexandria, VA 22310
Tel: 703–971–7928
Attn: George Simcox

Montgomery County Ki-Aikido Society
Mailing address:
19004 Rolling Acres Way
Olney, MD 20832
Attn: Daniel E. Frank
Dôjô:
4511 Bestor Road
Rockville, MD 20853
Tel: 301–774–3477

New Jersey Ki Society
529 Howard Street
Riverton, NJ 08077
Tel: 609–829–7323
Attn: Terrence Pierce

South Carolina Ki Society
c/o Department of Philosophy
Furman University
Greenville, SC 29613
Tel: 803–271–9355
Attn: David Shaner

EUROPE

European Ki Society HQ*
19 Rue de la Cité
1050 Bruxelles
Belgium
Attn: Kenjiro Yoshigasaki

*With branches in the U.K., France,
Sweden, Yugoslavia, Finland, Holland,
Germany, Italy, and other European
countries, including:

Ki und Aikido Berlin
32 Blücherstr
1000 Berlin 61
Germany
Tel: 030–694–3585

Ki und Aikido Heidlberg
Heltenstr 1
6906 Leimen
Germany

Centro Ki-Aikido Torino
V.M. Coppino 138/10 Torino
Italy
Attn: Rocco Mileto

Ki Aikido Mestre
Via Milano, 12 Mestre
Italy
Attn: Carloh Rehata

Ki no Kenkyu Kai Italia
P.O. Box 3003
Firenze 26
50100
Itary

Meishin Kan Novara
V. le Allegra 26
28100 Novara
Italy
Attn: Gioconto Giovanni

Ronin Ki Aikido Novara
Via Visconti 1
Cre Enel Novara
Italy
Attn: Maul Bruno
        Volpe Maurizio

Firenze Ki Dôjô
Via Gordigiami 36/C Firenze
Italy
Tel: 055–362090
Attn: Giuseppe Ruglioni

Ki Society of the U.K.
5 Hopkins Rd.
Counden, Coventry
CV 6, 1 BD
U.K.
Attn: Philip Burgess

Rhondda Ki Society
Trederwen Gwaun Bedw
Cymmer Rhondda
Mid-Gran S. Wales
U.K.
Attn: Richard Gardiner

Ki Society of the Netherlands
Ijsselstein Stratt 26
5212 TS Den Bosch
The Netherlands

Ki no Kenkyu Kai Västerås
P.O. Box 422
72108 Västerås
Sweden

SOUTH AMERICA

Ki no Kenkyukai Sao Paulo Dôjô
Pua Sebastiao Carneiro, 501-AP 71
Aclimacao 01543
Sao Paulo-SP
Brazil

PACIFIC REGION

Australian Ki Society
P.O. Box 412
Byron Bay, NSW 2481
Australia
Tel: 066–85–6389
Attn: Michael Williams

North Queensland Ki Society
P.O. Box 413
Mossman, Q 4873
Australia
Tel: 070–98–1722
Attn: Robby Kessler

Brisbane Ki Society
P.O. Box 842
Springwood, Q 4127
Australia
Tel: 07–208–9472
Attn: Michael Stoopman

Red Hill Ki Society
100 Bowen St.
Spring Hill, Q 4000
Australia
Tel: 07–832–1671 or 07–369–0920
Attn: Wayne Murray Driver

New Zealand Ki Society
P.O. Box 1140
Auckland
New Zealand
Attn: Mike Stanford
Dôjô:
North Shore YMCA
Akoranga Drive
Takapuna
New Zealand
Tel: 480–7099

Singapore Ki Society
53 Paterson Rd.
Singapore 0923
Tel: 737–4839
Attn: (Francis) Chong Hong Siong

Ki Society of the Philippines
90 Women's Club Street
Santol, Quezon City 1113
Philippines
Tel: 61–69–97 or 711–84–31
Attn: Ernesto Talag
        Nestor Perrin

Indonesia Ki Society
Yayasan Kilndonesia
Jl. Bendugan Hilir Raya No. 31
Indonesia
Tel: 570–3071
Fax: 584–190
Attn: Takehisa Kinoshita

Appendix *C:* References for Further Study

Although readers are recommended to contact the Ki Society Headquarters, or one of its local branches, there are also several books available on the subject for those who wish to do further reading, published by the Ki no Kenkyûkai and Japan Publications, Inc, as well as the author's own earlier books on the subject.

Tohei, Koichi:
• *Ki in Daily Life*. Tokyo: Ki no Kenkyûkai, 1978. A classic text, available in several languages, which has helped introduce many people to Ki principles. This book provides detailed instructions, with a large number of photographs, showing how to do many Ki exercises and Ki tests, as well as Ki breathing. The book also provides useful advice on Ki philosophy and its application in daily life.
• *Book of Ki: Co-ordinating Mind and Body in Daily Life*. Tokyo and New York: Japan Publications, Inc., 1979. A nice supplement to the first book, with a greater emphasis on specific applications which strengthen mind and body. The book is well illustrated and contains many anecdotes, including episodes from the author's early life and training.
• *Kiatsu*. Tokyo: Ki no Kenkyûkai, 1983. A practical manual on how to do Kiatsu therapy. This book provides specific instructions on how and where to press, as well as describing the therapeutic applications of Kiatsu.
• *Ki Sayings.* Tokyo: Ki no Kenkyûkai, 1981. A small pocket-sized book with twenty-one short lessons which contain the essence of Tohei's teachings, written in poetic prose, in both English and Japanese. These sayings are usually read by the instructor and the group at the beginning of each Aikido class.

Maruyama, Koretoshi:
• *Aikido with Ki*. Tokyo: Ki no Kenkyûkai, 1984. A practical manual of Shin Shin Tôitsu Aikido, written under Tohei's supervision by one of his top students, Koretoshi Maruyama. This book explains in detail all of the basic Aikido arts up to the first degree of black belt. It is well illustrated with photographs. A revised edition by Tohei Sensei will soon be available.

Reed, William:
• *Ki: A Practical Guide for Westerners*. Tokyo and New York: Japan Publications, Inc., 1986. A description of Ki principles and their specific applications in various aspects of Japanese culture, the traditional arts, as well as daily and professional life.
• *Shodo: The Art of Coordinating Mind, Body and Brush*. Tokyo and New York: Japan Publications, Inc., 1989. A comprehensive guide to the art of brush calligraphy, based on Ki principles, and covering technical, aesthetic, historical, as well as psychological elements of the art.

Note: The entire Aikido curriculum, including the Taigi arts, has been put on video tape. These tapes will be available soon, with English translation.

Index